LEADERS

By the same author:

Industrial Democracy
The Atlantic Management Study
Government and Enterprise in Ireland
In Good Company
Out on Their Own
Boardroom Practice
Talking to Ourselves
Freedom and Order

LEADERS

Conversations with
Irish Chief Executives

Ivor Kenny

Published by Oak Tree Press
19 Rutland Street
Cork, Ireland
www.oaktreepress.com

© 2001 Ivor Kenny

A catalogue record of this book is
available from the British Library.

ISBN 1-86076-221-2

Printed in Britain
by MPG Books, Bodmin, Cornwall

For Maureen with love

Contents

Acknowledgements

I am indebted to the 18 people who helped me write this book — 17 chief executives and my friend and colleague in UCD, Gillian Acton.

David Givens and Brian Langan of Oak Tree Press are a pleasure to work with.

Introduction

"Know then thyself, presume not God to scan,
The proper study of mankind is man."
                    — Alexander Pope, 1688–1744.

In the following pages, 17 Irish chief executives talk, uninterrupted, about what they know best — their backgrounds, their businesses, their failures, their future and their motivations. Otto von Bismarck said, "Fools say they learn by experience. I prefer to profit by other people's experience." There are many years of experience in the book, but anyone who expects a handy list of rules for success is best warned of the disappointment that awaits. Cocksureness is not a characteristic of the conversations. The immodest purpose of the book is to bring together the experience and wisdom of men who saw what needed to be done and did it, so that others might be helped in that seeing and doing.

The title is *Leaders*. A leader is someone who has willing followers. Without followers, there can be no leaders. Leadership is a combination of character (who you are) and competence (what you can do). The leaders in this book are the people who carry the ultimate responsibility. They are personally accountable for *results*, not for the elegance of their arguments.

Most managers operate within existing ways of thinking. Leaders challenge those ways — even a cursory glance at the following pages shows they are happiest when they are changing things. They are seldom content. They never arrive.

And they are all different. Among the most effective leaders I have worked with over 40 years, some were gregarious, enjoying people and parties; others were solitary, preferring the sanctuary of their families. Some were nice guys; others were affectionately known as right bastards. Some were impulsive and moved too quickly; others took ages to decide. Some were warm and welcoming; others were distant and aloof. Some were vain and sought publicity; for others publicity was pointless — the chairman and CEO of one major Irish company would not go to the AGM. Some were austere — a decent suit and a modest car — others were ostentatious to the point of vulgarity. Some sought adulation; others would be embarrassed by and suspicious of it. Some were introvert and, having listened to advice, would work things out inside their heads; others were extrovert, thinking out loud and changing their minds as the discussion progressed. The one thing several of them did *not* have was charisma.

I have come to the conclusion that charisma does not matter a damn. If you have it, it can be helpful for getting attention but it can also be showbiz, self-indulgent and overpowering, inhibiting genuine communication.

I'm almost minded to start an Anti-Charismatic Movement. I am not suggesting that business schools should run courses on How to be Dull and Boring — we can manage that without help — but there is a certain obsession with celebrity and charisma. The line between fame and notoriety is unclear. We are confronted with a jumble of celebrities: the talented and untalented, heroes and villains, people of accomplishment and those who have accomplished nothing at all. The criteria for their celebrity are that their images give enough of the *appearance* of leadership — wealth, success, glamour and excitement — to feed our fantasies. A lack of concern in questioning the qualifications of people to be celebrated is a perverse phenomenon — for we are who we celebrate.

The charismatic leader's style can be superficially attractive. But charismatic leaders are unreliable. You do not know until the final act what their real purposes are. Perhaps they do not know themselves. I revisited *Brideshead* recently and came across this: "Charm is the great English blight. It does not exist outside these damp islands. It spots and kills anything it touches. It kills love, it kills art." Charisma and charm are near-synonyms. Substitute charisma for charm and Irish for English and you will see what I mean.

For as long as I can remember we have faced a crisis of leadership. (We seem also to be always at a crossroads.) The more our political leaders clamour to expose themselves in the media, the more their frailties become apparent, especially to the young. Our current leaders may well be no worse than their predecessors, but they *seem* worse, which amounts to the same thing. Scepticism about authority, an old and worthy tradition, is healthy. Cynicism and its bedfellow, apathy, are dangerous. We have, however, no business blaming those of modest ability who rise above their proper level of capability. They simply fill a vacuum created by the indifference of abler people.

However, to bring the matter down from the heady heights of politics to the level of this book, neither should we blame the shop steward in a company where the manager is stripped, by technology and management "theory", of all realistic authority.

A cynic might say to me there are only two questions I need ask of the managers when I enter an organisation: "How long have you been here?" and "What harm has it done you?" Leaders and their organisations can do bad things to people.

A better question to ask is, "How many bosses have you had in your working life?" Some managers turn out to have had many. Then I ask, "Which ones do you recall with gratitude and affection as really good?" The most I ever get is one or two; at any rate, a tiny minority of the whole. Last, I ask them to describe those good bosses.

By far the most common description is "Tough but fair". This is not a scientific formulation. The important thing is that everybody seems to recognise it. Nobody says, "Fair but tough" or even, "Tough and fair". Tough comes first, expressed as a necessity, then fair. You have to be tough, but the toughness is OK if it is fair as well. People who are remembered as "good" bosses have a certain kind of intelligence, a particular way of thinking that makes them memorable. Their virtue is that they do not consciously exercise charismatic influence. They simply keep their eye on the ball, with a certain humility, but nonetheless grow in the fullness of time to have *earned* respect and influence.

Leadership is a quality of character and intellect, not a condition or empty honour. The indispensable ingredients are the ability to sense the future, to understand the aspirations of followers, to discern the limits of possibilities and to select the lines of advance which hold the best promise of success.

Leaders are judged not by tactical nimbleness but by the robustness of their strategic designs. Good designs will be new, because they must contend with new circumstances. Any successful organisation is a monument to old problems successfully solved. Its very existence is proof of a good design in the past. But unchanging behaviour in rapidly changing conditions can cause a leader to look like a tree on a windswept heath. Those who can't change their minds, can't change anything. Hard-headed men who have made their perilous ascents to leadership have unbounded faith in their own beliefs, but those of them who change things penetrate the surface of events and break through inherited rigidities. Leaders barren of ideas are caretakers. Ideas uncoupled to the will, passion and skills of leaders are intellectual toys.

We do not know it all and we never can. The race between incessant demands to act now and our own ignorance calls for a mingled curiosity and faith in what is known as "learning". It is hard enough for an individual, but when we are told — as we are increasingly — that organisations must learn, we are carried beyond common sense. Organisations are created by humans. A learning organisation means that the individuals who give allegiance to it grow in knowledge and skill under the guidance of enlightened leaders.

We know enough now to answer the increasingly silly question: are leaders born or made?

It was Dean Inge, not Oscar Wilde, who said, "Nothing fails like success." It is clear from many of the following pages that one bit of experience essential to becoming a leader is failure. That is where there is real learning. A participant quotes the sign hanging in Joe McHugh's pub in Liscannor: "Experience is what you get when you didn't get what you wanted."

Leaders are not born full-blown. Neither are they made like instant coffee. They are slow brewed in the circumstances of the time.

It would hardly be possible to put between two covers a wider variety of businesses and backgrounds. There are two missing ingredients. The first is state companies, or as they are erroneously called, semi-state. I had the good fortune to work with, and to learn from, some of the pioneers of the state sector. It is sad to witness over the years the slow disembowelling of state company chief executives. On the one hand, they are faced with uniquely powerful public sector trade unions who are crystal clear about what they don't want. On the other, accountability is lost in the labyrinths of governance. The adjustment of state companies to a competitive economy will be slow, painful and wasteful. To paraphrase a distinguished Irish economist:

they who have made the ground barren blame the grass for not growing.

The second missing ingredient is women. While there may be anecdotal evidence that women are beginning to break through, few indeed have reached the top floor — women constitute two per cent of the chief executives in the leading 100 Irish companies. It would have been an insult to indulge in tokenism.

The method is the one used for the companion volumes, *In Good Company*, *Out on Their Own* and *Talking to Ourselves*. The conversations took place in the participants' offices or homes. They lasted, on average, three hours. I had no hesitation in giving an assurance that nothing would be published without the participants' consent. The danger in doing so is that an anodyne, unpublishable script would be returned, bearing the deadly marks of the public relations consultant. That did not happen with the previous three books and it did not happen here. Changes were minor and were about accuracy or concern for the sensitivity of third parties. Footnotes are my own. They refer to the companion volumes or recount developments since the conversations were recorded.

There is transmutation between the spoken and the written word — even more so when questions or interjections (which were few and far between) are eliminated as superfluous. Some participants felt that what was written read like an ego-trip. There is no way people can talk about themselves without liberal use of the first person singular and anyway, you, the reader, will form your own judgement. This was a particular phenomenon with the other books, where every reader I met had different "favourite" chapters — and where those who knew well the participants had their likes or dislikes reinforced with even-handed prejudice. Books like this do not change strongly held opinions.

Ivor Kenny
Woodview
University College Dublin

3 September 2001

1

Richard Burrows

Pernod Ricard

"There was a time when, if I did not get The Irish Times *and the* Irish Independent *early in the morning, I would feel naked. Of course, now I can get into them through the Internet — but it's less of an obligation."*

George Richard William Burrows is joint managing director of Pernod Ricard.

He was born in Dublin on 16 January 1946. His father was George Burrows, a journalist. His mother is Daisy Beamish. He was the eldest of a family of four — a brother and twin sisters: Johnny, Jane and Rose. He is married to Sherril Dix, who worked in the Creation Group. They have four children: Emma (27), Karen (26), David (23) and Samantha (21).

He was educated at Wesley College, Dublin. He then became an articled clerk and subsequently a chartered accountant.

His first job was with Stokes Brothers & Pim (now KPMG) (1963). He then worked with Peat Marwick Mitchell in London (1969); he subsequently joined Edward Dillon and Company, wine and spirit importers (1971); and Old Bushmills Distillery as managing director (1972). He became general manager of Irish Distillers in 1976; managing director in 1978; and chairman in 1991. He has been joint managing director, Pernod Ricard, since 2000.

He is a director of the Bank of Ireland; a former member of the board of management of the Royal National Lifeboat Institute; and chairman of the Irish Olympic Sailing Group. He is a past-president of IBEC, the Irish employers' body. He won the Flax Trust Award in Northern Ireland and is a Chevalier of the Légion d'Honneur.

The conversation was recorded in Richard Burrows' home in Portmarnock, County Dublin, on 18 March 2001.

Richard Burrows

The thread I would draw is the long involvement I've had with the drinks industry. It started when I was doing articles with Stokes Brothers & Pim. I was put on the audit for John Power & Son and then, following the merger that created Irish Distillers, I was involved with Jamesons and Cork Distilleries also as a young accountant. That was how I met Kevin McCourt,[1] the first managing director of Irish Distillers, appointed in 1968. I worked closely with him. He was trying to organise Irish Distillers which, at that time, did not really want to become a cohesive company — each one of the family companies that had merged wanted to retain its separateness and identity. This ran somewhat against Kevin's plans, which were to achieve the objectives of the merger: to create a single strong entity in Ireland, capable of defending the home market and, therefore, capable of developing its export business, which had fallen away to almost nothing over 50 or 60 years of neglect.

Working closely with Kevin was an interesting time for me because, even though I was the auditor, really I did rather more than that. When David Dillon, a friend of mine and the financial controller of Irish Distillers, became ill, I was drafted in to fill his shoes for a period. I got an inside working knowledge of Irish Distillers. I then went off to Peat Marwick Mitchell in London. Stokes Brothers & Pim had a relationship with Peats and wanted to start a consultancy service. I went to Peats for some training. I thoroughly enjoyed myself in London. Then, one day, the idea of the four-way merger between Irish Distillers, Waterford Glass, Carrolls and Irish Glass Bottle was mooted.

Kevin McCourt was new in Irish Distillers and, from the very outset, had the gravest misgivings about this merger as a strategy for Irish Distillers or, indeed, for the shareholders. The only strategy that was ever put forward for it was simply one of size — if you had eco-

---

[1] *Out on Their Own*, p. 2.

nomic scale, everything else would be possible. It came at a time when Carrolls was at its peak and when Waterford Glass was riding the crest of the wave. Irish Glass Bottle was the poor relation and for Irish Distillers the best years lay ahead. Kevin whistled me back from London to work on a defence strategy, which meant building a long-term plan for Irish Distillers — on that basis the board would be enabled to take a view as to whether or not the merger made sense. I worked on the strategy for five or six months and, the more I worked on it, the more obvious it became that for Irish Distillers this was going to be disastrous. Finally, the whole concept collapsed — by mutual consent.

I went back to Stokes Brothers & Pim for a period and then Kevin approached me again, indirectly through my uncle, Nigel Beamish, who was managing director of Edward Dillon. Irish Distillers had taken a shareholding in Edward Dillon as part of the strategy of defending the home market. Since there would always be products imported into Ireland, it was better to have a stake in the strongest importer and be in some position to influence rather than to ignore. Irish Distillers bought out the Dillon family. I was invited to go in as assistant to Nigel with a view to learning the trade. The initiative was a joint effort between Nigel and Kevin . . . anyway, I was quite close to Nigel. After I went in, we bought a little company, Fitzgeralds, then operating out of Westmoreland Street and which had run into financial trouble. I did a job on it, effectively winding it down and merging it into Edward Dillon.

No sooner was that done, than I got a call from Seagram to become managing director of Old Bushmills. Seagram had bought Bushmills with a view to selling it to Irish Distillers in return for a shareholding. There was great nervousness at the time in Bow Street about investing in Bushmills. It was 1972 and the troubles in the North were at a serious level. There was a feeling that Irish Distillers moving into an investment in Northern Ireland would be rejected. It was decided that Seagram would be the leader for Bushmills for some time with Irish Distillers playing a backseat role, but Seagram needed somebody to go and run the thing. Kevin nominated me and I was invited by Jack Yogman to be the first managing director of Bushmills in Seagram's time.

I ran it from 1972 to 1976. Irish Distillers became more confident and ultimately were able to integrate Bushmills fully — Bushmills became a wholly owned subsidiary of Irish Distillers. It's interesting now to see so many people in Seagram whom I knew and worked with back in those days. It's a feature of the drinks industry that people tend to stick around for a long time.

In 1972 there was just me and Sherril. It was a bizarre time; there was a great fear both in Irish Distillers and in Seagram about what was happening in Northern Ireland. I got my instructions from Jack Yogman in New York to start in Bushmills on 1 November 1972 — he told me that I would be introduced by a man named Harold Currie who was then managing director of Chivas Brothers, based in Paisley near Glasgow. I got instructions that I was to go to an old military airbase outside Coleraine. There was absolutely nothing there, concrete slabs with nettles growing between them. Harold was to come in there, we'd drive to Bushmills, and I would be introduced. There had been no prior announcement that all this was going to happen. I left Sherril in Dublin, stayed in Belfast overnight, and duly met Harold Currie the following morning; we drove to Bushmills and he rounded up the management. They were, of course, aware that Bushmills had become part of Seagram. He introduced me as the managing director and said he was off back to Scotland, that I had better select an office for myself.

The facilities in Bushmills were fairly basic. Having had a look around, I decided not to disturb the existing management and took over as my office what was a visitor reception room. That was it — I was in position, in charge. They knew I was from Dublin and, in true Bushmills style, it took them about 30 seconds to work out that I was a member of the Church of Ireland and that I was married to a Catholic — I had a foot in both sides! The selection of the office was not without drama. There was a fine big table cut from a slab of oak. The chief blender, John McLernon, laughed every time he came into the office. I could not figure out why. He finally revealed to me that, the night before I arrived, they had had a reception in the distillery and he had found a male staff member on top of a female staff member on top of the table.

In those days Bushmills was a fascinating place to be — by integrating it into Seagram, we were opening up markets all over the world. It had had a good business in the United States and some pockets of business elsewhere but not too much. Bushmills was then the best known Irish whiskey in the States. There was a relationship with a Colonel Kaplin who had an importing company in New York and whose relationship with Bushmills went back to when the distillery was owned by the Boyd family during the Second World War. Isaac Woolfson bought Bushmills on a tax deal from the Boyd family and sold it on in the early sixties to Charrington Kinahan. Bushmills were used to different owners, though there were still some members of the Boyd family in management when I went there in 1972.

The period from 1972 to 1976 was a time of terrific development. I reported directly to Jack Yogman, a funny old Seagram way of doing things: the managing director of each of the subsidiaries reported directly to the president of the company. Jack wanted Bushmills doubled in size. It was a learning experience for me: I was getting involved, for the first time, in project management, in sales and marketing, which I had never been involved in. When I went to Northern Ireland the product was distributed there by Bass Charrington, the brewer, relating back to the Charrington Kinahan thing. I felt we could make more progress and a lot more money by doing it directly.

This ties back in to my first meeting with you, Ivor. I knew nothing at all about sales and marketing and decided I'd better get myself on a sales course pretty damn quick. I enrolled in one of the modular courses in the IMI and did three days a month. During this time, I was also recruiting sales people and a sales manager! Each session of the course would end with a dinner and you used to come to them and give a perspective on management and that course opened up for me what the role of management was. People like Ken Whitaker[2] came, people who were putting up big signposts for economic development in Ireland. At that time, there was either State enterprise or family business. There was an absence of a management class. The IMI successfully promoted in those days the concept of management as a distinct profession.

By virtue of the troubles in Northern Ireland I was really left to myself to get on with things; rarely was there a visitor to Bushmills from Seagram. We did have a board; the nominee from Irish Distillers, Clem Ryan, the production director, faithfully attended. I met Kevin McCourt regularly to keep him informed — that usually meant meeting him for breakfast in the Shelbourne Hotel at eight in the morning. I'd drive down from Castlerock where we lived and be back at my desk by eleven o'clock. The initial stake Irish Distillers had was

---

[2] *In Good Company*, pp. 279–305.

25 per cent. Over a period, they took more chunks as they became more confident about their acceptability as shareholders. It's hard to transport the thinking back to that time, but it was pretty rough for business.

Ian Paisley was one of the first people to come to meet with me in the distillery — he was MP for the area. There was a little road that ran through the distillery connecting Bushmills Town with a farmland behind. When I embarked on the development of Bushmills, which involved considerable capital expenditure, one of the issues was security. We had visits from the RUC and a lot of local politicians became interested in what we were doing — it was clear that there was going to be a significant increase in employment. Bushmills as a town was largely dependent on the distillery. There was little else apart from farming and a couple of pubs and a hotel. There were about 125 working in Bushmills when I joined. Ian Paisley arrived and wanted to know what I was doing about security. He pointed out the danger of this road going through the heart of the distillery. Those were the days of massive car-bombs. He said, "Let's get the road closed", and in jig time the road was closed. We put an entrance at the town end and closed off the back end. For the first time, the Bushmills site was integral and protected. Ian may have had an aversion to the devil's buttermilk, but he understood about employment and was extraordinarily helpful.

We did, in fact, have a bomb in our Belfast warehouse. We had offices in Waring Street and a big bond there where the whiskey was assembled for shipment. We must have had 30,000 or 40,000 cases of product in that warehouse. The terrorists came in, planted a bomb, gave a warning and I got a call from Harry Adams, our warehouse manager. I got in the car, shot down to Belfast and arrived just after the bomb had gone off. I went in with the soldiers and the place was awash with whiskey — the bomb had shattered all the bottles in all the cases and it drained onto the floor. Harry was a rather nervous man and we got to his office, a little cubby-hole at the back of the warehouse. We were paddling in whiskey. We sat at his desk. He started to light up a cigarette and his hand was shaking. I shouted, "Harry, for God sake . . .!" and stopped him before he blew us all to Kingdom Come. That was the end of that warehouse — it was no longer needed; we'd ship direct from Bushmills.

We had a lot of fun in Bushmills. We had many visitors — I encouraged customers to come. We took, as a tourist attraction, an old kiln which was under the malt house — when I went there Bushmills had its own malting floor where the germinating barley was turned by hand. The essence of Bushmills was the craftsmanship of people who had probably followed their fathers and mothers. You did not have to tell anybody in Bushmills the techniques of making whiskey. Malting barley was not at that time an economic activity, so I closed down the facility. In the kilns were great coal-burning fires used to dry the malting barley to kill the growing process and in 1975 we opened the first visitor's centre. The Giant's Causeway was another big Northern Ireland attraction, not far away. We had a co-operative arrangement with them — they would send busloads of tourists to us. It was so successful that, on that basis, we subsequently developed visitors' centres in Midleton and in Dublin for Irish Distillers.

It was a time of great activity. Sherril moved up. We found a house in Castlerock on the sea looking north into the Atlantic — on a good day you could see the Orkneys. And that's where we started our family: we had two daughters, Emma and Karen, while we were there. We enjoyed the North, once we got established. People were friendly. We still have a lot of very good friends there. Castlerock was west of the Bann, so the population was somewhat more mixed but still had a strong Unionist tradition, strong Twelfth of July activities. On one occasion, I had to go away around the Twelfth and left Sherril in the house on her own with the two babies. Castlerock had a population of no more than three or four hundred people. There was a circular road that went around the centre. We were living on that road. Sherril was absolutely terrified because the band stopped at the gate and beat the hell out of the Lambeg drum, as they did outside every house where there was a Catholic living. It was a kind of ritual — I don't think they meant any harm, but it was an unnerving experience. I rang Sherril and she was in a dreadful state. You lived there in a close-knit community where everybody knew everybody else, everybody knew about my involvement with Bushmills and thought I had a pipeline running directly from the distillery to the house. But we had that little difficulty from time to time.

On another occasion, we were at a licensed trade function in the Stormont Hotel in Belfast. We had Emma, who was just a few months old, asleep in our room. We went to the function downstairs and, in the middle of the reception, there was a bomb scare in the hotel. It was a bitterly cold night and we were all immediately ushered out into a big car-park. We moved along with the crowd and then realised that Emma was in the bedroom. I had to fight my way back into the hotel because the soldiers were there and did not want anybody to go in. I brought Emma out to the car-park all wrapped in a blanket. Sherril sat in the car with Emma, and I opened the boot where I had a reasonable stock of Black Bush miniatures. We had a right get-together in the car park in the freezing cold. It was just the relief of having got Emma out of the hotel — everybody celebrated. It turned out in the end there wasn't a bomb and after an hour-and-a-half we all went back in and had a helluva party. Those difficult occasions tended to glue everybody together. There was a sense of shared re-sponsibility, shared revulsion at the violence.

The Bushmills business grew by leaps and bounds — we got profit-ability very substantially up. I was invited by Kevin to come back to Dublin. He had had McKinsey in and they had done a restructuring which was, among other things, to lead to Kevin's retirement in 1978. The McKinsey boys came to Castlerock to meet me. Derek Finlay came — he was not too subtle about his real agenda — and I was in-vited to become general manager of Irish Distillers working directly under Kevin. I was responsible for IDL, the main trading arm in Ire-land; its principal preoccupation was completing the building of a new distillery in Midleton. There were also the major shareholdings in Bushmills and Edward Dillon — that constituted the Irish Distillers Group, of which Kevin was managing director. We were closing down the old smaller distilleries. Those were the days where we began to understand scale and the necessity to get your costs of production down. It was the time of specialised distilleries rather than people trying to do everything.

Back in Dublin and plunged into IDL was a very different experi-ence, very political, with a number of people jostling for the managing directorship when Kevin would retire. I think Kevin had conspired with Frank O'Reilly,[3] the chairman, to have a pretty open competitive situation to see who would come through. The rumour mill had names of outsiders chucked into it every now and then, which added a bit of spice. In 1978, Kevin stepped down and I was given the job. I

---

[3] *In Good Company*, pp. 259–278.

was 32. Kevin kept saying to anyone who said I was very young that that was something time alone would cure!

I learned a lot from Kevin in that 1976 to 1978 period. I'd follow him around the world. He saw the United States as Irish Distillers' Klondike; cracking that market would be the answer to exports. He saw a significant role for Seagram — Seagram had built up to a 20 per cent shareholding from their original 10 per cent. Charles Bronfman represented them on our board, followed by Mel Griffin. It was a contentious enough issue because there was a strong feeling, not just among Irish Distillers' shareholders, but among politicians and others, that it would be terribly wrong if Irish Distillers were sold to a foreign company. Irish Distillers should remain in Irish ownership. Seagram were held at 20 per cent by a strong agreement which would limit their right to buy any more shares and, in fact, they could vote only 15 out of the 20. There was a concern that it could be a creeping takeover. Seagram were very relaxed about that, they felt they were playing a long-term game: they wanted to develop the business. When I say Kevin saw the United States as the Klondike and Seagram as the big partners, it didn't happen. Seagram were the sole importers of Jameson in the United States, with Brown Forman importing Bushmills. Bushmills and Jameson moved pretty much in tandem but neither achieved the sales figures we had hoped for. Kevin was disappointed about that. We were fighting against a negative perception of Irish whiskey. Sales growth was disappointing relative to the effort and investment that went in.

Kevin had run Irish Distillers on the basis that the home market was where the profits were made and he was prepared to plough every penny of those profits into the development of export sales. That was fine through the seventies when the Irish spirits market doubled in size on the back of our joining the European Economic Community. There was a huge increase in the financial well-being of our farmers. The market grew steadily and then doubled, but, by 1980, things were starting to turn against us nationally. The Government were looking at alcohol and tobacco as the cash cows to sort out any budget deficit. In a period of four years, we had four duty increases. The market fell by a third between 1980 and 1984. That forced us into a radical review of what the hell we were doing. Suddenly, exports had to pay their way — we could no longer go on building exports in the hope that some day we would make money out of them.

In 1984, the definitive export marketing strategy for Irish whiskey was put in place. It was a tough process. The only course open to Irish Distillers as an independent company was to adopt a premium price position against Scotch. A premium price position had to be supported by product and packaging — a full range of marketing tools. We were confident enough about the product — the Midleton distillery had performed very well. We were producing a product that was quite definitely superior to Scotch. We went for things like emphasising the triple-distillation, the fact that there was no smoke in the drying of the malted barley — which meant there was no smoke in the end product, which enhanced its smoothness. We had to change our packaging radically. And we had to educate all our importers around the world that they would have to take substantial price increases. Since 1984, that is still the foundation of the Jameson marketing strategy.

It also required us to focus absolutely on Jameson. This was a difficulty because the family members of the original distillers were still on the board. They paid lip-service to marketing — that may sound harsh, but I believe it's true. Their interest was whether *their* Jameson or *their* Powers or *their* Paddy was getting the promotional money. Bushmills was the orphan. Anyway, the focus went onto Jameson and Black Bush as premium whiskeys and we de-emphasised our investment behind the other brands. We really had to build *a* brand in an export market. There was a lot of confused talk and thinking about building a category. If you built a brand, you built a category. If you built a brand of Irish whiskey, you were building a category of Irish whiskey. That had to be the way it was but it caused internal debate and was a tough sell.

Indeed it was probably one of the things that caused us and Seagram to fall out a bit through the eighties. Seagram did not really have a focused marketing strategy at all. Seagram threw brands at markets; some of them worked and some didn't. They had the resources of their home market in the United States where they had a leadership position, hugely profitable. Their traditional brands included Seagram's VO, a Canadian whiskey. They built out of that Crown Royal, a premium Canadian. There was Seagram's Seven, an American whiskey, an important brand in the seventies and eighties, and Seagram's Gin. They bought Martel Cognac. They had Chivas Regal. Sam Bronfman had bought Chivas and built it as a very significant brand in their portfolio. They were involved in just about every sector around the world — it was a scattergun approach based on a successful North American business. Seagram diversified into entertainment under Edgar Bronfman Jr., which has now led them on to this merger with Vivendi and the sale of their spirits and wine business.

About 1982, Frank O'Reilly decided he would retire. He had been chairman since the formation of the company in 1966, having previously been chairman of John Power & Son, the most influential of the companies. He thought by then he had done enough. He was a tremendously engaging character and one of the most unselfish men I've ever known. He oversaw Kevin, he oversaw me, oversaw the divisions between the different family members and he hardly took a penny out of the company himself — he made no attempt to maximise his own wealth. When you look at some of the family involvements in public companies today, you could contrast them with the way Frank O'Reilly ran Irish Distillers for the benefit of *all* the shareholders and managed a difficult board. Michael Killeen[4] was signalling his retirement from the Industrial Development Authority and was invited to become Frank's successor. Michael was a stimulus, coming in with a fresh mind, very much in Frank's style, and with the other board members in his sense of the mission to defend the home market and build exports. He was a great help in pushing through the marketing strategy I talked about earlier.

In 1984, we secured a duty reduction in the home market, having made a substantial case to Alan Dukes, then Minister for Finance. He cut the duty on spirits by, I think, 25 per cent. Within about 15 months, the rolling rate of revenue for the Government was above what it had been prior to the cut. It stimulated the market and stopped a lot of smuggled product coming in. In 1984 also, we opened up Fitzgeralds again as an import company, because wine drinking was becoming popular. We had been progressively reducing our shareholding in Edward Dillon, the original import company. We started new product development — we launched West Coast Cooler successfully, first at home and then in Australia.

---

[4] *In Good Company*, p. 2.

Of course, we tried lots of other things that were not so successful. We bought BWG because cash-and-carry was becoming a significant channel for product to our customers. BWG was the second cash-and-carry company after Musgraves. Progressively, we sold off the bits of BWG that did not fit — Mahon & McPhillips, builders in Kilkenny, United Drug, and focused on the cash-and-carry side. The strategic thinking which led us to buy BWG evaporated very quickly. The duty reduction meant the market became much more orderly. What had been happening was that publicans had to buy their beer from the brewers because it was a draught trade in kegs. Their black economy ventures were spirits bought through cash-and-carry for cash, no records. I think it was Bertie Ahern, as Minister for Finance, who started to change that — he made it mandatory that all cash-and-carry transactions have an invoice and a VAT number. He subsequently introduced a tax-clearance certificate, which meant you could not renew your publican's licence unless you could produce the certificate saying that your affairs were in order with the Revenue. That had a significant impact on the business, moving a lot of cash-and-carry trade into the legal economy. However, we retained BWG and subsequently developed it in a rather different way. That was all happening between 1984 and 1986.

Then, of course, Michael Killeen lost his battle with cancer — that was a devastation for us. He really was a splendid character to work with. It took more out of me than I realised. He was a most encouraging kind of chairman, someone who would back you at a board meeting. If he thought you were right, he was prepared to take on all comers at the board. In the latter stages of his illness and for a little while after he died, Jack Lynch was chairman. Jack was a great chairman. He didn't really have to do a lot of work — his presence was enough. He was a representative chairman for Irish Distillers. He would come to all the staff functions, where he was idolised. I don't know whether any other Taoiseach has had the same kind of affection. Then Joe McCabe came in as chairman — he had retired from Irish Ropes — a different style of man, a different approach, low-key and private. Again, someone very supportive of management, much more interested in the detail of what was going on than either Jack or Michael or indeed Frank.

Joe was there for the ending of the relationship with Seagram. We had a rights issue while Michael was in the chair. We were suffering badly from the huge decline in the Irish market, we wanted to keep our export effort going, we had this fledgling marketing policy when it was difficult to make the investment necessary to support a premium product in parallel with an effective price increase. The upgrading, which was not going to show any immediate return, together with the purchase of BWG, led us to the rights issue. Seagram wanted to underwrite it. We saw that as a generous offer but, in fact, an easy way to creep their shareholding at a cheap price. We said no and they took it rather badly — the fact that we would pay underwriting fees outside the company when they were prepared to underwrite internally. I believe they misunderstood.

The relationship at corporate level started to go downhill and finally, about 1987, Seagram came to the view that, if they could not increase their shareholding with our support, they would sell their shares. This was at a time when Seagram itself was going through a lot of change — they were starting to invest heavily in entertainment — and they needed cash. One day we woke up to find that they had placed the rump of their holding into the market. That's what led to the position taken by DCC and Fyffes, who became significant shareholders in Irish Distillers.

The haste with which that was done and the lack of co-operation between us and our major shareholders, was, to say the least, unhelpful, and our brokers did not cover themselves with distinction either. It knocked the share price back and, when the emergence of Fyffes working with DCC became clear, suddenly the market was agog that this would lead to a takeover bid. Fyffes and DCC were clearly arbitraging their position.

Black Monday, 1987, followed shortly after that. Everything fell like a stone. Fyffes and DCC moved in and increased their holding quite significantly, a good play for them, as was proved when in 1988 there was a bid from GC&C, a company formed by Grand Met (G), and Cantrell & Cochrane (C&C) which was jointly owned by Guinness and Allied Domecq. Three major British drinks companies had come together. They made their bid in May. The DCC/Fyffes holding made us vulnerable. It was perfectly obvious that they were going to use that as a stepping-stone for somebody to acquire us.

In terms of our marketing strategy, it was obvious to us that, while we could do a lot of things, we were finding it very difficult to get a channel to market — the industry was consolidating. The independent importers we had been working with around the world were no longer independent — they were being bought up by Guinness or by Grand Met or Allied, or Seagram indeed, to become vertically integrated companies from producer right through to distributor.

We needed some kind of connection or affiliation. We talked in those days with Bols, the Dutch gin producer with whom we had a very long relationship on the trading side. We actually got to the stage of working on a merger proposal with Bols. They were about the same size as us with similar problems. The failure we had in the US in the seventies was followed by a decline there in the US market. We effectively switched our focus out of the United States into Europe. Whiskey drinking was beginning to grow in almost every European market. It was a new category, seen as international, and was moving along in an economy which in the eighties was a lot stronger than the US economy. Bols were strong in Holland, Belgium and Luxembourg, in Italy, a strong foothold in France, in Germany. It was a good match for Irish Distillers. Jan Hubar, the chief executive of Bols, got cold feet and would not go ahead. That led us almost exactly up to the point where GC&C made their hostile bid.

That happened at the beginning of May 1988. The Irish players were people like David Dand, Gerry Dempsey[5] and Tony O'Brien — Guinness and Allied were 50/50 partners in C&C, with Allied having the controlling share, so Tony O'Brien represented both. We had a tremendously hostile period but the friendship I had with David Dand and Tony O'Brien survived once the fighting was over.

At this time, I was running around spending my time more on corporate affairs than on managing the business. Within 24 hours of the bid being announced, I had a call from Thierry Jacquillat, President of Pernod Ricard, whom I had known for some years. I'd go to Paris to the rugby matches and Thierry would always host a lunch or dinner. He asked me if there was anything he could do and I said I did not know. The following Monday was a public holiday. By then we had armies of bankers and lawyers, all sorts of professional hangers-on around a defence situation. I went to Paris on the public holiday and met with Thierry. We talked the thing through — they were interested to help but not in any combative way against GC&C.

---

[5] *Out on Their Own*, pp. 59–74.

A feature of the GC&C bid was that it was based on breaking up Irish Distillers into its component parts: Guinness would take one brand, Allied would take another, Grand Met would take another. The company would be dismembered. That got the staff of Irish Distillers very exercised. The main reason the bid was rejected was that they pitched it at a stupidly low price. We got "Keep the Spirit Irish" going, but the underlying reason for rejection was the price. We talked with quite a number of other independent companies with whom we had contact, people like Suntory in Japan. Nobody was prepared to move against the combined strength of Allied, Grand Met and Guinness. We formed the view that this was a cartel and that was the basis of our submission to the European Commission. It led to a decision by the Commission to block it; Peter Sutherland[6] was the Commissioner at the time. The bid was blocked but they allowed Grand Met to proceed on their own. They came back into the fray and increased the offer pretty substantially. Now we were back where we were, but fighting Grand Met alone. You ask why we did not relax and enjoy it — because the price was still insufficient and there was a lot of momentum behind our objection to it.

The London Stock Exchange allowed Grand Met to continue on the condition that they could make one final bid and that would be it — it would either stand or fall — unless a competing offer emerged. They came in at something like £4.00 a share; the original bid had been about £3.15. It was a step up but not where our advisers were telling us it should be — somewhere over £4.00. That led to Pernod Ricard getting a lot more interested and coming over here. They would make an offer if it were supported by the board, and if they could secure irrevocable commitments in advance of making the offer. We worked out a plan with them that they would make an offer at £4.50, we could get irrevocable commitments signed up for 50 per cent, and then go public with the offer. That worked, except that during the weekend of getting the irrevocable commitments, Grand Met became aware of what was happening and, over that weekend, got clearance from the London Stock Exchange to intervene. Gerry Dempsey made his famous RTE broadcast on the Sunday at lunchtime in which he publicly increased their offer to £5.25 a share, while we had a string of people lined up in

---

[6] See Chapter 16, pp. 313–334.

our head office ready to sign irrevocable commitments for an offer at £4.50 from Pernod Ricard.

The queue stretched all the way up the stairs from the basement and outside. We had teams of people all over the country digging shareholders out to get them to sign up. I must say it is to the credit of a great number of small shareholders that they stayed with us. The bigger play was going on in discussions with DCC to try and get their agreement with Fyffes to the signing of the irrevocable commitment in respect of their shareholding. Similar talks were going on with Irish Life, all of which is documented, and led finally to the court cases and the handshake between Thierry and Neil McCann of Fyffes on his acceptance of the offer of £4.50 for his shares. Jim Flavin of DCC subsequently tried to unravel that so they could accept the Grand Met offer of £5.25. The handshake held through the High Court and the Supreme Court and was the foundation of Pernod Ricard's bid being successful. That's how we became part of Pernod Ricard. Subsequently, Grand Met, who had been buying shares in the market, sold their shares at the beginning of 1989 to Pernod Ricard at the offer price of £4.50. That was it, over — we were 100 per cent owned by Pernod Ricard.

That started a period of really dramatic change for Irish Distillers. Suddenly, we had the access to market that we had been seeking. Pernod Ricard had been putting down its own footprint market-by-market. It had a structure that was strongly under-used in terms of distribution. It needed products to go through that structure. Their products were the original two, Pernod and Ricard, the founding company's products — Pernod Ricard had been formed in 1975 in a manner not dissimilar to that in which Irish Distillers had been formed in 1966. They were two family businesses — in the case of Ricard a single family headed by Paul Ricard who had established the business in the early 1930s, and, in the case of Pernod, three quite unrelated Pernod families who had merged 100 years before to form Pernod as we know it today. They all made the same product but in three unrelated companies. They were somewhat more diffuse than Ricard and, of course, Ricard was much bigger and more powerful. Ricard became the dominant member of the Pernod Ricard share-holding. They had developed the idea of trying to build anise sales around the world, so they formed distribution companies. That largely failed and they bought companies like Austin Nichols with

Wild Turkey, Campbell Distillers in the United Kingdom with Clan Campbell and Aberlour Scotch Malt. They bought Ramazotti in Italy. From an early stage, they had also diversified out of alcoholic products into things like Orangina, Pampryl juices, and a company called SIAS which, when they bought it, provided fruit preparations to the major yoghurt manufacturers. Pernod Ricard was made up of all those elements: the core business was spirits and wine, and soft drinks led by Orangina and Pampryl — and Yoohoo in the United States, a chocolate-based soft drink, very popular on the East Coast and consumed mainly by young to middle-aged men who like a little shot of chocolate — who's arguing! They bought a company called Orlando in the wine business in Australia, which subsequently developed Jacob's Creek as its leading brand.

Out of all of this came a terrific coincidence of timing — they had been building a structure, they needed products and Irish Distillers became part of Pernod Ricard when we had just completed this revised marketing strategy with Jameson and Black Bush. Jameson moved into the Pernod Ricard structure — it was like a sponge, just sucking it up. It was the first really good international brand that Pernod Ricard had. Pernod Ricard could see its merits and, as a result of that, in the 12 years since we became part of Pernod Ricard, Jameson has gone from 400,000 cases to 1.4 million cases, by contrast with what happened with Seagram in the seventies. A million cases would be regarded as the threshold for an international brand. Another threshold is 100,000 cases in any particular market. What you need for an international brand is that it sells more than 100,000 cases in half-a-dozen markets or so.

Pernod Ricard is a very decentralised company — a small holding company with virtually all the operating responsibilities devolved to the subsidiaries. From an Irish Distillers' perspective, in joining Pernod Ricard, Thierry Jacquillat and Patrick Ricard, the chairman, had sufficient confidence to allow me to continue running Irish Distillers. They did not plant any Frenchmen in the team. The reporting lines were short — I reported both to Patrick and to Thierry — quite French! Irish Distillers' profits back in 1988 were £18 million. Ten years later they were £75 million. The only difference was that with Pernod Ricard we paid one hundred per cent of after-tax profits as dividend.

We would have been one of the companies within Pernod Ricard with an appetite for capital expenditure. If you start to build a brand like Jameson at a rate of 10 per cent per annum, you're going to double every seven years and you have to have the whiskey there to meet that demand. The average age of whiskey is about five years. You were laying down a huge amount, probably more than double what you were selling. This drives the demand for casks, warehouses, distilling facilities, way ahead of your present level of sales — it's a feature of a growing whiskey business. It is quite capital-demanding. That was also part of the thinking in going for the premium price positioning — you can't do that kind of thing and earn a shareholder return unless you are generating sufficient cash off your present volume to enable you to invest and provide for shareholders. Pernod Ricard were tremendously supportive of our plan. In a way, we were the first company in Pernod Ricard to have developed an international marketing plan.

That was the experience on the drinks side. We also had BWG when we became part of Pernod Ricard. One of the conditions stipulated by Albert Reynolds, Minister for Industry and Commerce in 1988, was that Pernod Ricard would not sell any element of IDG for a period of five years after acquiring it. That went back to the break-up concept of the old GC&C bid. We set about growing BWG. The management began to develop the Spar convenience franchise and we also began to make progress on the wholesale-delivered side of the business as distinct from the cash-and-carry. We grew BWG from a position where it had a very modest level of profitability in 1988 to a point where, five years later, it was a significant contributor to Pernod Ricard and so found its own position. It became another leg of the Pernod Ricard diversified strategy. Today it is making €45 million on sales of €1.25 billion. BWG is a company with a well-established business in the island of Ireland, North and South, and has a market share of about five per cent in Britain in the wholesale sector.

For me, life changed in June 2000 when Thierry Jacquillat announced his intention to retire on 1 July 2001 — he will be 60. Patrick Ricard invited me to become the joint managing director of Pernod Ricard with Pierre Pringuet; Pierre had been running the non-French European side. The two of us are now in joint harness in Boulevard Haussmann, where the head office is. Almost on the day the two of us were asked to get involved came the sale of the Seagram's spirits and wine business. We formed a partnership with Diageo to make a joint bid. The bid was accepted by the Vivendi board, having merged the entertainment business with Seagram Universal — and that's where we are today. We're awaiting regulatory clearance on the Seagram acquisition. It has to be cleared in Brussels, Washington and Canada. The effect for Pernod Ricard is to double our size in wines and spirits and stretches us to the pin of our collar to pay for it. Part of our strategy in the funding is to sell all of the non-core businesses and assets of Pernod Ricard — that includes BWG.

For Pierre and myself, it has been a much more hectic start to our joint managing directorship than it might otherwise have been. The Seagram opportunity has allowed us really to refocus the strategy of Pernod Ricard on our core business, wines and spirits, and move out of all the diversifications. By August/September we hope to be through the regulatory side and we should be well advanced in selling BWG, SIAS and our soft drinks business, for which latter we are in discussion with Cadbury Schweppes. It's going to be quite a busy six months.

The joint managing directorship is a formalised relationship under French company law. Essentially, the board has delegated authority to Pierre and me in a formal mandate. Our mandate does not require two signatures — either one of us can commit the company. It does require that we work very closely together. When Patrick invited me to become involved, the Seagram dimension and its effect on our strategy was not envisaged. The original idea was that I would continue to live here and spend maybe two or three days a week in Paris and Pierre would be based there. We were not long into it when we realised that that was completely impractical — we both had to be based in Paris. Since last July, I fly out on a Sunday night and spend my week there, or else I'm travelling, which is more the case of late. I come home on Friday night. It's the only way to work — there has to be continuous contact between the two of us. In terms of the management of Pernod Ricard, we have split the business into two. A number of subsidiaries report to Pierre and a number to me. That's just for ease of management of the subsidiary operations, but in all of the major decisions we both get involved.

I really enjoyed being president of IBEC. It opened a huge number of windows for me. For now, I would say that it is going to be difficult for Ireland to sustain the economic growth we have enjoyed. Foot-and-mouth will have a deeper effect than we are anticipating and we are exposed to what happens in America. I'd be nervous about America. On the other hand, in France, in the heartland of Europe, there is good continuing economic growth. I'd be optimistic that that can tow us along a bit but it will get rougher here before it gets better.

It's surprising how quickly one can become disconnected. There was a time when, if I did not get *The Irish Times* and the *Irish Independent* early in the morning, I would feel naked. Of course, now I can get into them through the Internet — but it's less of an obligation.

The business of Irish Distillers is going very well. BWG is going well. We have a new managing director in Irish Distillers, a Frenchman, Philippe Savinel. Philippe was sales director of Ricard in France, an accountant by profession, made the break some years ago. Dublin will be quite a change for him but he will do well.

That gets us to today but I would not like you to go away with the impression that life here is just about business. I really do enjoy family life and I really do enjoy competitive sailing. Sailing has been a major leisure-time activity for me over the last 40 years. One of the highlights was my son David's participation in the Olympics, both in Sydney and in Atlanta. My daughter Emma has sailed quite a bit with me, Samantha is quite keen; Karen doesn't like it at all — like her mother! So one of the other things we do is a lot of hill-walking. Karen and I walked the Wicklow Way a couple of winters ago. It's a wonderful walk — we did it over a series of weekends from start to finish. It was really one of the most enjoyable things I've ever done – we did it in the October/November period before it was really cold, the dogs with us.

Does that give you a picture?

2

Bill Cullen

Renault Distributors

Photo: © *The Irish Times*

"When I think back to the tenements and all the things we did as kids to raise a few bob, it does not depress me. I feel great about it. I got a better education on the streets and with my Ma than I would ever have got at college and did it an awful lot quicker."

Bill Cullen is the chairman and chief executive of Renault Distributors in Ireland.

He was born in Summerhill, Dublin on 19 February 1942. His father was Billy Cullen, a docker. His mother was Mary Darcy, housewife and fruit seller in Moore Street. He was third in a family of 14, seven boys and seven girls. His partner is Jackie Lavin, former fashion model, boutique owner, now running a health and fitness centre. He has two children, Anita (32) and Hilary (30), and two grandchildren, Callum (5) and Aidan (2).

He was educated at Gardiner Street School, St Canice's School and O'Connell School. He started as a messenger boy with the Walden Motor Company (1956); by 1964, he was general manager, then managing director (1966). In 1973, he set up his own Ford dealership company. In 1986, he bought the Smith Group.

He was chairman of Children's Hour; he is deputy chairman of the Irish Youth Foundation, having been chairman for four years; and a trustee of Children's Trust. He works with the Links Golfing Society, which raises money for charity. He was presented with the Lord Mayor's Award (1998).

The conversation was recorded in Bill Cullen's home in Osbertstown, County Kildare on 28 March 2001.

Bill Cullen

My earliest memories go back to Summerhill. I remember going to school at two-and-a-half years of age and I remember the War ending in 1945 and the celebrations. The poverty in Summerhill was exactly the same as in McCourt's book about Limerick, *Angela's Ashes*, but the difference was we had a great time. We did not know we were poor — everybody was the same. My mother was so positive — up at 5.30, get her Mass, get her children up, go down to the market, get her fruit out, sell all day, try and get home to make a bit of dinner during the day and get home for the tea in the evening. She was a human dynamo. I couldn't believe it when she died — I thought she would live forever. She died at 74 in 1986. Her mother outlived her. The Granny was the central figure in the whole family, my mother's mother, Molly Darcy. (We called the pub in our hotel in Killarney after her — Molly Darcy's. She never drank or was in a pub all her life — we told her it was a restaurant!) She was widowed at an early age. She had nine children and she survived seven of them — she lived to be 100. She gave a tremendous balance, to me in particular. When I was three or four years of age, she lived across the road and I used to go and stay with her because she was a widow. Here was my mother feeding all these kids and she would put together a little dinner: a bit of mash and cabbage and whatever there was, put it between two plates and I would bring it over to her mother. My mother was my Ma and my grandmother was the Mother, because that's what my mother called her — if you can understand that. I'd spend the evening with her and it was great for me to get out from the mass of humanity living in two rooms. We started in one room. Then we got two.

Summerhill was tenements — big four-storey-over-basement houses. You smelled the poverty — the urine in the hall and up the stairs. We would have had what we called spunkards. A spunkard was a drunkard, a wino. They would come in in the evenings because there were no hall doors on these tenements. The front door was gone and the basements were rat-infested. The spunkards would come in with their methylated spirits so there was always noise at night. There was no electricity; we had oil lamps. Some had gas lamps if you could pay the gas bill. No running water or sanitary facilities whatsoever; there was one privy down at the back of the garden.

In 28 Summerhill in 1946, when I was aware of things and counting, there were 98 people living in that house. There were two rooms on each floor so in eight rooms you had 98 people. We had a big room. There was a wire across the centre, wall-to-wall, and another wire running from the middle of that first wire, so the room was divided in three: two quarters and a half. The first quarter had a door and that was the reception — in which you had a bike, a pram, the logs and turf, the coats, everything. The second quarter was the children's bedroom, one big double bed. The half comprised the kitchen, the living room and the parents' bedroom. The wires had sheets hanging from them and the sheets were made from sugar sacks and flour sacks stitched together. The dividers reached only six or seven feet up, so that mass of humanity lived together. I remember in the film *My Left Foot*, the boys sleeping in the one bed and shouting, "Would you ever get your foot out of me mouth!" I remember it well. Later on, as the eldest boy, I would go to bed last and eventually I got a sleeping bag from Alpha Bargains in Liffey Street and I'd roll in under the bed rather than get into it.

The point I'm trying to make is that we were all very happy. My mother was always talking — the Granny was the balance with her wisdom. She was very wise — and told stories. Neither my grandmother nor my mother could read or write. My greatest achievement in life was in 1952 when my mother read to the family the front page of the *Evening Herald*. I taught her to write her alphabet, taught her to read, starting off slowly. Eventually she got very excited when she could say, "I can read, I can read!" The most important thing she read was about the *Flying Enterprise*, a huge story in Irish life, the first big event after the War. A ship sinking in mid-Atlantic — it was the first global event covered by the media. We had no television; you had the wireless and the newspaper — the *Herald* and the *Mail*. It was on the front page of the *Herald*. When it capsized in mid-Atlantic, the captain, Kurt Karlsen, gave the order to abandon ship but stayed on board himself. He tied himself to the wheel. For the first time, RAF planes refuelled in Shannon, flew out to the ship and took pictures and they were on the front pages of the papers. We had never seen anything like it — it was exciting and it went on for fourteen days. A tug went out from Portsmouth to tow the ship back to England. The pictures showed a line being attached to the *Flying Enterprise*, a guy going over — and his name was Darcy, my mother's maiden name. He helped the captain to keep the ship afloat. I can remember it all as if it were a film — we followed it up every day. That was the first thing my mother read.

You got your tea in the evening about half-six — tea and bread. My father got his dinner because he took a lunch to work — he got his egg and his rasher. We had to wait till he was finished and then we all knelt down and said the Rosary. Then the kids had to be washed and put to bed. Before that I said, "Da, can I borrow the paper for a minute?" My father jealously guarded his skills and abilities — he would often say, "Why does the Ma need to read, can't I do it for her?" He could play the spoons. He was a great tap dancer but he would not show me. He was a great guy but he liked to be the star of the show. I got the paper off him and gave it to my Ma and I told everybody to be quiet. And she read, "The *Flying Enterprise* in mid-Atlantic . . ." That's the thing in my life I remember most — it was coaching, training. I'd love to be a teacher — and that's what I think I do in much of my work. That sparked off in me the trait of trying to help people, to work with them, trying to get things done through other people and trying to get people to realise their potential.

At the Eucharistic Congress in 1932, my Dad, having been in the Army, had helped Alfie Byrne, the Lord Mayor, to set things up in the Park. He was also a Sodality man in the Pro-Cathedral. He knew all the priests and the Archbishop. Alfie Byrne got to know him well and when the Congress was all over, my Dad got a lovely reference from him. Alfie sent him down to Mr Brooks in Brooks Thomas and he got a job. But Brooks Thomas closed down during the War — they were in builders' materials and there were simply no ships coming in.

May 31 1941 was a significant date in Dublin's history — German planes bombed the North Strand and we lived only 500 yards away. My father, then being in the Local Defence Force, gathered up all the troops in Buckingham Street School. They went down to the North Strand to go into the rubble — people don't remember now that 36 people were killed and 140 injured. It was heavy stuff. My father went there on Friday night and did not come back until Sunday evening.

My mother told me this story one night — I used to stay up late with her. She told me the Da came back, covered in grime, his fingernails ripped to bits, his hands in a terrible way. She took him out to the back yard with Dettol, the Sunlight soap, the basin and the scrubbing brush — and she scrubbed the grime out of him. We always had a big black stew-pot on the open hearth. In the pot were bones, carrots, onions — a vegetable stew running all the time. She had put the kids all down with the Granny and she gave my Dad his stew. He was very morose, naming all the people who had died, friends, neighbours but, in particular, one lady he knew well, a gorgeous girl who was there, dead, covered in rubble. When he went to lift her up, it was only her head. He never found the body. He broke down and cried. As my Ma tells the story, she took him to bed and nine months later I was born. She said, "Whatever the Germans did in bombing Dublin, you were the result of it."

My father was a keen Army man and kept all his Army contacts. He plotted everything that happened that night — where the bombs fell. The plane had made two or three runs up the Liffey. Was it lost? Did it think it was bombing Belfast or Manchester? Belfast had suffered a huge blitz three months earlier, hundreds of planes. De Valera sent fire brigades up from Dublin, Dundalk and Drogheda. One of the fire brigades that went up was from Buckingham Street, two more went up from Dorset Street and my father maintained that the Dublin raid was Hitler trying to blow up the Buckingham Street and Dorset Street fire stations. If the plane had been flying 300 yards more to the East, those are what it would have got — my father showed me on the map. He believed that. What people did not realise was that a last bomb fell in the Phoenix Park. It did not explode — my father knew that from his contacts in the military. He maintained it was the Germans trying to get the Ulster Protestant President, Douglas Hyde, in his house. My father maintained that all his life. In 1998, there was an article in *The Irish Times* — I still have the cuttings — an Irish research assistant in Munich, going through the German archives, held the file on Operation Roman Helmet: strict instructions from the Führer to make sure that Mr Irish de Valera did not interfere again.

After the War, 1947, I used to go down to the markets with my Ma, half-six or seven o'clock. I was five or six and would see her buying the apples, bananas and oranges — bananas were a new fruit in Dublin in those days. We took to them — you would buy the bananas in packs and they were green. We'd take them home and put them in the wardrobe full of clothes. Nothing hung in the wardrobe — it was stacked with all sorts of bits and bobs. We'd push the bananas in and in two or three weeks they were ripe. It meant that if you ever wanted to eat something, all our lives there were bananas — we were raised on fruit. To this day I have a banana sandwich for my breakfast.

I saw my Ma doing the buying and selling. I learned how to guess how many apples there were in a box because what would be written on the box would be one thing; when you opened it, it would be another. I learned by the weight whether it was full of paper or apples — there were times when they would have the box half full of paper. It was a street education.

I had to go to school at half-nine and come home at three o'clock and straight down to help my Ma finish off. I used love my three to six, where I learned to sell: "Get your apples! Get your oranges! Two for thruppence!" I also learned to have a hard neck. My Ma wanted all the kids to be independent and that meant having a hard neck. On Friday night, my father would come home and put his wage package on the mantelpiece. He never opened it. And it would just vanish — we could never see where it went. Then she'd send us up to Mr Riordan's shop with ten shillings and the list of messages. When you returned she'd say, "Take that bottle of milk back and change it and change that quarter-pound of sausages." "What do you mean, Ma?" "Just change it." "What'll I say, Ma?" "Tell him what you like." You'd go up and say, "Mr Riordan, this bottle is too cold." "What do you mean, too cold?" My Ma would have put a tiny mark on the silver foil cap. "And these sausages are too pale, have you got redder sausages?" Or, "These sausages are too red, have you got paler sausages?" When you would come back, she'd say, "Well done." Some of my brothers and sisters couldn't do it and I'd have to sneak out with them and tell them what to say, "The bread is too hard, it's too stale. I got the wrong bread. I wanted the other bread. I don't want Johnson Mooney's, I want Kennedy's." And so on. That was to give you a hard neck. You had to learn about confrontation: don't get into an argument, just get what you want. You have to sort it out in your own mind in your own way and the way Liam does it is different from the way Noel does it is different from the way Brian does it. The girls, of course, would go up and say, "Mr Riordan, can you change that for me, please?" And he would say, "Certainly, love." My mother was really teaching us all the time.

The tenements were condemned in 1948. I remember the Lord Mayor, Alfie Byrne, standing in our hallway saying, "Yiz are going — we're knockin' them all down!" And we had Ballyfermot and Donnycarney to go to. Cabra and Marino were probably the first estates built outside Dublin but Ballyfermot and Donnycarney were really the first places to house the inner city and, in particular, the inner city of Sean McDermott Street, Summerhill down to Rutland Street. We got the keys to a house in Ballyfermot Road (not far from my offices now) and out we went. Now, when you say out we went with Mary Darcy, you walked. We walked from the Five Lamps to Ballyfermot Church, which took one-and-a-half hours. When I went into the house, it was a palace. There were three bedrooms and a bathroom upstairs. There were lights, an indoor toilet. I had never seen a bath before, a fitted-out kitchen, with a gas cooker. "Ma! Three bedrooms — can I have one?" She said it was too far out; she couldn't afford the bus fares. So we got keys to Donnycarney — the same thing. She eventually took a room at the top of a little house in Portland Row, at the junction of North Circular Road going down to the Five Lamps. We moved down there and stayed for four years. When she had over nine kids, we got two rooms. One room became the kitchen/living-room/parents' bedroom and the other room was two beds, one for the boys and one for the girls.

In 1952, we moved down to the North Strand flats — they are still there, James Larkin House. They were terrific when we got there first, lovely three-bedroom apartments but, by the time that the last of the 56 tenants went in, all it takes is one bad apple in the barrel. Having come out of the tenements, the first thing the bowsies did was to chop down the doors for firewood. They used the hallways as toilets. We lasted four years there — great neighbours, great friends. I honestly think my time there fashioned my ambition to get places, to get out of the poverty. Those four years I was between the ages of ten and 14.

The Da had it very simple. He came home every Friday night and there were the wages, what more did she want him to do? He worked six days a week and gave her every penny he earned — that was three or four quid and the out-goings were eight quid. So my Ma, as Chancellor of the Exchequer, was left to make up the difference — she sold fruit and applied our minds to any other way of making money. The ways we made money are just unbelievable. We used make artificial flowers from crepe paper with wax and gilt paint. To this day I can make a rose. It was an assembly line. One fellow cut the paper, the other fellow turned it, the other fellow made a flower, the other fellow put the wire on it — we were like an arts and crafts department. My job then — the eldest with the hard neck — was to go out to the houses in Marino, crawl into the gardens and break the hedges to get what we called "a bit of green". You put the little branch of a bush onto the wire stems. You sold them for a shilling. The only cost we had was the tissue paper — you bought dozens of sheets for a tanner.

The Granny sold fish on Wednesdays and Fridays in Summerhill and later in Moore Street. My mother negotiated with the Christian Brothers a three-day week for me: "He's my eldest son, we've all these kids and he has to work with the Granny on Wednesdays and Fridays." I went to school Monday, Tuesday and Thursday. On Wednesdays and Fridays, we'd go out to Howth on the quarter-to-six train from Amiens Street, we'd go down the pier and buy the Howth herrings. They put them into a flat box about five feet long. It had a metal strand at each end to lift it with. We'd buy 60 to 80 Howth herrings. I would jump down into the trawler and Molly would say, "Get down there, son, and get 60 of the biggest, fattest herrings you can find." We'd buy them for a penny each, I'd throw them up and she'd pack them in the box, which we would drag to the railway station and put into the cargo van. As Gay Byrne[1] said, that's where he used put his bike — and the smell of the fish off it . . . We'd get into Amiens Street Station at about half-seven, where we would have the pram parked. The box went on top of the pram and off we'd go through the streets selling fish. She would cry, "Howth herrin's, get your Howth herrin's, thruppence each." That's where I began to learn about supply and demand. In the morning you might even get a shilling for three fat herrings, late in the evening they would get cheaper and cheaper. There was nothing you could do with them — you'd either eat them, or throw them out, or give them away. That's the way it worked.

Then, every evening, four o'clock, down to Princes Street to the *Evening Herald*. I sold newspapers every evening from the time I was six. I'd buy them off what they called "the shopper" — the shoppers

---

[1] *In Good Company*, pp. 37–55.

were the people who'd take huge quantities, maybe a hundred dozen and he'd give me three dozen. I can remember clearly the prices — he'd buy them for a penny-farthing, I'd buy them off him for a penny-halfpenny and the list price was tuppence. I used get three dozen, would not pay him, sell them and come back and pay him. As I learned then, I was making a return on a nil investment, wasn't I? I learned then too that there was such a thing as volume because he said to me, "If you took ten dozen, Bill, I'd give you a bit of a rebate, a shilling back." So I got my two brothers and had what were called stringers. I would give them thruppence for the night and I would get the profit and the extra shilling from your man. As a newspaper boy of seven, eight, nine, ten, I was making nearly as much money as my father was on a weekly wage in Brooks Thomas.

I remember vividly the launch of the *Evening Press* in 1954. I sold loads of papers. You had to get a pitch to sell papers. I started selling with a guy who had a pitch at Sunset House pub at the top of Portland Row. I then moved up to Gill's pub on the North Circular Road on the way down Rutland Street to Croke Park. Brendan Behan's aunt lived across the road and Brendan lived in Charles Street. He was a good friend of my mother and I knew him well. He'd always buy papers off me but he would not pay me for some time. I'd be told I was short and I'd say, "Mr Behan bought three off me and he'll owe me." He'd give them to people. I'd have it in my little book — when he came to pay you, sure he'd give you ten shillings. I could actually afford to give him papers for nothing because I had been pre-paid.

As a result of the papers, I joined the Belvedere Newsboys' Club. Here's another one of those circles in my life that keep happening. The Newsboys' Club was two doors from the Marlborough Street Pro-Cathedral at the time. It's now re-housed in Buckingham Street as The Belvedere Youth Centre. It was run by the Jesuits from Belvedere College, up the top of George's Street. I was there only for three months when the senior boys from the College, including Tony O'Reilly,[2] had to come and give two or three hours to the kids. Tony was a boxing instructor in Belvedere Newsboys' Club in 1952! His whole career was just starting — he was a hero. We had just moved to the North Strand flats. We were out of the poverty trap. We were living in a lovely clean apartment despite the immediate surroundings. I

---

[2] *In Good Company*, pp. 155–170.

started to read books in the library. For one reason or another, a number of us moved up to the Brugh Mhuire — there was the Brugh Mhuire, the Brugh Phádraig and the Brugh Lorcáin — three Catholic Youth Centres. That started all the wonderful things in my life.

Sean Moran was a social worker in the club. He was a schoolmaster in East Wall and he came every night on his bike — he devoted his life to that club. There are literally thousands of young fellows who will say that Sean Moran and Brugh Mhuire made the difference in their lives. He got us playing soccer and table-tennis — I became a Leinster table-tennis champion. I became a professional soccer player. We had a gymnast there, Tony Myles, who had been in the 1948 Olympics for Ireland — I don't think we've ever had one since. He was a wonderful man who could do double hand-springs, he could walk on his hands, he could do parallel bars. We had never seen anything like this in our lives — I wanted to be an athlete, a gymnast, a soccer player; all those things opened up for me.

From 1952 to 1956 was a fantastic period in my life. I was working every morning in the markets, going to school three days a week — school was a puddin' for me for some reason. I think it was because I started school when I was two. My sister, Vera, who was two years older than me, was my minder. My Ma was out most of the day so Vera took me everywhere but, at four, she had to go off to school and I remember lying on my back and stamping my feet and Vera said, "I'll take him to school, Ma." Ma said, "Take him. I won't be here. You needn't bring him back. Tell the nuns they can do what they like with him." I went up to Gardiner Street School with my two elder sisters and Vera, hard neck, said, "This is my young brother, Liam. Me Ma's gone out for the day and we can't leave him at home. Can we bring him in?" So I go into the girls' school and stay in my sister's class from September to Christmas, sitting there, doing my CATs and colouring, and then they moved me into the boys' school full-time and I jumped ahead a class or two of everybody. They got me at a very early age and opened my mind. How early can you start developing somebody's intelligence and eagerness and curiosity? That's what happened to me. It was like a crèche today, something that was not there in those days — you went to school when you were four or five. Everything came easy to me — mathematics, algebra, solving puzzles. To this day I amaze people with mental arithmetic. We were up in the American Embassy last night with the Links Society — there was a list of about 12 charities getting different amounts. Somebody asked how much was there and I said £552,000. I can look at numbers and give you the answer. I can't use a calculator — it's too slow! Even with the banks, I'll have the interest worked out per annum, all rounded to the nearest thousand or ten thousand.

In 1956, I had a kind of trauma in O'Connell School. I had got a Dublin Corporation scholarship from St Canice's to O'Connell's. I had gone to Canice's in 1948, the same time we moved house down to Portland Row. Canice's was a national school run by the Christian Brothers, wonderful. I had found the nuns kind and generous — they could be firm, but I was used to that. It's one of the attractions in women for me — that they have to be firm. My mother was a disciplinarian, no messin', do what you're told or else. The nuns were pretty similar and Jackie is the same — generous and kind but here are the rules and make sure we all know them.

When I went from the nuns to Canice's and the Christian Brothers, it was very different, probably because I was then far more conscious of everything that was going on. I was able to assess the good and the bad Brothers. The bad Brothers were the fellows with no confidence, insecure. I laid down the ground rules myself because one of the things my mother had said to me was, "Never let anyone put a hand on you, son." The first day with the Christian Brothers we all had to stand up in turn and say what our ambitions were and so on. It was done in alphabetical order so, with a C, I was near the top. The third fellow who stood up, Brady, stuttered. The Brother went over to him and pulled him by the hair-lock. The next fellow was Caffrey, so he was before me. Without any ado, the Brother went over to him, pulled him by the lock, and held him like that during his monologue. He turned to do the same thing to me and I backed off. "Don't put your hand on me." World War Four! He tried to hit me a dig, I ducked and put my fists up — I was six. "Get out!" And he tried to give me a boot in the ass out the door. Up to the headmaster, Brother Gallagher. He said to the headmaster, "I'm not taking this fellow in my class. Put him somewhere else." They were having this dialogue between themselves when I said, "Excuse me — I've no problem, I'll go to his class but he's not going to hit me or pull my hair." "I didn't touch you." "No, but you pulled Caffrey's and Brady's hair like this — what do you think we are, robots?" I stayed in his class but, as you can imagine, I got the leather every day. They had leathers two inches wide and an inch thick. He gave me about 18 slaps that day so I told my Ma about it. She told me to sort it out myself but if he overdid it I was to let her know. I asked her what too much was. "Does it hurt?" "Not really." I had very tough hands from working in the streets.

We had a kind of pact — he realised I had ability. I always got first in the exams even though I did not do any studying. I had a natural gift for all the mathematical subjects. I loved history and Molly, my Granny, had told me all these great stories that started with Cuchulainn, the greatest warrior that ever lived. She would say to me, "You are my little warrior." That put tremendous confidence in me, which is why things happened at an early age. I loved my time with the Christian Brothers, saw some of the activities that you would be aware of today, never saw sexual abuse, but saw things that could have led to it. All I really saw was where they were strict and hit people. I was in sixth class, the scholarship class, at the time and the teacher threw the *glantóir*, the duster for cleaning the blackboard, at a boy called Max. Max ducked and the *glantóir* went out the window. Max was expelled. I went up to the headmaster and said, "He could not answer the question, the teacher threw the *glantóir* at him, he ducked and it went through the window and he was expelled — where's the justice in that?" This probably goes back to the subject of this book and to what my Mother had always said, "Never be afraid to speak your mind."

In 1986, I was sitting with her two or three nights before she died and we did not know she was really sick. I said, "Ma, you gave us some terrible hidings." She said, "I did, son, and you in particular. You were very strong-willed, you know. I had to keep you under control." "Why did you hit us, Ma?" "Do you think I had time to sit down and reason with you lot? Remember, son, every time I hit you, I was telling you I loved you." That was the natural wisdom of these two women I lived with, Ma and my Granny. My Ma never went to school but she was in the hurly-burly of life all day, every day. From her I get my sense of people, my sense of timing, when to say things and when to shut up. She knew who to trust — Jackie has a wonderful instinct for that, more than I have. Jackie will say, "Watch your man", or "He's a nice fellow". She'd be right all the time. She sits in on interviews with me. In a brief look she can see inside people. My mother would do that.

I was in Canice's from 1948 to 1953. Once a year, the social work-ers came round and the poorest kids in the class got a bit of help. There was the *Herald* Boot Fund — they gave out pairs of boots to the poorest kids in the class. You got a voucher to go down to Guiney's to the value of £1-10s-0d. My Ma would go down to Guiney's and maybe put a couple of bob with the voucher and buy vests and runners for all the family — the only time she got boots was the first year. I said, "Ma, they won't fit me." She told me they weren't meant to fit me, they were the biggest size — 13. I said they wouldn't even fit my Da. She said she knew that, but they would make the most in the pawn. They would go into the pawn on Monday morning and come out on Saturday together with my father's suit for going to Mass. The idea was to get something as valuable-looking as possible. That was an-other instance where the *Herald* was a great supporter of the family between me selling the paper and the boys getting free boots.

In 1956, O'Connell School was great — a huge playground in which you could play soccer during the different intervals. It was closer to home than St Canice's — my job was to go home at dinner time and feed the younger ones. Brother Gallagher, who came down from Canice's to O'Connell's, was a kind man but I fell out with the head-master, Dr Carew, because a picture appeared of me playing soccer, winning the Under-14 Schoolboys' League. I was also playing hurling and Gaelic football with the school. Dr Carew said, "You're not to play soccer." One thing led to another between us. He said, "You're going to come to school five days a week." I told him I couldn't because I had to sell fish on Wednesdays and Fridays. I had done all my exams, I had been in the top three in every class. He asked again if I was still playing soccer. I told him I was. He said, "You're not a person we want in this school." At that time you could be thrown out of school for playing soccer — Liam Brady was. Dr Carew and I parted com-pany.

Between the jigs and the reels, I got a messenger boy's job. (We now have a messenger boys' bike rally every Bloomsday — we raise about 30 grand each year.) I used work as a messenger boy for the three months of the summer. I worked in the Monument Creamery, top of Henry Street, Liptons who had shops all over the place, Home and Colonial Stores, HCR Chemists and, one I still have a connection with, Findlaters, at the corner of Cathal Brugha Street. Alex Findlater today is a very special friend of mine — he does the messengers' bike rally with me; he has his old Findlater's bike with my initials carved on it in 1953. He can remember vividly the day he was first brought into the office in the back of the Austin Princess with a chauffeur. He was then Master Alex. The messenger boys would be lined up — you had the messenger boys with the bikes and then the men who drove the dray with the horses. We had to say, "Good morning, Master Alex and good morning, Mr George", and we were to look at the toe of our boots — you don't look the bosses in the eye.

It was still hard to get a job in Dublin after the War — it was not what you knew but who you knew. In those days, I always felt, why could I not be a boss? I told this to my Ma and she said, "You look in the mirror every morning and you'll never meet a man better than you because you have a heart — you're a good lad." I often think of that and the confidence it gave me. I used watch everything that went on in any of the places I worked as a messenger boy. A typical example was HCR Chemists. They had 24 branches in Dublin. I worked in the Henry Street branch most of the time. You'd come in in the morning, clean the windows, dust all the shelves, sweep and wash out the floor. You'd get the cigarettes and the few cakes for the break for the girls who worked in the shop. Then, at a quarter-past-ten every morning, you got on your messenger bike with the stock list to go over to the head office in Grafton Street, where McDonalds is now, where you'd get your stock for the day. So did 24 other messenger boys, so we were there for three to four hours, playing cards, reading comics, doing nothing. I said one morning, "Hey, mister, why are we all coming here every morning and sitting around like eejits? Why don't I come at nine o'clock and he comes at a quarter-past and he comes at half and we'd all be here only 20 minutes?" "Who said that? You shut your mouth and mind what you're doing. You're here to be a messenger boy. You're not supposed to think. Get out!" I went back to the shop and said the same thing. I used leave at a quarter-past-ten and get back at half-two for something that took 15 minutes.

It was things like that that convinced me I could do a lot of things better than a lot of people. In 1956, having gone through trauma at school, I started answering ads for jobs. I wrote about 720 replies to ads without ever getting a response because our address was Larkin House, North Strand Flats. In August of 1956, I was talking to Sean Moran, the social worker, and he said, "Yeah — I suppose address has something to do with it. Use my address, Vernon Avenue, Clontarf,

Dublin 3." The first time I used that address, eureka! The Walden Motor Company invited me in to talk about a messenger job. I went to be interviewed by the company secretary, Michael Cole; he now lives in Booterstown. He told me I needed to be good at sums. Remember those old calculating machines — he did a sum on one, pulled the handle, gave me the sum and kept the answer. I got the bit of paper with pounds, shillings and pence on it. I told him the answer was £39-14s-8d. He said, "How did you do that? You should add up the pennies and then the shillings and then the pounds." I said, "No, I do it all together." He said, "Stand over at the door" and he gave me a longer one. I did the same. He said, "William, come in here, take this young fellow for a little walk and come back here in five minutes." We went back in, and he said, "Now, do that sum." I did the same again. He said, "How do you do that? William, is he able to see the reflection in the window?" I said, "I can add up." "You have the job."

The Monday morning I was to start, we got our six o'clock Mass, went down the market and had to be in Walden's at eight. I popped into the Granny. She said, "Son, I want you to remember one thing. No matter what you're given to do, do it better than anyone else ever did it. If you're asked to clean windows, clean them so that nobody would know there were windows there. If they ask you to sweep the floor, sweep it so that a king could eat his dinner off it." That first day, there were 80 or 90 fellows working there and you'd go round and get a list of what they wanted for their break. I was back in 15 minutes. The break was at half-eleven and the other fellow would not be back at half-eleven, so they used to say about Cullen — that fellow is back before you even know he's gone. Curiosity — I watched everything that went on in the place. As soon as anyone was out sick, I'd ask if I could give a hand. I learned to type, I did shorthand, worked the accounting machine, started to do mechanical work, went into the parts department to learn how to do the stock. Within four years, there was nothing I could not do. I gave up going down to the markets in the morning and I'd be in Walden's at seven, tidying up from yesterday.

Billy Wallace was the boss, he owned the place. He was going home one night very late after a party and saw a light on in the office. I would have been about 17 at the time. He found me there and asked me what I was doing. I told him it was the last day of the month and I had gathered the invoices up from the different departments and was posting them into the debtors' ledger and I'd get all the statements out and down to the GPO that night. The sooner I did that, the sooner I could start ringing people for the money. Before, the bills used not go out till the fifteenth of the month and I could not get the money in and I was getting given out to because there was too much money outstanding. I had two piles of envelopes, one for the GPO, and one that I would hand-deliver on my way home or in the morning so that I would save on the stamps. He took me home that night; the wife was with him in the car; it was two o'clock in the morning. It was New Year's Day — he had been at his New Year's Eve party and he said, "There's a young fellow, on New Year's Eve, in my office, looking after my money — and I want him running this company as soon as he can." I got the job of general manager when I was 21 years old with 200 people on the staff. I went from messenger boy to general manager by observing everything and saying, "I can do that." I was always looking for something to do.

The motor business was backwards in the fifties. You did not need any qualifications — you still don't. There are very few professionals in it. I would think I brought a professional mind to the industry at that stage in that company. I just used common sense. What I say to the trainees here is, "Make yourself available and make yourself invaluable." That's how you climb up the ladder — become noticed for what you do. "Do more than you're paid to do and eventually you will be paid more for what you do."

When I came off the messenger job and went into the office, I had to buy a tie, because there was no tie in the house.

Like my father before me, I would put my unopened wage packet on the mantelpiece but, now that I had a job, I got my dinner like my father, my egg and my rasher. I was now seen to be one of the providers of the family. One day, my Ma said, "It's time you got a suit." We went down to Louis Copeland's, the present man's father — he was a great friend of my mother. He was in Capel Street and we used bring the fruit out the back of the fruit market, through Mary's Abbey, swing around and Louis Copeland's was there on the right. We would pass his place every morning. When I was making my first communion at six, I had this lovely white suit — white jacket, white pants, white socks and white shoes — which every one of the seven boys had for communion and confirmation because the suit went up and down to fit the occasion. It was big when you were making your communion and small when you were making your confirmation. Louis

Copeland made that suit for her — I was tailored by Louis Copeland
at the age of six. He was never paid — there was great generosity of
spirit there. Every Saturday morning, I'd give him a half-dozen bananas in a brown paper bag. I asked, "Ma, why doesn't Mr Copeland
pay me for the bananas?" And Mr Copeland got his half-dozen bananas every Saturday morning for as long as I was there. He made me
a beautiful grey flannel suit. When I went into Walden's on the Monday morning, there were wolf whistles and, "Who does your man
think he is?" But I looked well and grey is still my favourite colour.

I started going to night school in the Parnell Square Tech. I did
bookkeeping, marketing and English — six to ten with a spare hour in
between, so I did shorthand and typing as well rather than do nothing. In a recent talk to the Chamber of Commerce, I said, "I'm delighted the Chamber of Commerce has invited me to lunch and I'll tell
you why." In 1958, I was awarded the Usher prize for getting top
marks in the Tech for bookkeeping and commerce. We were invited
to lunch in the Ouzel Galley, where they had their chambers. Reflecting the status at the time, the boss drove over in his big Zephyr
Zodiac and I walked across the Ha'penny Bridge. I waited for him and
we went in the door together and there was a porter, "Good morning,
sir." "Wallace, Chamber of Commerce." "Thank you, sir." The porter
told me to stay put and he'd be down to me later. The porter said,
"You're not Billy Cullen's son, are you? I knew your Dad in the Army.
You're not invited to the lunch — it's your boss goes to the lunch.
You'll be getting the presentation afterwards. Have you anything to
eat?" We went under the stairs in the Ouzel Galley where I shared his
sandwiches. I went up then and got my certificate and £20.

Even in the tenements in 1948 I can remember reading. When we
moved down to Portland Row, we had electric light and my Ma took
the bulb out of my light because I'd stay up all night reading. I had to
buy a flashlight so I could read under the bedclothes. If anyone were
to ask me what was the basis of my success, I'd say it was reading and
expanding my knowledge. Sean Moran in the Boys' Club had a little
library, three feet wide, about 150 books. He said, "Bill, start at A and
end at Z", and every Saturday night he would give me an exam. I
could read a book a night. I did the same thing at Charleville Mall Library on the banks of the Royal Canal at the North Strand Bridge. I
would read everything until I found what I liked and what I didn't
like.

I got an invitation yesterday from John Stafford, the former Lord Mayor, to join himself and Bertie Ahern in Cusack's Pub on the North Strand, because they're starting a fund for the St Agatha's organ restoration. St Agatha's was the church beside the library. I was told to bring my cheque book. We call Agatha's Church William Street Church. My brothers and I were altar boys there all our lives, Lourdes Church in Sean McDermott Street before that and St Joseph's in Portland Row — it's not a church any more.

We had a devout Catholic upbringing. I went to Rathfarnham Castle every year for a silent retreat. I was absorbed in the Old Testament and the Gospel. My bedside reading for years was the Gospel according to St Luke. St Luke fascinated me. He was not an Apostle. He never saw Jesus Christ. He was a physician in Rome when Christ died and Christ was dead two years before St Luke went to the Holy Land. He went round and spoke to a lot of people before he wrote his Gospel.

It was kind of like history — I got fascinated with heroes — Cuchulainn, whom we've mentioned, Finn MacCool, Brian Boru, Robert Emmett, Michael Collins — they would all have a very special place for me. I have all their books here. There's a girl, Morgan Llewellyn, who has written historical novels about those people. I wrote to her recently and got a lovely letter back and we'll meet soon. She's an American girl whose father used tell her about these Celtic heroes.

Molly Darcy, in 1902, when she was ten, was a downstairs maid in a magnificent house on Mountjoy Square, when those houses were very like Merrion Square today. As a downstairs maid, you came in and went out the back basement. The only people allowed upstairs were the butler and the upstairs maids. I bought this house where we are today in 1990 and brought Molly Darcy down here. If you look at this room, the guests would come in through this door at my back and the servants would come in that other door from downstairs. Molly Darcy sat here and the pull handle for the bells was still here. She sat here and cried: "To think that a grandchild of mine would be living in one of these houses."

In 1968 I became the managing director in Walden's. It was a family business from Billy Wallace's father before him — I was the first outsider to be the boss. Billy had two sons going to Trinity, young Billy and Vincent, fine lads, great personal friends of Richard

Burrows.[3] Vincent Wallace sat right through school with Richard
Burrows. The old man was very tough on the two young ones. They'd
often come in to me from college to say there was a dress dance on
Friday night — they needed a few quid and a car. I told them I would
organise things for them but that they knew the rules — you didn't get
anything without working for it. They would come in on a Thursday
afternoon and I would put them in the office doing something. We
had a situation where, if someone introduced a customer to us, they'd
get a fiver — I used that to cover up the few bob I was giving them.
Billy Wallace found out and I was nearly fired — how dare I interfere
with his parental role: "Those kids have to work for every penny, just
like I did." I said, "Mr Wallace, you had to work hard just like I had to
work hard. My kids won't have to work as hard as I did and yours
won't either." Eventually, common sense prevailed and we put the
lads on a small stipend. But it was a reflection of the times and the
discipline that was there — and the way everything was starting to
change.

In 1972, Vincent was finished college — I remember him coming in
with Richard Burrows. It was time for him to come into the business
but he was going to do another year in philosophy in which he still has
a huge interest. I said to the boss, "I think it's time I moved on to make
room for the lads." He said, "No, you're staying here." "Let me put it
like this: I've been running the company for the past four years; it's
now their turn to do it and, I'm sorry, but I won't be able to work for
them." We agreed privately that I would stay on for 12 months so that
there could be an overlap with Vincent and that's what happened.

You learn about timing, don't you? I left on Friday, woke up on
Saturday morning and the Six-Day War had broken out in Egypt. I
had arranged finance for my own garage, I had bought a site in
Tallaght, I had a dealership commitment from Ford, I had a credit
line organised with the banks and on Monday it was all gone. Do you
remember the time when you could not get a gallon of petrol? October 1973. The banks went away with their credit line, I could not buy
my site, there were no Ford dealerships being given out and I ended
up in Ballymun, where I opened a used-car lot at a service station. I
went through the rigours of being a one-man band. I did that for
three years until things recovered in 1976 and then I went ahead with

---

[3] See Chapter 1, pp. 7–27.

the plans that had been shelved for three years. We built a big dealership in Tallaght and we became the biggest Ford dealer in the country. I worked as a Ford dealer from 1976 to 1986 and then I got the opportunity of the Smith Group.

Paddy Hayes, the managing director of Fords, was very close to me. I had spent 30 years with Fords. When I heard that the Smith Group was being broken up for sale by Waterford Glass, of which Paddy was then chairman, I rang him and told him that I would like to buy one of the garages in Templeogue. It was a Renault garage that I was going to turn into a Ford garage. I offered a hundred grand — they wanted two. I rang Paddy again and said, "This guy is looking for too much — have you no influence?" He said, "Bill, what are you doing buying one garage? Why don't you buy the lot?" I said there were 20 garages. He said, "I don't mean that — I mean the whole Smith Group." There were 47 companies in the Group — they had Rucon, building construction; they had CRV, commercial road vehicles; they were making railway carriages for CIE; they had Hodges, which was wallpapers and paint; they had finance companies and everything. I said, "Paddy, how much is this being sold for?" He said, "A pound." February 1986, I went down to meet him in the Shelbourne. He said, "Bill, the other side of the coin is we have £18 million worth of debt — you'll have to find someone to fund that." What I did not know at the time was that Waterford had got a credit line of $100 million in New York, one of the conditions of which was that they had to sell their loss-making subsidiary, the Smith Group.

Des Peelo was my financial hand-holder through it all. What I had to go on was my common-sense instincts of deal-making. We eventually got the money from Barclays with Waterford's help — none of the Irish banks would touch us. I had one banker who said he would not give us 18 pence, never mind £18 million. I was originally negotiating with Paddy's financial controller, Tony Brophy, who was easy to deal with because he was anxious to get rid of the company, but then Paddy brought in Gerry Dempsey,[4] who was a tough negotiator. The whole pattern of the thing changed. Halloween, 1986, we were concluding the deal in the Smith Group head office in Fitzwilliam Street and the next thing Gerry said, "Bill, this deal has to be concluded by ten o'clock." We had been at it three days there, day and night. Gerry

---

[4] *In Good Company*, pp. 59–74.

put it up to us, he said, "That's it lads. I'm drawing a line in the sand. If you want to buy the company for a pound, that's the balance sheet you're buying. Now make your mind up in the next 15 minutes." Des Peelo turned to me and said, "Bill, what do you want to do?" I said, "You tell me." Des said, "You need £1 million in there." Gerry Dempsey said, "You're not getting it. Make your mind up." And he walked out. I probably had a net worth at the time of £300,000 or £400,000 and I had to put everything in — the house, the keys of the car, the savings account — the lot.

I said, "I'll go out for a walk — I'll be back in a minute." I walked out of the beautiful house on Fitzwilliam Square. It was drizzling rain. I turned up my collar. It was about 8.30, Halloween, very dark. The next thing: "How are ye, luv — are you looking for action?" There were three English ladies of the night standing under the lamplight with one umbrella. I went over, "How are ye, girls? How's it going?" "It's very quiet and it's very cold — if you have a car you can have it for nothing." And I thought, wouldn't it be great to bring these three ladies back to the house where a bar was set up in the basement for the legal eagles and the accountants and we'd have a bit of fun.

I wandered off and thought to myself, what have I to lose, when you think of these poor girls trying to make a living out here — what's life for, only taking a chance? I went straight back. There was an oratory in the house — it had been the Lord Lieutenant's once upon a time. I said, "Gerry, the boys said I had to get £1 million into this balance sheet." "You're not getting it, Bill." "I'll do the deal if you put in half-a-million and I won't if you don't. It's as simple as that." He said, "I won't." "All right, we're walking." He said, "Hold on a minute — we'll put in £250,000." "You won't, you'll put in £400,000." He said, "I'll put in £350,000." We shook hands, he opened the door and shouted, "Right — we've a go!" Then he said, "Where's the phone? Where's the phone?" It was nine o'clock and it was many years later that I learned that they had until five o'clock in America (five hours behind) that Friday to confirm the sale of the Smith Group or $100 million for Waterford was gone. I always think I could have stuck out for the million and got it!

We bought the company and the first couple of years were horrendous — we were living on a knife-edge. I told you that the Smith Group consisted of several companies, including making railway carriages for CIE. The first day I'm in the company, I'm told that we have a great order for 20 wagons for CIE — about £1.5 million. I asked how much we were making on it and was told they did not know. Des Peelo and I figured out that we were going to lose 15 grand on every one of those wagons. We folded that company. They had a depot down the quays, not far from my friend Harry Crosbie's Point Depot. We sold it to him and he's probably sitting now on £10 million when we would nearly have paid him to take it off our hands. We sold off all the properties. We had two businesses in Northern Ireland in the paint and wallpaper business. It all goes back to the fact that Con Smith was a magnificent entrepreneur. You remember, he died in 1972 in the Staines air disaster. Gemma, his wife, had to sell off the Renault bit to pay off the death duties — as indeed the magnificent home in Killiney was sold for £42,000. It would now sell for up to £8 million. Waterford Crystal, with Noel Griffin — and the McGraths[5] were involved — just bought things. All we did over two years was to reduce it to the core distribution. We kept about six or eight of the garages and leased them to dealers.

Renault had done well in the early eighties — they had the Gordini and the Renault 18, which was very good. In 1981, they had ten per cent of the market — by 1986 it was down to two per cent and the company was practically bankrupt, reflecting the fact that, in France itself, Renault was bankrupt and was being bailed out by the Government. Renault was 50 per cent owned by the State.

Year One, we made 200 grand against a loss of £2 million the previous year. That stabilised things, but we had not made much progress in selling off the assets and we were paying the banks between 18 and 24 per cent interest. I remember waiting for Jackie in the Stillorgan Park Hotel in 1989, when we had things on an even keel, and a beautiful girl tapped me on the shoulder and said, "Hello, Bill." I did not know who she was and I saw Jackie coming in and this girl says, "Do you not remember you owe me a nice big brandy?" Jackie comes over a bit frosty. I say, "Hiya, love, this is . . ." She turned to Jackie and said, "I'm Gemma Boylan — in actual fact, he's never met me. Tom Boylan in Barclays handled his account from 1986 up to last year and he owes me a brandy because my husband used to walk the floor every night screaming about the Smith Group and the £18 million they owed him."

---

[5] *In Good Company*, pp. 77–93.

It was Patrick's Day in 1988 that I felt we were really getting our head above water. For me, spring, Patrick's Day, is the beginning of everything. One of the things that was strangling us was that we were in that big premises on the Naas Road that SDS/An Post are in now. The Smith Group had built it in 1981. We could not take that asset on to our balance sheet because it stood them £3 million and we'd have to take that on with bank borrowings. They leased it to me for 400 grand a year. I said we had to get out of that big mausoleum and get a smaller, more cost-efficient headquarters. January 1988, Fiat closed up in Ballyfermot and put their premises up for sale. We bought it for £500,000 with bank debt, so I had costs now of 60 grand a year rather than 400. We never looked back.

Today I'm turning over £250 million in the company with a strong product range. Renault have bought Nissan — that further strengthens the company. I'm looking forward to the next five or ten years and seeing Renault become a major player in the Irish vehicle market with a reputation for excellence. That's our mission statement.

I sit here with you today and look at where I am, think how lucky I am. When I think back to the tenements and all the things we did as kids to raise a few bob, it does not depress me — I feel great about it. I'm never afraid to talk about it — I feel it's what gave me all the basics of business. I got a better education on the streets and working with my Ma than I would ever have got at college and did it all an awful lot quicker. I got a compressed education — by the time I was 14, I could do a deal on anything, I could buy and I could sell. Another thing I learned from those two wonderful women was, "You're not really selling anything, son; you're helping people to buy." I preach that now to my young colleagues. I say to them, "If you show trust, sincerity and integrity, people will buy off you." There was a shop in Parnell Street, Duggan's Pharmacy, opposite Walden Motor Company. A Mr O'Sullivan owned it. I went in there as a messenger boy because the fellows would want Aspro and Alka Seltzer. Mr O'Sullivan had his daughter, Ciara, working there, a beautiful girl. She became a Rose of Tralee and married John Byrne. She was the apple of my eye but the thing I shall never forget about her father was, behind the counter in his shop there hung a sign: "The price of everything you buy includes the integrity of the man you buy it off." I carry that thought with me everywhere. I never sold anything in my life, but people will buy anything off me, because they believe me, trust me, I look after them and never let them down. You exceed expectations, you go the extra mile, you keep all your commitments. These might be trite sayings, but I've always tried to live them.

That's what I tell these kids out there in the training centre, and they love it. The motor trade is scarce of professional talent — it's not an attractive industry. Four years ago, we put an ad in the paper. We said we were looking for young people who were cheerful, honest, liked dealing with people, had an outgoing personality and wanted to work in the motor business with the Renault company. We got 680 applications. I invited the whole 680 of them into the Burlington Hotel for the day. We took a ballroom and had buffets going. I addressed them and told them all that they had the ability to be what they wanted to be. I told them that, unfortunately, we could take only 20 — we'd take 60 for the next interview and then we'd take 20. I think I got over 500 letters from those kids. We picked 60, we got 20 and we took them down here — we have replicated that through the years.

You should go up to Liffey Valley to see the future of the motor industry. If you go there, you will meet a dozen sales consultants, three-quarters of them young girls — and they're all helping you to buy your car, with honesty, trust, sincerity, commitment and integrity. That's how we are developing the Renault network. We'll be starting a course next week. They become very loyal to the company: this is Renault and this is Bill Cullen — and this is Jackie. Jackie will be popping in and out. I'll try and motivate them to realise their potential. I'll say to them, "It might be that you won't stay with us, that you will go on to bigger and better things". When the young people walk around the lovely gardens here, I say to them, no matter what position you are on the totem pole, you can aspire to this. I tell them it's all about their own ability.

The motor trade gets into your blood. It's a great business to be in because you meet so many people — everyone has a car.

Success is not all about financial success, as we know. The first priority is your health. Molly Darcy used say to me, "Stay strong and fit, son, you know you are the eldest and we rely on you — so you have to look after yourself first. Don't think that's selfish. You come first. A lot of the others are not as strong as you, so you have to mind them." I've ended up in that role with the family as well, lucky enough. So there you are.

3

Mark FitzGerald

Sherry FitzGerald Group plc

"Running right through the business from day one has been a sense of innovation, focused not just on today and tomorrow but on the day after tomorrow."

Mark FitzGerald is chief executive of the Sherry FitzGerald Group plc.

He was born in Dublin on 23 June 1957. His father is Garret FitzGerald, former Taoiseach (Prime Minister). His mother was Joan O'Farrell. He is third in a family of three, the other two being John and Mary. He is married to Derval O'Higgins, a solicitor. They have five children: Ciara (15), Garret (11), Erinne (8), Loaise (5) and Meadhbh (2).

He was educated at the College of the Sacred Heart, Leeson Street; Gonzaga College; and the College of Commerce, Rathmines (Auctioneering).

In 1975, he was apprentice auctioneer with FitzGerald & Partners; in 1979, he qualified as an Auctioneer; in 1981, he was made associate director in Fitzgerald & Partners; appointed to the Board in 1982. Later that year, he was one of the five founding directors of Sherry FitzGerald; in 1986, he became managing director. When Sherry FitzGerald became a public company in 1999, he became chairman and chief executive. He is now chief executive only.

He was Chairman on An Bord Iascaigh Mhara from 1996 to 1997; and National Director of Elections for the Fine Gael Party for the 1997 election.

The conversation was recorded in Mark FitzGerald's home on Palmerston Road, Dublin on 5 March 2001.

Mark FitzGerald

Here I am at 43 years of age and I have to ask myself, how did I get to be here discussing my career? I suppose the starting point is that I was born into an academic, middle-class Dublin family, the last of three children. There was a positive, creative and exotic environment at home — my father had an ever-changing and eventful career. He brought a sense of optimism and hope into the house — it was always full of young people, in part because he was a university lecturer. From that environment, I learned to be an optimist and open to change. Ireland was changing in the sixties, seventies and eighties and my parents were very much part of that change. My brother and sister excelled academically but that did not interest me particularly and I probably became an under-achiever at school.

At the age of ten, in my father's study, I came across a 1926 street directory of Dublin. I was fascinated by who lived in the different houses on Eglinton Road where we then lived. Like other children, I was interested in sport and collecting cards from different games and Scalextric. However, from the directory I developed an interest in houses and in architecture. Not being artistic or mathematical, I decided that I would like to sell houses. I would cut out from the newspapers all the house ads and put them in a scrapbook. I probably tailored my schooling towards being an auctioneer. To gain entry into the auctioneering course, a very low hurdle at that time, all you needed was a pass Leaving Certificate.

I was a difficult adolescent. My parents found me very challenging but they did know what I wanted to do. So, after an indifferent Leaving Cert, I got into the auctioneering course and also got a necessary apprenticeship — in September 1975, at £6.00 a week. That's how bad things were in Ireland at the time, but I was very committed. I loved houses and I loved people, so I found my métier, something I had not found in formal education. It was really only when I got into the business and enjoyed it that I got the self-confidence to do it. Looking back, perhaps I should have paid more attention to my formal education — you would not get away now with what I got away with then. Once I got into business, I had to make up for lost time — any education I've got is self-education. I began to read a lot — that broadened my horizons and developed my mind. With the house full of books, with my brother and sister academically inclined, I suppose as a child I had rebelled — the more my parents wanted me to study, the less inclined I was. Now, I would regard myself as an innovator, so I would see myself as better in the area of innovation and leadership than in pure management. I've had to work at management — it does not come naturally to me. A sense of focus and self-discipline is something I have to work on and I'm continually in arrears.

It's easier to lead if you have a natural empathy with people, listen to them and understand them and see the advantage in bringing together their diversity on one team and getting the best out of them, delegating to them and helping them develop an organisation. A manager, on the other hand, has to have a singular focus, a person who has a plan and understands that management is about action *now*. Good management is about implementation. Management is concerned more with processes than with people. The trick in leadership is to get people into situations where they make the processes happen easily. We have a very good management team — they are not the same as me, they complement my skills. The challenge I have is to lead them to be good managers. Good leadership is about upwards, downwards and sideways communication. Whether it's family or business, you can't communicate enough.

It's no use *telling* people something has to be done. You have to discuss with them what the issue is, knowing clearly what you want done. You have to bring people around to the same conclusion, developing and tweaking it. Then you have a much better chance of getting implementation.

When Sherry FitzGerald was founded I had to take on real responsibility, having enjoyed myself for my first quarter century. That was in a country that had a growth rate of minus two per cent and a mortgage interest rate of 18 per cent, with inflation of 17 per cent. I still lived with my parents and, when I came home, there were really not a lot of people I could share my problems with because my father had a worse problem — he had to take responsibility for running the country.

Many of my generation were forced to emigrate and the choice was to stay at a relatively low standard of living with few prospects — or go. I did consider going but decided to stay and make the most of it.

There were a lot of auctioneering firms in Dublin and no barriers to entry. There were many professionals who wanted to finance a standard of living but had little business strategy. It was a purely re-active business based on connections. People in the business were GPs — they did everything in terms of property. They had a number of skills but there were very few specialists in any one area.

My objective was housing and I came to the conclusion that not many people in Dublin approached that market in a customer-oriented fashion. Not through any grand design, but through one event after another, I decided that, if we could offer a quality service at a time of the day that suited people, they would give us the busi-ness. In other words, we had to give benefit before we got the busi-ness. I don't think anybody had quite thought of the business in that light before. The starting point was to assemble a team of people who could offer a high-quality service that would be different from what other auctioneers were offering.

Being young and in a small enough city at that time, one tended to know people who were able and like-minded and were hungry: the team we put together consisted of people in their early to mid-twenties. It was easy enough to recruit people. They had two alterna-tives: they stayed in the businesses they were in or they emigrated. There were few prospects in the businesses they were in, so it was easy enough to sell when the plan was outlined — we were going to do something exciting together, creating a really great business.

From early on, I saw it as a social democratic business — to win, we were prepared to be generous-spirited in involving other people. I had no problems with sharing equity — I thought that was the best way to retain people. A thing I learned from my father during the 1981–82 elections was the need to motivate people by giving them a cause — enthusiasm and a sense of commitment. Fine Gael managed to do that in the early eighties even with so boring a subject as the elimination of the national debt. The second thing I learned, going around 41 constituencies with my father and my mother, was the changing role of women in Irish society. The marriage ban had not been long lifted from the civil service and Fine Gael had a number of women candidates. I could see that the older men in grey suits in the party were rather sceptical about women standing in an election, moving on from making tea and sandwiches and licking envelopes. They were surprised when the women did very well in the election. I saw the new dynamic women brought to Fine Gael, helping my father to change the party and Irish society. I knew from my reading that women in America had been very successful in real estate. They had the organisational skills and the important empathy.

I wanted to prove myself. My father was and is different, and is quite competitive. As I grow older, I see that some of that competition has rubbed off on me. The customer-centred proposition was my philosophy. There was a city of a million people. My job was to make them want to use us — by giving a different service, by opening seven days a week, by having committed young people, people of high ethical standards, people who were prepared to work very hard, who were prepared not only to sell a house to somebody but to offer them wise counsel, realising that buying a house was a traumatic event. And being interested in selling a house for the maximum price because ultimately that's what the business was about; otherwise there was no justification for people to use you.

The period from 1983 to 1987 was the formative years — a number of key people joined the business; they are still its foundation. We have about 45 senior people in the company and fewer than five have left in 15 years. It's like David Ogilvy said: "Create a brand, hire people brighter than yourself and let them get on with it."

In the late eighties, things began to pick up in Ireland and we managed to start growing the business. We opened our first branch in 1989 in Terenure, a big event. Then we were hit by the Gulf War. The currency crisis in the early nineties was a difficult time. We knew we could succeed in a big way if we got a break economically — we used the recession to our advantage. We knew we could grow market share in difficult times because the opposition were not as focused as we were on being competitive — they were more focused on survival. We used those difficult times so that, when there was a turnaround, we could rise with the tide. I would not say we were doing *well* during the recession, but we were very focused on winning and getting more boards up.

Running right through the business from day one has been a sense of innovation, focused not just on today and tomorrow but on the day after tomorrow. The brand, Sherry FitzGerald, stood for selling a semidetached house. In 1982, Sherry FitzGerald did not mean anything to anybody — seven years on, it was a brand. Meanwhile, the competition could be doing a landlord-and-tenant case in the morning, letting a flat in the afternoon and dealing with a house sale in the evening. Nobody in Dublin had been associated with ordinary housing for ordinary people because they were either a general practice or were associated with higher value houses and tied into the Establishment. The Sherry FitzGerald brand at that stage stood for ordinary houses for ordinary people — and still does: civil servants, teachers, guards. They were the people we were selling houses for and to. The number of houses sold at the top end of the market was very small. We filled a vacuum that no one else filled.

We then began to develop the commercial business. Being innovative — and being seen to be innovative — was important: seven-day opening, bringing out our own property magazine, revolutionising the standard and style of advertising, bringing out a lot of consumer information in terms of mortgage rates that were not published at the time — and then developing the whole area of property research, informing clients and the public about what had happened and what was likely to happen. We were the first property firm to hire an economist — research has been a key part of our strategy.

In the mid-nineties, when things were taking off, there were two routes we could take: we could milk the cow for all that was in it or we could milk the cow and try to recycle the milk by further investing in the business. I was in a fortunate competitive position — we had assembled a great team of people in their thirties who were coming into their own. I had the benefit at the Sunday dinner table of free economic advice — my brother John is a senior Research Professor in the Economic and Social Research Institute. My father's optimism about the future of Ireland in the mid-nineties was such that, even if he and John were only half-right, it was clear there were great opportunities.

We had the people, there were the opportunities, so maybe we should move things on. We continued to open branches and, in the mid-nineties, we began to shape the vision of what Sherry FitzGerald is today. We now had the residential and commercial businesses established. We had to address the problem that the Sherry FitzGerald brand was a semidetached-house brand. We wanted it to become the core umbrella brand. There was substantial inward investment in

Ireland but the big international companies would not have seen us as the automatic choice — they had international property advisers.

We approached a firm in London called DTZ, a public company, which resulted in the formation of DTZ Sherry FitzGerald which is now a well-established brand, looking after commercial property. From that business, we have already spawned other businesses, like DTZ Pieda, a firm of economic and town-planning consultants.

Having seen the two brands established and having Dublin choke on its own prosperity in the mid-nineties, a thing that caused me to change my view of Ireland was my chairmanship of An Bord Iascaigh Mhara, the Irish Sea Fisheries Board. I had to resign that chairmanship when I became director of elections for Fine Gael in 1997, but it was a year of my life that I enjoyed immensely. It was a complete contrast to property in Dublin. You were dealing with people involved in the fishing industry who lived literally on the periphery of Ireland, people who had been marginalised, who did not connect with Dublin and did not feel that Dublin connected with them. They had suffered from, as distinct from benefiting from, EU accession. I spent a lot of time travelling round the country looking and listening and I felt that there was a new wave of confidence even among those people on the periphery. There was something happening out there that people in Dublin did not fully realise. There was a dynamic to be tapped and exploited. During my time as chairman, we appointed a very good new chief executive, Pat Keogh, who now has an excellent management team and a restructured organisation. I learned a lot from that time.

With that experience and with the experience gained in travelling around the country at election time, I came back to Sherry FitzGerald with the vision that property outside Dublin could be quite exciting. We developed the idea of a franchise business to help us implement that vision.

Ireland has a low-density population, about 130 per square mile, against a corresponding figure for the UK of 622. If we were to expand, as the banks and building societies had done, we could end up with large fixed costs and not a great return on capital. People who are self-employed are generally highly motivated. Franchise was the way to go — with people we knew. We studied other franchising operations, particularly in America, because nobody had franchised the property business indigenously in Europe. Franchising was a way of exploiting our brand and offering a service nationally. People were buying their videos and their groceries from national service providers yet they could not do so for the most important purchase (or sale) of their lives. We gave them the facility in Dundalk to buy a house in Galway. We believed the Irish people would respond to that service. With expert help, it took us about eighteen months to develop the franchise model. We would open our own business in the major cities — Cork, Limerick and Galway — while we concentrated the franchises on the medium to larger towns: any town or city with less than 50,000 people, we would franchise.

In January 1999, two years ago, when we launched the franchise, we had one great courageous man in County Clare, Dermot McMahon. I have known him for twenty-odd years. He ran an established firm, Michael McMahon & Son, in Ennis. He agreed to join us. We were looking for people who shared our values — people who saw that Ireland was changing, who saw there was one growing marketplace throughout Ireland. People were moving into Ennis and buying property and people were moving out of Ennis into other parts of the country. Whether the franchisee was first, second or third in their town was not so much the case; what was important was that they shared our values. Two years on, we are one of the top four or five advertisers in the country and we're one of the best-known brands. When you travel the highways and byways of Ireland, the boards are there to be seen by everybody.

We have 960,000 people between the ages of ten and 24 in Ireland. We have 930,000 aged over 50. The housing stock, depending on who you talk to, needs to increase by anything between 30 and 40 per cent. We needed to increase the stock from 1.2 million houses up to something closer to 1.7 million. Those new houses are not all going to be built in Dublin because Dublin is running out of land. The need for people to live in Dublin has to be reduced — large regional centres have to be developed. That is continuing to happen, though not at the rate I would like. It is in this context that our strategy is based.

We floated the company in April two years ago and, shortly after that, we bought Ross McParland New Homes. Overnight, that made us the number one new homes agency in Ireland. That was very important. There were fewer Victorian homes being sold in Dublin, homes that Sherry FitzGerald had dealt with, while Ross McParland were selling new homes. Ross McParland has kept its name — we own

80 per cent of it and there's a 20 per cent earn-out over five years. We are now poised to meet the upswing in housing with the young generation coming through. We have bought another business in Cork, Burton Crowley & O'Flynn. We now have 20 per cent of the Dublin house market, 15 per cent of the Cork market and 15 per cent of the Limerick and Galway house markets. Three years ago we had eight branches — now we have 50 franchised offices plus 17 branches of our own. We have grown to 67 outlets over a three-year period. In all, including the franchise outlets, there are about 600 people employed.

In the last couple of months, in association with two of our competitors, Gunne's and Douglas Newman Good, together with AIB Bank, we created from nothing a "property portal" on the premise that the customer comes first. The Internet makes it possible to centralise all the information about the house market, but that could happen only if all the industry came together and agreed to a centralised marketplace. Gunne's and Douglas Newman Good shared our philosophy and we put together a business plan. AIB agreed to invest £1.8 million for 23 per cent of the business. We created a business worth £9.6 million before we even started. It was launched earlier this year, headed up by a very able man, Jim Miley. The project is going to revolutionise the house-search process. The children and grandchildren of Ireland will literally be able to visit the marketplace from anywhere they are. American experience has shown that it has cut the viewing time from having to go and see eight houses down to four. It brings our costs down, too, because we will depend less on newspaper advertising. Auctioneers from all over Ireland have now joined up with the three original shareholders. There are other portals but we were off to a flying start — we welcome competition. A significant proportion of the Irish house market will be on this portal. With its geo-mapping system, you can go to the town, to the suburb that you want: you can see all the houses available in Dundrum or Rathmines. If you want to send your children to Wesley College or you work in Citywest, we will be able to show you a route planner. You can see the crèches available in the area. It costs only £50 a house — the cost of advertising a house for auction is about £2,500. The portal is customer-centred.

I subscribe to the philosophy of David Maister — he is the leading guru for professional services firms: it's fundamentally about working as a team, no stars, no egos, do our utmost to offer different services to our clients. The client comes first, the firm comes second and the individual comes third. It's a strategic as distinct from a tactical way to run a professional services firm.

It's a crying shame, now that we have got so much right in the country, that we still get some fundamental things wrong. There are two housing markets: Dublin and the rest of Ireland. Long-term, interest rates are likely to stay low. The rest-of-Ireland housing market is reasonably good value and accessible to our young people. Dublin is, however, a difficult market for a young person to get a start in.

What happened is this. A generation emerged from the Second World War and our fathers and mothers and their brothers and sisters had to emigrate. Things were dismal — people don't realise how bad things were then. Fifty years ago in Dublin the kids selling newspapers had bare feet. When you paint a picture like that, maybe people today understand how far Ireland has come in the intervening 50 years. That generation were patriotic people, partly because they were the children of people who were born into a new State and partly because they had seen so many of their friends and relatives emigrate, not having any choice in the matter. Emigration in those days was a much more final matter than it is today. That whole generation was focused on developing our economy, primarily through inward investment and becoming an industrialised society. We had to look outwards rather than inwards as we had done. We had to create more demand for our products and services. It started in the mid-fifties with Ken Whitaker[1] and John A. Costello. Sean Lemass is the person most synonymous with the change in direction in the post-de Valera era. He was ably assisted by Donogh O'Malley with the introduction of free education in 1968. Probably because we never had a history of success, nobody foresaw its implications. Because we had stability, because we were English-speaking, because we were good Europeans, we changed from a blue- to a white-collar economy and got involved in the high-tech area. We underestimated our success and all the investment was brought into the Dublin region. We had little or no infrastructural investment. We had an agricultural country that hadn't changed its infrastructure in 100 years. Whilst we had the educated people who could tell a good story and were able to work, we were bringing these high-tech industries into Dublin which had come from

---

[1] *In Good Company*, pp. 279–305.

having five per cent of the population to having 30 per cent, with no infrastructural changes. If you compare Dublin in the year 2000 with the Dublin of 1900, we now have a worse transport system. You then had the Harcourt Street railway line. Now you have three times the number of people with a public transport system that is the result of decade after decade of dismal economic performance and no investment. If people want or need to live in Dublin they have to commute farther and farther distances either by car or by a poor transport system. Their quality of life has deteriorated. While their jobs may be stimulating, they are working for survival rather than for prosperity.

This is particularly unfortunate when every city in Ireland is, in European terms, close to Dublin. Cork, which is farthest from Dublin, is a mere 160 miles. There was a man in charge of the roads in Dublin, P.J. O'Sullivan, who wrote an interesting paper. He said we had to have motorways by 1986. He wrote that in 1961 and we still don't have them. I was 16 when we joined the EU in 1973. I'll be at least 49 *if* they do deliver a motorway between Dublin and Cork by 2006. It will have taken a third of a century of EU membership to have a motorway between our two major cities. On a good day, it would take you two-and-a-half hours to get to Limerick by train. If you travel from Le Mans to Paris by TGV, it takes one hour to do the same distance. Granted we have a low-density population, but we do have sufficient riches to be able to link our major cities: Dublin, Cork, Limerick and Waterford. We should be able to do that within a five-year period by bringing in international contractors. If we did that, it would be possible to study in Trinity and live in Limerick. In that way, you would make the property market much more equal. What shapes the property market is our transport system. If we got that right, everything else would follow in the right direction.

We can't just wring our hands about the problems we face. If we care about future generations we have to think about what the solutions are. We know what the problem is. We know what the vision is. What we lack are the mechanics to make it happen. For a start, we need planners and engineers — those are the people who are actually leaving the system. The reverse of what should be happening is what's actually happening. Governments have freedom to act when they wish to do so. When we were approaching the millennium they found ways to pay extra to the essential IT people working for government departments. They have done the same with the Air Corps to keep pilots, because commercial airlines were paying them £100,000 a year. We simply have to pay more money to engineers and planners whether they are working inside or outside the system. Through the media, we have seen these grey areas where people in local authorities have supplemented their incomes and this has undermined the credibility of the system. You have to sympathise with people who are trying to bring up a family on a relatively meagre income. If they are prepared to work those hours, why doesn't the State pay them to work those hours? Then the State as well as the families get the benefit.

Ranelagh is now like Kensington. The media often portray the Irish market largely as Victorian Dublin — which it isn't. There are 1.2 million houses in the country as a whole and there are 35,000 Victorian Dublin houses. Victorian Dublin is three per cent of the Irish housing market. If you see a house in Victorian Dublin getting a big price, it is economically irrelevant. The fact of the matter is that, because our wealth base was so restricted, and because we did not have the industrial revolution, Victorian Dublin was small. Victorian Dublin is in demand because it is so scarce and has become very valuable. In relative terms, it's easier to buy a Victorian house in Wolverhampton than in Dublin. Only 60 houses were built in Rathmines, Rathgar, Dartry, Terenure and Templeogue each year over the 40-year late Victorian/early Edwardian period. That's how slow-moving things were. Nowadays you could see 600 houses built in 18 months in just one estate.

Moreover, with the geographical restrictions of the sea and the mountains, not to mention the Phoenix Park, which is over twice the size of Hyde Park and Regent's Park put together, and the airport to the north, combined with no proper public transport system and a small amount of Victorian housing — those houses in good locations are going to be like jewels. With newfound wealth and a history of private ownership, you have a concoction that pushes prices right up.

Having been in the business now for a quarter of a century and having spent so much of my waking life working, it is extremely important that one does enjoy it. It's important that there is a sense of balance in one's life. I have enjoyed it but generally I have not had enough balance in my life. I'm going to work at that, looking after myself, developing other interests in other areas, but I suppose what's important to me is that I have not only enjoyed the business but I have enjoyed working with the people in it. It's one of life's great journeys to build a business with like-minded people and to be able to look back together and to say that we have created some lasting value — without being self-important, it is good to be able to say that we brought about some progressive change that has benefited consumers. I readily accept the fact that the perception of people would be that firms like ourselves can be responsible for the problem rather than for the solution. People can blame auctioneers for high prices. I would make no apology for that — when somebody comes to us, our job is to get them the best price but that is not to say that we cannot see ourselves as responsible citizens. Society needs to change, so that not only do some of our children get a chance, but all of the nation's children get a chance.

The creation of lasting value is something that's very important to me and to the people I work with. I would hope that we have done our bit to make a more consumer-led Irish house market. The great challenge ahead, now that we have this network together, is to turn ourselves into a financial services and property firm, rather than just a purely property firm. There are two routes — the quality route and the efficiency route. I see ourselves going very much by the quality route. When people come to us with such significant business, our relationship with them deserves to be a quality one rather than one that's based on pure need and efficiency. I can quite understand why a fast-food business is run on the basis of need and efficiency and turnover. Our business has to be based on a relationship that goes deeper so that we become advisers not only to the client but also to their family and friends. Nothing gives me greater pride than to see people and their families returning to us again and again, happy that we have helped them negotiate through some of the more difficult and important areas of their lives.

4

Sean Fitzpatrick

Anglo Irish Bank Corporation plc

"It may not have been the Harvard way. I have a very healthy disrespect for very bright people. It was always about the fact that this is a simple game. What you need are people who are absolutely focused and want to be part of a real team."

Sean Fitzpatrick is Chief Executive Officer of Anglo Irish Bank Corporation plc.

He was born in Bray, County Wicklow on 21 June 1948. His father was Michael Fitzpatrick, a dairy farmer. His mother was Johanna Maher, a civil servant. He was second in a family of two; his sister is Professor Joyce O'Connor. He is married to Caitriona O'Toole, a former secretary in a consultancy company. They have three children: Jonathan (24); David (20); and Sarah (16).

He was educated at Presentation College Bray and UCD (BComm). He qualified as a chartered accountant in 1972, having served articles with Ernst & Young (1969 to 1972), and worked in what is now PriceWaterhouse Coopers (1973 to 1974).

He joined Irish Bank of Commerce as an accountant (1974). It was taken over by City of Dublin Bank (1978). City of Dublin Bank, with the encouragement of the Central Bank of Ireland, bought Anglo Irish Bank (1980) and Sean Fitzpatrick became general manager. In 1986 he became chief executive of Anglo Irish Bank Corporation plc.

He is President of the Irish Bankers' Federation; a member of the Council of the Institute of Chartered Accountants; a director of the Dublin Docklands Development Authority, of a funds management company, Singer & Friedlander, of Lithographic Universal, and of Drury Sports Management Limited.

This conversation was recorded on 31 January 2001 in Sean Fitzpatrick's office in Anglo Irish Bank Corporation plc, Stephen Court, 18/21 St Stephen's Green, Dublin 2.

Sean Fitzpatrick

I was born in Bray in 1948, the second child of Michael and Johanna Fitzpatrick. My mother is now 88 but still very much in touch. She would query why Tiernan O'Mahoney and Willie McAteer were photographed at the recent announcement of our results. Was I losing control? When things went wrong in Waterford Crystal a few years ago, she telephoned me and said, "Make sure you do the accounts every second month in the bank." She's very much alive.[1] My father is dead.

I went to school in the Loreto Convent for a year with my sister. She continued on in the convent and I went to Presentation College, Bray. Presentation Bray was a small school and, when I was doing my Leaving Certificate in 1966, there were only 15 in the class. It was very intimate — you knew the people ahead of you and behind you. Academically, I was at best mediocre. I played a lot of sport — captained the junior and senior rugby teams. We met with some success — we never carried off a Leinster trophy, but we did get to the semi-final, which was incredible for a school of our size. School was happy and, in the fifties and sixties, Bray was a brilliant place for a young person. You had rugby, golf and swimming, and in summer an influx of British tourists, typically from Yorkshire and Liverpool, coming across for their two weeks' holidays. This was before they discovered Spain. At a very early age, we were exposed to people from different cultures.

At 13 and 14, I did casual jobs in the Amusement Arcades on Bray Promenade. I was in charge of the bumpers, where I met my wife for the first time! My sister, Joyce, worked in a guesthouse — it was a happy, simple life. We were not poor but we were comfortable. There were times when my father had a car and there were times when he didn't. We never went away as a family on a holiday, ever.

Joyce was the apple of my father's eye. It was difficult growing up in her shadow. She was very bright and academically inclined. Maybe that's why I devoted all my energies to sport! She has done very well.

---

[1] Sean Fitzpatrick's mother died on 27 August 2001.

We would have left our teenage years with a real understanding of the value of money and a strong work ethic. Money was an issue with me in my twenties, less so with Joyce.

My mother was a typical country mother, keen on the family. She was dominant but she would give up everything for her two children — she made enormous sacrifices for us all the way through her life. That's something that both Joyce and I would be very aware of. Will we be thankful for it? Sometimes, yes, and sometimes, no. It's a burden as well as a comfort. You were always expected to succeed. You'd come home and say, "I ran the best race ever and came second." The first question from my mother would be, "Who got first?" That hurt at times but it was also a driver. I don't blame her for that — she had very serious ambitions for us.

When I was in fifth year, I went to France to work during school holidays — that was unusual in those days. I went by myself. There were only four of us in the French class at school and the teacher had put me in touch with *Etudiants de Travail*, an organisation that would find work for students. The Aer Lingus fare to Paris in 1964 was £15 return. When I got off at Orly Airport I did not know where I was to stay that night. I rang the Irish Embassy. It was closed. I asked somebody how I could get in touch with a church. He gave me the number of a Catholic priest in a monastery in the centre of Paris. I telephoned and said, "Je m'appelle Jean Fitzpatrick. Je suis étudiant irlandais. Je voudrais rester avec vous parce que je n'ai pas d'argent." It was 14 July Bastille Day, I got a train in and stayed with the priests for the night.

My father did not have my mother's pragmatism. He was a small farmer — a small farmer in Shankill, County Dublin was very different from a small farmer in the West of Ireland. We owned two-and-a-half acres and we had conacre of about 15 acres around Shankill, not all in one field. I remember bringing the cows home, helping with the milking and putting the milk into churns and bottles and selling it with my father during the weekend. Everything was done manually. We had a small dairy called Tillystown Dairy.

My father was a Dublin guy, warm and outgoing, who grew up as one of the boys. My mother was reared and educated in Tipperary. He lived more for the day rather than the future. My mother, on the other hand, believed that we had to forego today so that we would reap the reward in the future — study and you get your exams, work hard and you'll get rewarded. My old man would say, "If you've got the money, spend it now." In some people's eyes he might have been feckless but he and my mother were a great combination.

I'd say I had a bit of the sparkle of my father and a bit of the cuteness, drive and ambition of my mother. She was almost a puritanical Protestant in the sense of a work ethic. My father was much more relaxed, almost a British sense of taking part in the game, not so much the winning of it. Whatever about her Protestant values, my mother was very much a Catholic, faithful to her church, while my father might have been more relaxed in such matters. He got more faithful as he got older! It was a bit of an embarrassment when I was young because he would not be at Mass on Sunday with us. My mother would say that he had his own way of dealing with God. It was great to see them grow old together and stand back and appreciate their different qualities.

My father died at 70, quite young. I never saw him as an old man till the day before he died. It was the first time death came to me. He died of cancer — quite quickly, because, after they opened him up, he was dead within three weeks. There was no lead-up to it. That was a pity: he had done so much for Joyce and myself. You go through life without realising how much you love your parents and how much you owe them.

My wife, Triona's, mother, is 79. Triona's father is dead. Every Sunday the two grannies and our kids come to lunch in Greystones. It isn't that they always have a great time — there are some Sunday lunches when hardly anyone speaks, sometimes we have general rows and sometimes we have great fun — but that's all part of it. We're not an idyllic family — but we're close. I would certainly be closer to Joyce today than I was when I was growing up. I used to envy her. She was an all-round sports person and was captain of her school hockey and basketball teams. She got seven honours in her Leaving — I got one, in French. I passed honours maths but failed to get an honour in it and the rest I struggled through. However, I got into university because I had five passes in the Matric and went on to do a Bachelor of Commerce Degree in UCD. Joyce went off to do Social Science there. She became the Auditor of the Social Science Society. She became a big name in college and then went on to do a doctorate. As the Head of a third-level college [*National College of Ireland*], we have many issues in common, such as handling financial and management problems.

I knew my limitations academically but, with a bit of my mother's practical common sense, I would have looked hard at the system and realised that college was quite simple if I got all the lecture notes. The nuns were great at taking notes. I was the only one who'd have a cup of coffee with them and I ended up with the best set of (nuns') notes in college. I got my examinations, doing very well in the end.

Sport was a huge part of my life, particularly rugby. Growing up, everything was sport — and I could not play anything without being competitive. My father used to say, first person upstairs gets a six-pence, and we'd dash up, have a bath, and see who would be first into bed. He encouraged both Joyce and myself to be competitive, even if he was much more relaxed and fun-loving himself.

I well remember my final year in college. Lectures finished in early May and the whole summer stretched before you to revise for the fi-nals in October. I actually worked very hard, maybe too hard and, coming near the exams, I couldn't remember a thing. This was of great concern to everyone — including me. My mother went to daily Mass but praying failed to sort it out. My father gave me £20 and told me to go off into town and enjoy myself and he would see me on Monday morning, the day of the exam. He had great understated wisdom. The tension and the build-up were because I was afraid of my life to fail. In the event, as I said, I got the exam.

My father would have borrowed money from the City of Dublin Bank before I joined it. As time went on, he got out of dairy farming and sold the two-and-a-half acres. He was left some of the conacre when the owner died and he also sold that for building development. With the money, he bought machinery and became a tillage contractor.

At that time there were some gentlemen farmers around Shankill, like Pakenham-Walsh in Crinken Lodge and the Tyrrells whom he enjoyed working for but, of course, all the farms were eventually sold for building and other development and my father was out of a job towards the end of his life. In hindsight he was not a great strategist.

I would often say to my kids, "Don't worry about how well you do in the exams." As an employer, I'm never really interested in what students get academically, nor am I interested in whether they did an arts or a business degree. It's all about their interpersonal skills, how they shape up in an interview.

My best friends are people I met at school, in university and through playing rugby. When I went to university, all of my rugby contemporaries from school days were there too: I knew people from Terenure College, Colm Jenkinson and Michael Mahoney, and from Gonzaga College, Tadhg Gleeson and Donal Forbes. All of those I would have played rugby against from the age of 12. And then from my own school, Brian Hargan. He was the only one who gave me a superiority complex because he was even worse than I was at school and is now a Fellow of the Royal College of Surgeons, and a very good friend. Other friends of mine from Pres Bray were Jackie O'Driscoll who now has a thriving pub business; Cormac MacAlinden who owns a printing and publishing company; Eddie O'Beirne who is a local Solicitor; and Tino Cassoni who has his own bakery business in Bray.

I played rugby with UCD until I graduated in 1969, and then I joined Bective Rangers. Bective was probably the most cosmopolitan rugby club in Ireland during the seventies — members were drawn from all walks of life, students, accountants, lawyers, doctors, builders, self-employed and unemployed. We also had members who were charming chancers, and we even had one we suspected was a member of an illegal organisation! There was no such thing as a typical Bective person. It was a melting-pot of different characters — yet, when they put on the Bective jersey, they were moulded into Bective players. I left Bective, probably too soon, to come back to Greystones, which had just emerged from junior ranks to become a senior club. I had to come back because now I was married and living in Greystones and there was pressure to return to the local club directed at players who had played senior rugby with other clubs. I was moving from a cosmopolitan, outward-looking club to Greystones, which was a bit parochial in those days. All of us playing in Greystones grew up together and knew too much about each other. On reflection, I should probably have stayed a bit longer in Bective. However, I enjoyed playing rugby with Greystones and I continued playing until I was 38, way past sensible retirement, but I wanted to play because I got so much fun from it. I was CEO of a publicly quoted company but still playing rugby with kids of 20 years of age and that kept me in touch with a different generation, both in a social and business sense.

In two weeks' time I'm going off to Glasgow to watch Celtic play Rangers. The day after that I'm going to Turnberry and the three guys who are going with me on that golf trip were at school with me. That's how enduring those friendships are. That doesn't mean I meet them regularly — but they are my friends. Everybody must have a place they can return to, their home, or the local pub, where they are not worried who's in there. They can open the door with the courage and the conviction that they are going to be well received. These are the places that you go to sometimes at Christmas, sometimes when things are difficult. It's in places like these I feel most comfortable — with people that I know well, people who will cut me down to size, give me advice, have a joke, people I can rely on because I know they're not just playing to me.

There are just a few business friends that I would rate as close friends. There are some I would rate as acquaintances and some I have got to know and like, but not in the same way as my school friends. I'm 52 now — not old by any means — but I know that, when I retire, the invitations will dry up the day someone else takes over here. That's life, that's the way it is. My school and college friends are the people that you can go back to. I won't pontificate any more on that! Remember I talked about Brian Hargan — I used to mitch from school with him occasionally and go into Dublin for the day or play golf out in Greystones. When I look back now, we were very innocent. They were innocent days and simple times.

Even before I went to college I decided I was going to become an accountant. In the mid- and late sixties, the only jobs that were paying big money seemed to be for chartered accountants. I had decided I was going to get a job that would pay me good money. In 1969, on leaving UCD, I obtained Articles of Clerkship with a firm of accountants, Reynolds, McCarron & O'Connor, which, after a series of mergers in the nineties, is now part of Ernst & Young. I had really serious ambitions when I went in there — I wanted to become a partner. The partners seemed to be doing very well. I worked hard, but the big thing in articles was to get your exams. When I finished my period of articles, I was the only one let go, a big disappointment to me at the time. However, there was no problem getting another job and I got one straight away with Atkins Chirnside & Co., a Cork firm, with a branch in Dublin. Shortly after joining, they merged with what is now PriceWaterhouse Coopers. I got great business experience there.

In 1969, I met Triona again, whom I told you I first met briefly when I was 15 and was running the bumpers in the amusement arcade in Bray. When a bumper car got into trouble, I was like Superman jumping aboard and sorting things out. It was the type of job where girls noticed you. I asked Triona to go for a walk with me up

Bray Head, which was normally what we did with English or Northern Ireland girls. She said no. I did not meet her again until I was a student at UCD in Earlsfort Terrace and she was a schoolgirl in Loreto Convent, Stephen's Green. Two years later, I asked her out; we got engaged in February 1973, just after I qualified as a chartered accountant. We married in September 1974.

I was then working in PriceWaterhouse Coopers and could not get a housing loan, even though I had deposited money with the EBS for two years. In those days, unless you had up to 15 per cent of the cost of the house on deposit, they wouldn't even give you an application form for a loan. During our engagement, Triona and I would deposit two or three pounds each a week but, when it came to the crunch and we wanted the money, the building society told us no loans were being given out for a further six months. This was when my mother suggested I join a bank and get a cheap loan.

One of the people I was working with in Pricewaterhouse Coopers at the time was Charlie McCreevy. I told him I was going to leave practice and join a bank, and he told me he was thinking of going into politics. I didn't see him again for about ten years, just as he was achieving notoriety challenging Charlie Haughey, and beginning to make a name for himself in national politics.

In 1974, I applied for a job as accountant in Irish Bank of Commerce. I went through three interviews and was called back for a fourth and final interview with Michael Sheehan, the managing director, and Gerry Watson, the Finance Director. Their office was in Fleet Street. I was ushered into a boardroom with a very impressive boardroom table. It must have gone on for 50 feet and there was Michael Sheehan seated at the far end. He waved regally at me and I walked the length of the table, shook hands, and he said "Well, Sean, you've got the job."

I thanked him, said I was thrilled to be the chosen candidate and then he said, "I believe you want to buy a house?" I told him the house I wanted to buy in Greystones would cost £6,800. He said, "We'll give you £7,200". I told him I didn't need £7,200, what would I do with the extra money? He said, "Well, you could play the gilt market." I told him I had never heard of the gilt market. I remember shaking hands and dashing for the nearest phone to ring my mother to tell her that I'd got the job at £3,750 per annum and a loan of £7,200, of which £400 was to play the gilt market. She asked me what the gilt market was. I told her I didn't know either but I was sure as hell going to find out quickly. That was the first time I got any sort of sniff of corporate Ireland. Michael Sheehan drove a Jaguar; I was very impressed. Gerry Watson drove a slinky Citroen.

Michael Sheehan, Gerry Watson, and Terry Carroll (who now works with us), all of them had secretaries — and even I had a secretary. It was just incredibly different from the atmosphere and working conditions in Pricewaterhouse Coopers. I was truly on the path to success.

On my first day at work on 1 April 1974, I shook hands with all my new colleagues and was led to my office where there was an *Irish Times* and an *Irish Independent*. I picked up the phone and rang my mother and told her, "I've got this huge office and *two* newspapers and I've got a carpet with such a deep pile you can't hear anything." I left the office at ten o'clock that night and every night for the next number of weeks. At Easter, I worked Good Friday and Easter Saturday — in fact I worked Good Friday and Easter Saturday for the next six years of my life.

My first assignment in my new job was to prepare the company accounts for the year ended 31 March 1974. These showed we were making a loss. The natural reaction to that was to doubt the messenger. I was under strict supervision from Gerry Watson, one of the brightest people I've ever met and the mentor who probably had the most influence on my business life. He was a man of great integrity and creativity. He is now an independent consultant and amongst other things advises corporates on their art collections. He grilled me on everything to do with those accounts. Eventually, I was able to prove to him that it wasn't me, the accounts were right and the Bank was losing money.

Then the main shareholder in Irish Bank of Commerce, Jessels Securities, went bust. A liquidator was appointed and he effectively controlled 65 per cent of our Bank. That was September 1974 and I was getting married. It was a difficult time. Gerry Watson in particular was fantastic at that stage. It wasn't that the Bank was trading badly — in fact we had turned the corner into profitability. It was simply that our largest shareholder had gone into liquidation and people were naturally worried: would there be a run on the Bank by the depositors? We had to arrange standby lines from Bank of Ireland, which were supported by the Central Bank of Ireland.

The Central Bank was magnificent. At that time there were a few small banks that could have gone to the wall and if that had happened it would have had a huge negative effect on the Irish economy. The Central Bank, by being proactive, helped a number of small banks and in that way protected the Irish banking sector from potential serious losses.

Gerry Watson taught me many things but in particular to tell it as it is. Now we in Anglo Irish Bank have a reputation for being open and transparent with our staff. We still give as much financial and other information as we can to all the people in the Bank so that they know exactly how everything is going. The benefit reaped by the Bank from that policy is that all the staff are and feel very much part of the Bank. For instance, when we are announcing our interim and final results, we always bring all our staff together in the Shelbourne Hotel the night before the results go out. The staff are the people who put it all together and they should know first how the Bank has done. We believe passionately in that and I believe that is why we have staff willing to run with us and help create a unique culture and ethos amongst Irish banks.

Back to Irish Bank of Commerce. Let me get the chronology right. As I have already said, six months after I joined Irish Bank of Commerce, its largest shareholder went bust. Irish Bank of Commerce was then taken over by City of Dublin Bank. Two years later, City of Dublin Bank also bought Anglo Irish Bank. So now you had City of Dublin Bank (a finance house) owning Irish Bank of Commerce (an investment/merchant bank) and Anglo Irish Bank (a middle market business bank).

A French Bank, Crédit Commercial de France, wanted to buy an investment bank in Ireland and eventually targeted Irish Bank of Commerce, but they did not want its fellow subsidiary, Anglo Irish Bank. Initially they bought 20 per cent of Irish Bank of Commerce from City of Dublin Bank. Anglo Irish Bank was a halfway house between a finance house and a merchant bank. Anglo Irish, therefore, filled the gap between the other two banks in the Group.

I had been told by Gerry Watson to get Hay MSL to draw up a list of suitable candidates for the role of chief executive for Anglo Irish Bank. The previous chief executive, Pat Casey, had gone to Sedgwick Dineen. Before I went down to Hay MSL, it struck me that I could do that job. Even though I was now financial controller in a senior and influential position, it was very unlikely that I would become general manager in Irish Bank of Commerce in the foreseeable future. On the other hand, while Anglo Irish Bank had gross assets of less than £500,000, I would be the CEO, I would hire new talent, and, over time, together we would grow Anglo into a serious bank.

The Mammy and the Da would be so proud of me, and I'd now be the youngest general manager of any bank in Ireland! I went back to Gerry Watson and asked him if I could have the job. He said, "But you don't know enough about banking." I told him I had learned a lot from him, I was as cute as they came. I was well able to lend money. I had got a great practical education growing up in Presentation College, Bray. I will always be grateful to Michael Sheehan and Gerry Watson for sanctioning that decision.

I immediately hired a few people, including Peter Killen, who is still with me as a fellow director of the Bank. We decided on a strategy of becoming a Bank focused on the business market and, after a few years, we were earning more profits than either of the other two banks in the Group. In 1985, Anglo were making £600,000, yet the group results were only £175,000.

I picked up the phone to Gerry Murphy (who was CEO of City of Dublin Bank) and asked, "How could the group make only £175,000 when we made £600,000?" He said, "Well, we have a lot of bad debts and so on." I then said, "Gerry, can I go on the Group Board?" Gerry said, "Yeah, I will support you, but Tom Kenny (the Chairman) will need persuading." Gerry pushed and I shoved and shortly thereafter I became a director of the Group Board although I was still running the subsidiary Bank.

In the summer of 1986, I again went to Gerry Murphy and suggested we merge Anglo Irish Bank and the City of Dublin Bank, making one bank trading under the name of Anglo Irish. Within a few months we had the new Bank operating; Gerry became chairman and I became chief executive. We started off on a great voyage.

This was back in 1986, when our market capitalisation was just over €1 million; today it's over €1 billion.

We decided to get out of the finance market because we were not very good at leasing and hire purchase. Instead we concentrated our resources on business banking. We hired people from different banks with different skills and immersed them in our culture, giving them a very clear vision of the type of specialist bank we wanted to be.

And we worked and we worked all the hours possible — we fought battles, we won some and lost some. Those times were very difficult, our backs were to the wall, but we were young, hungry, tenacious and enthusiastic to succeed. This commitment sowed the seeds for what is now the culture in Anglo today.

Right from the time I first played rugby I knew that the key to achievement was to have the right people around me. Certainly in the early days it was difficult to find the right people and then to get them to join the Bank. I was constantly faced with the question, "Why should I leave my very senior job in Bank of Ireland and go to Anglo? It may not be around in three years' time — that's not a good career move."

Sometimes it was as well that these people did not join me, as they would have been just as unhappy with me as I with them. I always wanted a person to understand the commitment expected from them once they signed on. Sometimes I ended up recruiting younger and less experienced people than I had intended to and giving them the responsibility to run their own teams. That was always the attraction for someone joining Anglo — that they were given far more responsibility much quicker than they would have got in another bank. They would be encouraged to act, to take it on and go for it. By and large this worked well — people develop quickly when they are stretched.

Before long we had built a great management team. This sounds like the usual trite statement that every CEO makes, but it is true in the case of Anglo. There is no way that anyone would be able or allowed to run a bank of our size (now the eighth most profitable company in Ireland) without having excellent people throughout the organisation. Undoubtedly the single best job I have done for Anglo was the recruitment of entrepreneurial managers who have delivered.

Whilst I am the public face of Anglo, the success of the Bank is down not to the individual but to the strength and commitment of the senior executives. The Bank now runs day-to-day effectively without me. The whole thing here was about belief — we wanted like-minded people to whom we would give a platform from which they could develop. If they were not capable or committed, we got rid of them. I was driving, not the business, but the people, and trying to create a culture that was going to be different. I was determined this was never going to be just another bank. I have huge respect for the likes of AIB and Bank of Ireland, but that was not what we were trying to be. We were going to be a different Bank, with a different culture and a different way of doing business. In our Bank, the customer was genuinely going to be king.

Reverting to the 1980s, I can remember the IMI Annual Conference in Killarney — it was always a popular event in the corporate calendar. However, I did not identify with that part of corporate Ireland. I saw them as establishment, dull, grey, consumed with Harvard Business School rubbish, people who never understood real customers.[2] They would spend their time talking about macro issues when they did not know what was going on inside the heart of their own businesses. I wanted our executives to be seen as being different from the typical IMI delegates. It was going to take time, but we were going to build professionalism and a unique culture in our Bank. I wanted us to end up where we would become the envy of our peers, not because we were more aggressive than they were but because we were different and more professional.

What was different about Anglo? Well, for a start, everything was built on relationships. We never used brokers — we always use word-of-mouth. There was no lending by formulae or credit scoring; every deal was different. We gave a lot of autonomy to our lending officers. They were the people the customer would meet face-to-face and they were the key decision-makers. Sure, their recommendations had to come to the credit committee but it would not be usual for them to be shot down there. We lost a few bob here and there — we had to struggle to overcome problems and we had to duck and dive, no question about that. But the fun we had — you've no idea.

For instance, Bernard Somers rang me one day to tell me that the Goodman Group had gone bust and that he had been appointed administrator. He said, "Sean, there's no bank in the world that will lend money to Goodman today notwithstanding that the loan will effectively be a secured debt from the European Union." I asked him how much he wanted. He said, "£40 million." Our loan book at the time was £100 million. I charged a large fee at a time when we were making profits of around £900,000. We got the first four months out of it and then all of the banks came pouring back in. This was all because, unlike the other banks, we wanted to do a deal.

It would be wrong to think that it has all been plain sailing. I made mistakes along the way. Two years after I had taken over as chief ex-

---

[2] The author was director general of the IMI at the time.

ecutive I was full of confidence (over-confident indeed) and ready to take on the world. The operations had turned around nicely and we were now beginning to make a reasonable profit. I met a car dealer who operated from several centres in the UK Midlands. He had the effective placing of the finance business on all the cars he sold. The concept he broached me with was that the perfect combination was a bank and a car sales operation, a fifty-fifty joint venture. He would supply the customers, we would supply the finance. In hindsight, this never worked, and bad debts began to grow. We closed it in 1990, took our loss and licked our wounds.

I am not sure I would ever go into a joint venture again. They are by their nature transient and not long-term propositions. I probably stuck with the joint venture for too long. We should have packed up and left much earlier — a lesson learned.

In 1989 we ventured in to stockbroking, buying two firms, Solomon's and Porter and Irvine — two fine stockbrokers indeed, with people of integrity. However, my timing here was impeccably wrong. Within a year of acquisition the business had gone in to a cyclical downturn and, while we weren't losing money, we certainly were not making any and there was no light at the end of the tunnel. What was most difficult was the amount of management time that the stockbroking absorbed. It was diverting us from the profitable core business of lending. Once again I had to take the difficult step of closing down a business and letting the staff go. I did this just as the stock market was picking up.

It would be unrealistic to blame bad luck on either of these mistakes. It was more an error of judgement. I have always felt the key is not about avoiding mistakes but how you deal with them. While mistakes were made I believe that there was no funking the difficult decisions at the time. It makes you wiser next time out.

If things were going wrong, we looked under every stone. We did not sleep at night for wondering and worrying if we thought we were going to lose money on a deal. The other banks started at nine o'clock and finished at five o'clock with long lunch breaks. It was never that simple for us. Why? Because the culture of our bank is that each lending officer is taught to believe he is lending his own money rather than the Bank's. We never travel first class anywhere — we always go back of the bus. It's part of our culture. I'm ten years here and I never use the Bank's money to buy a new car. (It is actually false economy!)

We always bought second-hand cars. We would encourage our people not to go to the large dealerships but to the local garage and try to cut a deal. It was always about it being your own Bank. That was the style we brought to Irish banking.

It may not have been the Harvard way. I have a very healthy disrespect for really bright people. It was always about the fact that this is a simple game. What you need are people who are absolutely focused and want to be part of a real team. That's what drove everything in the bank, absolutely everything. It's as simple and as complicated as that. Sometimes I'm asked why I don't talk about competitors. My response is, "What do I want to talk about them for?"

I don't see myself as a traditional leader. I feel I am intuitive and see myself as being, thankfully, in touch. I'm very lucky to have had tremendous support in my life: my mother, my Dad, my wife Triona, my children, my sister Joyce, my friends and my colleagues. When someone asks me, "How did you think all this out?", the truth is that there was no thinking it out. It was just getting up and trying to survive and getting on with it. Each day brought new challenges, maybe to issue a new loan, maybe to put one over on the other banks. It was almost like a game — that could never be lost. It was not simply to make money — I couldn't really give a damn about money, now that I've got some. That never was the drive. It was being part of a team that could build a financial institution that could be meaningful in an Irish and an international context. We are well on the way to this goal, and we now have operations in Ireland, UK, Austria, Switzerland, Germany and the United States. It's very different from what it was even five years ago.

So what now for the future? With the growth of the Bank I can no longer know every loan that's on our books, nor would it be right that I do. The issues I now have to deal with have changed over the years. More of my time is now spent on strategy and top-level over-viewing — but some things will never change. We must continue to protect the culture and uniqueness of our bank, which has brought us to where we are. An Anglo Irish Bank with a market capitalisation of €10 billion and a significant international division to its business does not now seem so difficult or distant. I know we can achieve this by applying the same basic principles as we did in the past. I still believe that commitment, dedication and hard work, not to mention a little luck along the way, will overcome obstacles and take us farther along the road.

5

Donal Geaney

Elan Corporation plc

"It's fatal to confuse the process with the objective. The process is only important if it gets you to the objective. You have to be intellectually ruthless — perhaps a better word is honest."

Donal John Geaney is chairman and chief executive of Elan Corporation plc.

He was born in Dublin on 21 January 1951. His father was Daniel Geaney, a wholesaler. His mother is Maura, a dress designer. He has one younger brother, Patrick. He is married to Anne. They have three boys: John (18), Richard (14) and Danny (13).

He was educated at the Franciscan College, Gormanston, County Meath, and took a Bachelor of Business Studies Degree in Trinity College Dublin. He is a chartered accountant.

Following college, he joined Stokes Kennedy Crowley (SKC) with the intention of eventually joining his father in the family business, post-qualification. His father died in the middle of his articles and Donal stayed with SKC. He continued with SKC (which became KPMG) and was a partner in the firm when he decided to leave to join Elan.

In 1987 he joined Elan, which had been his client, as executive vice-president for strategic planning. Subsequently, he became the chief financial officer, later president and chief operating officer, and joined the board in 1992. The founder, Don Panoz, retired as chief executive at the end of 1994 and Donal Geaney succeeded him as chief executive. In 1997 he became chairman and chief executive.

He is chairman of the Irish Aviation Authority and a member of the Court of Directors of Bank of Ireland. He is on the board of the Trinity Foundation (TCD). He has recently been appointed chairman of the National Pensions Reserve Fund Commission.

In November 1998, he was awarded the Outstanding Achievement Award from The Ireland–United States Council for Commerce and Industry.

The conversation was recorded in Donal Geaney's office in Lincoln Place, Dublin, on 11 January 2001.

Donal Geaney

As I came from a family business background, we had business for breakfast. Even when I was going to primary school, business was always part of everything I did. When I was 13 I got my first job — maybe not a real job — packing boxes with Mr Crichton. He was an awfully proper man who ran the warehouse. A Corkman, he had fallen on hard times and my father took him on. He was particular — you had to pack those boxes very carefully. That sort of business does not exist any more: nobody breaks bulk like that and there are no small shops to supply. You had to dust all the boxes and, by the time you got to the end of the warehouse, you started all over again. It was an early lesson in humility.

When I was a bit older, I used to drive the delivery van. We had the Clery's wool account. Clery's was the biggest knitting wool emporium in Europe. We had to be outside the side door on Sackville Place at 8.15 in the morning with our first delivery. We also used to go to what is now the Point Depot from where cartons were shipped to the country.

Our bookkeeper left during a bank strike. I was trained in how to write up the books. We had a country book and a city book — all sorts of amazing things from the past. We reorganised that — instead of writing out something ten times, we used duplicates.

When I was 18 or 19, my father sent me out to spend a week with a sales rep in the south, visiting small shops. There were typically three parts to each shop: the shop itself, then the bar and finally, at the very back, the snug. It was pretty obvious that distributing to such shops was not going to be a long-term option. Dunnes Stores was just coming as a big threat. I decided that, sure as hell, I did not want to spend my life trotting around those small shops. I wanted to do my degree.

I signed on for a BBS (Bachelor of Business Studies) in Trinity. At that stage, business studies were not nearly as popular as today. The training — no, I should call it education — we got at Trinity was very broad, unlike what you would get in a business school today. There was a lot of economics, we did one year of psychology, and indeed many other subjects. In the final year, for the degree, one of the critical papers was the General Essay. You had three-and-a-half hours to put into your essay everything you could think of from all the modules of all the courses you studied. It sounds onerous but we had none of the pressures that people have today. It was not difficult to gain entry to the course, and once you were in, you did not have to work from 8.00 a.m. until midnight. Of course, you had to perform, you had to know your stuff. I had not done as well as I could have in my Leaving Cert. I became more serious as I got older and did much better as each year progressed. Believe it or not, there was a teachers' strike that year and there was kafuffle about a paper that had been leaked.[1] We had to resit that particular paper.

I don't believe in dossing. It's a waste of one's time. You have to understand that you have some talents, however limited they may be, and that you are obliged to use them. If you sit around doing nothing, then you're not going to be a happy person. I was always a doer.

While I was at Trinity, I was interested in rallying. With some friends I bought a car — we built one really. We did not do particularly well. We were not all that skilled nor did we have the budget. Liam Lynch was the other half of the team. He had been at Gormanston with me and was doing medicine at Trinity. He is now president of the IMO. Rather than sit there talking about rallying, we actually did it. My father had a great expression: "If it's worth doing, it's worth doing today." You took completely for granted that it was worth doing well. Don't sit on your butt, get on with it.

Don Panoz, who founded Elan, always said that he would forgive people sins of commission, but he would never forgive sins of omission. People who do things certainly make mistakes, but they can put them behind them and then get on with it. I've often wondered what makes people successful. I don't suppose there is any one answer, but not doing things sure as hell won't make you successful.

Trinity was a very pleasant time to think and to talk. I made friends there — it was a small university then. There were only 5,000 students — there are over 11,000 today on much the same campus. It was a generally more leisurely period — before the oil crisis, which fundamentally changed many things.

---

[1] ASTI, the Association of Secondary Teachers of Ireland, was on intermittent strike when this conversation was recorded.

I was with the accountants, SKC, when you built the splendid IMI headquarters in Sandyford. During that particular time we had a wonderful experience with inflation accounting, of which the late Don Carroll[2] was the major proponent. We had to adjust the numbers to deal with inflation. How that had any relevance to the IMI was beyond me, but it had to be done for such a prestigious body, leading the charge. The annual report was printed and circulated. A chap from Cork wrote to SKC asking them to explain how the adjustment was made to the working capital. Somebody dashed off an answer but this chap persisted that it could not be right, that the IMI must have had one of the strangest cash flows, must have been doing incredible financial engineering to get back, at the end of the year, to what the historical accounts showed. At that point, they came to me in SKC and I looked at it and said, "This is wrong." What had happened, of course, was that someone had made the entry the wrong way round: they put the debit where the credit should have been and vice versa. Nobody noticed because nobody thought it was relevant. It had gone right through our firm, right through the IMI. It was very embarrassing — what were we going to do? I had to go in to Lawrence Crowley, who was the partner in charge, to explain that we had screwed up. We immediately contacted Jim Byrne, the Financial Controller in the IMI, a very nice fellow, and explained what had happened. We went with trepidation to the annual general meeting where we would have to explain ourselves to the great and good of Irish business. We were prepared to pay for the reprinting of the whole report to rectify the matter. I well remember Donal Flinn, a distinguished accountant, at the meeting saying, "Thanks very much for 'fessing up. We would never have noticed." Gordon Lambert of Jacobs — he was also an accountant — supported Donal. Our relationship with everybody in the IMI improved immensely as a result of our having to eat humble pie. The lesson was that you should never sign off on something you don't understand.

When I finished Trinity, I needed training and experience and SKC were the first to offer me a job. The first offer received was the one I took. I must say, I enjoyed my time at SKC. There were an awful lot of good people. Niall Crowley[3] was the man in charge at the time — I did

[2] *In Good Company*, pp. 307–330.

[3] Ibid., pp. 215–236.

not know him particularly well — Lawrence Crowley was there, Bill
Foley, Declan Collins, a very bright man. David Roe was the technical
man, the man who understood the new developments in accounting. I
was lucky in that, at that time, there was a lot of very basic work to be
done. You had, for example, to write up the books of investment
companies so you really got to understand what was going on. As I
had some business background, I always saw accounts as a reflection
of the business rather than something in themselves. Later on, when I
had trainees working for me, I used to take them out to see the fixed
assets, the plant and machinery. You had physically to do a year-end
stock-take, but you had to understand what it consisted of, not just
count it: midnight in beef plants, making sure there was actually fillet
of beef in the boxes. Shaklee came here and never really got off the
ground. It was subsequently bought by Yamanouchi, the Japanese
firm. Shaklee had a business in cosmetics. They were located in Leixlip. Part of their inventory included large drums of fructose. I was
sent out to do the year-end stocktaking. I said, "How do I know it's
fructose?" They were very irritated with me because I made them take
the drums down off high racks to view the contents. It's amazing how
people don't do that, how they don't try to understand what's behind
the numbers. You get the John Cleese caricature of the accountant,
wearing a green shade, just ticking off the numbers. You can't use
numbers unless you can see beyond them.

When you're presented with surveys or numbers, you really have
to ask yourself what is behind all this, what it really means. How do I
really interpret these things, as distinct from the obvious, superficial
interpretation? Take employee surveys: one group will say that, on a
scale of one to ten, we score nine on innovation; another group will
say we score six. What does that mean? Does it mean anything? Sta-
tistical errors are a big issue — as the politicians have found out. Mr
Bush and Mr Gore certainly figured that recently!

Looking beyond the figures was what helped me progress, first
through SKC, where I learned to be helpful to a client and not just the
pest that came around to do the audit. I qualified in 1976. In those
days, the pass rate was much lower than today. When I did my finals,
17.6 per cent of candidates succeeded. I got through first time — you
don't require any huge intellect to do that stuff: what you need is application. There was a vast amount of material to be covered and, I
suppose, you had to be reasonably good at doing exams. An analogy:

the driving test is a *test*, it's not about driving. You should not try to improve on what is required in the test — that, I think, is why a lot of people fail. You have to be clear what the objective is. The objective of a driving test is to pass the test, not to become a rally driver. A lot of people don't focus clearly on what the object of the exercise is. We regularly do that here in Elan: hold on a minute, what are we really trying to achieve? If you keep asking yourself that question, it helps a lot. You get through a lot of dross that way.

You can see that in research programmes. When people don't get the right answer, they go back and reinvent it and reinvent it and re-invent it. They don't ask the question, what was the original objective? For example, is the objective to get a cure for Alzheimer's disease, a real objective, or is it to prove that this theory will lead to a cure for Alzheimer's disease? Two quite different objectives. What we're interested in is to *get* the cure for Alzheimer's disease, not *how* we get it. We're not wedded to any particular theory. We'll kill a project if it's not making the milestones. It's fatal to confuse the process with the objective. The process is only important if it gets you to the objective. You have to be intellectually ruthless — perhaps a better word is honest.

I find myself regularly doing this when I'm chairing a meeting. If things get off track, I will say, "Ladies and gentlemen, let's pause here and get back to the point: what is it we're trying to achieve?"

In SKC, I was involved in several different situations which were helpful in learning about the process of management and about business generally. One of those experiences was with the TMG Group, chaired by Michael Smurfit,[4] run by Maurice Buckley. It was a high-flyer in the seventies and then it ran into trouble — a bridge too far. It taught me how you have to keep all the pieces in balance. This is particularly true in a high growth situation where you can't afford to leave any of the pieces out. You must have a strong balance sheet: you can't take risk unless you can afford to take risk. That may sound obvious but if you think about it it's true. It is not appropriate to go around to the local branch manager and ask him for an overdraft to do some research project that has as much likelihood of failure as of success. You will not be able to pay him back and you will go out of business. It's very simple. You have to fund that sort of project with

---

[4] *In Good Company*, pp. 195–214.

equity that you are prepared to lose. Or, as we are doing in Elan, trying to build a significant international business, you have to have the
management skills to do that. *I* don't have all the management skills
to do it — and even if I had, I can't be everywhere. You have to build a
team. Or, if you're trying to find a cure for Alzheimer's, you are not
going to succeed unless you understand the medical scenario, the
pathology of the disease itself: you have to have a team of scientists
who understand the biology and a team who understand the chemistry. All these components have to come together for success.

What I find somewhat frustrating with the investment community
is that they tend to focus on the issue du jour, this quarter, or short-
term goals. The issues du jour won't get you to where you want to be
in the longer term. You have to have the overall capability. Take the
Jefferson Smurfit Corporation. They started from a very small base
and now they have a hugely significant international company in a
highly competitive industry. You could criticise them on this or that
decision, but you can never take away from them the fact that they
have created a world-class international business, a difficult task.
Take CRH — putting that organisation together is an incredible
achievement and it's not just that they bought this particular business
or were able to do that deal. They got all the parts in balance so that
they could compete on a world level — just as the Kerry Group have
done.

A lot of companies have done very well but the key thing is to have
an integrated, a total approach. You cannot underemphasise any of
the bits, even those that are not particularly rewarding at the time,
the things that are not sexy, that don't give you a buzz. For example,
at present we're working through our Dura acquisition. It's a laborious process, analysing sales and territories and pulling people together. Doing the deal or making the acquisition is where you get the
headline. That's the sexy bit. But the value is really created afterwards
where you do the hard work piece, shaping the organisation to meet
longer-term objectives. It's very difficult to get over the market's
short-term view. That is why you have so much volatility. Look at the
highs and lows on the New York Stock Exchange for the year — the
lows are at least half the highs. There are huge variations, even in the
best blue chips. The market is always imperfect — it is only perfect
over time. When I say the market is imperfect I mean that it does not
value things correctly at any point in time: it is either over-valuing or

under-valuing. Very few companies are ever valued spot on. If you take Elan's share price today, it's probably 30 per cent below what it should be relative to its peers. If you look at interest rates, or the economy in general, or any particular industry sector, and then if you take the relative valuation within that sector, that's about all you can do to say whether the market is efficient or inefficient. You have the double effect of whether the market is assessing the prospects for an industry sector, which sets the overall level, and then whether it's correctly assessing the value of a particular company in that sector. For example, the tech sector was over-priced but now it's probably under-priced, at least some of the stocks are.

The quality of the analysts is variable. There are some very good analysts who do their homework and who really understand the industry. Then there are others who are essentially lazy. But by and large, these guys live or die on the value of their recommendations — people won't listen to them if they don't give them good ideas. The funds will walk from them. This is relevant for you and me because it is our money that is managed by the pension funds. Twenty years ago the management of such funds was very local; now it is much more global. The better people are getting rewarded which, I suppose, is as things should be. Fidelity, the largest fund managers in the world, as you know, has stakes in many Irish companies. There is now a definite trend of money coming out of the lower-performing funds into the higher performing funds and this is accelerated by transparency. In the 1970s, if you wanted a pension you went to Irish Life or maybe New Ireland — it was probably a question of who you knew in one or the other or which salesman hit you first. Nowadays that would not happen. Pension trustees have firms of professional advisers. All of this puts pressure on people to perform on the investment side which, in turn, leads to more money being available where the opportunities are — but more risk, because the two go together.

It's now much more difficult to get follow-on funding unless you are successful — with the result that there is more pressure to perform in the short-term. When you are running a company you have to recognise that fact and you have to fund at the point where you are able to deliver in the short term. Elan, by its very nature, is not in it for the short term, but we have to use the financing windows that are available.

We are in the business of constant innovation. There is no simple answer to the question as to the length of a product life cycle or the value of a patent. There are several ways to skin a cat. There are, for example, several ways to treat blood pressure: you can use beta blockers, you can use calcium channel blockers, you can use ACE inhibitors. They all compete with each other in the marketplace. However, generally speaking, you're talking about a 10- to 15-year life. You may say ten years is not too bad — but it often takes you 12 years to get there! Ten years after an investment of 12 years is not a great life. Take our current research on Alzheimer's, where we are targeting the beta amyloid protein: it takes a number of years to look for compounds that affect beta amyloid. You start with bench experiments, then go into animal models, and then into human clinical trials. It is essential that product safety is established at an early stage. Then you have to establish the effective dose of the compound. We can make some educated guesses but we're not going to know until we do the work. Recently, there was an interesting piece about Merck in the *Wall Street Journal*. They were talking about their product Vioxx. It's a new compound called a Coxx-2 inhibitor. When they got to Phase II of their research, they ran a study at 1,000 milligrams. It eventually turned out that the correct dose was between 12½ and 25 milligrams. The larger dose was not effective. The patients tolerated it but they had overloaded. Like alcohol, there is only a certain amount you take if you want to feel that life is wonderful but you can overdose to the extent that you become a drunken fool and miss the therapeutic benefit you were looking for. On the other hand, if you were doing it only for digestive purposes, then half a glass is probably more than you need. Then there is another complication in that you can get different effects for the same dose with different people. Again, alcohol is a great example of this. There are some people who can drink a bottle of whiskey and walk out the door, while others will have two whiskeys and become babbling idiots.

Anyway, when you have established what the effective dose is, you do a Phase III trial. All this can take years and then you must go through the regulatory process in order to gain product approval. So the average time to market, as I said, is 12 years and the average cost is $500 million.

The time and cost to bring a drug to market has implications for the size of drug companies and for the cost of treatment. You have to recover the cost, so it is unlikely you are going to get a ten cent tablet. This has particular implications for rare diseases, narrower disease areas that are often genetic. There are many awful diseases where there are only 10,000 patients — what about them if it's going to cost you $500 million to get to the product? It is not feasible with a patient population of 10,000 patients to recover the cost solely from the patient. Maybe society can afford to spend $500 million to treat the relatively small number of people who suffer from these diseases, but society needs to make that call.

What we as an industry have to do is to find ways of speeding up the whole process, doing it for $250 million as opposed to $500 million. Still, the cost of treating people with, for example, blood pressure, is going to be infinitely less than people with motor neuron disease.

Take Alzheimer's: our estimates show anything from eight to ten million sufferers today in the world with projections of 25 million sufferers by the year 2020. Alzheimer's was defined as long ago as the early 1900s. The reason we are more aware of it today is that people are living longer. You are less likely to die from a heart attack if you have controlled blood pressure as we can do now. You are less likely to have a stroke if you monitor your bloods. Infectious diseases are much less a problem than they were in the 1950s — many children died before antibiotics were introduced.

There are about 20 major pharmaceutical companies. It's a free market. When we get to certain critical stages in the development of a new drug, such as the clinical trials or, eventually, acquiring a patent, all that material is in the public domain. While your competitors are not free to duplicate what you are doing, they can see the path you have chosen. So, as soon as relatively expensive drugs such as Losec or Viagra appear, you can be sure that, within a short time, other similar drugs will appear and this will force the price down. You cannot get a premium price for a product if there is an equally effective product at a lower price, regardless of the development costs. Competition is good. It keeps everybody on their toes. Unless Elan is constantly bringing out new products with incremental value, it will not be able to compete. You have to bring something to the table which has real value. You have to remember that our products are sold to a very educated customer. New products are usually first adopted by specialists, opinion leaders. If, for example, the leading cardiologists are persuaded that something has incremental value, then they will prescribe that. Pfizer bought Warner Lambert for Lipitor, a cholesterol-lowering drug that is on track to be a $5 billion product. That drug could not have got there without passing the scrutiny of the doctors. Ultimately, our customer is the patient, but the patient is not sufficiently knowledgeable about what he or she needs. The doctor is the real decision-maker. In any event, things are so transparent now that no features of a product can be ignored.

Productivity is a fundamental issue in Ireland. The current teachers' strike is a case in point — as were the gardaí and the nurses previously. The productivity of these groups has simply not increased in line with the productivity of the rest of the economy. Take one of your managers in the Kerry Group in Listowel. The level of productivity expected from him is infinitely higher than that which would have been expected 20 years ago. You get things *done* overnight by e-mail now whereas it took weeks for a letter to arrive from San Francisco. The level of productivity in Western countries, including Ireland, has improved dramatically over the last ten years so the rewards that people get are much higher. You have jobs at Microsoft or Intel, or Elan for that matter, where people have good salaries and stock options — rewards for productivity. The public sector has not dealt with this issue. Nor does it seem to want to deal with it. The big issue with the teachers is that they will not have any performance-related standards. Performance is a code word for productivity. Why should teachers be exempt from productivity or performance? There's no reason why good teachers should not get 30 per cent or more, but there has to be some way to measure it. The teachers who work in private institutes of education get rewarded appropriately — they also get fired if they do not measure up. Teachers are not prepared to take on the other side of the equation and, until they are, we'll be stuck.

Early social partnerships between trade unions and employers, including the private and the public sectors, were designed to improve the overall situation. Now what we see is groups looking for "their share" of the wealth created by the Celtic tiger. Let me tell you who were the first people to get "their share" of the Celtic tiger. It was the unemployed. The Celtic tiger is the difference between a 5 per cent unemployment rate and a 20 per cent unemployment rate. Nobody says where that share went. Why? Because nobody cares about the unemployed. The unions don't give a damn about the unemployed —

they are not their members. Now that we're down to 5 per cent, the early aspirations of the partnership process are lost — now it's down to *mé féin*.

However, there are fundamental alterations that will change the situation forever. Selfish unions or public sector employees — or private sector employees for that matter — cannot be immune from globalisation. Competition, free trade, transparency, fundamental political adjustments are all coming together. The speed at which information is moving around — people's ability to buy goods from various countries — all these things are coming together to enforce productivity. For example, with price transparency, you will not be able to hide inefficiency any more. Monopolies are beginning to crumble.

A classic example of a State monopoly is air traffic control. If the controllers stop working, the place closes down. Up to now, every country has had its own little monopoly in air traffic control. That is not going to be the way in the future. It's too inefficient and expensive. Airlines can no longer afford to pay exorbitant and unnecessary prices for the service. However, the inefficiency is worse than the price. The European air traffic situation at present is a real mess. It's not unusual at all to have two-hour delays going into Europe. Think of what that does to Ryanair. It has an aircraft sitting there which should have gone some place, unloaded and 45 minutes later it should have been full again and coming back, and it hasn't left yet for its original destination. That's a whole flight lost and you can never get it back. Ryanair is a great example of a company that has succeeded by cutting its costs and being competitive. The fact of the matter is that you cannot sustain uncompetitive costs in the long term. The situation in European air traffic control can't last. The question is, what providers will survive? That depends on who's willing to be productive. That is why the British are privatising their air traffic control system. They are privatising it not for profit but for productivity. They are trying to become cost-effective. There is a consortium of airlines bidding for the operation who intend to run it as a trust. Their objective is to get the costs down and still run it more efficiently. We are going to see more of that in other industry sectors.

Of course, in some areas you do need regulation. The drug industry is a very good example of that. It is completely in the hands of private enterprise but regulation is totally in the hands of the State.

Regulation is rigid and specific and it works pretty well. Irregularities are picked up quickly and stopped. In the drug industry, you don't mess with the regulator. Regulation of air traffic control is very important but it is not a reason to maintain gross inefficiencies. Let me give you a specific example. An aircraft arriving at the edge of European air space, just 15 degrees west of Ireland, could not be routed directly from that point to Dusseldorf. You have three people handling it, one in Ireland, one in Britain and maybe one in Dusseldorf, when one person could handle it all. And we have the technology and the people here in Ireland to do it. Think about it for a minute. If somebody can handle an aircraft going from Galway to Dublin, surely they can handle it going on to Liverpool? In the US, the National Flow Control Centre is just outside Dulles Airport. There's a huge wall with a map of the US, Europe on one side, Asia on the other and all these little dots of aircraft coming along. The point of this discussion is that there will be more and more demand for people to be transparent and efficient. And if people want to increase their personal take, then they have to be prepared to increase their productivity. That is what has happened in the rest of the economy.

Not until the last year have we had a significant level of inflation. The primary causes of inflation were the weakness of the euro and oil prices and the fact that we have a stupid housing boom here that makes no sense. Beyond that, inflation has not been driven by huge cost increases over productivity — or at least it has not been up to now. If we get back into that situation we will see the end of the Celtic tiger very soon.

You have to have growth to provide the opportunities that you'd like to give to people. Managing is very difficult if you don't have growth. Growth allows the number of jobs and the jobs themselves to expand. The size of the challenge increases as you develop. In the pharma industry, when companies go ex-growth, their innovation is failing and they are not producing new products necessary for survival. They get taken out and the process starts again. Examples of this are Marion Labs who were bought by Merrill Dow and became Marion Merrill Dow. That did not generate sufficiently large new products for the merged entity to survive on its own. It was then acquired by Hoechst and became Hoechst Marion Roussel. Even this was not sufficient — so it merged with Rhone-Poulenc who, in fact, were a combination of a lot of other companies. The new company is now Aventis. If you go back to the beginning of all of that there was a company called USV which was bought by Revlon Pharmaceuticals which was bought by Rorer which was bought by Rhone-Poulenc. So you had maybe ten chairmen and CEOs replaced by one chairman and CEO and one director of research. That process continues: if you don't win on innovation, you get taken out. Every one of those mergers or acquisitions drives people out simply because the situation was not productive. Then those people find their way into other companies who have the right circumstances at the time. Pfizer are on the top of the hill at the moment. So long as they innovate they will continue to do brilliantly. If they falter, they'll get taken out. The people who are leading will be retired. If you are not productive, you get fired.

"People are our most important asset" is one of the more pious statements we hear in companies. It is actually true, particularly in our business, which is all about intellectual capital. What you have to do in our business is to create an environment where people have an opportunity to do something useful, an environment where they can contribute, be a player. They have to be able to see where their contribution fits into the totality. You have to have clear objectives which people can understand. You have to be able to articulate the company's mission and that part of the mission which is relevant to them.

The most important thing in developing people is to make sure that what is expected of them is absolutely clear. That is the greatest development tool. If you say to someone, "This is what is expected of you", they can turn around and say, "Well, if that is what is expected of me, then I need these assets and this training." Mutual expectations have to be clear. There needs to be a clear career path and clarity about what kind of experience is needed to get there. For example, I have a person who's just done a good project for me. So both of us have to articulate and agree on what his next step is and where he sees himself in the future. There is an onus on people to be able to articulate what *they* want to do, otherwise it will be difficult for us to help them. Alternatively, and unfortunately, there are times when you have to say that their ambition is not realistic within the organisation and that we do not see a continuing role for them. At this stage, you can either change the expectations or they find another place to pursue their goals and we help them to do that. You have to be honest with people.

Of course, we have Human Resources but the principal thing is for people to be able to see where they can contribute to a mission or a goal that they think is worthwhile. From that point of view, we are in an easy business, whether it is in drug-delivery or in the direct pharmaceuticals part of our business. There are clear benefits for people: we can make a better medicine for you and reduce your side effects and get whatever condition you have under control — or we can cure your condition with some new medicine. That's a noble objective. It might be a bit more difficult if we were making sausages. Maybe not. For most of our people, the real satisfaction is in the work itself and in the recognition of that work. If our people discovered a cure for Alzheimer's, they would be in line for a Nobel Prize. That's an advantage we have over other industries. You could see it too in software development where the developers can see that they're going to bring a real benefit. It's harder to see that in some of the older industries.

What is important to me personally is the success of Elan. We do not consider ourselves successful yet. We have not yet achieved critical mass — we certainly need $5 billion in revenues and this year we might struggle to achieve $2 billion. I suppose that's damn good considering where we started from! The reason we need to get to $5 billion is to make enough profit to fund long-term R&D. We would like to be a significant player in the disease areas that we concentrate on and, as a result, a significant player in the industry, in the top 20 bracket. There is no reason why we can't do that if we are good enough. That's work-in-progress, not work complete. I'd be a happy man when we get to that point. And I would have done what I can do for this company. Once you cannot see clearly how you can reinvent yourself, then it's time to get out. You will not have the passion and the drive and the vision. There are times when you get to the end of a road and that's the time you should change course.

Years ago, I was driving down to Sligo to review an audit and was listening to BBC Radio 4. A woman was being interviewed. She had just started to learn ancient Hebrew. She was 82. Every ten years in her career she stopped: she had been a surgeon, an archaeologist, all sorts of different roles. She reinvented herself every ten years. So I don't see myself wedded to any one thing forever and a day. You also have to let other people have their chance.

Don Panoz used to quote from *Antony and Cleopatra*: "They have their exits and their entrances; and one man in his time plays many parts . . ." There's a time for your entry, a time for your piece — and a time for your exit, which you should do before somebody tells you it's time.

Don Panoz is a great character, a huge visionary. He had a great influence on me and many others. He could see things that nobody else could see. He would make two and two equal five — there would be a missing step, but that could be figured out later. He was utterly fearless. Failure was never an option, never. Look at what he's doing today. He's challenging Porsche, BMW, Mercedes in sports car racing at Le Mans. Only a real visionary or an utter nutter would do such a thing. He is certainly not a nutter. He has proved that he can compete with these people. The best way to motivate Don is to tell him that it can't be done. He is a great person to be around, always moving on, always doing things — and he is also great fun. We had a lovely period in Elan when we were a small team with relatively easy challenges in the context of today's challenges. They might have been just as diffi-cult where we were coming from, but they were more containable, touchable. It was just great craic. It was not like work at all. I still don't see this job as going to work — if it was like work, I would not want to do it. Another thing about Don was that he would listen to your suggestion and, if he thought it was a good one, he would back you up. Don was someone who could absorb information like a sponge. He now knows all the people in the racing business — he's probably on Michael Schumacher's Christmas card list. He's generous to a fault — he would never offer you anything less than the best bot-tle of wine in his cellar.

What made Don and me such great collaborators stems back to when Elan tried to go public in 1983. That is when I first got involved: I was still with SKC. We tried to raise money in London and Dublin and do a stock exchange listing. We were turned down. Devastation back in Athlone. Where were we going to get the money to finance the plant and finish the products and all the other things that needed to be done? I said, "Why don't we go to New York?" I had never been to America. Don grasped the idea with both hands. This was on a Thursday and he said that we would set up the meetings for Monday. On Saturday, I went into the Aer Lingus shop on Grafton Street to get

my ticket and we were in New York on Sunday. It took us from June
to the following January to get the job done, but we did it.

There are very few things that we have done that I regret but there
are several things that we have not done that I do regret. That probably describes Elan. Up to that time my thinking was very much
bounded by Ireland. However, when you go off to New York for the
first time and you show up on a Monday morning and try to persuade
people of your crazy notion — and pull it off — that changes the way
you go about things. Now we have no fear of going anywhere to ask
for whatever we want. Why should we?

6

Chris Horn

IONA Technologies plc

*"Initially I was hesitant about delegating but, as I got into it,
I delegated more and more actively and the more I delegated
the more I learned I was doing the right thing."*

Christopher John Horn is a founder and executive chairman of IONA Technologies plc.

He was born in Redhill, Surrey, on 30 November 1956. His father was John Horn, a tennis coach. His mother is Angela Mitson, professional housewife. He is the eldest in a family of four; he has one brother and two sisters, Peter, Caroline and Sally-Ann. He is married to Susan Pakenham-Walsh, another professional housewife. They have four children: Stephen (14), Jenny (12), John (10) and Linda (4).

He was educated at Avoca; Avoca and Kingstown; and then Newpark. He then went on to Trinity College Dublin (BA, BAI, PhD).

His first job was as a university lecturer in TCD in 1979. He completed his PhD in 1983, resigned from the university, and joined the European Commission in Brussels as an advisor on the Esprit Programme, which had public funding for computing research across Europe. He rejoined TCD in 1984. He co-founded IONA in 1991 under a campus companies scheme and finally resigned his college tenure in December 1993.

He is a member of the Board of Directors of the Object Management Group, an industry-wide standards body. He is a member of the Board of Directors of the Irish Brain Research Foundation and Vice-Chairman of the Council of the Irish Management Institute. He was a Scholar of Trinity College, 1976, and was awarded an honorary Doctorate of Science by the University in 2001. He was awarded Fellowship of the Institute of Engineers of Ireland, 2001.

The conversation was recorded in the IONA Building, Shelbourne Road, Dublin 4, on 12 and 26 January 2001.

Chris Horn

I was born in Surrey of English parents. My father was an amateur tennis player representing the UK in the Davis Cup and playing at Wimbledon. My Mum never made the international circuits but was a county tennis player. They married in the early fifties. About the time I was born, my Dad wanted to step down from the amateur circuits and become a professional. There wasn't then the sponsorship of the game that there is today. He was looking to build up a coaching/ teaching practice based in London, but he discovered the market there was already saturated. He got an invitation from the Irish Lawn Tennis Association to come over to Dublin to play a series of exhibition matches. He found there were no tennis professionals in Ireland at that time. He decided immediately to emigrate. We lived first in Bray and I'm told I was brought around in a carrycot and parked on the side of tennis courts. My two sisters and brother were born in Ireland. We lived in Bray until I was eight or nine and then moved to Blackrock. I started school in Avoca, as it was then, and stayed there until my Leaving Cert. The school was only half-a-mile from home. The things I remember about school were the changes it went through as, first, it merged with Kingstown School, Dun Laoghaire and then went comprehensive — so my fifth and sixth years were spent in Newpark. I was always keen on sport but, frankly, not very good at it. There was an expectation outside my family that I would become a fantastic tennis player like my parents. They were good enough to recognise that that was not ever going to be the case — they put no pressure on me at all. Of course, one of Dad's concerns was passing on the business that he had created, teaching tennis around the schools, particularly in the Dublin area. In the event, the business passed through Caroline and my younger brother, Peter.

I was always keen on mathematics and the physical sciences. I had a very good maths teacher, John Harris, who became the headmaster in Newpark. John was responsible for introducing transition year to Ireland. I was keen on acting and there we had another inspiring teacher, Derek West, who taught English and is the current head-master of Newpark. I remember Chris Sealy, a physics teacher, Roy Rohu, teaching Irish, and Derek Langran teaching geography and history. John de Courcy Ireland, very well known in Dun Laoghaire and in maritime matters, taught history and French. It was a happy school.

In 1973 I had to decide which course to take in university. My parents had never been to university — they were both only children so there was no extended family, no aunts or uncles. They had left school when they were relatively young. But particularly John Harris and Derek West were encouraging me to go to university. In my ignorance, I decided that if I were to take science and mathematics, the job prospects coming out the other end would be limited. I felt there would always be positions for engineers. Being in Dublin, then there was the question of UCD or TCD. What pushed me towards Trinity was the different approach the two universities took to engineering at that time. Both had four-year courses but, in UCD, there was one year of general science, followed by three years specialisation in a branch of engineering: chemical, mechanical, civil and so on. Trinity had the opposite approach: three years of general engineering followed by one year specialising. Since I knew nothing about engineering, I felt that, having to specialise after a single year, I might not be able to make the right choice. In 1974, I ended up in Trinity; I graduated in 1978.

I was terrified in my first term about what the academic standard was. Whereas I had been in the top 20 per cent in school, I was now with my peers from all the other schools around the country. While I joined the Trinity soccer club and the engineering society, I found the amount of course work we had as engineering students was pretty intense. I could cycle every day — it didn't make sense to live away from home.

Trinity had an introductory computing course for engineers in their first year. The man who took the course, Neville Harris, took an engineering-oriented view of computing. It was very much about understanding how a computer worked, rather than jumping in at the high level of programming languages and techniques. We programmed computers by literally flicking switches on/off on the control panel. That fascinated me because I could understand how this thing, at an electronics level, worked.

I was interested in the history of computers, early programmable computers like ENIAC and the Manchester University early computers which were very influential on the industry, things like the Enigma machine built by the Germans during the war and how that was cracked by mathematicians both in Poland and in England and by people like Alan Turing.

In retrospect, second year was broad but shallow. I sat the Scholarship exams at Easter. My tutor, Ronnie Cox, strongly recommended that I go forward for "Schol". I thought I was not good enough and didn't bother to complete an application form. Ronnie Cox was astonished when he found out and made me complete the form right there and then in his office. To my surprise — not having worked hard for it — I got it. There were four Scholars in Engineering and I got the fourth place, just scraping in. A scholarship meant the university sponsored the fees. (My father was thrilled.) Plus rooms in college, an evening meal and a book allowance. The following year, 1976, was my first time away from home. I lived in college Monday to Friday and brought home the washing at weekends.

The pressure was intense in my final year in Trinity. Unlike today, you had only one bite at the cherry and your career depended on it. It all came down to seven three-hour exams. Remember, Trinity was three years general, one year specialist. I chose electronic and electrical subjects, topics that were not specifically in computing. I felt that going into a software career, I'd be stuck in an office all day, sitting in front of a computer screen — and that was not for me! I wanted to be out in the field doing real engineering. Nevertheless, I felt I should keep my eye in in the computing area, so for my project, an essential part of the exam, I chose computing. My project, under Neville Harris, was to study how a small computer could monitor the behaviour of a large computer. This was at a time, 1978, when microprocessors had just been introduced. The small computer had electrical probes that you would attach to the guts of the large computer to monitor the electrical signals flowing through the large computer, analyse those signals and work out where there were inefficiencies in terms of idle time, etc. The project was successful and I enjoyed it. Unlike the Schol exam, I put a lot of work into the finals and ended up with a First overall. I don't think I was at the top of the class but I was probably in the top 5 per cent.

I promised myself after the finals that I would never ever sit another exam. The Schol was for five years to encourage students to stay on and do post-grad. My Schol had three years left to run. I started a Master's, intending to transfer to a PhD if the Master's was going well — you could do that in Trinity. I spent the first nine months trying to decide on an area of study, with Neville Harris trying to guide me. I did not find anything I was really happy with. I was getting a bit disillusioned. I began to look around more widely and talked with Michael Purser who had lectured me in my final year. His specialty was networking of computers, connecting computers together using telephone wires and writing software to make computers work in that scenario. I became very interested indeed in what he was doing and started working with him. He also had some external work — I remember working in the Meteorological Office, the pyramid building in Glasnevin. Michael and I worked on the small computers that connected with the very big computer in Glasnevin that gives the weather forecasts. This was a real world where you could see the real benefits and the need.

Michael had a company at the time called Chaco which was doing consulting work on computer networking both in Ireland and overseas. Chaco is a physical region, like Munster, in Argentina — Michael is a fluent Spanish speaker, and has worked extensively in South America.

At that time Trinity started a BA in computer science. The course was to start in October but the money from the Higher Education Authority came through only in July with no students and no staff. Somehow, the university managed to divert people from the courses they had registered in into this new course. They were stuck for lecturers. I became a junior lecturer and had to switch to a part-time PhD. That was my first full-time job. We were literally one week ahead of the students in terms of course notes. When the first years went to second year, we had the same thing. And so on. The main lesson I learned from that was not to panic! Instead of finishing my PhD in three years, it took five.

I became more and more fascinated by the idea of using a collection of small computers, microprocessors, to behave as a team collectively and to offer the power of a very large computer. At that time, a mainframe computer would have cost £1–£3 million, whereas you could string up to 50 microprocessors together for maybe £50,000.

Michael Purser's interests were, and are, on the telecommunications networking aspects of computers. I became increasingly interested in how you get computers to split or partition their work, how you organise a network of computers so that, if one fails, the others can take over the work, or, if you want to increase the capacity of the system, you can just insert a new computer. This was an area that Michael was not particularly interested in and it was where I wanted to specialise for my PhD. I ended up, full circle, back with Neville Harris as my PhD supervisor.

There's a company called Sun Microsystems which was established in the late seventies in California. "Sun" stands for Stanford University Network. Academics led by Dave Cheriton had built a network of computers that were working together doing things like jobsharing and load balancing, and using a technology called Ethernet as the network between them. Some of Cheriton's research students saw the opportunity to exploit Ethernet technology commercially. Neville Harris knew Cheriton well and had spent a sabbatical year in Stanford. Neville brought back to Trinity some of the early Sun computers. I think we had the first of them anywhere in Europe. They were the computers on which I prototyped my dissertation. I remember physically handing in my PhD on a Friday afternoon. The following Monday I was in Brussels, working for the European Commission.

Michael Purser, through Chaco, knew the Commission were looking for people to act as consultants on an initiative they were starting called Esprit. It was a ten-year programme really formed in opposition to the Japanese Fifth Generation Computing Initiative. Both the Americans and the Europeans were surprised by the amount of investment in Japan. One of the major concerns of Esprit was to link the research communities across Europe with the major European companies like Philips and Siemens, Nixdorf and ICL and Bull, each of which were national champions and not good at co-operating together across national boundaries. The Commission wanted to form a solid European computer industry.

I ended up working for Nick Newman, an Englishman, whose particular responsibility was computer networking technology. To get computers to talk to each other was quite difficult technically at that time.

There were two elements to the job — one political, the other technical. Nick Newman was a full-time Commission bureaucrat. The

Esprit programme itself was highly political because the Commission had 20 directorates-general, effectively ministries. The question was which ministry should own it. It ended up that the Esprit programme was not put under any ministry. It was its own taskforce. There was some resentment from the ministries and some of the high-fliers from those ministries had left to join the taskforce. I joined it in its early days: a small team of 20 people. After three years that same team had grown to 200. At that early stage, people were jockeying for positions and starting to build pyramids beneath them. I expected to find each country fighting for its turf, but national boundaries didn't come into it at all — it was a question of personalities. That was re-freshing.

My job was as an assessor, to organise peer reviews of some of the running projects and sign off on cost-statements, and also to assess proposals for new projects. The head of the taskforce at the time was another Commission bureaucrat, Horst Hünke, an interesting guy, overworked and stressed. Part of my job was to visit various companies and research institutes throughout the Community, such as INRIA, the French research centre, but what was frustrating was that my peers and managers were spending time in Brussels in-fighting both with each other to grow the organisation and also defending the organisation against the 20 DGs. They were spending insufficient time out in the field. Naively I felt that the whole purpose of Esprit was pan-European collaboration and yet the Commission itself was not actively spending much time doing that.

Following that first year, I had the opportunity to become a full-time employee of the Commission — I had been an employee of Chaco. I decided not to join the Commission — one, because of disil-lusionment and, two, because I met other Irish people there, particularly Barry O'Shea, who, together with his family, were very kind to me. Barry had been a career civil servant in Ireland and I could see people like him becoming lifetime civil servants in the Commission and finding it difficult to leave — the pay was good, it was tax-free; there was a VAT-free supermarket inside the Berlaymont building.

I came back to Trinity as an academic on the undergraduate computer science degree course, fully intending that that was a stepping-stone. I was not quite sure what job I wanted, maybe with a multinational computer corporation, maybe with an Irish software company. But Neville Harris, in the nicest possible way, quickly got his hooks into me and sought funding from the European Union for an Esprit project in Trinity. We got involved in a very large and well-funded project. We were collaborating, in particular, with Olivetti, ICL and Bull, specifically in the areas of getting their computer systems to work together. This was precisely the area of my PhD.

I had come back in September. By Christmas, I realised that I wasn't going to rush out and look for a job elsewhere. The Esprit project was commercial in its approach — it wasn't purely theoretical. Eventually we had a team of 25 in TCD alone, all funded through the EU. There were about 150 people across Europe working on this single project. What we were doing was known in Brussels as "pre-competitive", because the EU could not fund something which had a direct commercial application. And the results had to be available to all other participants in the Esprit programme. Certainly the companies with which we collaborated could take the results of the project and exploit them in their product lines, but they didn't. I think this generally happened across all of Esprit. There were 400 or 500 Esprit projects and you could count on the fingers of one hand those that had been exploited. Millions of taxpayers' euros were being put into the Esprit programme with few commercially exploited results. This was becoming a political issue: where were the results, where were the products, where were the improvements in the European computer industry vis-à-vis the Americans and the Japanese? Brussels' response was that it was going to take another five years before the "pre-competitive" R&D was turned into something commercial. The whole life cycle was very long and the computer industry moves so fast. The results produced by Esprit were probably becoming irrelevant as the technology moved on. Esprit was excellent in fostering European collaboration but, in leading to commercial results, it achieved very little. Now the Commission's programmes are about competitive R&D, not "pre-competitive". Esprit was disappointing.

So there we were in Trinity, five academics and 20 researchers. Then, in 1989, the Object Management Group was formed in Massachusetts by some people who used to work for Data General in Boston. Data General had been getting into financial difficulties. They had a software group that had been looking at what is called object technology, a technology which promised a new style of designing and building software, very much like Lego building bricks, like chips in hardware circuits, where you have reusable chips and building blocks which you string together. Up to 1989, software had not really been built in that way, incredible as that may sound. The Object Management Group had been formed to try to set industry-wide standards for this new style of computing — frankly, in response to Microsoft's announcements at that time. Microsoft had announced that they were going to do object technology and the industry said, "My God, we can't let Microsoft own this new and exciting software. We need to band together. We need to try to force Microsoft to conform to standards which we have agreed."

Back in Trinity we knew very little about the Object Management Group, but the guy behind it, Richard Soley, now the president and chief executive, visited the Esprit Annual Trade Fair in Brussels. He came to the Trinity booth and saw what we were doing.

In 1989, the Object Management Group issued a solicitation to the industry for proposals for what could be the new standards. Bull and ICL were the only proposals from Europe — there were about 20 from the States. The OMG were left with the problem of how do you rationalise, coalesce, decide between these different proposals. We started to participate in the assessment committee. What it all means is that if two companies implement the same standard, then their respective products can be connected together: it's basically about compatibility. There was a tremendous move in the eighties from proprietary to industry-wide standards so that a customer is not locked in to a particular supplier. Standards defined by consensus across the industry became a very important theme. There was both customer and vendor pressure, together with the competitive threat from Microsoft. What that means for a vendor is: I must implement industry standards but maybe I can do so in a way that is better, cheaper, faster and more reliable than my competitors. The impetus came both from concern about Microsoft and from the customers who did not want to be confined to one product. Customers want to be able to mix and match their equipment. Middleware is something that allows you to connect things together — things that would otherwise be incompatible. At the time we are talking about, companies would have in-house their home-brew software/middleware. There was no standards-based external product on the market.

The OMG published their first standard, called CORBA. This was as a result of coalescing the various proposals that had come in the previous year. The OMG would not publish a standard unless there was one commercial prototype somewhere in the world. After OMG meetings, in the corridors or in the pub, talking to the engineers, we did not see any mad rush on the part of the commercial companies to implement the standard. However, we knew there was customer interest in it — we being the five Trinity academics in Esprit. At this stage, 1990, Esprit was being wound down.

An active campus company scheme was initiated in Trinity. There had been some earlier campus efforts, like Mentec, very successfully operating in Dun Laoghaire, headed by Michael Peirce. He's now the chairman of Parthus, which has recently gone public. Eoin O'Neill was appointed by TCD to administer the campus companies. At the end of 1990, we decided to form one to implement the new standards, based on the eight or nine years of Esprit research. The question arose as to who was going to lead it. I believed that this could take off and that you couldn't lead it on a part-time basis. Down the road it would need serious commitment. Six Trinity academics signed up as shareholders but only two of us were committed to it full-time, Sean Baker and I. The other four were Neville Harris, Vinnie Cahill, Brendan Tangney and Alexis Donnelly. One of our research assistants, who had not been on the Esprit project nor a full-time academic, was Annrai O'Toole. He was interested, so essentially it was Sean, Annrai and I who took the lead in forming IONA. Brendan Tangney was also very supportive. He helped steer the proposal through Eoin O'Neill and the Trinity Board sub-committee that approved the projects.

IONA is not an acronym — it doesn't stand for anything. One afternoon, we went through a list of names, and liked IONA for its Irish connotation and because it could be recognised multinationally. We also chose IONA *Technologies* — IT, a play on Information Technology. We formed the company on 19 March 1991, started in a tiny room in the Innovation Centre on Pearse Street. All we could fit in was a desk, a chair, a broken filing cabinet and a telephone.

For the first year Annrai, Sean and I put together a business plan looking for outside investors to bootstrap the company. We said we could implement this new CORBA standard faster than the Americans. That sounds great until you ask who are the Americans — and they are Sun, Hewlett Packard, IBM and Digital. We had talked to those guys, we knew they were not going to enter the market until 1996 and we thought we could do it in 1992. You could see potential investors' eyes glaze over: "It sounds like a good idea — but you're

going to compete with *who*? And, oh, by the way, Microsoft don't en-
dorse this?" At that time, indigenous software companies had not
been particularly successful in Ireland. There had been Memory
Computers which went head-over-heels and left a sour taste in the
private investor community. Another major issue was the fact that we
were a Dublin, Irish company, going to compete against the Americans.

There was, however, in our minds, one shining example, a role
model, Glockenspiel. It was formed around 1995 by John Carolan
who had worked on object technology with AT&T/Bell Labs in the
States. John had taken, with full permission, one of their early "products". He became quite a well-known name for selling this product
back into the United States from Glockenspiel in Dublin, Ireland.
John's problem was how to penetrate the US from Dublin. The way
he did it was to agree a distributor/partner who sold his product ex-
clusively, leaving John and his team to develop the product in Ireland. There were apparently disagreements between Glockenspiel
and the distributor and around 1990/91 Glockenspiel got into financial trouble and was acquired by Computer Associates. John was very
honest and open with us and told us what had gone right and what
had gone wrong for him. We decided not to sign an exclusive dis-
tributorship for the US. In retrospect, we were fortunate in our timing
compared with Glockenspiel. By the time we had our first product in
1993, the Internet was much more developed — it was possible to sell
through the Internet to a US technical audience. Had it been there in
the 1980s, Glockenspiel would have been a brand name as much as
IONA is today.

I also talked with Mike Peirce in Mentec. He was very helpful,
particularly in telling us about his relationship with the IDA. And, at
that time, Chaco had partnered with a company called Systems Dy-
namics and built a third company that was going to be the marketing
and sales arm for them both. That new company was called Baltimore
Technologies. Mike Purser was on the Board — I had also been on
that Board since I returned from Brussels and, as a non-executive director, got some insight into building a high-tech company in Ireland.
In forming IONA, the external influences on me were those three:
John Carolan, Michael Purser and Mike Peirce.

We spent about a year talking to private investors, banks and BES
investors but we were just not credible in what we were trying to do —

a bunch of crazy academics with no business experience in a high-tech area which nobody really seemed to understand, and potentially competing with the American majors. We made some forays into the UK and France, talking to venture capital companies, but they had no interest. We realised that we could get this thing going only by using cash flow from operations. For the first three years, we did consultancy work, one-off projects, and used the money from that to hire our first couple of engineers to build Version One. We worked with the Met Office, with the UK Customs and Excise people, we gave courses in object technology to ICL, we helped people to get printers to work from Macintoshes to PCs — anything to raise money. We continued to have a participation in the Esprit programme, small but very important to us.

We had by early 1993 reached the stage where we were ready to launch our product, Orbix — not commercially but among friends who could provide us with qualitative feedback. Between January and Easter 1993 we gave away about 20 copies of the product. ICL here in Dublin gave us a lot of feedback. We were about eight or nine people. Colin Newman, a friend of Annrai's, joined us to help with marketing. Jim Mountjoy, who had been brought in by Michael Purser as CEO of Baltimore, advised me always to have three months' cash in the bank and to have another three months' money owed to you. If you had *more* than three months' money in the bank, you were not expanding sufficiently aggressively. That was the way I was leading IONA. Incidentally, there had never been any big discussion, or event, about my becoming chairman and CEO — I may have got the job because I was ten years older than Annrai and about two years older than Sean! It just happened.

By June of 1993 the OMG were having their annual trade fair. We used that show to launch our product. We built our booth here in Rathmines and air-freighted it out to California. We flew out almost all the staff — that show was make-or-break for the company. My three months' cash flow was down to about two weeks. Thankfully, at the show a few companies saw what we were about — we were the first company in the world to implement this CORBA standard in full: not only had we implemented it on Unix machines from companies like Sun but we also had implemented it on Microsoft's Windows software. This was unique. We had also used a programming language called C++, which was very trendy at the time. We caused quite a stir.

I remember we had to buy four Sun computers at a cost of £12,000. Of course, we did not have the cash. We had to sign lease agreements and get personal guarantees. I had to give a guarantee against my house. Michael Peirce had told me never, ever to do that, that he had to do it and it was the most stressful period of his life. But we had no choice.

Anyway, the launch was successful and we got our first few customers. Sun Microsystems were at the show and were interested. They were now a multi-million-dollar corporation. They did not have a full implementation of the CORBA standard. What they did have worked only on the Sun computing equipment and, in particular, did not work on the Microsoft Windows computing environment. We did not know it but, at the time, they were looking for a business partner to help solve the problem, when, out of the blue, along come these Irishmen who had done it.

The Sun CEO apparently had a diktat at that time that no one in the company could have a Microsoft Windows machine inside Sun anywhere. That meant there were no engineers in Sun who understood Windows. They had partnered with one of our competitors, Hyperdesk, who had started up in Massachusetts with extensive venture capital. Novell had also invested in them, so they were well capitalised. In 1993 they had a product on the market which was competing with ours. They were about 150 people. We were about eight. They were the company to beat. Hyperdesk had been slow to deliver on Sun's expectations, so Jim Greene, Sun's project manager for CORBA, flew over to us from California. He liked what he saw and said Sun was willing to invest $600,000 for 25 per cent of IONA. The implicit worth of the company was $2.4 million. Our revenues were about £30,000. What he wanted from us was that our CORBA product would work with his on Sun's computing equipment. And he wanted two board seats. I responded positively to him but, in parallel, we had been talking to the IDA.

William McBride in the IDA had told us that, yes, we might have something, but we needed a major industrial sponsor to be credible. When the IDA checked out Sun, they became interested too and were willing to put up matching funding. That meant we would get $600,000 investment from the IDA — for us, it was just incredible.

The IDA investment turned out to be partly in job grants — the first 56 jobs we created, we got $6,000 per job. That amounted to about half the $600,000. The other half was in the form of a repayable loan on which we paid interest. The IDA took a 7 per cent equity position and, as a campus company, Trinity insisted on having 15 per cent for no financial investment. That meant that 47 per cent of the company was held outside the promoters. I felt this was untenable. Annrai and I negotiated with Trinity for the company to buy back a proportion of the 15 per cent. Their investment was reduced by 12 per cent to 3 per cent. We also had a formal agreement with Trinity that they had no claim on intellectual property. When Sun came to do their due diligence in winter 1993, they found the company clean and everything well documented. We signed the agreement with Sun on 23 December 1993, the day before Christmas Eve. We cracked open the champagne in William Fry's solicitors' office.

Motorola at that time were interested in our products but were worried about our size and durability. When they saw that Sun had invested in us, we got a contract from them worth $600,000.

We moved out of Trinity and into Percy Place in Dublin. Sun were setting up a development centre in Ireland and their first offices were there. Dick McQuillan was the local Sun man. He came on to our Board along with Jim Greene from California. The IDA had the right to appoint a director. At that time, Kevin Melia[1] was forming his company, Manufacturers Services Limited. Up to that time, Kevin had been the CFO of Sun Microsystems. The IDA were happy to accept our suggestion that Kevin be their nominee. He joined the Board in 1994.

Things began to happen. We did joint marketing with Sun. Motorola became a major customer. Barry Morris, now CEO, joined us from Lotus in Coolock. Barry and Annrai and Colin Newman responded to a quotation request from Boeing. Up to that point, Boeing had played with and evaluated our technology — and that of our competitors. They liked the Motorola endorsement but, perhaps more importantly, Boeing got a problem solved in a very short time. In February 1994, we opened an office in California to be close to Sun. Annrai went there for a year. The eight hours' time difference made things difficult and I took a decision to relocate the office to the East

---

[1] See Chapter 10, pp. 191–208.

Coast. We shared offices with a partner, Stratus, but they were 40 miles outside Boston, in a beautiful place, but very difficult to get the American staff we needed to commute there. So we moved to Cambridge, Massachusetts. The Boston office was very much marketing and sales with the engineering being done in Dublin. Our product was easy to use. We could ship it in a FedEx box to a customer — they did not necessarily need to have an IONA person there to tell them how to use it.

During this time, some American competitors came and some went. A company called Visigenics, which had started out as Post Modern, rang us one day and asked us for a copy of our product. To our chagrin, we subsequently found they were competitors. They copied some of our ideas — though we implemented the CORBA standard we had also extended it with some proprietary and clever features. We hadn't patented them and Visigenics reinvented a lot of what we had.

Hewlett Packard decided to close down their development centre which was working on a product competing with us. That was in Chelmsford in Massachusetts, just up the road from where we were. We negotiated with HP, some of their key engineers came and joined us, they gave us access to some of their test suites and one of the key people we got at that time was Steve Vinoski, who is now our chief architect. That gave us the impetus to start an engineering centre in Boston. In 1996, we also started an engineering centre in Perth, Australia, because of David Glance. He worked for a partner/competitor of ours, Tibco in London. Tibco and we had a joint customer in Nomura, the big Japanese bank in London. We did not know it at the time but David was setting up a renegade engineering group separate from the Tibco headquarters in Palo Alto. Palo Alto tried to close down what David was doing so he wanted to join us. He had lived for his early years in Perth and wanted to go back there. Knowing that the Western Australian economy was depressed and that there were some very good graduates there and knowing that Perth was in the same time zone as Tokyo and Hong Kong, we thought, why not? That's how we came to have three different engineering centres.

By 1996, we began to think seriously about doing an IPO. The only market we could think about was the Nasdaq. Easdaq did not exist in Europe at that time. We did the usual beauty contest and went with a boutique bank, largely because of the expertise of one of their analyst in the software area. He was, in fact, a brand name. He then unfortunately committed suicide — he climbed to the top of the building and threw himself off. When that happened, they put a junior research analyst on to us. I was not happy with that and we ended up with Lehman Brothers as the lead investment bank. Lehmans were interested in entering the high-tech market and gave us terms considerably less than the normal 7 per cent of the money raised in the IPO. They were also prepared to pull out all the stops.

Sun said, "You're not going to go public — we want to buy you." I gulped and said, "What sort of money are we talking about?" They sent their advisers to run the rule over us and Annrai and I ended up in a meeting in Mountainview in California with the senior manager to whom Jim Greene reported. Sun's bankers presented their analysis to us running various models, all ending up at a valuation of IONA of between $50 million and $60 million. Our revenues at the time would have been about $8 million or $9 million. Lehmans had told us that, if they brought us public, they would value us at about $200 million.

The senior manager said, "Look, Chris, this is great. I'm willing to buy you at $65 million. You guys will all be very rich and it's a huge success story. What do you think?" Annrai and I immediately said no. He then stormed out of the meeting, feigning great upset and the veto came down, "You guys are not going public." This was something they could say as a 25 per cent shareholder. Even if they didn't have a legal veto, they could have upset the IPO. We needed Sun on board. How were we to get them to change their minds?

Andy Mallick from Lehmans and I met with the senior manager and with Sun's CEO. At the time, Sun were developing a new division to promote the Java technology which they had invented. There were some internal rivalries for the ownership of Sun's software strategy. To an extent, we were caught up in those wars. I approached some of the outside non-executive directors in Sun, including one of the venture capitalists who had bankrolled Sun in the early days. The essential proposition was, "You invested in IONA because of CORBA technology and the OMG. Now your whole strategic direction is changing towards Java and away from CORBA. Therefore IONA is not as strategically interesting to you as it was. If we are to do an IPO, your 25 per cent would be worth $50 million." After some time, they came around to that decision and overruled the senior manager and let IONA go public.

When you do an IPO, you prepare a prospectus, you then do a roadshow over a number of weeks, visiting prospective investors. They place tentative orders with your bankers, then, when you have finished the roadshow, based on the tentative orders, you "price" the deal. There is what's called a pricing meeting literally on the night before the IPO. Sun said that if they could not be guaranteed a price of $60 million for their 25 per cent, they would veto the IPO. That meant that, right at the very last moment, Sun could pull the trigger and say that we were not going ahead. In a way, they were calling Lehmans' bluff. They also insisted that for three years after the IPO we would guarantee that our products would support Sun equipment — that was no problem at all for us. They also insisted on a right of first refusal if anyone were to offer to buy us for two years after the IPO. In other words, if, say, Microsoft were to make an offer, Sun could match that offer and buy IONA. That had to be publicly disclosed in the prospectus and effectively stymied any takeover bid. This also meant that the investors were aware of Sun's right — in a high-tech industry investors normally would pay a premium for the stock in the expectation that the company would be taken over.

None of IONA's senior managers had experience of running a public company and we were potentially weak operationally, particularly as we grew. We were riding a wave, doing very well, but being a public company was something else again. The Board, but particularly Kevin Melia, were keen that we should have a person of substantial experience. Kevin's nomination was Mick Prokopis. In August 1996, Mick joined us from Digital Equipment Corporation. Mick brought in Lindsey Kiang, as our legal counsel, and Teresa Kelly on HR. Mick insisted that we invest in the SAP financial management package before we went public.

We went public in February 1997. We did not expect at all the level of interest in Ireland — suddenly there was this Irish company that nobody ever heard of going public. My wife Susan rang me while I was on the IPO roadshow in the US to say that there was a fuzzy photograph on the front page of the *Evening Herald*: The Multi-Million Dollar Man — who was this Chris Horn?

I feel that everybody should do an IPO roadshow at least once in their lifetime! It's something you would never forget. The tiredness —

eight meetings a day, some days three cities, Boston, Philadelphia, Pittsburgh, getting red-eye flights at ten o'clock at night, getting in at six o'clock in the morning to start off again. I remember a three-hour drive in a pelting rainstorm in Chicago. (We were flying back and forth across the Atlantic by Concorde.) One of the surreal times was in a stretch limo, asking the driver to take us into a McDonalds, pressing the button for the black window to come down to get a Big Mac for breakfast.

We were 11 times oversubscribed. The initial price was $14 to $16. Then we raised it $16 to $18 and eventually opened at $22. Sun got their money.

Mick Prokopis was both CFO and COO. With his agreement, we subsequently agreed to split the roles and, in the summer of 1997, David James joined us as CFO.

In 1999, we had a profit warning — we missed Q1. At the time we had gone public we were using primarily telesales. The average deal size was about $5,000. After we went public, we started building up a field sales team, primarily in the US but also worldwide. Our deal sizes began to increase to about $15,000. We now had a relatively large number of relatively small sales and small numbers of much larger deals, even some $1 million deals. There were two different target markets for those deals. In Q1 1999, we had been over-optimistic about our ability to close large deals. Our field sales team was not as mature as it should have been.

We had a huge embarrassment. I remember being disappointed but, at the same time, philosophical, saying to myself that it was the same company today as it was yesterday. What I did not expect was the turnover of staff that ensued, as the headhunters in Ireland and the US put their claws into us. They were devastating our ranks. There were some people, particularly on the sales side, I was not un-happy to see go, but we also lost some very good people.

There was a fair amount of doom and gloom around but the core of the company remained optimistic and in Q2 1999, we bounced back. The reaction of Wall Street was it was too early to make a judg-ment. The share price had dropped by about 50 per cent and it was at this time that the distinguished author of this book joined the Board! In quarters three and four of 1999, we continued the bounce-back and Wall Street began to take notice. The tide began to turn. An ana-lyst who followed us, John McPeake, told me that we had been very honest with the investors — and we were not the only ones who had a tough year. Some of them were blaming it on the run-up to the Year 2000 (Y2K) transition and a slow down in investments by the corporates. We said the reason we missed was internal execution — mea culpa. Incredibly, we did not receive any class action lawsuits from the shareholder community. However, we took a lot of stick in the Irish market and that affected morale in the Dublin office. The morale in the US, on the other hand, was pretty buoyant. While, in the second half of 1999, the Y2K phenomenon took up an inordinate amount of engineering time, we felt it was overblown.

I believed the company had now got to a size and complexity that it would be appropriate for me to step down as CEO. I took that decision as a New Year's resolution — that some time over the course of the year, I would split the roles of chairman and CEO. I'd done the job for almost ten years. I travelled an awful lot. My children were growing up — my eldest was 13. These were the key years for the family. There were two or three candidates internally and one or two externally but, coming up to Easter, in my own mind I had come down to one particular candidate. I had obviously taken soundings with the Board and in May, I told them that we should split the roles and I felt Barry Morris was an excellent person for the job. As we look back now, it was a great decision.

I had very mixed feelings in June. I had psyched myself up for it. There was certainly a sense of relief that the mantle had been removed from my shoulders, I wouldn't be travelling so much, I could see my family, but there was also a feeling of some anxiety as to whether Barry, who was at that stage untried as a chief executive, could do it and concern that I could give him every possible support but without interfering with him on a day-by-day basis. There was a sense that I had to be ready if things went wrong. And, finally, there was a sense of slight disappointment. I had built this thing up for nine years and it was a pity to let go but then I couldn't continue forever. Very mixed feelings. I had my annual two weeks in Connemara to think things through and came back feeling more optimistic. And here we are today, at the end of January 2001, and it's been fabulous. Barry and I have clearly got a great number of challenges ahead but we are confident and he's doing a great job.

As chairman, I had a stronger feeling of what not to do than what to do! What not to do was to be involved in any way operationally —

that is entirely Barry's domain. It is important not only that Barry is let get on with it but is seen to be let get on with it, particularly inside the company. Externally, I probably had a higher personal profile in the Irish media than he did and it was important that his profile in Dublin be raised. So I've tried to take a bit of a back seat. He's now got more traction than I have in the US media.

What I wanted to do was to continue to meet with senior customers, to help in the investor relations effort which, by the way, has always been under the CFO's domain. American investors expect to see the CEO and CFO more than the chairman, so my job was to be in a supportive role. I'm comfortable about being number two to Barry's number one.

I wanted to spend time promoting the company in an indirect way with trade associations, business organisations both locally and internationally. I also felt strongly that I — and the company — should get involved in some sort of philanthropy — we had had a philanthropy budget but it tended to be *ad hoc* and uncoordinated. We needed a rallying call for all the staff around one particular cause. Just as I was mulling over this, Maura Quinn, who runs UNICEF Ireland, walked into my office. I hadn't realised that IONA had become the largest contributor to the UNICEF Christmas card scheme in Ireland. The actor, Liam Neeson, is the patron of UNICEF Ireland. He had suggested to Maura Quinn an auction of movie industry memorabilia, but he needed a cause. Maura Quinn, who had travelled extensively in Africa, suggested HIV/AIDS as a cause.

The AIDS situation in Africa is awful. It's a different strain of the virus from that in the West. In the West there are drugs that can slow down or even stop the progress of the virus but they are inappropriate for the African strain and, in any event, would be far too expensive. However, some new drugs have come onto the market which effectively block the transmission of AIDS from mother to child during childbirth. While they don't do anything for the mother, at least the child is born free of the disease. A child born with AIDS has a high probability of being dead before age four. All of the other self-help programmes in Africa are becoming meaningless because of the spread of AIDS. Whole segments of the population have been devastated. The teaching profession in primary and secondary schools and in universities has virtually disappeared because they're dead. The civil service has broken down. It's black and white, rich and poor, middle class, working class — across the whole community. It's everybody. The social fabric of the countries is disintegrating. It's so horrendous that you might think there is nothing we could do, that it is only pouring money down a drain hole — we should forget it, it's hopeless. But these new drug treatments, which cost just $4, could stop children being born with AIDS. And education becomes most important — in Zambia, in the 15–20 years age group, there has been a change in AIDS penetration from very high to reduced levels.

I went out to Lusaka with Maura in October last. I wanted to understand what UNICEF's work was really like on the ground. I did not want to hear it from UNICEF people. I wanted to meet the Zambians themselves. The last thing that people need is Westerners coming in and telling them how to do things. UNICEF is held in high regard there but the education is done by the local people themselves, mostly through drama and music, local Zambians going out and giving positive messages to their peers.

I admire the work of Goal and Trócaire, but our international staff would need as a rallying point an international brand name charity. By the time this book is published, the auction will have been held on 6 March in Manhattan. I have been astonished by the strength of the feedback from some of our people, several of whom have had direct experience of AIDS either through having a brush with it themselves or through knowing people. It's great that the company as a whole feels it can contribute to something.

Back in 1993/94, we felt it was us against the world. That could have been misinterpreted as arrogance, but really it was from a sense of helplessness. We felt we did not need to hire people with 20 years' experience. We felt the young people coming out of college would be just as good and would be fired up. One of our best sales people had been a baggage handler for Aer Arann. Another guy's father had a furniture shop. He learned through selling furniture. Neither of them knew anything about software or computers — but they were driven. Well, at some point, that management philosophy began to unravel. I realised that I had been incredibly lucky but I had over-promoted inexperienced people and the company began to get into trouble. We needed more maturity — that was one clear lesson.

I'm so glad that I did not form the company on my own, that we formed it as a team. It would have been horrendous not to have somebody to share the ups and the downs. I could not have done it without having Sean and Annrai to talk to about my fears and worries. They would lift me up. Equally, there were times when they were depressed. A good decision was that we did not really socialise together — and we still don't now. When we came to the end of a working day we would go our separate ways. We were not great drinking buddies; we did not go on holidays together or have each other around for meals. We had our own lives to live. We could shut the worries away — we were not carrying the load 24 hours a day.

Initially I was hesitant about delegating but, as I got into it, I delegated more and more actively and the more I delegated the more I learned I was doing the right thing.

A bigger change than the chairman/CEO one, which was almost a natural progression, was back in 1995 when I was chairman, CEO and head of engineering. I was coding and developing some of the products myself. I stepped back from that because I just knew I was becoming a bottleneck for that team. Software engineering is incredibly detailed and intensive. You need to have a clear perspective over the whole product suite and you need to be 100 per cent devoted to it. I was not 100 per cent devoted because I had everything else to do and I was beginning to increase my travelling. People were waiting for me to make decisions. As a result, the engineering team was slowing down. Letting go of the technology was a wrenching decision but I knew I had to. A lot of the engineers — and Annrai in particular — believed I would continue to dabble. I didn't. I said, "I'm out of here", and we appointed a new engineering manager. That was one of the biggest management decisions I had to make. I found it difficult because I enjoyed software development so much.

IONA is an Irish company with its headquarters in Dublin. I've always tried to recruit locally — Japanese staff in Japan, French in France. The last thing I wanted to do was what some American companies do — parachute in an American from headquarters. We have some 800 people worldwide of whom about 600 are non-Irish nationals. When you look at the executive team, we have many more non-Irish than Irish, but it is still an Irish company with an Irish culture and ethos, albeit very much multinational. We've consciously tried to nurture a multinational ethos with, perhaps, an Irish perspective on business and that comes down to service, friendships, commitment — but also slightly the underdog competing against some of the major American corporations in this space.

One of the most startling questions I ever got was from one of our first US members of staff, Steve Deane, who said, "How do I know that, as an American, I am not going to be treated any differently or worse than an Irish member of staff?" We went through a period in 1996 where we had to recognise that we were no longer all-white, all-Roman Catholic, all-male, all-Irish. We had to sensitise things like the internal company newsletter and make sure we didn't offend people of different cultures. Today that's no problem at all.

Ireland has to move away from being best at process to being best at innovation, bringing new products to the global market. Ireland has become a global manufacturing base but there is no reason why, for example, the Czechs and Poles won't catch us up in five years time and build a tiger economy in their countries. As of now, Ireland's patent portfolio, Ireland's GNP, are way way down below other countries. Ireland tends to have copycat products. Ireland has not yet been particularly innovative in our technology products. We have the venture capitalists, we have the financial support. The distribution capability is clearly here — not least leveraged by the Internet. It's a matter of confidence, and getting down and doing it, and innovating.

It's very rare in the computer industry that you get quantum leaps. The software industry is more about incremental moves. It's evolution — not revolution. And it's not just the innovation you need, it's also the marketing ability to carry off the innovation in a worldwide market. That's an extraordinarily difficult thing to do. I guess I'm taking a middle-of-the-road view: yes, we must innovate but not in a spectacular quantum-leap kind of way but in a way that is a natural evolution from where the industry is today. And we need to be leaders rather than followers — as a nation and as a company.

When you look about at the condition of some of the State services, transport and roads, you need first a vision of what might be and then milestones along the way to that vision. But to get there you really do have to identify the low-hanging fruit that gives early victories, that, for relatively little effort, achieves quite a lot and helps build confidence that you can achieve a lot more.

7

Eddie Jordan

Jordan Grand Prix

*"The most satisfying thing in my life was to survive.
In normal businesses, they look at the balance sheet every
half-year. In my business it's every two weeks. In one race,
you're either a complete tosser or a giant."*

Edward Patrick Jordan is the chairman and chief executive of Jordan Grand Prix and Jordan Holdings.

He was born in Dublin on 30 March 1948. His father, Paddy Jordan, was an accountant with the Electricity Supply Board. His mother is Eileen Mahon, a housewife. He was second in a family of two, with an older sister, Helen. He is married to Marie McCarthy. They have four children, two boys and two girls: Zoe (21), Miki (18), Zak (14) and Killian (11).

He was educated at Synge Street School and at the College of Commerce in Rathmines, where he did very little. He started as a bank clerk with the Hibernian Bank, now incorporated in the Bank of Ireland, then drove racing cars and now runs Jordan Grand Prix.

He has several directorships, all linked to Jordan Holdings. He is a patron of several charities, his favourite being CLIC, Cancer Leukaemia in Children, of which his wife is chairperson. He was Entrepreneur of the Year (2000); Sporting Ambassador for Ireland (1998–2000); Ernst & Young World Entrepreneur of the Year Award for Global Leadership (2001).

The conversation was recorded in the Berkeley Court Hotel, Dublin, on 25 April 2001.

Eddie Jordan

Imust say that I had a particularly privileged childhood. I was
brought up in Dublin, with aunts and uncles who lived in Bray,
where my father's family home was within 100 metres of the sea. We
lived in Dartry Road and it was a short walk down Temple Road to
pick up the then train to Bray. I'd go out after school in Synge Street.
For the first five or six years of my life I was extremely ill with what
was known as pink disease, an infantile disease, painful redness in
your extremities, caused by mercury poisoning. Miraculously, I was
nursed back to health by my mother — she tells the story better than
anyone else.

My father's twin sister was Reverend Mother at the Irish Sisters of
Charity. When she was Mother Rectress in the Merrion Hospital for
the Blind, we would be brought there every Sunday. That was the beginnings of my desire to help other people who were less fortunate,
particularly children, with charities such as CLIC, of which Marie is
chairperson. Of all my faculties, sight is the one I would want to lose
least. Last week in Dublin, I saw a band called The Blind Boys of
Alabama. They were Gospel singers and they had an aura about them.
The same thing with Stevie Wonder and Andrea Bocelli.

I was never a great scholar. I always had my mind on other things.
When I was 16, I would work during the summer holidays — I worked
in Perri Crisps stacking boxes into delivery vans, ten-hour days. That
gave me enough money to get me going — I saved some of it. I
worked in Palm Grove, stacking ice-cream boxes in fridges, which
nearly killed me — I was the lad on the trolley. I earned enough to buy
my first Honda 50, so I was the coolest guy in school when I went
back in September. I didn't ride it into school that often because it
was mostly in bits — I modified everything from the exhaust to the
top of the cylinder head. Even then, at 16, I could feel this lure towards speed. My mother banned me from riding it but I used to sneak
it out.

My other passion was music. I used to fake going to sodalities to go down to the 5 Club, one of the first nightclubs in a basement. Brian Harris, one of the best guitarists I've ever heard, played there. I'd get my pocket money and was allowed go to a dance once a month but I wheedled my father to make it once every two weeks. I'd end up in Templeogue Tennis Club, which was pretty wild. My aunts were quite good to me and I'd have ten shillings and you'd get four pints for that. When you are a young fellow and you're fit — I was playing a lot of football for the school — you could drink three or four pints, get the bus to Templeogue, you'd have to walk home. You'd be absolutely blasted and half the kids in the place would be getting sick outside the club.

On leaving school, I had a little flirt with dentistry in which I really had no interest. It was a sort of fashionable choice — my Dad's two cousins and his father were dentists. It was either be a priest or be a dentist — I did not want to be either, though, like every Irish Catholic boy, at 13 or 14, you feel you have a calling, but, dare I say, that comes more from indoctrination by the school or the family. I don't know whether I would have made a good priest or not. I did think about it, though. I went to the Jesuit Retreat House in Rathfarnham and spoke to the priest and, for me to actually do that, I must have felt something.

My Mum and Dad were both keen golfers and captains of Bray Golf Club in their time. At the age of 16, I was a five or six handicapper playing in junior scratch cups. The great John O'Leary and Roddy Carr were around.

It was a quiet, normal upbringing, very well cared for. My mother was tough on me but she was very fair. My father was a soft man and kind. I could not have had a gentler father; he never once raised his hand to me. They made up for that in school. I'm not being critical of Synge Street — it gave me an education no other school could have given me because I was not a great student. People now talk about them hammering it into you, but they probably needed to — 60 unruly kids in a class. Now, when I have to speak in different places around the world, I can confidently tell them that Irish education is superior to any other, certainly in Europe. Schools like Synge Street have produced winners — people like Dermot Desmond,[1] whom I

---

[1] *Out on Their Own*, pp. 75–89.

have a great regard for. He came from St Joseph's School, similar to Synge Street.

When I got to 18, my mind was slightly scrambled. I was quite good at golf, I was a reasonable footballer, played Gaelic football for the school. I also played for Herberton United in the Sunday soccer leagues. My Dad was a great footballer. He had trials in England — he was called Snitchy Jordan and played for Shamrock Rovers. I did not feel the need to be pushed into university. I had got my Matric in fifth year in school, so I had the entrance pass to Trinity. At that time, as a Catholic, you could not go to Trinity without the Archbishop's permission. I did not want to go anywhere academic. I wanted to earn some money so I could go out and graft and do things.

At that stage, I was already a wheeler-dealer. I was making money out of things that I did not have to work at — and that was always an attraction. I was a buyer and a seller. I'd have three marbles and I'd swap them for two bigger ones. I don't know why it is, it's an inherent thing. My Mum says she got the wrong baby; with the colour of my skin, she thinks I'm a gypsy! There's no disgrace in being a gypsy . . .

I spent a bit of time in various hospitals with crashes off the motorcycle, the original Honda, on which I was a lunatic. At that time, I did not get involved in racing but a friend of mine from school, Jackie Fagan, owned the Gem Motorcycle Shop in Ranelagh. He raced on a 50cc. I got a ride on his bike every now and then. Mondello was not there at that time. The races were in Dunboyne, where they would close off the roads. Poor old Kenny McArdle was killed there; and people don't remember that Michael Smurfit[2] drove an E-Type there.

Michael was a great support. We were on the bones of our backsides and Michael put on a gala dinner for us in the top room in the Hotel de Paris when we went to Monaco with our Formula 3 Team. We had never been inside anything like that in our lives. The food and the wines were exquisite. Michael has a passion for motor racing and is still a great supporter. People don't see that side of Michael too often — there is a sweet side to him.

My parents would have liked me to be a top-line amateur golfer but the lure of rock-and-roll and girls and engine noises soon put paid to that. Only recently have I come back to golf. I play with Marie

---

[2] *In Good Company*, pp. 195–214.

and it gives us an opportunity to have time together. That's not often the case because motor racing can be incredibly demanding. I started cost and management accountancy in the College of Commerce in Rathmines full-time and then decided to do it as an evening course. I can only imagine that the reason I got into the bank — the bank was the next best thing to university — was through the influence of my father's sister who, by then, was Superior General of all the Irish Sisters of Charity based in Milltown. She probably had a word with her bank manager — it was too big an account to refuse me a job.

I started in Mullingar with the Hibernian Bank, later to be absorbed into Bank of Ireland. I continued to play golf there and met Denis Shaw, a solicitor. He was starting a karting club. Just at that time, there was the bank strike of 1970. I always had my own little agenda. I wanted a better car. When I arrived in Mullingar at 18, the bank manager would not allow me to park because it was unheard of for a bank clerk to arrive in a car. But I had worked for it — it was a grey Morris Minor. I took the hubcaps off and painted the inside of the wheels yellow. I had two white stripes going over the top of the car. It looked hideous. I had a run-in with several bank managers who told me, you can do what you like, but don't park your car outside my bank — it gives the wrong message. It was like the circus was in town. The Morris Minor became a Mini with a straight-through exhaust that made it sound like a rocket machine. I lowered the suspension and had wider tyres. I was a cool kid. You'd rock up outside the County Hall in Mullingar on a Tuesday night with whatever band was playing and, with a jazzy machine outside the door, you always had a better chance of pulling. That was me. My nickname at that stage was Flash — Flash Jordan (remember *Flash Gordon*?). Thankfully that stuck only for a short time. I always wanted to see if I could make money for the things I wanted — the family did not have the money. It's not necessarily the money now, it's being able to conclude a deal or seeing it become successful.

During the bank strike, I went to Jersey. I went on my own when many bank staff went in groups — to London or wherever. I'm not a loner, but I'm clear about what I need to have. I worked during the day as a clerk in the Jersey Electricity Company. I worked in the Bristol Bar at night. I was back to work in the Jersey Electricity Company at 7.30 in the morning. I never had any problem about working — I was a grafter. However, I'd never work on Saturday and Sunday, one or the other. I'd go to St Brelade's Bay where there was a kart centre. I was hooked. It was mind-blowing — you put a helmet on, you were about an inch from the ground and you were going quicker and quicker.

When I came back, I again met up with Denis Shaw with the Mullingar Karting Centre. He runs a successful practice down there now, J.A. Shaw. I met him a couple of weeks ago, first time in 15 years. We used to go out to Lough Ennel. There is a walkway around the lake. In the evening, nobody was there and we used run the karts around in preparation for the race wherever it was that weekend. We had two little trailers. That was the needle in the arm. It was an out-and-out drug — I could not shake it even if I wanted to. Everything suffered — girlfriends, drinking, nightclubs — I was hooked, gone. The only time I had to be a normal person was in the winter when the season had finished.

I was still holding down the bank job and, in fact, opening more accounts than anybody else. I had lots of front, but I was bloody use-less at anything else. They'd never put me on the machines or filing cheques or planning somebody's advance. My concentration skills were useless. Because I could open so many accounts, I was always in the Cash. I was, however, giving out loans for cars and it struck me, why should *I* not sell some cars? I went into the mini-car trading business. If I could offer them a better deal with the car I had, why should they not buy mine? That became quite successful.

I need to go back a year. When I first started competitive karting, I had a horrific accident and broke my leg in about eight different places — I've broken my left leg in about 15 places throughout my ca-reer in racing. I have a plastic ankle but it has not done me any harm to date so, thankfully, I'm still able to exercise. But, after that first accident, I thought this was very silly. I had just missed out on sum-mer, locked in a cast. It was an old-fashioned heavy cast right up the full leg. I had moved out because my mother could not stand the anxiety of waiting for me to come home — or, rather, not come home — after a motor race. I got a little house in Dundrum in a place called Ailesbury Grove. I shared it with a couple of guys. I would pay the rent and then sub-let the rooms — I was always that kind of person, a dealer. I needed to have control but I was happy to have people share.

People were telling me at this stage, "You've had your fun, Eddie. You're 22 — it's time you concentrated on what you are doing. There's a meaning to life. You can't aimlessly wander your way through it. It just doesn't happen like that."

During the winter following that lost summer, there were some karting trials. I said to myself, "I'm going to give this a real go." I wanted to see if I could still do it — sometimes you lose your nerve. But I had the initial signs that I was quite quick and quicker than some people with a reputation.

The following year, I bought the latest equipment. At this stage, to calm me down, the bank had moved me to Portumna. That worked out quite well. You would finish early on a Friday. I had the car packed on the trailer and, as soon as the bank closed, puff, I was out the door and off to the next race. In fact, Portumna was great, a super place on the Shannon but nowhere near as lively as Dublin, or even Mullingar. Neither Portumna nor Mullingar were ever going to be my home, but the bank job was quite productive because I was studying for the Institute of Bankers and Costs and Works Accountants in the evening, so it passed the time away productively.

To my surprise, I won a couple of races early on in the karting season. There's nothing worse than that because then you are defending a lead. I won the championship in 1972. After karting, I went into 250 — that was big, with five-speed gearboxes. They were like animals to drive, hugely fast — a great experience. I then met the man who looked after Ken Fildes, a well-known and successful racing driver. Someone was needed to drive the car because Ken was doing something else. I went up to Crossle in Hollywood, County Down and got a brand new Formula Ford car. John Crossle had been a very good racing driver, then became a great manufacturer. He was not widely known but he built the best Formula Fords and the Irish guys had them. I found it easier to win in England than in Ireland — at that stage, there were people like David Kennedy, Bernard Devaney, Derek Daly — a whole heap of young guys at the time Mondello had just been born. It happens, doesn't it, that at particular times there is a sudden blossoming of talent, where one drags another along and suddenly you have a higher standard. And we all lived in a certain part of Dublin — Dundrum, Dartry, Templeogue, Terenure. I said, this is ridiculous, how can I win races in Aintree or Oulton Park or Silverstone and I'm having difficulty winning races in Ireland? I decided to spend more of my time in England.

I bought a Volkswagen pick-up with a winch on it. At that stage, I had been transferred to the bank branch at Camden Street. I had broken my legs again in a big accident. From Camden Street, I was able to load the car on the pick-up, drive down to the ferry every Friday night and land at Liverpool at a quarter-to-seven. I'd always ask for late entry to the qualifying heats so I could make the scrutineering. Liam Nevin used come with me — his sister worked alongside me in the bank. Even to this day, they are both great supporters. When I came back on a Monday morning, Liam would work on the car all week to have it ready for the following Friday. I lived my life like that for about two or three years. It was too painful — I could not quite cope with it.

I was still selling cars, mainly to friends. I had an arrangement with several garages who did not want to bother retailing their not-so-nice trade-ins. I'd buy maybe four for £1,000. I'd put ads in the *Evening Press*, eight or ten cars. I'd sell every Tuesday, Wednesday and Thursday evening, from six to ten outside my flat on Dodder Bridge — I had moved from Ailesbury Grove because it was easier access for customers and it was on a hill if the car batteries were not so good.

I also knew Joe Eustace from The Floor Centre, and I asked him what he did with his carpet off-cuts. He told me they sold them off to the dealers. Joe would undercut everybody and had a huge business. I got the off-cuts from him, used his van when he was not using it on Saturday and all day Sunday. I set up a stall in the Dandelion Market where the Green Cinema used to be. It was cool, fashionable, to have a place there. If you had a stall at the Dandelion Market, you were one of the aristocracy — you got pints served quicker to you in Rice's and soup because you were always frozen. But we made money, particularly at Christmas, and had these lovely carpet remnants which I had not paid for — I paid for them when I copped the money, so it was a no-lose situation. I cut a friend of mine in on half the money and said, "You go and run the thing for me and you take half the profit." I had no expense, no outlay, no risk and I was copping half the profit. I put another guy in on another stall. When the season finished, October coming up to Christmas, I borrowed the van and went out to the Ashbourne Road and joined the dealers, with whom I became quite friendly. We pitched our places together and people came in their droves to buy all sorts of things, but particularly carpets. I was one of the lads. I made a lot of money. The Costs and Works accountancy did not quite fit in to that little programme; the Institute of Bankers was more or less completed.

I moved from Formula Ford, with which I had quite good success. Formula Ford is a normal Ford engine modified to about 120 horsepower in a very lightweight chassis, 250 kilos maximum. You had a car that could do 175 miles an hour — open wheel, single-seater. You had enough space for the fuel and the oil, you had the engine and the gearbox sitting on the back — all the weight was behind, so you had to balance the car. It's the first area where a racing driver really gets to understand about set-up, about balance, to get the shock absorbers and the springs to marry with the ride-height, with the controls, the turning in, whether the car under-steers or over-steers — and how to balance it all on roll-bars. It's a great education. It's like a guy becoming a fighter pilot — it's a training Formula. It was all hands-on. You did it yourself and you learned — you learned the hard way. It was great.

We then moved into Formula Atlantic. Formula Atlantic is higher again. It's the first of the slick tyres, much wider, no tread pattern. You had a different level of grip, greatly increased around a corner. It was also vastly more powerful — you had a car that would do nearly 200 miles an hour. If you are talking about danger, it was increased, if you're talking about competence, you certainly needed to have a couple of years under your belt driving Formula Ford. The ideal progression was: karting, from which most of the world champions have come; Formula Ford; Formula 3; Formula 1.

To my surprise, in my first year, we did particularly well with the car even though it was a bit of a junker, held together. It was a Lotus 69, a very old car. Maintenance costs were huge — it takes a lot to keep a Formula Atlantic car going. Every part was hand-made — Lotus had stopped making the cars. The expense involved prompted me to learn about sponsorship. The sponsors I had were Hogan's Meats — I had been at school with a member of the Hogan family — and The Floor Centre.

In 1976, Philip Morris were coming to launch Marlboro in the Irish market. They had a very successful Grand Prix motor racing team, with people like Niki Lauda, Emerson Fittipaldi, James Hunt. A friend of mine, Vivian Candy, decided to set up a team, with him doing Formula Ford and me doing Formula Atlantic. At this stage I would have been one of the favourites for the Irish Formula Atlantic championship. Vivian taught me a lot — he had come from advertising, press, PR and was very clever. He had a slick, professional manner.

We made a very special presentation to George Macken, who was the sales and marketing director for Marlboro, a tough Yorkshireman. He had been a professional footballer with Grimsby. For the following ten years he was one of the most influential people in my life. He still lives in Oxford, near me. He decided he could sponsor Jordan and Candy — this was the first ever time that a major international company would invest in motor racing in Ireland. We launched the sponsorship at the RIAC in Dawson Street and Vivian sold a secondary package to Captain America's — the owner, Mark Kavanagh,[3] was a cool guy around town. To have a car sponsored in red and white Marlboro with Captain America's on it — we were just the coolest. Now we had to deliver on the track.

Vivian had some problems with his car. He was quick enough and I won a number of races. I finished second or third in the championship. That was enough for Marlboro in 1977 to say to me that they would like to take me on professionally. I applied for leave-of-absence from the bank. Then I was able to concentrate on what I was doing, I was able to travel. George Macken kept me in Formula Atlantic, which was good for me because it was quicker than Formula 3. I was older than my main international competitors but younger than the Irish competitors — the reason for that is that in Ireland everybody paid for it themselves. In England, it had emerged as a profession, people who were really good — young, quick lads — got sponsorship enabling them at an early age to go on to be great.

I was caught in the middle — I was too old for anything at junior level. At that time, there was a European Formula Atlantic Championship — and I won that. The car sales and all that had now gone. I was on a paid contract with Marlboro. My parents were horrified. Since when did children pay a lot of heed to their parents? Certainly, my children don't pay much heed to me. You give your parents respect and comfort but you have to follow your own life, for which there is no action replay. This is it — you can't turn it back.

---

[3] *Out on Their Own*, pp. 137–164.

Winning the Formula Atlantic Championship was a big boost. It was a turning point when I was not just playing with things or having fun. Winning was a big coup for George. The reason he liked me so much was that I was very loyal to him. He brought out a brand of cigarettes, Raffles, in 1978. He got me to be understudy to James Hunt — James and I would do all the nightclubs to help launch the new brand. It was in a black pack and was successful for a limited period. That experience gave me an insight into the launching, marketing and development of a brand. This was hard-nosed selling, giving the night-clubbers samplers of the cigarettes and a chance to meet the racing drivers. It was very tough — you were owned by Marlboro, but, in return, you were getting a car, the maintenance of that car, travel and a life that had a huge horizon. You were also getting invaluable experience — of seeing first-hand how you create, launch and drive a brand and make it successful. That's the biggest marketing experience that anyone can ever have. It was easy for me to soak all this up because I loved it, because inside me is a natural salesperson. But this was something different — you first had to create the demand for the sale. It was pure marketing.

Gone now was any idea of golf — motor racing outweighed anything else. I had met Marie in 1977 in Dublin. She had been going out with a man who had a knowledge of motor racing and, when I saw her, I fell for her. She was a tall schoolgirl, an international basketball player. I thought to myself, well, motor racing is fantastic, but let's be serious and put some time into this. We became friends. I was 28, she was 18.

At the end of 1978, I had won the European Formula Atlantic Championship and helped create the brand, Raffles, alongside the main brand, Marlboro. Marlboro was becoming popular in Ireland, so the message was getting back. I had created and registered a team, Marlboro Team Ireland, which became a famous identity. The Irish newspapers would give a disproportionate coverage to any success I had. In fact, we got a lot of general media coverage — for the brand, for the team, for me, but for the sponsors as well. I learned how to work with the media.

Early January 1979, Marie and I decided to get married. We got married on a Saturday. On the Sunday I did a photo shoot — in other words, on the first day of my marriage, I jumped out of bed to do a photo shoot for Nissan cars. Small wonder Marie was furious.

Nissan were giving me a free car to drive around for the season: "I'm Eddie Jordan. I need to get places with speed, reliability and in comfort — and that's why I pick a Nissan." It really was rubbish. And Marie and I drove off on our honeymoon. The reception had been in Lamb Doyles and we stayed in the Dublin Sport Hotel on the road to Enniskerry. If you ever do not want to have relations come to a wedding, you should have it somewhere like Lamb Doyles on a mid-winter evening, with glassy roads. Some people didn't actually make it.

George wanted me to enter the European Formula 3 Championship. I could see this was going to be *tough*. I'm looking at the names — Nelson Piquet, Nigel Mansell, Andrea de Cesaris, Philippe Alliot, Michele Alboreto. Anyone who knows motor racing knows these are names that have gone on to Formula 1. That year they were all doing Formula 3 Championship. These were young kids beating the hell out of each other every week. It was *hard*: you'd just have a trailer with the car on it, you'd have your two mechanics, you were driving from one place to another like nomads — probably the best fun I've had in my entire life. There was immense camaraderie. The bonds of friendship that were forged in those years are the strongest to this very day. None of us had any money.

I did that for the first year of our married life. I had a couple of podiums — that means being in the top three. I had done enough for George to go to his board to recommend the continuation of the sponsorship for another year. This was now 1980 and I really needed to do something quite big. At the same time, James Hunt had become a regular driver at McLaren and had won some races in the Hesketh car. A couple of times, I was given the McLaren car as a test driver. That was as high up the ladder as I got. The competition was outrageous. As I told you, talented people often come in bunches — there were so many high-quality drivers, some of them still in Formula 1. I was running Marlboro Team Ireland and there were two other Marlboro guys; one was Andrea de Cesaris, who actually drove for me in my first year, 1991, in Formula 1 — he was that good. Twelve years after being his team-mate, he was still there as a Formula 1 driver and our first ever driver in Formula 1. My other team-mate was Stefan Johansson who now runs a team in the States — we became inseparable. Some of these characters are ordinary or boring, and some of them are mad, but Stefan was just good to be around. You were on the road with these guys, you were not able to categorise them, you did not know where they came from, where they went to school, what religion, if any, they had — no one gave a shit, all we wanted to do was go racing. It was so different from the Ireland in which I was brought up, where you would know everybody and whether they were Catholic, Muslim, Hindu or Jewish, and what pubs they drank in. It was like being on a different planet.

I would drive a truck with the car in the back and all the spares and the noses (the front of the car). George had paid for everything — I had a budget of over £100,000. One day, we turned up in Monaco for a Formula 3 race — Formula 3 was always the support race for Formula 1. I had qualified because I was just about good enough. Our eldest girl, Zoe, was a couple of months old. Marie and I travelled in the truck together — we had no home. We towed a caravan. John Walton, whom I persuaded to leave HB Dennis's in Dublin (and is today the team manager at Prost) was with Jordan for a long time. He was a devoted, loyal mechanic. John would travel with us and get local help wherever we were. The four of us, including Zoe, would sleep in the caravan. We had a Maori mechanic who could not sleep inside. He slept under the caravan. He had some strange habits, but he was very cheap. John Walton slept in a hammock in the front part of the caravan. John was such a handsome looking guy that he used pull birds from the trees. He is still a legend. He liked the fun, the craic and the drink — but only after slogging his heart out on the cars.

George Macken used to send us food baskets and stuff. He wanted me to be his guest at an extravaganza to celebrate 25 years of Philip Morris sponsorship of motor racing. They had taken over the biggest club in Monaco. I said to Marie, "How are we going to do this?" A tuxedo was not something I necessarily had in my little caravan and Marie did not carry with her a ball gown. Marie was tall and could wear anything and we all had natural tans from being constantly out in the open. She bought a ball gown in Oxfam for 50p. I got a black suit and a white shirt — and we went to the ball.

In Monaco, they had little regard for any of the teams except Formula 1, so we were parked up at the back of the tennis club where they have the World Championship tennis tournament. You could walk from it down to the beach. We had to shower on the beach to trim ourselves up. We went to the ball and we looked good. I went on the stage with John Watson, who's Irish, who has won five Grand

Prix, who has become a friend and now lives beside me. John was from Belfast and understood what I was going through and was wondering a little why I was putting myself through so much pain — there were easier ways to make a living. The total amount of clothes on our backs that night cost no more than a fiver. Marie's ball gown was reasonably antique — we would call it retro now — but, of course, the curious wives of the big wheeler-dealers thought it was brand new.

I spoke on behalf of the drivers. It seemed to go down well and, as a result, Philip Morris have never forgotten me. They have stayed loyal even though I have not been with them for years. To get out of Ireland in a sport which had no real recognition here was crucial. It would not have happened without George Macken.

Each year I was going back begging the Bank of Ireland to extend my leave of absence — at this stage I had a family and a very young wife. I was a nomad and I needed the bank to keep my position open. Eventually they got fed up and said no. Then I got tough with them and said I wanted my marriage gratuity — if a girl can have a marriage gratuity, so should I. I left under somewhat strained circumstances where they had to pay me money to get rid of a house loan but I felt very strongly about it. I have no animosity towards Bank of Ireland — they were kind to me in certain circumstances.

Into 1980, I probably didn't do as well at racing as I should. Into my thirties, I had a family, had to find a home, bought and sold cars. George was paying me just about enough. I got friendly with the bank manager at AIB in Northampton — he loaned me some money to buy a barn with an outside loo at the end of a house. I bought it for £4,000 and, within a year, sold it for £14,000. With the £14,000, I went back to the bank manager and borrowed some more and we bought a house for £23,000 in Silverstone. The first year I would cycle to work and Marie had the car. She worked as a packer in General Foods, which must have been humiliating for what she was — she had been doing science after school. In any event, she had to give it up, amongst other things to take care of Zoe. The £23,000 house had five bedrooms. We took in three full-time lodgers. Marie did all the cooking and laundry but it gave us built-in babysitters. Then Miki came along. We started to make money, made the repayments on the mortgage, sold the house for £45,000 and bought another one for £102,000, which we sold for £270,000, and that seems to be the sequence of my life. Fourteen years ago, we bought a house for £600 grand and we've never left it — it's just outside Oxford. It's probably worth two-and-a-half million now. I'm not mentioning those figures for any reason except to illustrate the fact that I have an eye for a deal.

Back to George. I told him I was over 30 and had a chance to get out of single-seaters. I drove for a semi-works Porsche team at Le Mans and found much more success in that — I was younger than the older sports-car drivers, people like Derek Bell, Jackie Ickx. I did Le Mans for a number of years. One year I drove for a team owned by Pink Floyd; Roger Waters was the leader. To this day, his wife shares a horse, Molly, with myself and Denis O'Brien.[4] They were doing a final concert in Earls Court the same time as Le Mans.

At that time, 1981, I still had no idea where I was going. We were planning more children. George said, "Eddie, I don't see you ever going back to banking. I see you more as an entrepreneur, a free spirit. If you are harnessed and categorised, you will not flourish." He was a wise man — and that's why I loved him. He arranged to help me financially to go to a company called Ralt to buy one of their cars. When there were Brabham cars, they were all called BT, which stood for Brabham Taurnac — after Ron Taurnac. When we went to Ralt, the car was called an RT3 — Ron Taurnac 3. Ron Taurnac is now well into his seventies — he was instrumental in a lot of things for me and still features in my life. He was at my most recent race. I bought the car and a little lock-up in Silverstone — I was the first person to be on Silverstone Circuit as a tenant. It had no loo, no running water, but it had a garage in which I put a mezzanine. John Walton was still with me and we decided to build EJR — Eddie Jordan Racing. This for me was a brand new venture — going into the race-car preparation business. We had little or no money; I would still cycle to work. We had another deal with Nissan and Marie would use the car. I was always looking for different things. I saw a new tyre company in Japan called Yokohama — and I had a Toyota engine. The Toyota engine was in the Ralt Formula 3 and I was giving odd drives to people to make some money. I'd go to Monaco, charge a guy £3,000 or £4,000 to drive the car, take a percentage of the prize money if there was any and the next night we'd go off to another race, maybe into Holland and then back to Sicily. It was worse than racing-driving — I never

---

[4] See Chapter 13, pp. 241–273.

had a week off. There were always races somewhere and I had to make the car pay. It was like a car-hire business. The car was quite successful — I always had an eye for a couple of things: one, for drivers, and, two, for new items.

At the end of 1981, I went to Japan to see if Toyota could give me a better engine. They introduced me to Yokohama and they took me on as their works team. Their tyres were better than anyone else's. In 1982, I had an English driver, James Weaver, and that was really the beginnings of it all. He won three of the four faces we did for Yokohama tyres — one at Silverstone, one at Nogaro near Lourdes, and one in Jarama, near Madrid. He came second in Donnington. I had spotted a driver, de Silva, and he blew my mind he was so quick. In a test drive in the car, he was quicker than Weaver had been in a race. I thought maybe it was a quick day, the atmosphere or the tyres or whatever. We put new tyres on and he was quicker. When people have outstanding talent, you don't have to wait around to see it — it's there. Eventually, he dropped the de Silva part of his name and went by the name of Ayrton Senna. His very first time in a Formula 3, Ayrton Senna drove for Jordan. That was 1982. The next time he drove for me was in Macau in 1983 in the Macau Grand Prix, which we won together. As you know, he went on to become world champion.

We have been involved in making three world champions. In 1985, there was a guy doing motorcycle racing, who had a more famous father, and I felt he should try single-seaters. That was Damon Hill. You, Ivor, rowed for London Rowing Club with Graham Hill, and Damon still has the London Rowing Club blue and white on his helmet, just as his father, Graham, had.

When you think of motor racing and engineering and engines and all that, you might think I am a things person. I'm not, I'm a people person — there isn't another team in the world that can hold a candle to us for the number of successful drivers we've had. We gave Michael Schumacher his first ever drive in 1991 in Spa. Hill, Schumacher and Senna — in recent years, they don't come any bigger. When you look at a Grand Prix race, more than half the competitors came from Jordan one way or the other. Ralf Schumacher started his life with me. One of my proudest moments ever — in the Australian race this year, every one of the top six had been Jordan drivers. I have given my all for those guys and it's nice to see the results.

In 1983, things got fast and furious as we went into the Championship. I'm on the road, I'm beginning to make a few bob, I get very brave and do a two-pronged attack. I go down to Ron Taurnac, do a deal with him for a whole heap of cars and spares, try and get a semi-works deal out of him so that I can get a special discount and, because I'm going to be competitive, he gives me the deal. I run two cars in Britain, one with a Canadian, Alan Berg, and the other with Martin Brundle, who is the current commentator for ITV. At that time, I was bitterly disappointed because Senna had gone to another team — that hurt me. In the big fight for the Championship, Senna was going to be the sure favourite — and we were going to stuff him if we could. There are 20 points in the Championship and Brundle led by one point going into the last race. Senna won. We finished second in the Championship but we won a lot of races. Suddenly, Jordan Grand Prix was getting good credibility. I was seen as a strong, hard, committed person always concerned to bring my drivers on.

I then became Brundle's manager. The following year, I negotiated to get him into Tyrrell, a Formula 1 team. In an 18-year period, seven drivers have scored points in their first race in Grand Prix — only seven. All those seven had come from us, every one of them — I loved that. Brundle was the first — he scored for Tyrrell. Suddenly, I was managing a guy in the top echelons of our business, so I had access to Tyrrell — they would have to negotiate with me. At that time, Grand Prix drivers got special discounts at Mercedes and Martin gave me a car. Rags to riches, here was I from driving a truck to driving a Mercedes sports car. Things got much better very quickly but for the right reasons — we were winning races.

In 1983, there was a young Irish driver whom I had a huge regard for, Tommy Byrne from Drogheda. The biggest disappointment of my life was not to see him world champion. He was so naturally talented that he didn't have to put into it anything like the same efforts as others did. As a result, he did not appreciate what he'd got or what most people would have given to have that talent. You can get away with talent for a certain period, you can't get away with it for ever. He's now living in Florida and turns up at the odd race and I love him with a passion, he was such a great man. But he was typically old-style Irish — the craic was more important to him than anything else, any kind of excuse to go wild. Once he didn't make it to the warm-up for a race in which he was in pole position. The clerk of the course was calling out the drives' names and they were answering "yes". When he came to Byrne's name, I replied "yes", and the drivers were laughing. He arrived half-an-hour before the race, sat in the car and won. He won it with such ease that the scrutineers would not pay us the money until they stripped the car down. They were bandits — if I needed a load of money to go to the next race, I wouldn't leave the track until they paid me. I didn't want cheques.

It took us until 1987 to win our first major championship with Johnny Herbert. I then managed him to go to Bennetton. He finished fourth in Brazil, got three points in his first ever race. He is also a key person in my life. There were some difficulties during that period. I wanted to build a bigger factory and I took on some drivers that I probably should not have, drivers who had substantial sponsorship and I probably concentrated on business at the expense of winning races. Every six or seven years, sparked by a crisis, I would have to rethink the whole situation. In 1986, I realised forcefully that I had to have the drug of winning. I took on Johnny Herbert, who had no money, and I said I'd go out and sell the sponsorship for him. Instead of a driver coming with his package, I'd take on the task. That, in fact, became the practice with major teams. I got the sponsorship, put Johnny Herbert in the car, and he won the Championship. I decided I would never move to the higher formula until I had dominated the formula I was in or won that championship.

The following year, I moved to Reynard and Rick Gorne — Rick was passionately supportive of Jordan because he could sell cars on the back of our success. He gave us a huge deal on a car to go for Formula 3000, just one step under Formula 1. The first race was in Jerez in Spain. I got Johnny Herbert to do the race — we had little or no sponsorship.

On the night before the race I called Duncan Lee of Camel cigarettes, whom I had been negotiating with and not really getting anywhere. Camel had just come into the picture with their yellow cars. I said, "Duncan, we're in pole position here and I've got no stickers on the car. I am prepared to put large Camel stickers on my car, which will be live on TV on a lot of European stations. I don't want a commitment and I don't want money, what I want is to sit before you on Monday morning and put my proposal properly to you if this car wins. Is that a deal?" He said, "I can't give you any money. I will give you the assurance that I will see you — go with the race."

That became history — to win your first ever Formula 3000 race at your first try with a driver and a team who had never done it before. That can't be beaten because it's the ultimate. I sat with Camel the next day and within a week we had a contract. I had three glorious years with them. I won more races than anyone else in Formula 3000, the following year winning the Championship with Jean Alesi who still drives for Alain Prost. My last year in Formula 3000 was 1990 and my drivers were Eddie Irvine, who later came back to drive for us in Formula 1, and my current driver, Heinz-Harald Frentzen. I hate losing people; it's something that really upsets me. I love loyalty and I want to be loyal to them and what you won't see in Jordan is staff flitting in and out.

That was the end of the Formula 3000. We had got to the stage where we had won more races than anyone else. I spoke to the Camel people and, in theory, Duncan Lee had agreed to help me fund Formula 1. Within a decade, from being totally penniless, I was managing three or four drivers in Formula 1. I'd had a good lifestyle, I'd moved to a proper house. We had three or four children and I was enjoying the fruits of success. I probably had £3 million or £4 million sterling in cash. Maybe I had made the right decision not to go back to the bank! We had a home in Spain. Miki, our second child, had very bad asthma and had been advised to go to a warm climate. Marie moved with her to Spain and Miki emerged a much stronger child.

I needed everything in place for an onslaught on Formula 1 in 1991. I had a serious chat with myself — something I do regularly. I put the pros and cons and evaluate things. With £2 million or £3 million, I didn't really need to do anything — why take the risk? Formula 1 is going to soak that up in two seconds. But Marie was very supportive: "If you think it's right, go and do it, but make sure you analyse it." That's all she would ever say. She was never negative.

We felt we were walking on water — I could never see the dangers, I couldn't even imagine failure. It wasn't on the agenda. I'm the total optimist. I have plenty of pessimists in Jordan Grand Prix to make sure things are balanced. The management team in Jordan has been together for a lot more than ten years, very unusual in Formula 1. My secretary has been with me ten years, she knows who to talk to and get things done. I don't have to be there. Maybe I didn't really appreciate the fun we had in the early years — Formula 1 was so different. There was a different level of pain — by that I mean financial pain, political decisions by people being unbelievably brutal if they needed to be. It was so huge there was no scale to measure it. The deal I thought I had with Duncan Lee of Camel was aborted by people outside his control. I went to Winston Salem, banged the door and had to be ejected because I wouldn't leave — I felt absolutely betrayed, I was left there with no sponsor. My £4 million was gone. I'd had to put together a factory and employ people, buy a 3D CAD system — Jordan was the first ever team to design a car without a drawing board. I think that's one reason the car was so good the first year. I took on Gary Anderson as chief designer. A guy from Coleraine, never had any Formula 1 experience. He stayed with me for 11 years.

Then I got a proposal from a person who said they couldn't give me a lot of money, but it was for a green car, which is what I wanted. I went back to Ireland to get a bit of support for that, which I did. I sat in front of 620 executives in the Carlton Towers Hotel in London — the marketing and sales executives worldwide for Pepsi Cola. I explained to them the benefits of being in Formula 1, how they could create extra value for their brand, create awareness beyond their wildest dreams. The person I was focused on was Paul Adams, the sales and marketing director for Europe for Pepsi Cola. 7-Up was a popular drink in Ireland and we had the 7-Up Jordan in places like Australia, Japan and Phoenix, Arizona. We opened up a new area of Formula 1 activity: dual branding. In Ireland and Europe, we were 7-Up; elsewhere, we were Pepsi Cola. It was for one year only because the following year Michael Jackson was doing a world tour and that's where all their money was going. If you remember, that was the year his hair caught fire. It turned out to be a near-disaster for Pepsi.

When I was with Camel, I had a proposal into Kodak because the Camel and the Kodak yellows were similar. I was trying to leverage one against the other. Then I thought, how am I going to see Kodak now that the car is green? When I asked Kodak if they could cope with a green car they asked me if I was crazy: "Our biggest competitor is green." So I jump on the plane to Japan to see Fuji films, make a presentation and I get triple the money from Fuji than I'm getting from Pepsi. As it happened, I was fairly well known in Japan. Before I could get the drivers into Formula 1, when they were finished in Europe, I would send them to the Japanese Championship — people like Martin Donnelly, Johnny Herbert, Eddie Irvine, Frentzen, Kenny Acheson. They were getting paid, I was getting a few quid commission. They were building their careers before they came back to do Formula 1. I had already been there with Toyota and Bridgestone and Yokahama tyres, as we talked about. The people in Japan knew me. I went to Densu Agency. They were the biggest advertising agency in the world. Through them I got to see the president of Fuji. How I sold it to him was that, at that time in Japan, you could not get the best staff. I had read why Honda had gone to Formula 1 — it was so that they would be attractive to young engineers with initiative and suddenly Honda were recruiting a much higher level of student. I got that message across to the president of Fuji — not alone would he get his name across the world, but he would attract a higher level of staff. At that time Japan was bursting with emerging companies — anything that was happening in new technologies was happening there. Getting Fuji was a coup and they came on with a lot of money.

However, Cosworth, who were owned by Vickers, were very tough with me. Cosworth were supplying me with a Ford engine for that year. At the end of the year, we were in serious financial difficulties. Ron Dennis said, "Eddie, welcome to the piranha club." We had finished fifth in the World Championships, the first time a new team had done that. We were in Spa and the bailiffs arrived and put the chains on the trucks and would not let them out of the garage. From a previous year, a man believed I owed him some money and had not paid it back. In Belgium, if a creditor believes you are going to skip the country, he can get a court order to stop you. I had to get £100,000 and Bernie Ecklestone came to my rescue. All the money that was paid at the gate that day was brought to the magistrate, paid over, and my cars were released. I felt the whole of Belgium was against me — I had a Belgian driver, Bertrand Gachot. While he was in London, he ran into the back of a taxi driver. The taxi driver got out and Bertrand thought he was going to hit him so he sprayed CS gas in his face. The law in England, or anywhere else, does not take kindly to people in public services being attacked. Bertrand was brought to court and, thinking that nothing would happen to him, was a bit surprised when the Judge gave him a year-and-a-half in the nick. This was the Tuesday before the Belgian Grand Prix and, with all my financial troubles, I needed a driver. Through an arrangement with Mercedes, I got a young driver, who had never driven the car before. He came seventh and suddenly everyone wanted to know what his name was — it was Michael Schumacher. His first ever drive in a Formula 1 was in Spa in 1991 in a Jordan 7-Up car — a car that had just been released by the court authorities. It was well known that Jordan was struggling to survive. At that time, there were no German drivers in Formula 1 and Bernie was desperate to get a German driver, so he put Michael into the Benetton team. We went on to the end of the season, ducking and diving, buying and selling drivers.

People often thought that I didn't care enough about the drivers. The driver is the most important thing to me. When I sold Irvine for $5 million to Ferrari, we needed the cash for a new wind tunnel. Irvine had only one more year left in his contract and he had confided to me that he would prefer to move on if he could. It made perfect business sense but the outside world saw it in a different way. He got what he wanted and I had got an extra $5 million that I was able to invest in a new premises and the wind tunnel I so desperately needed. However, we were issued with a winding-up petition, an Order 14. I know them very well, I've seen a lot of them in my time. That was in the High Court in London but my main concern was to get an engine. In my naivety I was not thinking that this judge could have me down the pan, big time. He was obviously a good judge of character, because he gave us a stay of execution and said that the Cosworth and Vickers' figures had not been accurate. It did not say that Cosworth had lost, it just needed to be readdressed. However, Vickers got such bad publicity out of this — it was a high profile case — we did a deal outside court. I told them I would give them the original Michael Schumacher car in which he did his first race: "You are going to run him next year with Ford. He will be a world champion and this car will be worth a fortune." I was able to put a massively high price on the car together with some repayment over a two-year period. I was breathing again.

I now had the Yamaha engine. I had met a guy in South Africa who had Irish connections. He said that, with the end of white rule in South Africa, the country needed to get its business launched on a worldwide basis. He believed the state oil company, Sasol, which made oil from coal, could be an opportunity. We met in the International Management Group offices, Mark McCormack's place, and we did a three-year deal for a lot of money — I think it was for about $28 million. That was our first major coup in terms of money. I had free engines and I had sponsors so I was able to go out and get some drivers. I hired one of my ex-drivers, Thierry Boutsen. It was not a great year — we struggled. I had some philosophies all starting with "S" — Survive, Stability, Success.

In 1991, there was a downturn in the market, much more severe than anything we are looking at now. There was total recession in most countries. Motor racing is one of the things that suffer most — because of the cost. There were 18 Formula 1 teams and eight or nine of them went into bankruptcy. A lot of the others had to be merged with bigger groups. Jordan has been the only one, to my knowledge, possibly Williams, that has been able to maintain to this day the name of the founder over the door. I think the fans like the romanticism of Jordan. It's a story that is not necessarily portrayed the way I like it but that's what sells papers. The year 1994 was the first time we won a podium with Rubens Barrichello, now driving for Ferrari. Rubens was a Brazilian driver who came out of the shadow of Ayrton Senna when he died in Imola. Rubens gave us our first podium in Aida in Japan, ironically enough, for the Japanese Grand Prix.

We never really looked back from there. We got a Peugeot deal and my two drivers were Irvine and Barrichello. We finished second and third — both cars on the podium with Peugeot. Sadly, Peugeot never won a championship even with Prost or McLaren but their best results were with Jordan.

In the outside world, people think we in motor racing are a bit crackpot, that there's something missing or that we've lost the dimension of life being a serious business. In actual fact, our business is very serious because of the amount of cash involved.

I never had any problem going into the top to whatever board — Peter Sutherland[5] in Goldmans. Formula 1 gives you that possibility; it breaks down such barriers. The same with Sony — I can speak to the president. The president of Honda was my guest at the most recent race. It seems strange that somebody like me is able to jump levels and go right to the very top. I think it's the lure of Formula 1 — it has huge appeal and it needs huge amounts of money to run. As I keep saying, it's a drug and people seem to want to talk to people at the top of Formula 1. That's more widespread today than it ever was in the past. No matter where we go, people recognise us as an Irish team. When we won our first race, they didn't have the Irish national anthem. I asked them to play the British national anthem. My mother

---

[5] See Chapter 16, pp. 313–334.

would ask, "My God, why did you do that?" Quite honestly, the British gave me a chance no other country would — certainly not France or Germany or, for that matter, anywhere else. There is nobody as welcoming to a foreigner as the English are. A lot of European countries have time only for their own nationals. But all future Grand Prix's made sure they had *Amhrán na bhFiann*. It's a tearful moment standing up before 350,000,000 people worldwide singing your home anthem, for a team that really should not have been there, because we're the little gangsters, the little upstarts, we're fighting the multitude of millions that Ferrari have or Mercedes.

I hate when people tell me that we've got less money than those big guys because that's a direct criticism of my ability. My job is to find the money to run the team. We now have a hard core of major sponsors — Gallahers, an Irish company, with their brand, Benson & Hedges — they have been with me now five or six years. Mastercard don't do continuing sponsorships — they do only events. The only sponsorship they do have is Jordan, the only exception. They have 700 million customers and it goes on from there — we've got Sony, we've got Honda, we've got Bridgestone. We have a Honda engine now. We were able to show them that we could win with an engine from a very small sister company of theirs, Mugen Honda — Mugen Honda is a son of the great Mr Honda. I now have a long-term deal with the Honda direct factory team.

They are all the people I'm pinning my hopes on to win a title and bring a world championship to my team, to my family and to Ireland. The commercial aspect is now no longer the strain that it was. We now have to refuse sponsorship. Nevertheless, you can never be complacent. We are lucky that we have contracts in place that will see Jordan grow from strength to strength. We are moving into a new 150,000 square feet factory on top of two other factories we have.

Jordan Grand Prix is now a powerful machine. In Canada you can buy a Jordan Honda. In England last year, the Jordan Civic was a special edition. There is now the emergence of the brand. If you drive from here to Galway and stop at a garage, you'll be able to buy EJ10, an energy drink based on what the drivers drink before they go out to race — a high intensity drink, but with no caffeine.

I'm fortunate. I've got my health. I've got my four children and I'm allowed to do a few other things, like indulge my passion for music. I play quite a lot — I've got two drum kits, one in the office and one at home. I play in a number of different bands — mainly for charity. Formula 1 has opened many doors — it means that I can assist with charities.

I am looking at the three protagonists for Eircom: O'Brien,[6] Desmond[7] and O'Reilly[8] and I sit here not knowing what to say because I own a share in a horse with each of them! The press would love that story but by the time the book is published that will be long since forgotten.

When I was 50, I promised Marie and the family that I would sell a portion of the business, a minority share of Jordan. It was the first time a Formula 1 team was able to attract a major financial institution, Warburg Pincus — they took a minority share for $70 million. That allowed me to pay off things, put some money into the business, put a pension together and a trust for the family which meant that, if anything ever happened to me, they were not all going to be out on the street, as would have happened in years gone by. When I think back, maybe my parents were correct. Would I let my kids do this? I would not. I continue to advise them not to — just like my parents did to me. But when you've got a will inside there, you've got to let the passion flow, otherwise you will live a lifetime of regret. We have a free spirit, not just in Jordan Grand Prix, but in our home life. Provided certain rules are agreed to, the kids can have their own freedom.

People often ask me what was the greatest part of my racing career. That first race we won in Spa, when Damon Hill won and Ralf Schumacher was second, was the first time ever that a team won a race and also finished second. People say that must have been my greatest moment. Yeah, that was very exciting for one given moment — it was a lot that I had lived for. To win a Formula 1 race took a monkey off my back. I then had only one target left in my life — to win a championship. That narrows down the objective. I won't stop till I do that.

The most satisfying thing in my life was to survive. The year 1991 was awful — it's the only time in my adult life I've been ill. There is nothing worse than financial stress and strain when you see the

---

[6] See Chapter 13, pp. 241–273.

[7] *Out on Their Own*, pp. 75–89.

[8] *In Good Company*, pp. 155–170.

whole thing crumbling around you — it's not just your family but also your staff who are going to be out on the street. Your very identity is collapsing. Some people can hide things but our business is transparent — you're either good or bad. In normal businesses, they look at the balance sheet every half-year. In my business, it's every two weeks. In one race, you're either a complete tosser or a giant.

I lived to tell the tale. I talked about the S's. The Survival lasted too long — I had to survive for four or five years. I was a better person when I emerged the other end. Then the stability of 1994, 1995 and 1996. In 1997 we really came with a vengeance, I had built good foundations. I'm not an airy-fairy person — I need to have a strong belief in what I'm doing. Along with the winning came a certain notoriety — there's not a country in the world in which we're not recognised. Sometimes that can be intrusive and difficult. Sure, the material goods have come. People in Ireland seem fascinated with the Rich List. They like to know where you are in the pecking order. They take great interest in whether I've got a plane or a nice new yacht, whether I've a new home wherever or where I ski. Yes, I have these things but they're not really important to me. They are just items that are there that I have acquired along the way. If I were to lose them, would I be very upset? I honestly don't think I would because I don't feel they have any long-term right to be there. They probably will be there because our business and the sport will endure. Do they make me a better person? Absolutely not — they just give me opportunities to get around easier and in more comfort. I have been one of the lucky ones. It's just that riches, in Formula 1, if you get it right, are quite amazing. I make no apology for that.

For a small fellow, I've always had huge amounts of energy, nervous energy if you like, but I still have it. In magazines in different countries around the world, when they are writing me up, I'm frequently described as frantic — and that has not changed. The more things I'm doing, the less chance I have of getting bored and the less chance I have to concentrate on one thing long enough to do it. I need to have lots of different things to do. That's what gets me through the day.

8

Stewart Kenny

Paddy Power

"You cannot be successful in business unless you are driven."

Stewart Ross Kenny is managing director of Power Leisure, trading as Paddy Power.

He was born in Dublin on 23 October 1951. His father was John Joseph Kenny, a Supreme Court Judge. His mother is Marjorie Baskin, who worked in an accountancy office. He was second in a family of two boys. His brother is Roger. He is married to Ruth Ogwu, housewife. They have two children: Nicky (21) and Kim-Ella (19).

He was educated at St Conleth's College, Glenstal Abbey and UCD (first year BComm).

At age 20, he worked with Ladbrokes in London, then with Jack Brown Bookmakers and then started on his own at age 22. He subsequently had partnerships with Alan Tuthill and Kenny O'Reilly and then Paddy Power.

He was Sunday Independent/BMW *Businessman of the Year in 1999.*

The conversation was recorded on 5 February 2001 in Stewart Kenny's home in Anglesea Road, Dublin 4.

Stewart Kenny

I was a sick child — I had asthma and eczema and that lasted for a good while until I went to a homeopath, Dr Goodwin McDonald, who cured my asthma. He mixes homeopathy with regular medicine and is magnificent. Now that I have studied psychology a bit, I can see the connection between being a sick child and being driven as an adult. You cannot be successful in business unless you are driven.

I went through Miss Ryan's kindergarten in Stillorgan — I have very happy memories of it. I then went to St Conleth's in Clyde Road — it was, and is, a wonderful school. Looking at my class coming out of St Conleth's, they had diverse careers but they all seemed well-adjusted, content but not self-satisfied, relaxed in themselves. My parents wanted the very best for me and believed the right thing was to send me to Glenstal. I was 12 when I went there. It was second-to-none but, looking back on it, I remember one of the priests saying that boarding school was really only for people from rural areas where there was no good secondary school or for people whose parents were living abroad or for people from broken marriages. I had no problems at Glenstal. They treated me brilliantly but, nowadays, boarding schools are not half so popular — we all feel we don't have enough time with our kids. I did not send my kids to boarding school, but my parents took the decision they thought was right at the time and it did not do me any harm — it started me into a flourishing bookmaking career!

I was not born into racing — my father enjoyed cricket. He was bookish, not a sporting person, more into music, art and books — and work and work and work. But, because I was a wheezy kid, he thought it was vital I get out into the fresh air. He asked some colleagues in King's Inns what was the best thing to do and somebody suggested, "Bring him racing."

I suppose I was always going to do something that gave two fingers to the Establishment. When I started bookmaking, it was not the thing a Glenstal boy did. I remember going back to Glenstal and telling the headmaster I was going to become a bookie. He laughed out loud and said, "No, but seriously, what *are* you becoming?" My mother always backed me but, she being a Methodist from a very respectable background, I'm sure her friends were horrified. It was as though I had put the neighbour's daughter in the family way!

My academic career was not great except for my pre-Leaving results because I was able to get in and get the papers in advance, which brought me first place in the class in honours English. That was the only academic success I've ever had. My claim to fame has been that I am the only person in Ireland who failed pass Greek twice — if you could write your name and do the alphabet, you got pass Greek. When I came to sit honours English in the actual Leaving Cert, the paper was stolen that year and appeared on the front page of the *Irish Independent*, having been on sale in Grafton Street the night before. I always had a huge admiration for the lads who stole it. I had been planning to do it but didn't have the ingenuity — it's probably just as well I didn't become a high-scale criminal, even though people refer to bookmakers as sophisticated burglars. In any event, we had to resit the honours English. Honours English was two papers, pass was one paper. Because it was on Irish Derby Day, there was no possibility of my doing honours English. Just as well, because I only scraped through the pass paper.

I went to Ladbrokes — it was a great experience. They were the best bookies in those days. They trained their staff brilliantly. They gave me a grounding in bookmaking that I would never have got anywhere else. It made me really understand it and it's kept me away from disasters. It's not a very complicated business but, if you get the fundamentals wrong, you end up with the kind of mess Corals Eurobet have made.

The fundamentals of bookmaking can best be described by my telling you about the day I first stood up at Harold's Cross Dogs. A great bookie, Seamus Farrell, came up to me and said, "Stewart, any fool can fill a satchel — it's filling it at the right price that counts." Of course, I was too young, too confident and knew it all, and did not get anywhere at Harold's Cross Dogs. If I could not get it at 6/4, I went 2/1, if I could not get it at 2/1, I went 3/1.

Betting has been destroyed by conning the public that you can make money from punting. All betting is is added entertainment to TV viewing. If you watch some boring soccer match, Southampton vs.

Bradford, real yawn-producing stuff — if you have a bet on it, it makes it so much more exciting. All I'm saying to punters is, "Come in. Give me a tenner on Saturday and I'll give you involvement in the soccer, the rugby, the Eurovision Song Contest, the lucky numbers in the Lottery — which is a huge thing — and horses and dogs. Go home and have a weekend's entertainment watching the bets on TV." That's all bookmaking is. I believe the con-job of telling people they will make money, number one, leads to social problems and, number two, it's selling a lie.

Richard Branson's autobiography had an interesting thing. He said that established businesses in the UK were trying to find the most profitable product they had and to push it into their customers. He started from the other end: "What do my customers most want? If I produce it for them, can I make a profit?" If bookmaking finds a profitable product, it's thrown so much at the customer that they get switched off: telling them they can make money out of gambling when they know they can't.

Twenty per cent of the Irish population bet reasonably regularly — 6 per cent of the UK population and 10 per cent of the Northern Irish population. And it's not because of our grá for horseracing — that's the usual illusion. In the UK, 7 per cent say they are interested in horse-racing — in Ireland it's 10 per cent. Racing is not that entertaining. Bring your kids racing and you'll see how quickly they are turned off it. Horseracing is a sport for the privileged — it is not really a mass sport.

Back to Ladbrokes. They were so good that other bookies were sending staff to them for a year's training. But, when I was a young manager in a Ladbroke's betting shop in London, I had no discretion whatever. That has been one of the successes of Paddy Power — we have allowed our managers be more flexible than our opponents'. However, as time goes on, and as we get bigger, I suppose they will have less flexibility. There would be greater need for controls.

James Osborne said an interesting thing to me — he said that one of the keys to management is how quickly decision-making is done. As businesses get bigger, decision-making gets slower — and he was talking about Ryanair. As Ryanair becomes global, another layer of management will be added and decision-making will be slower — and the same with Paddy Power. Our decision-making is not as fast as it was, but it is still faster than the opposition.

I think so long as I am there, decision-making will be quite quick — I tend to make instant decisions: betting decisions, "What special offer will we give today? What will we do today? How will we make ourselves different?"

I was on the Xtravision board and one of the great experiences is to be around something that did not work the way you hoped it would. Because Xtravision owed money to the banks, they were virtually dictating the pace at board meetings with the paperwork they were demanding. We never got time to talk about how we could make more profit. So, for Paddy Power, what board meetings are about is trading, trading, trading. If we want to get into accountancy issues, put it on the audit committee — that is not what board meetings are about. If accountants dominate a board they will tend to get into the minutiae of figures. Firms go broke from lack of cash, not from lack of paper profits.

Having got only as far as first-year BComm, I'm really a marketing shopkeeper and that's the way I want to stay. But you can only give so much of your personality to a business — I won't be there forever. Then we get a fresher, younger face.

When I came back from London, I worked for a go-ahead firm in Dublin, which did things differently. They did some things horrifically wrong and some horrifically right. At the time I didn't feel it but, in my subconscious, I was learning from them. The owner went off to do different things — people who do that really have balls. It's the safe option to stay at what you're doing, what you know best, what you've been successful at. I took a lease from him on two shops and the first day we were betting on Richard Nixon resigning.

Terry Rogers was doing that sort of thing. I suppose I broadened it a bit. He was doing Irish politics and a bit of American politics but only when there was an election. I did not want a this-is-Monday-we-must-be-doing-so-and-so attitude. There were opportunities before elections for betting. There are opportunities after elections. The most talked-about American election in the history of Presidential elections was the Gore/Bush one last year. The British betting industry stopped betting the day the votes were being cast. We never had so much publicity about an American election as we had the days and weeks *after* it. That's the time to really start betting. We paid out on Bush on the day of the first count — but we kept on betting. We got bundles of publicity — a huge book. They were all backing Gore.

American law does not let people place Internet bets — it's Prohibition thinking. What did Prohibition do? It made for secretive drinking, which led to problem drinking. It created the Mafia — and it will do exactly the same with betting, it will put it into the hands of the Mafia. When you get the business into the hands of the Mafia, you never get it out again. However, I don't expect a change with the new US Attorney General, who does not approve of drinking, gambling or dancing.

When I started on my own, I did a long line of PR gimmicks — betting on who shot JR. I had no competition so the papers were actually calling me: such and such is happening, have you got any betting on it? The papers were talking about Larry Hagman being in Tipperary staying with Phonsie O'Brien. A Tipperary man walked in and had £100 on Stone's widow as the killer — or whoever it was. I wondered if Larry Hagman had not let the cat out of the bag in a pub in Tipperary! We even had a BBC *Newsnight* coming over to do an interview. In all, it was thinking a little bit out of the box.

Any fool can say he knew the result of a Presidential election but it's only someone with a Paddy Power docket who can prove it! That's one of the lines we give. We advertise differently: the Pope to join Glasgow Rangers — that was a huge thing, it was controversy, it worked beautifully. Of course I got the belt of a crosier. The Catholic Press Office criticism was on the front page of the *Irish Times*. I'll give the Catholic church grants if the Press Office criticises us once a year.

Dad would have been a liberal Catholic. He was very academic. Some people might see him as distant but he had a kind heart, a soft and gentle person. He could talk to anybody. He was born in Limerick. His father was a builder — they moved to Dublin and, up to recently, houses on The Rise in Mount Merrion were always described as Kenny-built. His father was a brilliant builder but he had no clue how to price his houses. One of the things I was most proud of was Dad's Kenny Report on Building Land. Noel Browne was the only person who promoted it. We used laugh at the dinner table. Dad would say, "The politicians won't be able to avoid doing something about this report." I said, "You must be joking — they'll bury it along with all the other reports." Now we are seeing why reports like that were buried. It was quite radical — the idea was that the land essentially belongs to the State and the State should be able to take over building land at a percentage above its agricultural value. Why, if the

State were giving planning for land, should individuals get the bonus? The State was paying for everything — services etc. — and everybody else was getting the profit. Dad would have been left-of-centre in some ways, even though he started as a Fianna Fáiler when he was a young barrister. He was brought down to Limerick to make after-Mass speeches and he loved it. I've inherited his huge interest in politics and that has been one of the successes of Paddy Power — we bet on every political move and get constant publicity. In those days, Fianna Fáil was a broad church: left-of-centre and right-of-centre thinking. I believe I've inherited his slightly left-of-centre thinking. He used also think a lot of the time out of the box and that is something he has given me.

I always kicked against being brought up as a conventional individual — the son of a Supreme Court Judge could hardly be more conventional but, in some ways, in the best ways, Dad talked like a small farmer, but he did not have the conservatism of a small farmer. He thought the ban on Catholics attending Trinity College was ridiculous. He was pleased when he was given an honorary law doctorate by Trinity. He supported the anti-apartheid movement and was totally against the death penalty. The whole family were proud of the building land report. Perhaps you can see now why the only person who really supported it in the Dáil was Noel Browne.

I now had two shops — one in Wexford Street in Dublin and one in Athy. I got an overdraft for £6,000 from the Bank of Ireland in Stephen's Green — and I'm still with them. My Dad guaranteed part of it. Dad used tell me, "Build up a track record with your bank — they will know your ways." He would always welcome a new bank manager with a note saying, "You are my twenty-second bank manager."

At times when I became disillusioned with the business I tried to sell the shops and failed — you need luck in business. However, I soldiered on and formed a partnership with Vincent O'Reilly. We called the partnership Kenny O'Reilly. I was close to Alan Tuthill, who would have been the greatest bookie of them all, but he died of cancer at 40. He certainly thought outside the box. There was a great spirituality about him.

In Kenny O'Reilly we built upon the same theories — the way Paddy Power is run: getting into the papers, an emphasis on staff training, close to the customer. The name Kenny O'Reilly expressed the partnership but it could have been the name of a person — and that's where Ladbrokes and Corals go wrong. There's no personality in their names. We still have a most gifted person with people — Jimmy Mangan, first in Kenny O'Reilly and now in Paddy Power.

I was part of the campaign to bring the betting tax down from 20 per cent to 10 per cent. Charlie McCreevy and Brendan McGahon were for it and it was going well until they stood up on RTE one day and said the betting tax was immoral and they wouldn't pay it. From that point on, the tax was irrelevant. When two TDs from two opposite parties were saying they did not pay it, it fell into our lap because we had been saying for years that it was wrong to have a tax that nobody paid, that everybody evades. So far as the betting tax was concerned, all the business was under the counter. Then somebody was prosecuted. The State Solicitor said, "This is a serious offence. Six hundred million pounds is bet illegally in Ireland every year." And, of course, the official turnover was £100 million. Then the bookies went on strike in 1984 — they refused to pay the betting tax, not on the basis that the tax was too high, but because it was not being collected and it was a growing illegitimate business. If you had gone on strike to bring the tax rate down, you would have got no public sympathy. In fairness to Alan Dukes, the tax was brought down. In 1985 the turnover was £100m; it is now over £1 billion. The tax is now 5 per cent because Charlie McCreevy cut it again — and again, it was self-financing.

Reducing the tax to 10 per cent, the same as Britain, encouraged the British bookies to come in. We sold the Kenny O'Reilly shops to Corals and they multiplied the price of betting offices by a factor of four overnight. We started up again the day after they bought us out — the only constraint was that we could not compete within half-a-mile. The sale took so long that we had time to go off and buy new shops. We opened on the Monday, still as Kenny O'Reilly. Corals had the arrogance of their brand name — they believed that putting Corals over the door was all they needed to do. They should have bought the Kenny O'Reilly brand — that would really have done us damage. Now, the punters knew that Kenny O'Reilly had packets of money — it was all over the papers how much we got. Up to then, the one weakness we had competing with a multinational was that they had more money than us — so in fact Corals gave us money to compete against themselves. In England, bookmaking is highly regulated, so nobody competes. In fact, I find British business thinking quite dull and bureaucratic. That's why Americans find Ireland so good to do business in — there's very little form-filling, very little bureaucracy — we just get on and do the bloody thing.

John Corcoran, a man who has a great understanding of business, something I lacked, approached me and David Power to put an Irish group together. John has been and is a huge influence on my life. David Power was the biggest bookmaker on the track. John said to me, "You've got the marketing skills. We have more shops than you. We'll put the two groups together and we'll compete with the British at their own game." We came up with the name Paddy Power. Powers were as safe as a bank, they were there from the foundation of the State. Whatever else you knew about Powers, you knew the cheque would be waiting for you when you won big. We were competing against the British who had huge capital and we had to be seen to be as safe as a bank.

So we merged, and ran it along normal business methods for a while, cutting costs — we had 40 shops, 8 per cent of the market. There was a lot of management in 40 shops but they never left the management to me and never will! Whatever else I can do, I cannot manage.

We were playing the British bookmakers at their own game but we were never going to win. They were pastmasters at their game: increasing margins, cutting costs. My accountant at the time from Farrell Grant Sparks, John O'Callaghan (now an Appeals Commissioner), sat me down and told me I was off my rocker. He said, "There's only one way of getting business as big as the opposition — that is to build market share." John Corcoran had been at me for a long time about this.

One of the diseases we have is that people think those who have made most money are the leaders in our society. People come up and shake my hand and say, "Congratulations on the float." Making a fortune is only small talent — it doesn't last. Business people are forgotten very quickly when they die, and rightly so because, apart from their talent for making money, a lot of them haven't *left* that much to be remembered for. We are far too fascinated with business leaders. Kenny's bookshop in Galway, your folk, will be remembered when Stewart Kenny is forgotten. There's nothing wrong with that. The media now have this fascination with rich people. Seamus Heaney, Sister Stan, all the people who have built lasting things — Seamus

Heaney's poetry will last for generations, like Jack Yeats's paintings will last. Sister Stan is making a real contribution to future generations in the forgotten inner city. Society has become much too diverted by this money-making culture, as if the money-makers are the new leaders of society. It's a passing phase. They'll be forgotten. James Goldsmith is dead and nobody refers to him now. Who can name the famous businessmen in the forties? Nobody can, but everybody can name the famous artists, or the famous politicians. I feel that we've got much too diverted by money-making. We will become like every other society if we continue down that road. I often think of the drive that business people have — and have to have — to succeed — but I think they have read life wrong. When I say "they", *I* have read life wrong.

I was down in Castletownbere cycling between my bungalow there and the Buddhist Retreat Centre. It was lashing rain and I stopped to take shelter at a little pottery. The potter was showing me how he worked — how content he was. How much happiness he brought me that day. I said to him, "You wouldn't know what time it is?" He looked at me as if I had ten heads — why, in the name of God, in a beautiful place in West Cork, would you be worried about time? He said, "I don't know the time — I wonder if I have a clock here?" He went looking in a disused fridge in which he kept things. He found a clock and shook it and said, "I think it's four." I thought to myself, there's a man who has got life right. That man has as much to contribute to Irish society in his own way as I have. Maybe what he is creating will last longer. We're too caught up in the materialist morass. I know that's the "in" thing to say.

I spend a bit of time in that Buddhist Retreat Centre. Their message of spirituality is relevant to the present day. Their message, if you would call it that, is a yearning after the true way, but the beauty is that they don't believe there is only one, holy, true way. The Dalai Lama was asked recently about the yearning in Western society and the attraction of Buddhism and all its new converts — he was asked if Buddhism would sweep over the west. He said, "I'm not too sure that it actually suits the West. A lot of people in the West might be better off sticking with the religions they are comfortable with." I can't imagine the Pope saying that! Buddhism is very much an à la carte way of life. It gets you to look into yourself, searching for the truth and understanding the danger of attachments. If you buy a new car, the week before you buy it you're all excited about a new Merc. (I'm not a car person.) The first day, the smell of it, the feel of it . . . eventually it's just another bloody car. Attachments — wanting things — when you have them, they're no good to you but you want more of them because they are addictive. I bought this John Shinnors painting hanging there behind you. I still like it but it's just a painting. It doesn't change me, but it is nice to look at. A lovely sunset lasts longer with you than the attachments you have. Sure, art lasts longer than a great meal out or a new car. It's very hard to keep one's core in a city, with the media pushing the idea of money and possessions. I like the Buddhist idea of space for meditation, silence, not being afraid of our inner darkness. I was reading something Sister Stan said in the *Irish Times* the Christmas before last: our society has become very noisy, we're nearly afraid of ourselves and our inner darkness.

There is something that makes me very uneasy, walking through Dublin now and seeing so many people sleeping rough. John Lonergan, Governor of Mountjoy Prison, said that people's address is almost their prison sentence — the majority of people in Mountjoy Prison come from two Dublin postal districts. You may have read in the *Sunday Tribune* about a man whose three nephews and niece died from heroin addiction. If the drug addicts had been born in Nutley Lane like I was, and I had been born in Summerhill, who's to say one of them would not be running Paddy Power? I believe that I'd probably be a better criminal than them!

Every day you read on the front page about somebody who's made X million. I made a lot from Paddy Power and maybe I'm trying to justify it. What I don't like seeing is people, simply because they have made a lot of money, becoming cult heroes. Business is only business — it's only one talent. There's something ridiculous about me still working when I have got enough money to retire or do something else. However, I'm not talking about retirement — if I retired I'd die a death. John D. Rockefeller said, "I know what enough is — it is just one more."

Of course, there are huge inconsistencies between what I am saying about the pursuit of money and the fact that, over the long haul, the punter can't win, but surely it is the inconsistencies that are interesting? We have done surveys of the socio-economic groups that bet in Ireland and the Paddy Power punter is a perfect mirror of those groups. We have them all. Newtownpark Avenue has a betting shop —

so does The Goat. Fifteen years ago, those areas did not have betting shops. What we did was to bring a mainstream entertainment product to them. Of course, there are people who lose more money than they can afford, just as there are people in pubs who drink more than they can afford or is good for them. Of course, some people spend more money in Brown Thomas than they can afford, using their credit cards. Of course, banks give people credit which is going to leave them in penury for years. There are people who will always go to excess. All we give is entertainment, but I would not agree with endless credit, or, say, slot machines in betting shops, or lowering the age for betting — if anything, they should raise it from 18 to 21, as the US does for drinking. That age limit is strictly enforced here — we have had no problems with it. If you go into a betting office, you will not find anybody under 18.

Yes, there is huge inconsistency with my saying I'm uneasy about the drug problem, homelessness, *and* my spending money on art or hoarding money. I'm no different from the next man. At least I haven't gone "grand", God no. Are you joking? Just because I have made a success of a business, does not mean I have won the Masters in golf — I had a lot of lucky breaks. I think out of the box, but, if I had been trying to promote what I am doing now in 1960, it would not have worked. I happened to be here at the right moment. I was born into the right address. I had loving parents.

Some people, who have made it from poorer starts, often make the point: if I made it, anybody can make it. But loving parents make a huge difference. So many people who have had problem parents have the same problem themselves. When the whole family structure is broken up, when they did not have a structure on their childhood, they frequently pay the price.

There is no end — life is a journey. There is not a destination. I don't lead a Buddhist lifestyle — maybe it's only an escape, but, in Buddhism, you do learn to relax about yourself, to accept yourself as you are, warts and all, but keeping on trying to get more relaxed and searching for the truth. You never reach Nirvana — maybe you reach Nirvana only when you die. Is the Dalai Lama as unsettled as I am? Maybe so.

There's no point having a business unless it makes money. It's not a social service. People do have a fascination with how the wealthy spend their lives, so maybe the media are right, but I wonder do they fuel greed. Oprah Winfrey said that people in America were not too worried about not making a huge amount of money but they were very worried about their next-door-neighbour making a lot of money. Maybe capitalist societies depend on envy. If the media keep on shouting about people's wealth, the unwealthy may feel unsettled, that they're not doing very well. It is true, of course, that in this country we're not used to wealth and perhaps the fascination will go. It's the newness of the fact that there are hundreds of fellows with millions. But is it not wonderful to meet people whose lifestyle has not been affected by the millions? You do meet people who still go to the same grotty pub and you would not even know they had millions. There's something very refreshing about that.

One of the problems I faced in Paddy Power was that it was vital to publicise the business continuously. The PR advantage is what really made us. Fintan Drury is not only a great PR man but a great business strategist and a deep-thinking person. When I went to him first for Paddy Power, he said, "Stewart, the way to do this is to make you Mr Bookmaking — anything to do with betting, you turn up, even if it's not to do with Paddy Power betting." It's great for one's ego, constant appearances in the media and it becomes very hard, at times, to switch off from it. When you go to the pub, there's a shout, "What are the odds on this or that?" It's all an act, of course, me being the brash bookie. The danger is, it becomes me and eventually you lose touch with who you really are. At times, like the Lucky Numbers campaign when you're on the radio every day, you get hyped up, going from radio station to radio station and, when you get home, you have not quite switched off from it. And then you go out and people are slagging you. In fact, I am the public face of the brand. But there are a huge number of very disciplined managers behind that brand, a huge number of good marketing people there. Before the IPO, when the institutions saw the *business*, not just the public face, they saw that, if I were knocked down by a bus, the only thing that would be missing would be the public face. Over the next few years, you will see an increasing number of spokesmen for Paddy Power. We actually have a lad called Paddy Power, a young fresh-faced lad, with a lovely personality and he's made for the media. He will get in touch with the 25–35 group that I am not going to get in touch with. It is time for me to start rowing back a bit.

I hope I have helped to make betting an acceptable form of entertainment. Betting is nearly the wrong word: having a flutter is the word I would prefer. Betting has connotations of back-street. I would hope that having a flutter would be an acceptable entertainment for the masses, whether they are middle- or working-class. In fairness, Terry Rogers started it — I think I helped.

9

Bernard McNamara

Michael McNamara & Company

Photo: © Edmund Ross Studios

"You get more experience out of problems or failures than you do when things go smoothly. That's how I've learned most of what I know. I failed, or I did not get what I wanted, I analysed it and I had to take a different approach."

Michael Bernard McNamara is managing director of Michael McNamara & Company, building contractors.

He was born in Limerick City on 13 January 1950. His father is Michael McNamara, a farmer who moved into construction. His mother was Della Neylon. He is the eldest of four children, with one brother and two sisters: John, Shelly and Barbara. He is married to Moira O'Donoghue, a nurse. They have five children: Michael (20), Sinéad (18), Darragh (15), Cliodhna (12) and Ronan (9).

He was educated at Lisdoonvarna National School; St Flannan's College, Ennis; College of Commerce, Rathmines (Business Studies); Cost and Works Accountancy.

He was previously Cost Accountant with the Smith Group, first with the internal audit group and then with the construction group (1969–70). He joined his father's construction business in Clare (1971) and moved to Dublin in 1989.

He is a member of the National Roads Authority. He also served on the board of Great Southern Hotels (1990–94). His firm has won a number of building awards.

The conversation was recorded 7 February 2001 in Bernard McNamara's home in Ailesbury Road, Dublin 4.

Bernard McNamara

I was born in Limerick City — that's where the nearest maternity hospital was at that time — and reared in Lisdoonvarna. I went to St Flannan's College in Ennis. It was a big diocesan school, partly a feeder school for seminaries: their brief was to produce a certain number of clerical students, which they did. You could, however, keep totally free from that if you wanted to. Hurling was a big part of the college — half the pupils were from Tipperary, because the College was in the diocese of Killaloe. The hurling team regularly went on to the All-Ireland Schools Final. Football was not played that much, even though there was a good representation from North and West Clare. Two-thirds of the hurling team were from Tipperary with a third from Clare, and almost the opposite for football. It was a rough enough school, but Canon Cuddy began to change the ethos — bullying was targeted and stopped. Prior to that, there was a tradition of the seniors being the hard men and exercising significant control over the juniors virtually as of right — they could hit them. It was an environment where you learned to stand on your own two feet. It probably taught you how to live anywhere. You had to make your friends, earn your place. After Flannans I felt I'd never have any difficulty going anywhere. It was not well endowed in terms of library or music which, of course, it should have had. Free time was used up by going to Mass — you went to Mass twice every Sunday morning, at 7.30 a.m. and 10.30 a.m. — and you had games twice on Sunday. Mass and games were the Big Two. People would not believe nowadays that four fellows were expelled for going out over the wall to see Brendan Boyer and the Royal Showband in Ennis. There were some great priests in Flannans — Fr Willie Walsh (now Bishop of Killaloe), Fr Seamus Mullen and Fr Seamus Gardiner, all part of a new breed of priest coming into Flannan's after Vatican II.

I did not have a particularly distinguished school career — I got three or four honours in my Leaving Cert. I was heavily involved in debating in Flannans and continued to be so when I went to Dublin.

That was helpful to me in learning how to communicate with people and not being afraid of getting up if you have to say something. I was also involved in the drama society: when you go on stage for the first time, your knees are knocking. Doing that and debating, you *have* to get rid of your fear.

I went to the College of Commerce in Rathmines, partly influenced by my father in what I did. He had only a national school education because he was the eldest of 12 and remained on the farm until he was 29 — the rest of them got a secondary education. People forget that national school went up to 14 years of age at that time. It was a deeper type of education than what it would be now. He was not as lacking in education as people might perceive it in the modern world. He encouraged me towards finance and business studies rather than engineering. He always felt that, if I could get the money end of it right, the rest would follow or I could learn the rest of it but, if I concentrated totally on the technical aspects of the business, I might follow the path of a lot of builders who get into trouble because they think that cash flow means they own the money.

One of the big experiences I had in college was when I went to New York at 19 for £56 return — that included two nights at the Statler Hilton. I worked first as a waiter in Childs Restaurant. One of the guys had an uncle, a priest, who got jobs for four of us as busboys in the New York Athletic Country Club in Westchester County, which was great — you lived in a lovely environment. It was like a whole new world — people do not realise how dramatically different America was from Ireland then. America opened my eyes to a new society, to different standards of living. It was hugely developmental — the Americans are very open.

When I finished college, I worked in the Renault internal audit part of the Smith Group and then moved back into the construction end of their business. When I went back into my father's business, I virtually forgot about my education — I spent no time in the office. I was out on sites all the time. There was a bit of an upturn in 1971 and my father got three or four major jobs. That's how he persuaded me to come home. I had no interest in coming home. I was doing fine in Dublin, thank you very much, and having a better time. Clare was very quiet during the winter and very busy during the summer, like most tourist areas. I travelled about 50,000 miles a year mainly around sites in Limerick, Galway and Clare, leaving at 6.30 a.m. and returning at 8.00 p.m. each day.

At that time, the office was four people: my father and three administrative staff. There was a consultant quantity surveyor. I learned a lot by being out on the sites. It's one thing to know the financial end of it but out on the sites you learn that an ability to relate to people is important and it's important to break down the barrier of being the boss's son. If you demonstrate that you are willing to do anything, people will accept you much more quickly than they would if you don't go down a trench. I learned a lot from the foremen. We had a foreman who taught me something I remember every day. He said, "Everybody is good at something — the trick is to find out *what* they are good at." And he demonstrated that to me several times during the project we were involved in.

For four or five years, I hardly went near the office. I never went near the banks or involved myself in insurance — my father did that part of it. He is 93 now — at that time he would have been well into his sixties. He was anxious that I would learn as much as I could about the business.

Then a downturn came. At this stage, we were building a 50,000-square-foot office block in Limerick for about £1 million, 96 apartments in Galway, a housing scheme in Castletroy in Limerick, and we had some schools. What I found was that, when there was a bit of an upturn, builders bought plant, because there was tax relief on it. Most of them loved machinery. But, when there was a downturn, the volume of business contracted and the plant they had bought sat there looking at them. I began to see that this was a recurring cycle and going nowhere. I said to myself that I was not going to invest in depreciating plant — I was going to invest in performance building. Performance building means you get a solid reputation for building rapidly and to budget — you gain a reputation for deliverability and control of costs. That's a familiar piece of jargon in the trade now — it wasn't so much then. Don't forget that the time to complete projects then was two or two-and-a-half times longer than now. Builders employed everybody directly, whereas now it is primarily subcontracting.

A long recession came, which, to an extent, I had foreseen. On my way back from my honeymoon, I heard that we had got the extension to Galway Hospital, £3.5 million, three times bigger than anything we had done heretofore. At that time, we would not have got on too many tender panels of that size, so I took it as an opportunity for growth. It was a successful job and the Western Health Board put us on the tender panel for a Centre in Swinford for the mentally handicapped. That was a £10 million project — today it would be £30 million or £40 million. I took that as a further opportunity and I was probably £300,000 less than the next nearest tender. The other big builders predicted that I would fall on my face. It was a tricky site with silt and sand and bog and virtually every dangerous type of ground you could think of. We priced it in September and started in March. That gave me an opportunity to recruit a team of engineers.

We had also priced a number of jobs at Moneypoint power station. In three or four of the bids, we had been at the races. We had been interviewed — they always interviewed the lowest three, but we were not getting anywhere and I was getting a bit tired of it. We had now gone from £1 million in Limerick to £3 million in Galway to £10 million in Swinford. And I wanted to find out why we were not getting the ESB jobs, having reached the last three. Galway started in 1980, Swinford in 1982/83. When I got the feedback from Moneypoint, I heard that what they were saying was that there was just my father and myself with three or four people in the office and a consultant surveyor. They saw us as not having the in-depth management: "If your father and yourself were driving somewhere and had a crash, the ESB would be left with nobody." I got the message — it was probably the biggest single thing that affected my evaluation of how you manage something. Immediately, I recruited an engineer for Moneypoint even though I had not got a job there. I told him that I wanted to know everything about the next job that was coming up in Moneypoint even before it came out to bid. We got the Moneypoint job, so we now had a £3 million job there running together with the £10 million job in Swinford.

When we started Swinford, there were 33 buildings in it and we were the first people in Ireland to have computers on site. We put all the bill of quantities on disk, unheard of at the time. We also put the breakdown of labour, plant and materials so we could pull it in terms of what we got for labour. With the sub-contractors, we could compare their prices with our costs. That makes for very interesting negotiations. A fellow comes in and you can say, "Well, your price was not too bad but you have three or four crazy rates there", and he'll pull them back quite willingly.

I learned also the difference between the older operators and the current ones. For example, the sub-letting of the ground works was a package, where we had prices of £55,000 to £65,000. A man called Sandy Geraghty, back from England and the States, was very knowledgeable on plant. He walked in one day and said, "I'm fed up coming in here — I'm either going to get this job or I'm not, otherwise I'm just withdrawing my tender." "Fine, Sandy, but you're not the lowest." "My surveyor has been through it every which way." "Why don't we sit down and I'll write out the machines you think you need for the job and how long it will take you to do it." He told me what his concept of doing the job was — he'd need two D9 bulldozers and whatever else. I asked him what hire rates he'd need for them and he told me £18 an hour for this, £25 an hour for that. When I added it all up it came to £25,000. He went back and checked the list and could not believe that there was such a difference in the figure. I said to him, "I'll give you £27,500 to give you a bit of cover." He said, "No." "I'll give you £29,000, take it or leave it." He took it. He did well out of the job but it just shows you that, very often, building quantities do not reflect how a project is actually done. A lot of the estimators don't have a lot of technical knowledge or experience.

I went home to my father and told him I had got a great deal — remember, I was only 29 or 30 years of age. While he was a tolerant man, he might have thought I had cocked up such a big package. It took him about three days to agree that it was a good price.

I came through that project with a fear of failure. That's very important: the massive fear of failure people in my industry had — and have — when you could have a recession that lasts 15 or 20 years. At the time we were finishing Swinford, we had built up a substantial capability: we had a management team, we had invested in a significant overhead. We had to have work to feed the overhead. We'd start off the financial year with a cover of only 25 per cent or 30 per cent of our overhead. You had the very difficult choice of cutting your overhead and capacity and losing credibility — you could never be sure you would get on the bigger tender panels — whereas, if you did cut the overhead, it would be regarded as being safer. The overhead consisted primarily of people such as engineers and quantity surveyors. You either had to hold them because you had enough belief in yourself that you could win the work to keep them going or, if you did not get the work, you ended up with a major loss. If you took the short-term view and made them redundant, the next time you went for an interview you could not demonstrate that you had the capability to carry out large projects.

That's one of the reasons why the whole construction industry went so heavily into sub-contracting. We had 330 men working in Swinford and we had three weeks of snow. We had to cover all that bill ourselves whereas, in the current climate, you would have sub-contractors carrying a major portion of the risk. There has been a lot of change in the building industry since then. For example, we wanted to do the Swinford job in a year less than they had provided for. They would not let us do that. The wry thing about it was there were revenue cuts in Health at that time which Swinford would have escaped if it was finished earlier — the same thing happened with the Galway hospital job. That job was not opened for about three years, because there was no money for it. Similarly in Swinford, the job sat there empty for three or four years, then was opened only on a phased basis — and wasn't officially opened for nine-and-a-half years after we finished the construction. However, it's a fine facility and contributes to the town of Swinford. At the time, in the Western Health Board, there was a change of thought about whether these big centres were the right thing to do at all — whether or not they should be broken down into smaller centres.

After Swinford and Moneypoint, I said that the only way I could keep this size of business going was to open up in Dublin. In 1984, we opened an office in Adelaide Road a year before we finished Swinford. We made an eight-minute video, which we sent around to architects, engineers, surveyors and potential clients. People still joke with me about it — at the time a video was regarded as a bit far-out. It was a very quick way of showing people in Dublin what we had done. We were not well known in Dublin. There was a deep recession. It was difficult to get on tender panels — they were confined to about six established Dublin firms. The office was in Dublin 2, because three-quarters of the architects and engineers in Ireland were in Dublin 2 and 4. This was 1983/4 and we were there at least two years before we got a job. Initially we did not get on any tender panels. Our first job was the Social Club in RTE, about £600,000. The architects were Scott Tallon Walker. It had been hard to get to see Ronnie Tallon.

There were too many builders around and nobody wanted another one. When, eventually, I did see him, he said, "But you live in Clare — how do I get to meet you if I want to see you quickly? And how do I know what you're worth? Do you have the financial capacity?" "Ronnie, I don't mind any of those questions. If I can come back to you in two or three days' time, I will give you the exact answers." I realised that, because he had asked those questions, he was genuinely interested. I met him again, showed him our accounts, told him he could have copies of them, which he did not want, and he put us on the panel for the RTE job.

We then got the extension to Loughlinstown Hospital, about £1.8 million. Then we got the O'Reilly Institute in Trinity College. The building, as you know, is on Westland Row. Architects at the time felt it was fine to be building out in a field outside Dublin but building in the city was different. They believed that, if we did not have the experience for that, it would be very difficult to put us on a panel. Building the O'Reilly Institute, a prestigious job, broke down those myths. When I went into Trinity College to sign the contract, I was walking into a very august place and I was nervous. Dr Watts, the Provost, gave me a warm welcome and made me feel at home. He said, "You probably don't know that I know a lot of people where you come from — I take my students down to Lisdoonvarna and the Burren to Mary Angela Keane and to Ballinalacken Castle." He told me later that he was the man who acquired the controversial lands around Mullaghmore, which Trinity sold to the Office of Public Works to create a public park there.

When I came to Dublin, I found I knew an awful lot of people I had met at Renvyle House Hotel in Connemara, where we had gone on holidays for 12 years. In the Renvyle Hotel, I had not known what they did, but years later I found they were in businesses related to my own. My father had bought a house for £34,000 in Raglan Road in the mid-seventies when the family were going to college. After we got married, we spent a lot of time in Dublin. Moira had been nursing in Vincent's Hospital. I met more architects socially, whose office doors I could not get past, in the Shelbourne Bar with Moira on a Friday evening than any marketing guy going out knocking on doors.

Which reminds me to wind back a bit because, when I was 23 or so, in the quiet Clare winters, I got involved in voluntary organisations like the North Clare Development Association. I could never

understand why people in the West did not invest in themselves. A
friend of mine told me that in one bank in Ennistymon in the sixties
there was £7 million on deposit. There was little industry — people
were leaving the area. I got involved with people like Father Harry
Bohan and Micheál Vaughan from the Aberdeen Arms Hotel in
Lahinch (Micheál was heavily involved in Bord Fáilte) and Alec
Browne from Ennistymon. Alec, who since died, was involved with
the Vincent de Paul Society and many other voluntary works. I was
single and I had time. Then the Fine Gael councillor, Jimmy O'Brien,
a second cousin of my mother, died in Lisdoonvarna. The Fianna Fáil
fellows approached me to know if I would stand. The next youngest
councillor would have been 50 upwards. Derry Honan, husband of
Tras Honan, later the Cathaoirleach of the Seanad, and I were co-
opted on to Clare County Council. We were co-opted because it was
only three months before an election. Derry gave me a bit of advice,
"A young fellow like you, keep your mouth shut and see what's going
on here." Derry kept his mouth shut. I didn't. He did not get elected
at the next election. I did.

At that time you were put on different committees — I had written
a trenchant letter to the Vocational Education Committee. I was at
something in Ennis one night and a man called Paddy Doherty came
over to me. He said, "I believe you are Bernard McNamara." "I am."
"I'll give you two bits of advice: cut your hair and stop writing those
epistles. We will always beat you because we have more time." At the
following election, I got elected without any difficulty, even though I
was very young. Down the country, having a wide spread of relations
is helpful. It is not quite so dishonourable a thing as people might
suggest to have served on a county council. It was not driven by the
motivation that I would be on the inside rather than on the outside so
far as my business was concerned. In fact, it was a hindrance to my
business because, the more our contracts got spread throughout the
country, the more difficult it was to get back to council meetings.
They had this habit of having meetings in the middle of the day,
which suited teachers and publicans. I felt the meetings should be
held in the evenings. Joe Boland was a very fine County Manager.
There were no junkets like other councils. There were no Section 4s —
that is the statutory right of councillors to override the manager's
planning decisions. I went into the County Council because I felt I
might be able to do something. When you're that age you feel that,

with all these older fellows around the place, you can change things. When canvassing, I would use a dictaphone like you're using now. I'd dictate the letter on the way out the gate and chuck the tape into the office the next day. That was quite an innovation in those days, because I followed up on canvas issues virtually two days later, by letter.

After the second election, I was dragged away more and more by my work and was not so heavily involved with the Council, but Moira enjoyed dealing with much of the business for me. Now, when we're going to an opening of one of our completed buildings, people ask me how I know that deputy or senator — when you're a councillor, all the potential senators canvas you for your senate vote. Most of them would have been in my house at some stage, frequently at all-hours at night, as they canvas as late as possible when they are travelling the country. Similarly, going to a by-election in the sixties was as good as a holiday anywhere: the sing-songs, the fun, the drinking. I remember being in Westport and every night we went to bed at 4.00 or 5.00 a.m. For a fellow living down in West Clare, I developed a range of people I knew in different parts of Ireland. At the end of my second term in the Council, we had two or three kids, and it was time to give up and devote myself to them a little more.

Business goes in phases. When Dr Tony O'Reilly[1] was officiating at the opening of the O'Reilly Institute, which he funded, he remarked, "Mr McNamara made me really understand the meaning of accelerated cash flow!" We've done a lot of work in Trinity since, maybe eight or ten buildings. We have done a lot in other universities as well — not so much in UCD or DCU, I don't know why, sometimes it goes like that. We were reinforcing our acceptance as respected builders. Then there was a bit of an uplift and we were getting on more panels. Our turnover began to go up. There would have been times when it doubled, and there would have been times when it was halved. That shows you how cyclical the business is and how difficult it is to manage. In the last number of years, we have been among the top five builders, excluding the civil engineering part of Ascon Rohcon. One of the things that gives me satisfaction is the significant level of repeat business we do with our major clients, such as the universities, hotel groups, state bodies and private developers. I think this shows the quality of the people in our company and the stan-

---

[1] *In Good Company*, pp. 155–170.

dards we have achieved. It is also demonstrated in our relationships with financial institutions, where we do significant repeat business.

I started getting into property in the early nineties, which largely came about from the capacity to use tax breaks. My accounting background probably helped me there. In Mahon in Cork we did the Central Statistics Office, a 100,000-square-foot office building. That was designed, built and financed by us for the Office of Public Works, so you had to have, as well as the building capacity, the capacity to organise the finance. Our vehicle for that was a single-purpose property development company. The Office of Public Works leased the building for 20 years and eventually bought it back. The property company provided the construction funding through the bank based on the takeout by the Office of Public Works, which clicked in on hand-over. We had also started getting involved in student accommodation. In 1990, when student accommodation got the Section 23 tax break, UCD was the first one that went ahead with McInerneys, who were a plc at the time. We did UCC, UCG and the Royal College of Surgeons, accommodation totalling nearly 1,200 bed spaces, in about two-and-a-half years.

I served as a State director on the Board of Munster Chipboard with the late Amby McInerney. It was in a difficult situation for several years. It went into liquidation and was sold on to a Spanish company. It's thriving now. I gave Amby a lift back to Dublin and he was telling me about a chap who was very good at industrial relations. A couple of years later, when I had difficulty with bricklayers in Swinford, I rang Amby and asked him for the name of his IR guy so I could consult him. We had 300 men on site and 40 bricklayers withdrew their labour and stopped the whole site for five weeks. The bricklayers were earning £400 after tax at the time, very big money. I consulted with Amby's man, Jim Nugent, and he told me, "This is what you should do. You should send their last ten payslips by registered post on to their wives." The strike was over in less than ten days, as it was obvious their wives had never been made aware of their high earnings!

I have made considerable money on property development, primarily office, hotel and industrial developments. I have never taken a dividend out of the building side of the business — I take a salary. You have to build up the balance sheet of the company to improve continually your capacity for providing guarantee bonds, etc., and to grow accordingly. Property and construction give an interesting combination. I can produce things in different ways. That's the reason why I would have the guts to go into manufacturing new building products such as Acotec Concrete wall-panelling because I'm building a very large number of apartments and houses in my own developments. The same with brick-slips, a new method of brickwork. The combination — property and construction — enables me to be aggressive. You will remember the recent Vincent's Hospital Nurses' Home implosion, carried out by the UK-based Controlled Demolition Group — I was the first to use that technique in Ireland. We imploded the old Mount Salus Press site behind Fannins on Aungier Street — it worked beautifully, but, as we were coming towards it, people were getting nervous, there were buildings all around it. Some engineers in particular were saying to me that, if that went wrong, I'd be destroyed. You have to weigh things up very carefully. I said to myself, "If I funk this, I'll go back to being the safe guy that I have not been and I might as well roll over." You have to keep an edge to yourself. I increased my non-negligence insurance and said we'd go with it. It worked fine but, if something happened, I would have had egg all over myself. I must say, however, that even though the Vincent's job took 12 hours instead of three minutes, the implosion technique was well worth using there.

A lot of people warn you off doing things differently when it comes to the point. I think it's very important that you don't start getting too safe and saying, look, I've done all right, I'm going to be safe from here on in. We did the Mount Salus implosion pretty much on our own without involving any of the consultants because, if it had gone wrong, nobody would have liked to be associated with it.

There's a perception that building is a very low-grade business. It's not. The brainpower that builders have to employ matches any industry: the high calibre of engineers and managers who have to take the responsibility for our work. Kevin Kelly, former MD of Sisks, now with Treasury Holdings, said at a Construction Industry Federation Dinner, "Construction is like having to put on a symphony concert without knowing where the venue will be or who will be playing in the orchestra." It's an industry which is totally different from a factory, where you have the same people in the same place for years. We're moving all the time. And we may have to move to regions where we've never been before and we have to persuade people to come with us. We have

to provide our clients with collateral for bonds and provide sophisticated financial proposals for our business developments.

I think the industry does not sell itself well enough. There's a
feeling that we need to be watched because nobody trusts a builder. I
would contend that, if the builder was taken on board early on in the
negotiation of projects, particularly in the current market, he could
produce better value and spend the money better on a higher quality
building. It's impossible to convince people of that. However, that will
change. The builder can eliminate waste and take final responsibility
for costs, but only if he has the authority. You cannot have responsibility unless you have the authority.

I agree that survival in the modern world means constant innovation but there is a whole range of people — the advisors— who are
doing things the way they always did them, because nobody will force
them to change.

Let me give you an example. We are using pre-fabricated bathroom pods — they are lightweight concrete and the bathroom is totally finished. It's tested and certified to all the standards and you
simply plug in the water and power. The bathroom door is not
opened until the day everything else is finished. What that gives us is
a certainty of top-quality standards because it's made in a factory instead of out on a building site, bit-by-bit, where the tiler is standing
inside the bath which is meant to be fully protected, and where there
may not be proper light or weatherproofing. A lot of the people for
whom we could have used those pods would not certify the work. We
were able to use them initially only on our own property development
jobs. In an economy where you have a shortage of labour, where the
bathroom can be swung in on a crane, it is contributing to minimising
the effects of the labour shortage. We're now bringing in prefabricated kitchens. The plumbers and electricians who would traditionally be involved in that are free to do other work.

Official policy is fairly seriously misdirected in going out looking
for foreign labour. Builders are criticised on health and safety
grounds — how do you organise guys who can't talk English? How do
you tell them how to do things safely and make sure they understand
the instruction? I believe we can do the job quicker and safer with
these new methods, but the Government needs to facilitate this in the
building regulations. For instance, even though we are in the EU, the

Agrément European Product Certification System is not recognised in Ireland. This should be corrected.

It's not essentially the builders themselves who are inefficient; it's the whole method of procurement. For instance, we are doing a project where we wanted to use prefabricated bathrooms in student accommodation. We asked our bathroom-pod man to look at it. He said, "There are 14 different bathroom types in this project." So we could not bring in economies of scale. We rationalised it down to two or three different types. Why does the client not write that in as part of the brief? Why does the Minister for Health not say, when he is building a huge number of hospitals, that the designers should be instructed to have at the most one or two designs for all the bathrooms? Then whoever wins the contract can use the efficiency of the pods. There's a whole range of ways in which you can effect economies. Of course, they can be made to look different inside and beautiful. But the thing is to have them all the same modular size. If I suggest that to somebody, they'll say that's all very fine if you're building a block of flats, but not if you're building a hospital.

What I am trying to say is that people should stand back and take a developer attitude, something I have learned through my own property development. But there is resistance to that because people will say, "Look at the decentralised offices we got: the first ones were very low quality", but, at the time, you were *told* to build them at very low cost. The one we did in Cork, the Office of Public Works were paying a 20-year purchase rent of £4.59 per square foot. A purchase rent means you end up owning it, so it was paying back some of the capital as well — the site was free. It produced very cost-effective buildings. The first prison the OPW had design-built had a budget of £35 million. It came in at £23 million. It's a shame that bureaucrats and politicians will not admit that they should get builders on board earlier. Tender competitions could be two-stage. Clients often allow their design consultants decide a procurement method that is not the most cost-effective in terms of buildability, health and safety and building programme.

Let me tell you a story. I came across 50 acres of land in Finglas, almost by accident. I went there to look at land for industrial building. The auctioneer said, "There's a housing site here too but you probably would not be interested in it." I went down to have a look at it — it was near the new road coming from Blanchardstown to the airport, a splendid big motorway. I stood there as a countryman and looked at the grand green flat fields. I was told it had been zoned for 12 years but had never been built on because there was no sewerage and services and it would probably be there for another six or seven years. Nobody wanted to touch it.

We are supposed to have a shortage of housing in Ireland. I had been reading in the paper about people camping overnight in Drogheda to buy houses. I have five kids myself — I said, to hell with this, there must be some way of doing it. So I bought the land. I asked my architect and engineers to see what they could get planning for. We were told we would get planning for 40 houses — there was sewerage for only 40. I'm a great believer in starting somewhere so I told them to put in an application for 40. The application was not accepted. They told me there was no area action plan. I asked what an area action plan was. It was a new procedure they had come up with to get compatibility of design and in the way the landowners would use their land. I had no problem with that. I asked how we would get an area action plan. I was told the local authority had the responsibility but did not have the staff or the resources. There are no area action plans for most of the zoned land in Dublin. I asked Frank Benson, the Lord have mercy on him, to get his office to do it for me, at my cost. The local authority accepted it, did their own thing with it and then it was adopted. We then went to the local authority and said, look, the sewerage isn't there, we'd like to build a treatment plant because I would like to build the houses now. A treatment plant was not acceptable. The perception the public have as to why things are not happening or why the cost of housing has gone up dramatically is totally different from what the reality is. I'm trying to explain all the steps we had to go through. Would you believe, we had land in Limerick that my father bought in 1970 and it got planning permission only two or three years ago?

I met Bobby Molloy at a housing conference in UCD. I was going in when he was coming out and he said, "You were late for my speech." I said to him, "Bobby, all I wanted to do was to catch you to tell you what is going on in reality." I told him the story of my planning permission difficulties in Finglas. The civil servant with him knew exactly where I was talking about. Bobby said, "Come in and meet me tomorrow with some of my fellows." I had a brochure done for the scheme — it's amazing what a brochure achieves. Suddenly you're challenging them. You're saying, I'm here ready to go but I can't start the project. One of the guys said, "Sewerage is always a difficult thing. Could you turn it into water?" I told him I didn't know but I would find out. There is a new Japanese system where you can turn sewage into drinking water. It's a lot more expensive but we proposed it instead of the treatment plant. It frightened the daylights out of the local authority people. If I started to do that, everybody would be doing it. Then suddenly an advanced foul sewer popped up out of nowhere from Poppintree! The fact was, the Local Authority did not want to lose control. I later said to Department of Environment officials, who were trying to speed up housing starts, "Why don't you do two things: instruct all the local authorities to do an area action plan, which will take a year off the procurement period for housing; and why don't you give a three-year derogation for temporary treatment plants to get a set-off against the local authority levies?" At present, if you go out and spend £3 million or £4 million for a treatment plant, it will do the business for maybe 30 or 40 years, but you still have to pay the levies and the local authorities have been getting EU money for some of these schemes, so it's a double whammy for them. There's a whole area there where you'd wonder whether people were serious or not about speeding up housing starts to help moderate prices.

When the big burst of demand for housing was there, I could never understand why they were rezoning land when they were not dealing with the zoned land. I have never bought land that had to be rezoned. I can't understand why the local authority didn't buy the land before they rezoned it.

There are some hugely committed people in the local authorities, people the public service is lucky to have, but the ethos or environment they have, what they are trained up in, has always been to be dead safe and to protect their role. Similarly with the roads. When I joined the National Roads Authority, everything was being done sequentially, not in parallel. We lost two years of the roads programme because the Department refused £19 million four or five years ago for pre-planning work. That's the bottleneck. If they had got the £19 million that time, the designers could have done all the enabling work to bring things to the stage where they were ripe, to go ahead much more quickly and up to two years earlier.

I always try to present myself as a problem-solver. If I go to the local authority and they tell me there's no water there from Cappagh and it's going to cost £2 million to bring it down to Finglas and they don't know whether or not they'll get the money, I say, "Right — I'll put up a bank guarantee for half of it if that gives certainty of it going ahead." I know they are busy and understaffed and all that. I got Jerome Casey, the economist, who worked in Roadstone, to log the Finglas thing as it went along. I gave him access to the files. It was going on so long that I wanted somebody totally objective just to be aware and record. But when you go to the local authority guys, you can't just say this is bloody ridiculous, you have to be a problem-solver, you have to take some steps to help them in a totally above-board way. While it might be a bit different, you show them that you're willing to put your neck out as well and put your money on the table.

I probably learned a lot about interfacing with these fellows through being a member of a county council. Most people go in with an attitude that these guys are in mundane jobs when an awful lot of them are very bright people. When I was in school, a lot of these guys had done the Junior Ex, they were top of the class, but unfortunately to an extent they have been left behind.

Life teaches you a lot of important lessons. There's a sign in a pub below in Clare, Joe McHugh's in Liscannor, a long narrow little pub, and Joe was well known because he was a great character. The sign read: "Experience is what you get when you didn't get what you wanted." You get more experience out of problems or failures than you do when things go smoothly. That's how I've learned most of what I know. I failed, or I did not get what I wanted, I analysed it and I had to take a different approach. I'd come at things from any angle, I would think laterally — people laugh at me regularly for doing that. For example, people laugh at me on the National Roads Authority when I tell them it's going to take five years to get a motorway through Enfield. I'm a property developer and if I buy a site for £X, say two acres, and somebody has a little bit that I need but only a tenth-of-an-acre, and they want half of £X, I have a choice. I either have to pay them their money to get the business done or I have to walk away and leave it in limbo. If I was a dictator and I was on the NRA, I would have bought the left or the right-hand side of Enfield and shifted it to one side and run the motorway down the middle and they'd all be happy. That's regarded as a mad idea but in terms of macro-economic benefit, to release that traffic for five years is very important for the West. I hear loads of people saying they don't go to Galway or Clare any more or Connemara or Donegal for weekends because it takes too long to get there. It's very hard to get a creative approach.

On another occasion, I suggested that, in the interim period, there were ways around the small towns. If you are going through Kildare, you could turn right on the way down and come back out near the hotel. There is no problem in Kinnegad now since they put the little roundabout down. Loughrea — there's a low road going down by the lake — why not turn it into one-way for bank holiday weekends? They told me there were seven or eight different agencies involved. I learned an awful lot about this once when I missed a flight from Dublin to Shannon and I met Sylvie Barrett, who was Minister for the Environment at the time, coming out of Dublin Airport. He said, "How are you Mac?" "I'm like a bull — I missed a flight." "Well, I'm going down, you can come if you like". He got into the ministerial car. It was a Friday evening on a bank holiday weekend in the middle of summer. The driver had a load of back routes. I asked him where he had learned them. He told me they all compared notes in the ministerial drivers' pool. When I mentioned a few of these back routes at an NRA Board Meeting, people nodded and agreed with me — and nothing happened. The expertise that people have inside their heads is not *used*. Why not signpost the secondary routes for bank holiday weekend traffic? Why do we have to suffer absolute torture until the motorways are built when there could be good interim solutions, even if it's only for bank holiday weekends or peak periods? Perhaps it's too simple for rocket scientists. And there are too many agencies involved. NRA came back and said they'd have to get the agreement of about eight different agencies. You get tired at times. You feel you are looking like an eejit when you're talking like this, that you are too radical, that you're better off to sit down and keep your mouth shut.

You can see, there is still a bit of the angry young man in me, but I can't afford to let too much of it come out or I'd be shooting myself in the foot.

We are now getting involved in nursing homes, partnering with a Scandinavian and American company who have one of the biggest aged-care training colleges in the world. Their track record demonstrates their ability to attract people to aged community living centres, not as a last resort, rather as a place where they can enjoy their latter years in a secure, friendly and active environment and with day activity centres for the elderly people of the local catchment area. Uniforms are not worn and residents bring their own furniture. The room is theirs as long as they are there. Privacy is respected. Staff knock on doors before they enter.

Similarly, hospital hotels are a part of what we hope to do with this group — they are vastly cheaper to produce and run than full-blown hospital beds. There will be para-medical care and, if built close to, or adjoining, a hospital, emergency care will be available.

We also hope to do a number of day-surgery units similar to those in North America. These are partly owned by the surgeons along with ourselves and our US partner. Typically, a 15,000-square-foot unit costing £5 million to £6 million would have a throughput of 5,000 operations per annum. This would equate to releasing almost 40 hospital beds per annum, thus reducing waiting lists and saving substantial capital and revenue for the State.

Social housing is another area where, because it is perceived as a problem in Ireland, we have partnered with a company which has 20,000 "for rent only" residential units in America. These developments are rented to one-third full market rent tenants; one-third social welfare tenants; and one-third assisted income tenants. The management is supplemented by a significant social worker back-up and strong tenant involvement. This results in developments which have social housing integrated right through the scheme, but are also sought after by full market rent tenants because of their high quality and management. It is a surprise to most people when they learn that Eastern Health Board rent subsidies in Dublin are over £80 million per annum and that much of it is in poor quality accommodation. There is a sizeable business opportunity here as well as an important social requirement.

The construction and property industry is changing very rapidly. The social requirements in many areas are changing dramatically because of our changed demographics. It is an interesting time to be involved. Hopefully we can make a contribution.

10

Kevin Melia

MSL (Manufacturers Services Limited)

"Finding people who fit is the biggest challenge of all."

Kevin Christopher Melia is Chairman and CEO of MSL (Manufacturers Services Limited).

He was born in Ashford, County Wicklow, on 7 June 1947. His father was Richard Melia, a council worker. His mother was Mary Doyle, a homemaker. He was the third youngest, and the youngest boy, in a family of 11 — six boys and five girls. He is married to Ann-Marie Lally, a homemaker. They have four children: Carena (27), June (23), Sean (17) and Ryan (13). He was educated at the National School in Ashford and the De La Salle Brothers in Wicklow.

In 1965, he started as a wage clerk and storekeeper at the Celmac factory in Wicklow; in 1968, he joined Gaeltarra Eireann as an accountant, becoming financial controller of the knitwear division in 1971. In 1972, he joined the Digital Equipment Corporation (DEC) in Galway as management accountant; in 1975, he was financial controller John Daly & Company, a bottling company in Chapelizod, Dublin; in 1976, he rejoined DEC in the US as controller for a factory being started in Annecy, France; in 1977, he was plant controller for DEC in Galway; he returned to the US in 1978 as the group controller for a number of DEC factories. In 1983, he became manager of the supply chain operation for DEC worldwide; he became a corporate officer in 1986. He left Digital in 1989 for Sun Microsystems as executive vice-president of operations, becoming chief financial officer later that year. He became president of the Computer Systems Group of Sun Microsystems in 1993. In 1994, he left Sun Microsystems to start MSL; their IPO was in June 2000.

He is a member of the Chartered Institute of Management Accountants. He was founding chairman, now a director, of Horizon Technologies, and is a director of IONA Technologies plc; a member of the Board of American CEOs to advise the Taoiseach; a trustee of the Fenn School in Concord, MA. He was Ernst & Young Entrepreneur of the Year for New England in 2001.

The conversation was recorded in the author's home on 7 May 2001.

Kevin Melia

I was one of 11 children, five girls and six boys. I was the youngest
boy and the third youngest child. We lived in a small cottage on a
half-acre site in a village called Ashford, on the main Dublin to
Wicklow road. My father was a council worker and my mother looked
after the home. The home was always a hive of activity — my father
came home from work about 5.30; we would all have dinner; in the
summer evenings he would work in the garden; we would be sum-
moned to help. My father spent most of his spare time tending to the
garden, sowing and growing vegetables, my mother busy in the
house.

Our family was into sports. All my brothers played Gaelic football
for the local club team and a couple of them played inter-county football. Unfortunately, no such outlet was available for our sisters, who
were as interested in sports as the boys and were big supporters.
Most evenings and the weekends were taken up with football. My
parents would travel all over the county and country to support us. I
was introduced to the game at an early age and was good at it, playing
for my club and county. I also won running events at school and later
I ran marathons — I ran the Boston marathon seven times. I learned
a lot playing on the sports fields.

We were a close-knit family. My primary school was about a mile-
and-a-half from our home, a small school with two rooms and two
teachers, and probably about 60 students. I was back in the school
recently — the old two-room school is still standing; they use it as a
kindergarten. They have built a new school with 400 students, a big
change from my day. Being the youngest boy was a help; you always
had the support of the older siblings, and you learned from watching
them. You also knew how much you could get away with.

I was impressed by my parent's ability to raise 11 children on a
half-acre site. It required a lot of initiative. Every piece of that half-
acre was used productively. Like many families in those years, we
learned to be self-sufficient. Their ingenuity has always stayed with

me. My father could use his hands, had a green thumb; and my
mother could sew, make clothes, curtains, cook the finest of food, ca-
ter for a group, keep discipline. They both created their own fun and
pastimes and balanced the budget. They passed on a great set of values to their kids, hard work, be independent, take care of the family.
Idleness was not allowed. From the earliest time I can remember, I
had a job — I was out working or doing chores at home. When the
school year finished you were out to work the following day. You were
part of a team making a living. While I am sure my parents had
stresses and strains keeping us fed and clothed, I carry good memories of those years and learned a great set of values for life.

There was very little money. My mother was determined that the
youngest boy — me — would go to secondary school. Most kids left
school at 13 or 14. I went to the De La Salle School in Wicklow. I rode
a bike to school, about four miles from home. I did well at secondary
school, developed good friendships, played sports, and had a good
relationship with the teachers. I knew there weren't the means to go
on to third-level education. Teaching was an option, but not something I really wanted to do. My best friend at secondary school had
gone on to teaching college. I was tempted for a time to go with him,
but I decided against it. I wanted to see the world. Joining the Irish
Army Cadets was a way out. I liked sports and the outdoor life — and
I wanted to obtain a third-level education. I believed I could achieve
these goals through joining the Cadets. To my surprise, I failed the
physical. I kept myself very fit and I assumed I would pass the medical with flying colours, but I failed the eye test. I remember having to
come home and saying, "I failed" — my first memory of failing
something. That was hard — I was 17 and there weren't many choices
in the mid-sixties in Ireland.

My mother took the initiative — she went to see the Head Brother
at the school. She came home to tell me I had a job starting on Monday in a plastics factory in Wicklow town (Celmac Ltd.). They were
looking for a wage and store clerk. It turned out to be a great move.
My boss — John Divilly — was a chartered accountant and very supportive. The Head Brother at my secondary school had an insight into
my strengths — I was always good at maths, commerce and business
studies, so accounting was a natural fit. John Divilly encouraged me
to study it. I eventually did so and found that I enjoyed it and it
opened up possibilities for me. I had to figure out how I could pursue

the accountancy course. The alternatives I had were go to school at night in Dublin, which was not practical back then — we lived 30 miles from the city — or to do a correspondence course, which is what I did. Studying on my own was not difficult for me, as I enjoy reading and being on my own. My boss also helped me out. I remember well going to Dublin to take Part One of my exams — it was exciting but anxious. I always enjoyed taking exams. It was a lot like sports: be prepared and fit for the battle. I enjoyed the sense of anticipation before receiving the paper and seeing how many questions I could answer. I enjoyed trying to spot questions, where you trace the history of questions over the last number of exams and spot which questions were likely to appear at the next exam. My hit rate was good, but you could not depend on that to pass the exam. I was always well prepared.

I stayed in Celmac until 1968 and then wanted a bigger challenge, and a move to the city. I spent a year trying to find out at what level I could break into another company. In 1968, I joined Gaeltarra Eireann, a State company charged with the development of the Gaeltacht (Irish-speaking) areas of Ireland, mainly down the west coast from Donegal to Cork. I joined a great young group of accountants who had come in to Gaeltarra at that time, headed by Kevin McGoran. We were full of idealism and energy — we were going to bring employment to the Gaeltacht areas of Ireland. I joined up with my best friend from secondary school and found a flat in Dublin. It cost us £2.50 a week. He was studying for a BComm at night at UCD. I'd meet him after work and he would bring me into the cafeteria at UCD, which allowed me buy a hot cheap student's dinner, it also allowed me use the great hall at UCD to study for my accountancy exams. Thank God no one asked me for a student ID! Otherwise, I would have spent the night in a cold flat studying. I enjoyed mixing with the other students. I also realised what I was missing by not going to university, but I never let it bother me.

After joining Gaeltarra, I still had to complete my final accountancy exams. I was lucky with my boss, who was a chartered accountant returned from South Africa. Denis Mulligan was a great teacher and boss, demanding as hell, a stickler for detail and doing it right the first time. My first year or so was based in Dublin and on the four-hour trips to the west of Ireland I would have accounting questions to discuss with him. I had my own captive tutor. It was a perfect combination. I would say I am a very focused person, intense when I pick a goal. My accountancy exams are an example; from Part One until Part Five, I never took a break. I set out to pass an exam every six months. I knew I needed this foundation to create a career for myself. I still found time to pursue other activities I enjoyed. When you plan, set goals, organise and are disciplined, you can achieve a lot. You find time for the important things.

Gaeltarra headquarters were moved down to Furbo, three or four miles west of Galway City. They were looking for volunteers. I thought it would be a great place to move to; Galway had a rich tradition of Gaelic football. It was a university town, looked like a fun place to live for a 23-year-old. My father said, "There's nothing west of the Shannon. Why would you live in such a place?" Such were the views the east coast had of the west coast in the late sixties. I went and it was one of my best moves. I had also met Ann, my future wife, on one of my trips west, so I had an added incentive. My best friend at work planned to move, so it made the decision easy.

On passing my final accounting exams, I was made financial controller of the knitwear division of Gaeltarra. This meant moving to the headquarters of the division in Tourmakeady, County Mayo. In addition, I was involved in the division of Gaeltarra that provided grants to companies starting up. I really enjoyed helping start-up companies. As you know,[1] Gaeltarra was the lender of last resort — people came to us for grants and funding when the Industrial Development Authority or the Shannon Development Company had rejected them, so what you saw was the good and the bad. Unfortunately, there were more people with bad ideas than with good ones. People had not really thought through their business models, but I learned a lot, more from observing the failures than the winners, what not to do and avoid. But we were idealistic, trying to create jobs and I'm not sure we were rigorous enough testing the quality of the business proposals. However, at the age 23 or 25, it was an education to be representing Gaeltarra on the boards of these small companies, getting exposed to what it takes to start a business, win customers, manage cash, hire employees, evaluate people; it's the same challenge whether you are a big or small company. These experiences stood me well. They are the same problems today.

---

[1] The author was Chairman of Gaeltarra Eireann at the time.

I loved living in Tourmakeady — I stayed with the Heneghan family on Lough Mask. You woke up in the morning to a view of the Lough — the Heneghans were big into fishing and farming. Mayo was the Mecca of Gaelic football. Great times. As the financial controller for the knitwear division, I travelled up and down the west coast, from Donegal, where they knitted the Aran sweaters in their homes and you collected them, right down to Ballyvourney in west Cork. These garments and linen products were shipped all over the world. You got really exposed to people with great skills, trying to make ends meet, trying to keep families together, trying to create small enterprises, trying to survive in rural areas. Great people.

Trying to put jobs into remote areas was, to say the least, difficult. We were supposed to be trying to preserve the Irish language as a vernacular by keeping Irish-speaking people in their local areas. When you set up a factory, the first thing they would do was to put up a speaker system that played the BBC. They were learning more English than Irish! They were trying to earn enough income to buy a fare to set off for London — and create a new life. That was sad. And the culture wasn't exactly sympathetic to factory discipline. Sunday night was dance night, people would travel two hours to a dance, going to bed at all hours. You'd go to the factory at eight o'clock on Monday morning and half the workers would not have turned up. You'd get into the car, go up to their houses and try and roust them out so that you would have something like a workforce in the factory. It was a heck of an experience, but it was a forerunner to developing the workforce and the industrialisation that are so successful today.

In 1972, I married, and decided it was time to change my career focus. After qualifying as an accountant in 1970, I decided to continue my studies and undertook a joint diploma in management accounting granted by the accounting bodies in Ireland and the UK. During the course of those studies, I was introduced to the trend of computing in industry. This sparked my interest, and I decided to try and enter the computer industry. I was made a Fellow of the Institute and earned a joint diploma in management accounting in 1976.

The Digital Equipment Corporation had just come into Galway. It was then a $150 million American computer company. It was one of the first American companies to use Ireland as its gateway to Europe. I applied for a job. I also applied to a new company in Castlebar. I ended up getting two offers. We enjoyed living in Mayo, we were deeply involved in the local community, and I was playing Gaelic football — but computers were the attraction, so we moved back to Galway and I took the job in Digital.

Digital was growing fast — it was an entrepreneurial environment. They were at the front end of the whole explosion in the computer industry, growing at 100 per cent a year — a community of young engineers, probably some of the best and brightest people not only in Ireland but from the UK, all pulled together to start up the factory; long hours and many challenges. The Digital philosophy was to load lots of responsibility onto young people's shoulders. You quickly found out if you had it or not. I progressed quickly and then found that I was limited in what I could do locally. An opportunity came up to work with Digital abroad. We loved living in Galway and Ireland, but we had to deal with the big question: should we emigrate? In 1975, we were not ready. We had one daughter.

I got a call from Denis Mulligan, my old boss, now in Fitzwilton, and he offered me a job in Dublin. He had joined the John Daly Company, a Fitzwilton company — Fitzwilton was then a type of conglomerate. I took the job as controller of the Coca-Cola Bottling Company, a subsidiary of the John Daly Company. After six months, I was bored. They had a growth rate of 3 or 4 per cent a year. It was a nine-to-five job. We were living in Leixlip at the time and I could not imagine myself for the next 20 years driving between Leixlip and Chapelizod. I'd go berserk. The company was good to me but I missed the excitement of high-tech, the growth and the opportunities.

Thank God for Digital. I rang my old boss and told him we had decided to emigrate. He said, "Jump on a plane and get over here at the weekend, we'll talk about it and have you signed up." I flew over to Boston and they re-signed me. I was to be part of a team setting up a new factory in Annecy, France.

We spent a year learning French — let our house in Leixlip, rented an apartment in Annecy and, on 4 July 1976, went to the States for three months to join the other members of the team.

You will remember that, at that time, there was a resurgence of French nationalism, led by Jean-Jacques Servan-Schreiber, who wrote *Le Défi Americain*. They thought the Americans were going to take over the world and destroy the French culture. There was distinct anti-American feeling. There was no word coming from France that we were to move out. My boss came in and said, "I've got some bad news for you. The permit for the factory in France has been cancelled." We thought we were emigrating to France and there we were in the United States, myself, my wife and daughter, and a couple of suitcases. Our house in Leixlip had been let, our furniture was on its way to France. I said to my boss, "You have to come home with me and tell my wife that I don't have a job and we're stuck here." I bought a six-pack of beer — it was a hot August day outside Boston. We went over to the house, sat down, he told my wife and we drank beer for the afternoon and he said that everything would work out. I learned the important lesson of flexibility; my wife was great, she was not put out about it all. As happens in life it turned out for the best.

We stayed in the States for that year and ended up really liking it. When I visited the States — which I did a lot between 1973 and 1976 — I was not that enamoured of the lifestyle. When we lived there and involved ourselves in the community, we discovered we liked it. One of the attractive things about the States is the freedom, for better or for worse. If you take that freedom and opportunity and apply yourself, you can really do well; it is a meritocracy. It took us about three years to really settle into the lifestyle, and leave behind the longing for Ireland.

The US has become our home. We enjoy the way of life. We have four children and, while they have strong Irish connections, they are clearly American. We have decided that Boston is our base. The beauty of Boston is its proximity to Europe; a seven-hour flight will connect you to Dublin or London. In addition, the Internet has made the world smaller, you can stay connected real-time to any community in the world. Sports is still a big part of my life, and you can see live all the major sporting events in Europe. One of the great benefits of the Internet is the capability to stay connected to family and friends.

Digital asked me to come back to Ireland in 1977. I came back as plant controller for the Galway plant which was then really ramping up — it was a large facility with a couple of thousand people. We also helped set up a second factory in Clonmel. We came back to Ireland for just 18 months — that was the understanding, and then back to the States in October 1978. Digital had now come from a $150 million company to a $1 billion company and was growing at 100 per cent a year. It was clearly seen as a leader in the industry, a great environment to work in, lots of opportunity. Ken Olsen, its founder, was one of my heroes and his style was to give people lots of responsibility —

the best survived. When you're growing fast, as Digital was doing, you have to pick the best people and put your trust in them. I was on a fast track in Digital — every couple of years I had the opportunity to do new things. Digital was a great training ground for Irish managers — you can see throughout the Irish high-tech industry leaders who got their training at Digital in Galway or Clonmel.

I moved completely out of finance in 1983. As happens when you grow very fast, you eventually hit the wall — the systems just can't keep up with the growth. The company had a major surprise — they almost lost money in one quarter. At the time, they were the darlings of Wall Street. It was a shock. I remember well the atmosphere in the company, a humbling experience. The system was working primarily because of personal relationships. The company was re-organised and all those relationships were disconnected. The system came to a grinding halt — for example, orders from customers could not be found, you couldn't move orders from the sales organisation to the manufacturing plants. There was friction between sales and manu-facturing. I was called one morning at seven o'clock and given the as-signment to go fix the problem. I had to work with the sales people to find out how to quickly connect the sales and the manufacturing or-ganisations. I went in with staff responsibility because what I had to do was to work across a number of line organisations. The way Digital was organised in those days was that you had product lines with global responsibility and geographies with local responsibility. You had constant battles between the product lines, the geographies and then you had manufacturing which was trying to service both the ge-ographies and the product lines. I reported to the head of systems manufacturing, who had responsibility for making sure the ship-ments got out to the customers — and for making sure that the reve-nue for the company was achieved every quarter. It was intellectually challenging — to sit down and figure out the process. It was socially challenging because you had to solve the problems through people and get them to work together and make the processes run smoothly worldwide. We had a good team. We did it. It took 15 months. That was my first step outside pure finance into a line-type role. It was a big break for me — I took it and made it work. I liked the action — you were not counting the beans any more, or advising, you were making it happen. I liked setting goals and leading a team to pull them off.

From there I moved to having responsibility for inventory, logistics, materials systems and purchasing — Digital was purchasing about $2 billion of components a year. By then, 1984/85, Digital was a $5 billion company, growing at 50 per cent a year. We were adding a couple of billion dollars worth of business each year. Putting the systems in place and then managing them efficiently was complex — figuring out how to make a truly global company work with its different systems, its people, its business practices, its computer systems and connecting with suppliers. In 1986, I was made corporate vice-president — I was the youngest corporate VP in the company. I was on a fast track.

A company's most vulnerable time is when it's at its pinnacle — we did not spot, or we ignored, the discontinuity taking place in our industry. In 1984, the personal computer came along. In 1984 there were 1,200 PC companies. People talk about what has recently happened with the dot.com companies. That also happened back in 1984 in the PC space — of the 1,200 PC companies then, there's only one left today, and that's Apple. The PC leaders today came after this period. The same will happen in the dot.com segment. One or two will survive, but the real leaders will come along at a later stage.

Digital did not take the PC seriously. Digital had earned their stripes moving customers from the mainframe to the mini-computer, providing an alternative to the mainframe at a fraction of the cost — they were the mini-computer kings. What that meant was that they were beginning to distribute information away from the magic mainframe in the back room. The mini-computer brought the information down to the department where all the action was — and then to the PC. What surprised me was that we missed that next wave of computing. Disparaging remarks were made that the PC would never succeed. That was the beginning of the end for Digital — they never really recovered from it.

The lesson for me was that you really have to pay attention to the discontinuities that happen in high-tech. If you miss a cycle, it's very hard to get back in the game — not impossible, but difficult. If you have very strong management, you may recover, but its tough. Digital had grown very big. When I joined, it was 5,000 or 6,000 people — by the end of the eighties, it had 135,000. I think we became arrogant, believed our own press, and became internally focused rather than focused on the customer. That happens when a company gets very big and successful. There are phases — there's the $100 million phase, there's the $1 billion phase, there's the $5 billion phase, there's the $10 billion phase, there's the $20 billion phase — at every phase, the nature of the company really changes. If you don't change the organisation as you reach those thresholds, you end up in trouble. Digital's demise could be traced back to the mid-eighties.

In 1989, I left Digital and went to Sun Microsystems, a Silicon Valley-based company — two guys out of Stanford and one out of Berkeley. They were in their late twenties and they were going to change computing and change the world. One night at home, I got a phone call from the CEO of Sun — it was one of those frustrating days at work and I took the phone call! He told me he was going to be in Boston that weekend and would I meet him. There's never anything lost in talking, so I met Scott McNealy, we hit it off and I really liked what they were trying to do. At that time, Sun was a $1 billion company and it had also hit the wall — it lost money for the first time. It had grown very fast and went out of control; the growth stretched the systems and the experience of the people who were managing the company. Scott was wise enough to add some talent to the company — people who had seen the movie. It was similar to what happened to Digital in the early eighties. I think that's why he came after me. I moved from being the fast tracker at Digital to the old experienced head at Sun Micro. It was a big change. Leaving the Digital family after 17 years was very difficult, but it was time to move on. To have witnessed the demise of Digital over the subsequent years was not pleasant for those of us who had experienced the glory days of the company, but it shows you how a once-great company can fall from grace. No one is immune.

I joined Sun as executive vice-president of operations. I moved from Boston to Silicon Valley. There were two exciting things about that move — one was Sun and the other was the Silicon Valley system, a unique system for innovation and entrepreneurship. It's an ecosystem of its own.

I had five good years there — held three senior positions, initially the executive in charge of operations, chief financial officer, and then president of the hardware company. We grew the company from $1 billion to $5 billion with basically the same headcount. I had the opportunity to devise a strategy to use outsourcing of manufacturing as a way to compete in the marketplace. Sun was one of the first companies to do that. Up to then, most OEMs [*original equipment manu-facturers*] were vertically integrated — they did everything themselves, from the sand to the silicon, to building all the computer parts, to doing the installation. Sun was one of the first companies who said that we did not need to do our own manufacturing to compete — we would focus on our core competencies, which were product design, engineering, marketing and selling, brand and channel development. We would outsource all the elements that someone else could make as good as or better than us. This concept became integral to Sun's ability to grow into a global company.

That's where I was introduced to outsourcing. I clearly understood that this was potentially a large market and would grow very fast over the next decade. In 1994, with a partner, I decided to leave the security of Sun and start MSL. We decided on five objectives that have stood the test of time. One, very ambitiously: we would build a global company — in other words, we would start off as a global company. Second: we would provide a full range of services to the OEMs, provide one-stop-shopping for our customers in two dimensions — geographically and with a full range of services. If you as an OEM came to me, we could build a complete product for you and we could build it any place in the world you wanted it built. Third: we would make customer care our top priority — we would build the culture and the processes around the customer and reward people for servicing the customer. Fourth: we would invest significantly in IT and, over time, our IT would differentiate us in the marketplace. We had the simple idea that we would move information, not material. We would postpone the liability for material — we would acquire it as late as possible. We would de-risk the purchase of material, both for ourselves and for our customers — and even for our suppliers. We would use our systems to run the business really efficiently around the world for ourselves, our customers and our suppliers. Fifth: we would put together a management team who had experience running a high-tech, high-growth, global environment company — something that's easier said than done. It's hard to find people who are comfortable dealing with different cultures.

Early in my planning for MSL, I told Kieran McGowan of the IDA what I was thinking of doing. He said there might be an opportunity — there was a company in Athlone, an Ericsson factory where a group of managers did a leveraged buy-out and were open to a partner coming in. He introduced us and that's where I got started. We acquired 51 per cent of the equity. The first year we did $7 million, our portion of the revenue. Now we had a base from which we could build the company. We completed the partnership with the Athlone management in June 1994.

Objectives without capital remain objectives. We had to find a financial institution to back us. I spent some months on Wall Street. A number of institutions were interested and one of them decided they would put up $50 million and become our majority shareholder — Donaldson Lufkin & Jenrette, who are now Crédit Suisse First Boston. We did not want a venture capitalist; we wanted someone who would have the patience to build out a major player in the industry. It was going to take a number of years to put the foundations in place. It was a big risk.

Over the last six years, we implemented those strategies. In January 1995, we acquired a second operation in Minnesota; in September 1995 we acquired from IBM an operation in Valencia, Spain, quite a large operation — it was the big move for us. September 1995, we acquired a private company in Singapore and Malaysia. We wanted to enter Asia. We picked Singapore as our base — we were very comfortable with the processes, the people and the culture. We put our Asian headquarters in Singapore and then, 45 minutes away across the causeway, we set up our Malaysian operation. They were the three initial beachheads in the three different geographies. Since then, in Ireland we have expanded into Galway. Last year, we established our European headquarters there and the person who ran our Irish operations is now running our European operations. In Asia, we've gone into China, in the special economic zone of Shenzhen, about an hour from Hong Kong. Our headquarters in the US are in Concord, Massachusetts; we're also in Minnesota, as I said; Salt Lake City, Utah; in Chicago; in Memphis, Tennessee; in Charlotte, North Carolina; in Richmond, Virginia; in San Jose, California; in Westford and in Lowell, Massachusetts. We now have about 17 locations around the world, with 9,300 people.

In 2000, we took the company public, to get access to the capital markets and to become a public company. Large customers like to deal with public companies and employees like to work for them. Investors like public companies because it gives them the opportunity to exit their investment if they want to do that. This is a unique experience; a very small percentage of start-ups make it to the public markets in the US, so it was a major milestone for us. It's a year-long process and very challenging. It takes tremendous energy. To transition from taking a long-term view of the business when you are private to meeting quarterly targets and Wall Street expectations sharpens the skills of management. The stock price becomes the score that everyone watches. My attitude is: focus on the fundamentals of the business and the stock price will take care of itself. This is particularly true in the current period. We have invested a significant amount of capital over the last six years to build a global company; we have grown at a 57 per cent compound average growth rate; we now must continue to grow and achieve above-average returns. We have built the foundation — we must now build the rest of the house. It's a slow process to build a company, often two steps forward and one back.

Over the last six years, we have built a $1.8 billion company; we are number seven in our industry, 9,300 people worldwide with a diverse customer base — we build products for companies that put their own brand name on the product. I believe you must set high standards and then push yourself and your team to achieve them. I have observed that high achievers set high standards, whether it's in sports or business, and then they apply themselves to turn the standards into reality. The coaches and bosses I remember best and from whom I learned most were those that pushed me. I have applied that philosophy to my life.

You must have three conditions to have a shot at building a new company from scratch. You must have a large market. You must have access to capital — the biggest challenge for a start-up company is under-capitalisation. Husbanding the cash is very important — so many companies just run out of cash. I've learned that it takes longer and costs more to build a business than managers are willing to admit; managers are more optimistic than they should be in setting business plans. Number three is finding the *right* people. I say right people as distinct from good people. You can find good people but they may not fit the model. Finding people who fit is the biggest challenge of all. That's the delimiter to growth. It's very rewarding to see an idea turn into reality, to hire a group of individuals and see them grow successfully. To sow the acorn and see the tree blossom. You must believe you can win and overcome any barrier.

We've been affected, like everyone else, by the present downturn. Growth can cover many sins, but a slowdown tests you. Managers have to make the tough decisions and you soon find out who can make them and who can't. The most difficult action in a slow economy is to have to let people go, but you have to face reality and position your team to deal with the volatility of the marketplace. There are no guarantees. Many companies went through denial in the December quarter. Up to last February, they believed it was not as bad as it was. As a result, they were slow to act, and now must play catch- up.

In October 2000, on a trip around the world visiting customers, it began to appear to us that things were changing. As part of our planning process last October, we took a pragmatic approach to 2001. Our challenge is to manage our way through this very volatile market, take whatever actions are needed while not impairing our capability for the long term — more an art than a science. Forecasting what will happen is always difficult. Flexibility is key.

Looking back, 1999 and 2000 were two exceptional years for the high-tech industry. A number of factors came into play. You had Y2K momentum, which caused a lot of spending. In the telecom space, the spending on Internet infrastructure was exceptional — there was a tremendous amount of capital expenditure. The telecom companies around the world incurred a significant amount of debt — $150 billion. Then there was the whole Internet dot.com phenomenon. The venture capitalists fuelled that. They spent freely and then the equity markets became a source of VC funding — very unwise. The excesses of the last couple of years have been significant — it's going to take another two years for the telecom companies to right themselves.

The telecom space is in intensive care — companies who are building infrastructure for the Internet. You've got to separate that group from the rest. There are positive signs in other sectors. In our business, we have a diverse customer base. We build product for the retail sector, a segment that's doing quite nicely. If you go into a large store, whether it's a Wal-Mart, a K-Mart or a McDonalds, the checkout equipment could be built by MSL. That market is strong. If you use an organiser or a PDA [*a personal digital assistant*] or a palm-pilot, we build those products for that market and it will do OK. The PC is disintegrating — the functionality is been transferred to smaller devices. For example, I don't need to lug around a big PC with all this functionality in it. All I need is a device that can plug me into the network and give me my e-mail. So devices (fixed and wireless) that connect you to the Internet will continue to have good demand.

Today, electronics are in everything, whether they're industrial products, like elevators, or escalators, in automobiles, and across a wide spectrum. We build products for industrial customers — and they are doing well. The telecoms have all the attention. The media are focused on how a few are not doing well, versus the many out there that are doing well. Sure, some of the few are big, like Cisco, but other high-tech companies are doing OK. Growth is not 25 per cent or 30 per cent like it used to be, it's more like 10 per cent or 15 per cent. That type of growth is all right, people forget that. It's better than the 0 per cent to 5 per cent of the old-line companies. There are household names in the telecom space that may be suffering because of the excesses of the last two years — the market was over-priced. I have learned that things are never as bad or as good as they are painted, and for sure the experts will be wrong on the forecasts. It will take us till 2002 to put some of the major problems behind us in high-tech. The good news for the US economy is that inflation is low, unemployment is low by historical standards, and there are new products from high-tech companies coming along which will create new demand. Hopefully, Europe will show reasonable growth. So, 2001 will be a tough year, but we'll climb out of it in 2002 and 2003. The number of people connected to the Internet is still very small, and the Internet is changing and will change how industry does business. The Internet is in its infancy.

The dot.coms were just an unreal phase. I have had many arguments about the dot.coms' business models — if you can't see your way to making money, you should not be in business. Valuing companies based on revenue, based on the number of subscribers — and the idea that generating cash flow and being profitable does not matter — that just amazed me. The good news out of it is that it has stimulated a lot of innovation. It has forced companies to use technology in a more productive fashion.

There was no sentiment in setting MSL up in Ireland — you can't have sentiment in business. That does not mean that you don't care about people. You must invest in them. I'm afraid I believe the old saying: no good deed goes unpunished. Sentiment and emotion are the enemy of trying to run a business. I like to plan and run the business on data, collect it, debate it, think about it and complement it with your instincts. If, after that process, we feel good about a proposal, then we do it. I believe that you must also measure performance — marshalling data is key to running a business. When you are starting a company, you have an exciting idea, but you have to get traction. Otherwise, it just remains an idea.

I look back with fondness on the range of experiences I have had over my career — from small companies to large ones, to starting my own. It's been a privilege to have witnessed and participated in the significant changes and advances that have taken place in the high-tech industry — from the mainframe to the mini-computer, to the PC, to the network and finally to the start of the Internet. It's rewarding to have contributed to the growth of the high-tech industry in Ireland and to have seen the good policies and hard work by many people pay off. I do hope the current generation in Ireland appreciates what they have and the choices that are open to them today. I was inspired by the leaders in Ireland since the foundation of the State, people like Ken Whitaker.[2] Getting to this point may be the easy part — sustaining success will be the hard part. Developing the right policies for the future will be critical. I hope we see future growth and job creation come from indigenous companies. This will demand an environment where risk-taking is supported, failure is seen as a badge of courage, capital is available, and leaders can compete and win in global markets. My advice to young managers and graduates is to take risks early and help establish a culture of building successful Irish global companies.

The high-tech industry in Ireland has so much to be thankful for to those people who brought Digital to Ireland and the influence it has had on the high-tech industry. I am grateful for the doors it opened for me, and the experiences and success I have enjoyed by walking through them.

---

[2] *In Good Company*, pp. 279–305.

11

Michael Murphy

Dairy Farmer

"I'd like to see people coming into farming having a clear sense of strategic direction, a sense of vision, the ability to set clear objectives and follow through on them, to have their own plan — not one prepared by somebody else."

Michael Peter Murphy is a dairy farmer.

He was born in Cork on 6 December 1948. His father is Noel Murphy, a cattle exporter. His mother was Hilda Cagney. He was second in a family of five, three boys and two girls: Tim, David, Noelle and Judith. He is married to Geraldine (Dena) O'Brien, a nurse. They have four children: Michelle (26), Nuala (24), Niall (21), and Brian (18).

He was educated at Rathpeacon National School; at Christian Brothers College, Cork; he spent one year at UCD Veterinary College, and after three years round the world, he went to Warrenstown Agricultural College, followed by the Farm Apprenticeship Scheme. He qualified as a farm manager. He later did an MBA in UCC.

He joined the Norwegian Merchant Navy as a Deck Boy, eventually becoming Young Man (1967). In New York, 1968–1969, he was Deck Hand on the Alexander Hamilton, the last steamship that went up and down the Hudson; he was also a debt collector in Harlem. In 1969, he returned to Warrenstown and then the Farm Apprenticeship Scheme. He began dairy farming in 1974. He now derives 80 per cent of his income from non-farming activities.

He is a director of The Farmers' Journal; director of Binary Investments, a venture capital company; director of Blackwater Trading Company. He participates in the running of a Wealth Creation Course for farmers. He spends one-third of his time in the voluntary educational area for farmers. He was a winner of the Sir Charles Harvey Award as first in his MBA class in UCC; first in the Farm Management Cert. in Ireland; and a holder of the Farm Apprenticeship Millennium Award.

The conversation was recorded in the author's office in University College Dublin on 16 February 2001.

Michael Murphy

Even though I'm from a farming background, I was born in 1948 in Gardner's Hill in Cork City. I spent my first eight years there before moving out to the country in 1956. I was lucky that I was born into a happy family. I would not have seen much of my father in the earlier years. He was in partnership with his brother in five or six farms. He was also involved in the cattle business. He worked long hours but, in the summertime, I'd go out to fairs with him and to farms to buy cattle. My father was an entrepreneurial man with a good work ethic. From him I would have learned the psychology of negotiating. My mother was a remarkably intelligent person. She was first in Ireland in her exams and spent the last couple of years at school in England where she was also first. Both my parents were very keen on sports. My mother was an international hockey player. She had an international outlook, which was a contrast to Irish attitudes at that time. I was not exposed to the national inferiority complex and the anti-British attitude that was once so prevalent.

My mother was dedicated to the family, so we had a strongly supportive environment. She was a voracious reader, eight to ten books a week. I was interested in reading about sport, reports of matches or whatever. I was reading quite well at three years of age, before I went to school. Memories of childhood are happy ones. In a family of five — three boys of which I was number two, and two girls — we competed ferociously among ourselves at hurling, tennis, soccer, rugby. We were catholic in our tastes.

It was great when we moved to a big old house out in the country. It was surrounded by trees and was a marvellous environment to grow up in. We probably led a sheltered existence. At that stage, I had been at Christian Brothers College in Cork. When we moved to the country, I went to Rathpeacon National School and then, in time, back to CBC. We lived only two-and-a-half miles from the city. You had the amenities of the city and the freedom of the country. We did not live in an affluent way but we were quite comfortably off. I never

remember money being an obstacle. We would go for holidays to
Garryvoe and Youghal.

After the fairs with my father, we would go buying cattle in the
country. We were horrified by the poverty. You'd always be invited
into the house for a cup of tea. You'd be brought into the best room —
the parlour — and it would be damp. The housing stock was poor —
dark and damp. I was always impressed by the decency and friendli-
ness of people, but the circumstances in which they lived were difficult. It was better to drink tea rather than milk, because brucellosis
was endemic. You would get the best of what was going. I remember
one unmarried farmer who was living with a couple of his sisters and
was better off than most — with him you'd get four or five lamb chops
followed by raspberries and cream. He would then apologise because
he hadn't "anything decent to eat". My brothers and I reckoned it was
the best feed on the road.

Back in the fifties, cattle were still sold in the old way — people
liked doing deals, negotiating and swapping stories. The cattle trade
hasn't a great reputation but my father and my family have always
had a reputation for straight dealing. I would have got an appreciation for good cattle, straight dealing and a good, continuing business
— and an absolute rejection that you would ever pull a fast one on
people. That was ingrained in me from an early stage. My father
would call back on people year-in, year-out, so there would have been
a strong friendship between them. When you were negotiating a deal,
it would be a friendly contest. It was easier if the two of you knew
where the bargaining was going to end up, that is with people who
knew the value of their cattle. Problems would come with somebody
with whom you were friendly and who did not know the value of his
cattle — how were you going to shift him from this level to that level
in a way that left him feeling pretty good.

There's a story about a time my mother came out with us. It was
one of those occasions when the farmer had genuinely overvalued his
cattle — he thought they were heavier than they were. One of the
things you do when you are negotiating in a situation like that is not
to keep hammering at it but break off and ask if he thinks Munster
will beat the All Blacks or Cork will beat Tipperary and then gently
come back to the bargaining. This is what my father did and he said,
"What's this you were asking me? Was it £60?" And mother came in
and said, "No, no, it was £66." And all the psychology went down the

drain. In any walk of life, even in the cattle trade, the chancers don't survive over any length of time. Honesty, straight dealing, is the only way to do business over a period.

As well as sport and reading, I was hugely interested in current affairs. When I was in school I used buy two or three papers a day and one or two of the serious English ones. I was able to go through school comfortably without ever working at it. If the school syllabus didn't interest me, I'd read something else. I was reading, I was learning, but not necessarily what was on the syllabus. There were 15 or 16 Christian Brothers in the school and my memories of all of them, bar one, are good. They are much maligned and I think it's unfair — most of them were decent people trying to do their best. Men like Brother Gibson and Brother Reynolds were people of high integrity and gentlemen. I had the misfortune to have the bad apple in charge of me from second to fifth year. He just moved up as I moved up. He was definitely not an advertisement for the Christian Brothers. We had an all-out war for three or four years. I would look back on it as character-forming! I would stress, however, that he was not typical of the other Brothers. I majored in sport and was never particularly serious about my studies. I somehow managed to get honours English by writing the essay in the morning and studying Milton's *Paradise Lost* at lunchtime for the afternoon exam paper.

When I left school, I had no clear idea of what I wanted to do — except, perhaps, I had decided I did not want to go farming. For want of a better idea, I went up to Dublin to do veterinary. I didn't like veterinary much but I thoroughly enjoyed Dublin — that was 1966/67. At the end of the year, I was doing a physics practical. Dr Scott was the lecturer in charge. After 15 minutes, I was walking out and he asked me if I was feeling all right. He asked me if I would not stay and give it a chance. I told him there was no point, I had not been at the practicals. At that stage, I certainly was not setting objectives for myself. There was an element of finding myself — I did not look upon it as a wasted year.

The World Trade Fair, Expo 67, was on in Montreal in the summer of that year. I wanted to go to Montreal. I hadn't the price of it and I was too independent to ask. I went to England for the summer and, within two or three weeks, I did a bit of research and joined the Norwegian Merchant Navy, in particular a ship that was chartered out to Canadian Pacific, going up the Great Lakes with a stop in

Montreal. I suppose I got to Montreal through a bit of lateral think-ing! I believe a "can-do" attitude is the key to overcoming problems.

The Navy was a great experience. I was the lowest of the low: a Deck Boy. After a bit, I graduated to being a Young Man. (If I'd stayed on I would have become an Ordinary Seaman.) I left after six months and, looking back, working with people of different nationalities — Norwegian, British, quite a few Spaniards — gave tremendous aware-ness. Being at sea, I had to grow up quickly and look after myself. It was fascinating to see how different nationalities, different countries organised work. One of the ports we called to was London, which was then still the largest port in the world. It was incredibly inefficient, badly managed and under-invested. Labour relations were terrible. In Rotterdam, they were already containerising — the quality of thinking there was quite different. It was different again in the States where in some ports there was union labour and in others non-union, who were worked incredibly hard. What I learned was to get exposed not just to ideas in your own situation — whatever field you're in, find the best thinkers, nationally first, and then internationally. The port of London did not adapt to change and the seeds of its destruction were clearly visible. London probably does not now do one-tenth of the business it did.

Before it was fashionable, I went on a student visa to New York and stayed on — so I was illegal. New York in 1969 was a wonderful place to be single and to be young. It was exciting, always in top gear, and you could do anything — as a university of life, you were mixing and mingling with people from all sorts of backgrounds. I worked for three or four months on the *Alexander Hamilton*, a paddle-wheel steamer that used take two or three thousand people up the Hudson River from New York past Westpoint. Very close to Westpoint they had about 200 naval ships left over from various wars, all kept in perfect condition. Some of them, when I was there in the late sixties, would have been called into service for Vietnam. It was an indication of the wealth of the country that 200 ships, in perfect condition, could in effect be held for whatever emergency might arise.

I had been in situations where I had to be self-reliant — one of the more interesting jobs I had was as a debt collector down in Harlem. I had a huge amiable black man, Charlie Brown, as my bodyguard. Charlie fought for the World Heavyweight title in 1951 — he obviously didn't win! He was a very nice and very gentle man. This was at a period when there were major riots in Harlem. You also had riots in Watts, Newark and Detroit. There was unrest in the black ghettos and most white people would not go within a mile of Harlem. The only white people I'd meet would be four or six policemen together. Fire brigade calls — false alarms — would be put in regularly. The fire brigade and ambulances and police cars would arrive and they would be sniped at with guns, just for the hell of it. The sports stars were the kings and queens of Harlem and with Charlie Brown I was never subjected to hostility. Only once was I attacked physically and that was by a woman.

In Harlem, I would again have seen extreme poverty. I loved the freedom and enterprise of the States but equally I did not like the extremes of poverty. I've always been a strong believer in free enterprise but wonder whether there should be a little more support for the under-privileged in the States. One of the abiding lessons of working in the US would be the optimism and energy.

I went back to Ireland in September 1969. I wanted to be my own boss, wanted to work outdoors. Three years after I had decided that I did not want to be a farmer, the idea sounded attractive. I think I liked the challenge of farming. Bear in mind that what I had seen of farming with my father was an enterprising approach, since he and his brother were running six or seven farms and also running a business. They were not buried down on the farm. I use the term "buried down on the farm" to describe a mentality among some farmers that they have to be working long hours every day with their hands. I preferred to use my brain more and my hands less, so that I also had time for many other activities. My attraction to farming was not a romantic notion. Though I had enjoyed New York, I did not want to live in a city. I liked the people in the farming sector. I liked then, and I like now, the decency in them, the humanity and humility.

One of the things I liked about farming was that you could be in on the conception and implementation of an idea, you could go right through the cycles and, at the end, you were either successful or unsuccessful, depending largely on your own efforts. You could see cause and effect in a broad range of challenges. You could see the direct consequences of your decisions and actions. If I set myself particular objectives, there was no reason why I could not measure myself against them. If I failed it was down to myself, 100 per cent. And it's less difficult in the country rearing a family with a reasonable set of values. It's a healthy, sane environment, with a possibility of bringing up well-adjusted people who would have a reasonably broad range of experience. A farm is a wonderful place for family life.

Even people who are running pretty successful farms are generally held in low esteem by society. The people I mix with are very adaptable and do very well when they try different things. It's a good training to make balanced decisions. When I was on the MBA programme, we had to do a certain amount of project work in teams. I found my background helpful in assessing cases in policy, in marketing or whatever — running a very small business where you're responsible for a lot of functions is a good way to bounce things around and make decisions. That would not be the usual perception but it would be my belief that a good all-rounder is more likely to exercise common sense and reasonable balance in decision making than a highly trained — but narrowly based — specialist.

It's important to say that I did not drift into farming — I chose it. The idea was that I would do first a theoretical year — which I did. I thought I knew something but I lacked the practical base. I got frustrated at my lack of capability. There's always a danger in Irish farming that you become "The Boy" and never get the opportunity to use your initiative. I was first in Ireland that year at the agricultural college and I thought I knew something. Remember, I had *chosen* to go farming, so I really applied myself. I looked for more practical farm management training and spent three years, one year at a time, with three selected farmers. I had seen a bit of life at this stage and I had decided that, whatever I was going to do, I was going to do well.

There is a Farm Apprenticeship Board, with a full-time staff, who select some of the best farmers in the country. You spend a year living in turn with three farmers. You have to keep a diary, spend two weeks at a college each year. I was lucky to be exposed to one or two really good thinkers. It was a very practical training and you saw different ways of doing things. I was with a farmer, John Leeson, near Bray, County Wicklow. John told me *The Farmers' Journal* was having a trip to New Zealand in 1972 and under no circumstances should I miss it. The New Zealanders were the best in the world at low-cost grass-based dairying. I applied to the *Journal* for a scholarship — I would have been the leading farm apprentice in the country at that time. Paddy O'Keeffe of *The Farmers' Journal*, who became a great friend afterwards, turned me down — he did not know me from

Adam. And the Apprenticeship Board refused me leave of absence. It would have been highly unusual to have an apprentice on a trip like that. John Leeson suggested that I should pay the deposit, go on the trip and worry about the balance afterwards — which is what I did. I took the leave of absence from the Apprenticeship Board anyway.

We had a stopover in Hawaii and one of our party got into a bit of trouble swimming. I pulled him out, with the help of others. If we hadn't, the trip would probably have been cancelled at that stage.

The trip cost £535. I could afford the £135 deposit — I was making £11 a week. About two weeks after the trip, I was a last-year apprentice and I'd been cut back to £9 a week. I got a call for the balance, the £400. I was flat broke. I needed a car because I was doing a line with my future wife at that time. I offered to pay it back at £2 a week. Paddy O'Keeffe's secretary was to relay this fact to him. A strangled silence came back, "Mr O'Keeffe says to forget about it." Back in the eighties, I became an unpaid writer for the *Journal* and in the nineties a director — so I hope I repaid that debt in full.

The main point of the trip was that I would have been exposed to the people who went out there, the most progressive people in Irish agriculture. They had been carefully selected by Paddy O'Keeffe. And being exposed to the best thinkers in New Zealand was a seminal thing. It gave me an insight into the possibilities of really good grass-based farming. From that point onwards, I had a clear vision of the approach I wanted to take.

Dairy farming in New Zealand is not a way of life — it's very much a business. Given the economic environment, they have to be super-efficient. They have simple but effective systems, relatively non-demanding on capital. It was a great model to get at an early, impressionable age. I was repeating, at the farming level, what I had learned with the Navy — get out and see. That was a defining moment for me in New Zealand. Learn from the best and then try to do even better. I would strongly urge young people to get into "good company", positive thinkers in your selected field.

I qualified as a farm manager in 1973 and got married a month later and was keen to go and farm in New Zealand. My father and mother did not want me to go, so they signed over to me 127 acres, one of five or six units that were owned between my father and his brothers. It was highly unusual, in Irish farming terms, to be my own boss at 24. I had £200 of capital and no stock, so I had to borrow for stock and for machinery, for a milking parlour and paddocks — and build a house. I would have been heavily in debt then — £40,000, extremely heavy in those years. I bought 100 heifers and started. However, I was young and enthusiastic and, above all, had a clear vision of what I wanted to do. I had a huge belief in really low-cost grass dairy farming. It was an exciting period — we had just got into the EU and prices were rising. That first year I started, 1975, there was a big cattle collapse. Calves were virtually unsaleable. Everybody talked about a crisis. At the end of the year, I had paid off about one-third of my debt and I thought, "If this year is a crisis, it's not a bad business to be in!" Within four years I had cleared the debt — but I worked extremely hard — I was an Indian, not a chief. Through the eighties, I began to lease a number of farms. By the later eighties, I was dairy farming on seven units.

About 1984, I realised I needed some further training in management. I decided to do a post-experience MBA in University College Cork. On Tuesdays, Wednesdays and Thursdays, there were three hours of classes, 4.30 to 7.30. I was only 25 minutes away from the campus. I was hands-on farming at the time and I completely underestimated the amount of time it took to do an MBA. People who do an MBA tend to get a lot of their work delegated to other people. That wasn't really possible in my situation, so after 12 months, something had to give. I hired another person — it was not a planned move, it was a reaction to a particular situation, but it was a key success move. From that point, I became less hands-on and more into management. That, in turn, led to being a strategic investor. Under pressure, I simply had to organise things better, to find the time to study and learn. Time management is a critically important skill. I would suggest everyone should evaluate themselves. What have I contributed to my business this week? Have I used my time to best effect?

I believe the key to progress in any field of human endeavour is relevant knowledge. I had been working 90 to 100 hours a week and hardly seeing the family. From then on, I valued and measured the effectiveness of my time. If I'm a hands-on farmer, I'm worth £8 to £10 an hour. If I'm making decisions on farm management based on measurement, I'm worth £100 an hour. If I'm making decisions as a strategic investor, I'm worth £500 to £1,000 an hour. It was probably necessary to get overloaded to clarify all that.

I loved the MBA, particularly when we were divided up into teams to work through case studies. The MBA was done on the basis of the Harvard Case Study Method. I enjoyed the interaction and the different experiences and disciplines of the participants. The visiting lecturers were superb. I would have to compliment our professor about that — Leonard Wrigley, a Harvard doctor of business administration. I remember Howard Stevenson, the professor of entrepreneurship at Harvard. He strongly influenced me. I did a thesis which compared the then Kerry Co-Op, now Kerry Group, and Dairy Denmark, now MD Foods Denmark. The thesis was about the kind of strategies they each had to follow to enable them to grow successfully in different environments. Exposure to the clarity of strategic thinking of Denis Brosnan,[1] head of the Kerry Group, caused me to examine what I had been doing. I had been very successful but I had been largely opportunistic. Probably from that point, I became more strategic. Going through the Kerry story, where the Group had been exposed to commodity milk, something which is subject to the decisions of politicians, I very quickly made the connection in terms of what *I* was doing.

Denis Brosnan was very generous with his time and I studied carefully what he had to say. I could see the strategic implications for my own business. At that stage I would have been 98 per cent dependent on farming within the Common Agricultural Policy. It made me reflect on whether or not that system was sustainable — open-ended intervention at generous prices. Clearly it wasn't. I took a decision that, within three years, I would have 30 per cent of assets outside of farming. I believed that being in a highly regulated business which was 100 per cent dependent on the whims and actions of politicians was a position of huge vulnerability. I needed to change my tactics. And now, even though I'm still heavily involved in farming, 80 per cent of my assets are outside it. That proportion is likely to continue moving in the same direction. I really appreciated Denis Brosnan sharing with me his thoughts on that occasion. People with Denis's type of ability are remarkably open in helping others. It was an easy decision to invest in Kerry Group in 1986. I believe Kerry's success story is likely to continue for many years.

---

[1] *In Good Company*, pp. 57–75.

Back in the fifties, as I said, I had seen a lot of rural poverty. I took a decision that I wanted to be involved in helping the sector to be more efficient, more businesslike, and to face up to what I saw was an inevitable adjustment. The Common Agricultural Policy was driven by the great world wars where, in particular, Germany and France faced one another — that could never be allowed to happen again. Even though I had benefited from the CAP, I could see that this would reverse. As well as shifting my own business, I wanted to help the farming sector be alert to what it faced. It's a sector where we tend to allow other people to do our thinking for us. The CAP was good for Ireland in the seventies and eighties, but it distanced people from real markets and when that bubble bursts, there is a very painful adjustment period. My concern for the sector as a whole was not something out of the blue. I had been president of the Irish Grassland Association.

I was involved in several discussion groups. I had farm groups visiting my farms regularly. I was part of a group with Paddy O'Keeffe and others who strongly believed in the value of good research, sharing of information. So I set myself the objectives of developing my farming business, growing business rapidly outside farming, but equally to try to be of value to people in the rural sector generally.

To give myself more time, I had a bias towards fewer, bigger units where I could get professional help, which I could incentivise by having equity participants. I moved gradually down that path. Sometimes that was restricted by regulations — the agricultural sector is extraordinarily regulated: in farming, you're not allowed increase sales, you are a price-taker. It's very much a dependency situation.

Within the general business area, I had an objective of doubling net assets every four to five years. For many years I have been strongly influenced by the common sense and sound business principles of Warren Buffett — I strongly recommend a study of Buffett for every young person. And it was easier to get good returns outside farming. I also looked at farming outside Ireland and this led to my investing in New Zealand. Within farming itself, I wanted to be more efficient, to scale up to fewer units with better people whose interests would be precisely aligned with the interests of the business.

In the late eighties, I believed the farming sector had lost its way. The Irish competitive advantage is a climate in the path of the Gulf Stream. It's a climate ideally suited to growing cheap feed — a long grass-growing season. We had good skills and good research in terms of grassland management. The advantage was always that we were a low-cost producer. Then in the eighties, people began to drift, to lose focus, to build in extra costs. By the late eighties, the sector as a whole was going the wrong way.

In 1989–91, I went off on a planned series of study trips to New Zealand. I started in the warmer part, the North Island, with a climate unlike Ireland. It's the traditional dairy area. Then I went to the South Island, which is much colder, to see if the principles and practices developed in the North Island were relevant to a situation akin to Ireland's. Southland Province was virtually identical to Cork in terms of climate. The best practitioners were in the Waikato, a warm area. They were producing milk at 14 or 15 pence per gallon. In Southland, a cold area, they were producing milk at 18 pence. In Ireland, the average costs of production were about 60 pence, with the best people doing it at 40 to 45 pence per gallon. And yet the difference climatically between the Waikato and Southland was probably five times larger than the differences between Southland and Ireland. I felt there was something of real value there. I had always been on the low-cost end of things and highly profitable in an Irish context but I saw this as an opportunity to bring my own business to a higher level, really thinking through why, if the New Zealanders could do it, we could not. If we could not fully close the gap, we could at least close it partly. But I also wanted to see if it had a general application to the industry — to change the industry. You could see there's a bit of the missionary there!

I decided to try to do it at several levels. First, I wanted to put researchers in Ireland in contact with other researchers in New Zealand. Initially, I was extremely disappointed at the lack of a spirit of intellectual curiosity among researchers and the resistance to ideas from anywhere else, particularly ideas coming from farmers. That's now thankfully in the past. Moorepark Research Station is now well managed — the importance of good leadership at every level is critical. I became frustrated at my own communication skills and my inability to get people to change, so in 1991 I persuaded a couple of New Zealand Extension people to come over here — in Ireland we would call them advisers — Sharon Holmes and Alistair Rayne. They subsequently got married and are now dairy farming successfully in New Zealand. Instead of experts going out and telling people what to do, their approach was very simple — get people together in discussion groups. They focused on the *relevant* issues. On the day, they picked one or two relevant things and went into them in detail and got people discussing them and working them through. It was a gradual bottom-up approach — they were getting people to think for themselves. At first, it was a culture shock.

Now these took place with groups of 15 or 20 farmers out on the farm, not in a schoolroom atmosphere. Gradually there was a breakthrough as people began to *think*. Gradually we got people to become more businesslike — how would you extend the grazing season, how would you minimise costs? We have had New Zealanders here for ten years: as well as the original two, we had Leonie Foster, Ken Bartlett and Bryony Fitzgerald (from Australia) and a few more. It was so successful that the discussion groups proliferated. Teagasc has got in on the act and has partly improved their service. People began to think both operationally and managerially. Farmers managed their grasslands better, got their calves at the right time of the year and then began to make better investment decisions. That, in turn, led to a demand for information on investing outside the farming sector. Enterprise is now much more a feature than it ever was in the past. The best dairy farmers in Ireland are now the best dairy farmers in Europe and they are expanding their businesses outside farming. What it proved was that the way to communicate was to have a well-run farm in a particular location so that people could see for themselves and get reassurance that it could be done. If you're a farmer in Cork, it's not much use being told there's somebody good in Monaghan. You want a farm down the road so that you can see the possibilities in your own situation. It's always great when you can learn cheaply by seeing, hearing and reading about the mistakes and successes of others. Of course, human nature being what it is, much learning will be secured expensively through the mistakes we make ourselves.

I strongly believe that Ireland has the potential to be the New Zealand of Europe, to be extremely competitive in the longer term. If the industry got its act together, we could be the lowest-cost producer on a sustainable basis. To do so, the sector has to make a huge change. Government, and the farm organisations in particular, have a backward-looking attitude. They are trying to defend something that is not defensible — it's not sustainable, it's gone. Instead of having a clear vision of what we might become and try and work towards that, we carry on trying to resist change. It just won't work. It's a little like trying to hold back the tide of history. If we recognise that and if we decided as a nation that grassland farming had a sustainable competitive advantage within Europe — if we got our act in order, as and when free competition in farming comes in Europe, *we should be the ones to win that competition*. We can produce milk at a cost far lower than anybody else, both at an operational cost and at a capital cost. Milk from grass-fed cows is high in conjugated linoleic acid (CLA), a fatty acid found in milk fat which has considerable health benefits in terms of cancer and heart disease prevention — an extraordinary marketing advantage, which has not been communicated to consumers. The skills are there, but we need to commit substantial resources beyond the farm gate to both marketing and product development. We need to invest heavily in our future.

There is a problem with an ageing farmer population at a time when the economy was never more prosperous. Where people do not have a good living on a farm, they should be encouraged to look elsewhere. Treat them with dignity — but there is a necessity to adapt. There will inevitably be less subsidisation for farmers in the future but that message is not being spelled out to people. The profit they will make from a given level of farm production will be less and less in the future. Major change is inevitable.

The EU has created a culture of dependency. When I started farming, farmers were relatively independent — they did not get cheques in the post. Gradually, particularly in the nineties, we have got to a situation where farmers are completely dependent on those cheques. Their income is more dependent on farming the CAP than on using energy and initiative and being business-like. The farm organisations, as I said, are looking through a rear-view mirror, trying to protect the older farmers from change, instead of seeing that, if we want to have a lively farming sector in the future, we need to give opportunity to young people. That will take leadership and vision.

Decisions in and about the agricultural sector are short-term. Kerry and IAWS would be about the only organisations really "sensing" the future: they are thinking things through. "Sensing" the future is notably absent in the sector as a whole.

Irish people adapt well to a free-market situation — we're relatively energetic. I believe we're naturally enterprising. What we have in the sector is a lack of leadership, of visionaries, of clear thinking. We should turn our backs over time on beef and concentrate on the dairy industry. The beef industry is a dead duck. I would like to see us in 15 or 20 years producing twice, three or four times the present Irish quota. We would be the low-cost producers, we'd have a number of world-class performers at dairy company level. I'd like to see a young, adaptable workforce on farms. I'd like to see people who come into farming having a clear sense of strategic direction, a sense of vision, the ability to set clear objectives and follow through on them, to have their own plan — not one prepared by somebody else. We need farmers to be businesslike, to have a strong culture of measurement. Decisions must be based on good information. We need to move away from commodity meat and become a dairying country. We need to have a product that is well marketed, well understood by the consumers of Europe, a product that has strong health benefits, a premium product at premium prices, delivered at extremely low cost. I believe we have the possibility of a farming sector that is competitive, is adding value both for the country and for individuals, where people are using their initiative and enterprise and can live in a sane, safe environment and have decent levels of income. That's the kind of vision I have. We can do it if we have strong leadership, well-thought-through policies which are consistently implemented.

There is nothing I find more satisfying than trying to help people to help themselves, working with people who want to make progress. One of the lessons I've learned is that, if people are not interested in making progress, forget it. I like working with interested people who are very positive about their future, to help people take control, to clarify their sense of direction, to be good at what they do, so that they lead happy, balanced lives. There is a very enterprising segment — I emphasise *segment* — of Irish farmers who are now making five times the income that they would have made five years ago, by farming better and by using the free cash to grow in other areas outside of farming.

In some sectors, information is jealously guarded. Among the progressive farmers, information is freely shared and, once you get people thinking, it becomes unstoppable.

We have national agricultural policies that are almost geared to minimising talents. We need first a realistic evaluation of where we are and what the prospects are. In industrial policy, we're pretty good at targeting, for example, the high-tech and the pharmaceutical sectors — and those policies have been consistently applied with excellent results. If we, as a nation, realise that we have an indigenous resource that is absolutely sustainable and is capable of providing a huge income over time, then we need to position ourselves to be competitive, because that is the way the world is moving.

We have the possibility of having a superb dairy industry in the future. Have we the right people to measure up to that challenge?

Martin Naughton

Glen Dimplex

*"The kick I get personally is in the joy of making products.
There's a lovely satisfaction seeing a sketch on a piece of paper or
a wooden model and then to be walking down the street in Oslo
and seeing the product in a shop window, or going into somebody's house, or into a hotel, and seeing your products there."*

Martin Lawrence Naughton is chairman of Glen Dimplex.

He was born in Dublin on 2 May 1939. His father, Martin, was a garda. His mother is Mary Ryan. He was the second eldest and the oldest boy in a family of seven: Nuala, Kathy, Jo, Maureen, Richard and Gay. He is married to Carmel McCarthy, a schoolteacher, now chairman of the National Gallery of Ireland. They have three children: Fiona (32), Neil (31) and Fergal (24).

He was educated at the De La Salle College in Dundalk; then, while working with Hawker Siddley, did a five-year engineering apprenticeship at Southampton College of Technology. He switched to industrial engineering. He is a Fellow of the Work Study Society and Fellow of the Work Study Practitioners.

After Hawker Siddley, he joined SPS in Shannon as a work study engineer (1961); then joined AET in Dunleer as chief work study officer. In 1962, he was headhunted back to Shannon to Callins, which had broken away from SPS, where he worked as services manager. He returned to AET in 1965 as deputy works manager. In 1973, he left AET to form a greenfield company, Glen Electric. Glen Dimplex was formed in 1977.

He has avoided outside directorships. He is a member of the Council of State with which the President of Ireland consults. He is chairman of the Cross-Border Body on Trade and Business, one of the six bodies set up under the Good Friday Agreement. He is a member of the Foundation Board of Trinity College Dublin and a Trustee of Notre Dame University, Southbend, Indiana. He holds honorary doctorates from University College Dublin, Trinity College Dublin, The Queen's University of Belfast, and Notre Dame.

This conversation was recorded on 2 April 2001 in Martin Naughton's office in Glen Dimplex, Dunleer, County Louth.

Martin Naughton

My mother was from Galway and my father from Mayo but I would regard Dundalk as home, if I were to regard anywhere as home. That's where the formative years were. We were brought up to consider ourselves a West of Ireland family. Because my father was a garda, you kept a bit of distance from the community — you had to behave a little better. Everything I did in life, I was always the youngest by a long way. I joined the FCA when I was about 12; 18 was the proper age. I became a corporal at 14. I did the Leaving Cert. at 16. While I was still single, I had jobs running departments, I was travelling. The first comment you'd get was, "You can't be Mr Naughton."

Martin McCourt was running AET [*Aibhléisí Eireann Teoranta*]. He was president of the Confederation of Irish Industry. He owned Milestown House in County Louth. He was a man who influenced me greatly, a wonderful human being, a real entrepreneur. I learned from him as much about what not to do as what to do. He was one of these people who was an expert on everything. He was a father figure and a great travelling companion — we travelled the world together and he was a fund of knowledge. He opened all kinds of doors for me as a young man — he enjoyed the company of young people.

AET was one of those traditional Irish industries created behind tariff barriers. I remember Martin said to us, "Next year, duties go down to 50 per cent and at 50 per cent we have no protection." With the Common Market coming, the company bought a chain of retail stores, Tara Electric, throughout Ireland. Then they bought into a wholesaling chain. Martin believed that, if he was going to survive, he would have to control the distribution. If he controlled his own wholesaling and retailing, the factory had a guaranteed outlet. That did not work. Fóir Teoranta, the State rescue agency, came in and appointed new directors. Martin McCourt left the scene. I was works manager and was running the company. A group of us put forward a rescue plan — it meant cutting everything back. We had good products and processes and people — but there was dead wood. We wanted to cut it back to a core business from which we could grow it again. AET made for the Irish market every electrical appliance you could imagine — televisions, radios, fridges, cookers, washing machines, small appliances, heaters. It was the greatest university in the world for anybody in the electrical appliance business. We knew how to make every single product.

GEC, who were the main shareholder, gave the company permission to design and develop a range of our own products that we could sell in export markets. We sold those as yellow-pack products — good products, well engineered and you could put anybody's name on them. We had no brand. Even though we had sold millions of products round the world, we were unknown. Hence my affection for the brand and the brand image.

Our rescue plan was not accepted and that became the kernel of an idea — if this is right for here, it's right to go and do it ourselves. I led a small group of the management of the company, people with complementary skills: Doug Lally was in charge of tooling and engineering; Arthur Purton, technical; Ron Warren was our design director. We had a full-time designer but no accountant with us when we started — that showed where our priorities were.

At that time, I was newly married, two babies, but with total confidence in our own ability. We knew the products and the industry, we knew the costing — we knew what we were about. But, in some ways, it was probably our naivety that saved us. It's lovely sitting over pints or cups of coffee and *talking* about doing your own thing. It's a different matter to give in your notice and have no salary or pension. The idea of failing is not something you can contemplate.

On 24 August 1973, we formed the new company, Glen Electric, and one month later, on 21 September, we took over a small advance factory in Newry. Two months after that, on 23 November, we made our first product. We went to Newry because it was near where I lived — 12 miles — and also because the assistance we got from the Northern Ireland Government was better than we would have got here. AET was in difficulty here and the general feeling was that industries like that could not survive in the new world, trying to compete globally. We didn't believe that.

The plan we had was that we would build a company that in three years would employ 100 people, would have £1 million of sales and we would never, ever let it grow any bigger than that. But we would run that size of company better and better every year, tightly controlled. Our plan was: first year, £400,000; second year, £600,000; year three, £800,000 rising to £1 million. We would lose a little money in the first year, we'd break even in the second, and we'd be into profits in year three — a classic three-year business plan. First year, instead of doing £400,000, we did £410,000 and we made a profit every year since inception. What was critical was that we grew from our own resources.

When we began we had, first, to put our own investment in. Then there was the Northern Ireland Development Board, like a Northern Ireland Government merchant bank. Then they had the Department of Commerce, which gave grants. We were in the classic circle where the participants were waiting on each other to see who would put the money in first. Eventually, we got them around the table. It was high-risk.

Lochlann Quinn, who was with Arthur Andersen, was my financial adviser from the beginning. Lochlann charged £100 for his advisory work in helping set up the company — on the basis that Arthur Andersen would get the audit. That was a bit of fun when you think about it. By 1977, the company had prospered and the big opportunity came. Dimplex, who were the brand leader, got into difficulty following the first oil crisis. Dimplex was not insolvent but was losing money and the banks lost patience and put in a receiver. I told Lochlann that I wanted to go and see Dimplex and get as much information as I could: "I'd like you to come with me to give me the mantle of respectability as Arthur Andersen's." We went to Southampton, saw the company, asked for all the information from the receiver — costings, list of customers, everything. The management said, "You can't give these guys this kind of information." The receiver told them he had to. We had gone there really only for industrial espionage but when I got into Dimplex, it became an obsession. I had to have it. Nobody would agree with me. Lochlann pointed out that everything was going on the table — it could bring our whole company down and in a few more years we were going to get there anyway. But the Dimplex brand, from an established company, had just an unbelievable attraction — putting together young, aggressive, fast-moving Glen with the Dimplex Establishment. We ended up acquiring Dimplex from the receiver, put the two together and formed Glen Dimplex.

I found that, when Fóir Teoranta came into AET, they did not really respect the existing management — they were seen as failed. When we took over Dimplex, which had three years of losses, we kept virtually the same management. We earned the purchase price in the first year. Dimplex changed things an awful lot for us. In 1977, it was a major shock in Britain that an Irish company could buy an established British one. As we proceeded, we took over other companies. Derek Isherwood was running a company called Burco, a public company. He went to his merchant bank to find out how he could make himself bid-proof. His merchant bank went through his numbers and told him, "Derek, if you're not careful, the Micks will have you!" And we did. Today, any Irish company could buy any company anywhere in the world and nobody would bat an eyelid.

There was a year of bedding down for Dimplex and ourselves — it really worked. We had, as I told you, planned to stay at 100 employees and £1 million turnover, but a business takes on a life of its own and you can't stop it; it's got to go and you have to ride the tiger.

I know to the last penny what I paid for Dimplex, but I'm not going to tell you! Let's just say it was the first time I signed a cheque for over £1 million. They were enormous sums of money in those days. The night I came back — through Belfast (we were living in Blackrock, County Louth) — my wife told me there was a man looking for me from the Department of Industry and Commerce in Dublin and he wanted me to ring him. I said I was not going to ring him, that I was exhausted. Carmel said, "Well, he said he would wait for you, regardless of what time you came in." I rang the guy and he said, "You know AET. Would you agree it had some good products and some good people?" I said, "Sure." At this time, Fóir Teoranta were supporting AET and kept changing the management teams, bringing in new people. We would have been a competitor of theirs. They were still making a whole raft of products. This guy said to me, "If you would be interested in taking it over, we could structure a very attractive deal for you." I said to him, "Of all the days — believe me, I am not interested, good, bad or indifferent, under any circumstances. There will be an announcement in a few days and you will know why — but I really can't even think about it." He said, "We have had a consultancy report — will you come in and read it for us and give us a view?" I said, "Of course."

I went down to Kildare Street and sat in an office to read the report. Basically, it said that it would be better for the Government to keep giving the company £1 million a year rather than have people on the dole. It was going to need Government money constantly. Otherwise, you would have the horror of closing down the only company in mid-Louth — there were 1,000 people employed there, rather more than Dimplex and Glen put together. I agreed with the findings of the report.

AET struggled on and we met the Industrial Development Authority about nine months later and this time Dimplex was in really good shape. We suggested that the only way we would be interested in AET was if it were to go into receivership and we bought the assets. That's what happened. We bought the old AET, where we had started from. I had to be very, very careful that I was not doing it for sentiment but for real business reasons.

Immediately after that, I bought my old boss's, Martin McCourt's, house. I remained very close friends with him till he died a year ago. After Dimplex, I had a chat with Lochlann Quinn, who was now a partner with Arthur Andersen. We had dinner together in the Shelbourne and I asked him to come and join me full-time. This was 1979; Lochlann knew the company. Still for him it was a major risk to give up an Arthur Andersen partnership, but it led on to a great double-act. Partnerships like that often don't work — with Lochlann and me, it has worked very well. We get on well together — we have different skills. Lochlann is as clever a financial man as I have ever met — very opinionated, very strong views. We will argue about things — perhaps debate rather than argue — he'll begin here and I'll begin there, and we'll end up with my talking him around to my position or he'll talk me around to his, so we have to begin again! It's good and frank and it works very well for us. He is a friend as well as a colleague. He is great fun and a wonderful man to travel with.

Together, we have a lot of investments outside the company but we never mix up company and private investments. Anything we want to do that's not strictly business we keep absolutely apart from the company. One of the things we did was to get involved with Patrick Guilbaud's restaurant in the eighties. Things were not looking good for the restaurant and we came in to make sure it survived, because we believed that Dublin needed a quality restaurant, somewhere we could bring people with the same confidence you could

bring them to a restaurant in Paris or Brussels. The Merrion Hotel
was a similar sort of investment — we thought that Dublin needed a
hotel of that standard. They were fun investments that did not im-
pinge at all on the company — it was Lochlann and me personally.

When Lochlann and I are looking at another acquisition, our cri-
terion would be: if it goes totally wrong, and we lose our entire investment, will it inflict damage on the company? And we have stuck
to the business we know, electrical appliances. I find a lot of business
people become almost arrogant, thinking that, because they have succeeded in one little area, they know everything about everything.

I believe we learned a lot from starting a small, greenfield company, where you put in only the overheads that are vitally necessary
— and with your own money. You learn the discipline of respect for
money. Everything we do, we are writing a personal cheque. We don't
have any paper.

Money has never been a driver for me. I've earned money as a
consequence of doing more right things than wrong ones. And we've
been lucky — I have a little investment company for the children and
it's done well because of the boom in the economy. I remind them not
to confuse luck with knowledge or strategy — don't think we're very
clever. The company has been the driver. I could have stopped working 15 or 20 years ago. I work because I want to work, not because I
have to. I'm just beginning to realise that I am not 25 any more. We
brought in, as chief executive, a Corkman, Sean O'Driscoll, who was a
partner in KPMG. Sean shares our attitudes. He has great energy and
drive and has taken a lot of the workload.

The business has been my life — two of my children are now involved. The only conditions are (a) that they want to do it and (b) that
they are able to do it. If they are not, it's no good for the company and
it's no good for them. My eldest son, Neil, did an MBA in Columbia
and Fergal has just finished a Masters of Engineering in Stanford.
They are learning their trade. The only thing I would ask of anybody
is that they achieve their potential.

I don't carry the cross of an ego around with me. Harry Truman
always wanted to employ people who were cleverer than he was — I
would agree with that. When George Marshall brought out the Marshall Aid plan for the post-War reconstruction of Europe, he said it
should have been called the Truman plan, but Truman said, "It's your

plan — it will be called the Marshall plan." When you get honours like doctorates, it's gratifying, but no more than that.

I enjoy very much the involvement with Notre Dame. They are a fantastic group of people. Irish America fascinates me. There was a football game here between Notre Dame and Navy. When you go to the campus of Notre Dame it's the Fighting Irish — "Come on Irish!" The college was founded for Irish kids, many of whom came from the wrong side of the tracks. They were toying with the idea of opening a campus in Dublin and they had a lunch during the football game — I met some of the Trustees and the university officers. I asked them why it had taken so long for the Fighting Irish to come back to Ireland. I told them that, if they had been Jewish, they would have been in Israel, in Jerusalem, long before now. One guy said, "I can answer that for you. Our parents were so busy surviving, rearing and educating their children that they had no time to go back. We are the first generation of Irish to have achieved some affluence and the opportunity to go back. The scary thing is that our kids are the first generation to be born affluent and they are ten times more keen than we were to know about Ireland. They not only want to read Irish literature, they want to read it in the Irish language." There are two full-time Irish teachers on the Notre Dame campus. I helped them get things set up in Dublin — they are in Newman House on Stephen's Green. They will be sending 100 students over for a full year. They'll go to Trinity and UCD and get lectures in Newman House. These kids will be leaders in business and politics in the next generation. The fact that they have spent a year in Ireland, know it and understand it, will be of benefit both to Notre Dame and to Ireland.

Then they did me the great honour of asking me to become a Trustee of the University. For the last ten years, the Irish in America have really got involved in business — many corporations are run by Murphys and Duffys. It almost tracks what happened here in Ireland — as we run up, they would be parallel with us. They are very proud of their Irishness. They are trying a little to rewrite history. They don't want any more stage Irish; they want us to be leaders, Nobel Prize winners. *Riverdance* had a great impact. And they want to make Notre Dame the number one university in the world. The commitment of the Trustees is amazing — the time they give to improving the college in every way.

Fifty of us meet four times a year — you don't miss a meeting. If you give a commitment, you give a commitment. There are several sub-committees. The college has $3.7 billion of an endowment. Last year, it earned a return of $800 million. The Provost said all the pro- grammes were well-funded — the chairman of the Trustees reminded him that ballet and education were never well enough funded. We have people there like Don Keough, Ex-President and CEO, Coca Cola; Philip Purcell, who runs Morgan Stanley Dean Witter; we have John Kaneb, the boss of Gulf Oil; Bill Shaw, President and CEO, Marriott International — the Who's Who in America. I'm on the Aca- demic and Faculty Affairs Committee and we report regularly to the plenary meeting of the Trustees. The Trustees' meeting is a full-day event and around that there will be various get-to-know-you func- tions. In June, they're taking a ship from the Thames up the Nor- mandy Coast to Scandinavia for a week, all the Trustees together and their wives. One of our Trustees was Condoleezza Rice who is now the National Security Adviser. We had our last Trustee meeting in Washington about six weeks ago. The biggest supplier of brains to Government is Harvard; Notre Dame is number two. We had a lot of doors open to us in Washington. All in all, it's a very pleasing experience.

So is the Council of State. You have every previous President and Taoiseach, you have the present Taoiseach and Tánaiste and Attorney General, leaders of the High and Supreme Courts, the Speakers of the Senate and the Dáil. I have been at three of them now. The President chairs the meeting. She goes round the table and everyone has their pennyworth in it. The Council does not meet at regular intervals — it meets only for a purpose. The first time we met was when the Presi- dent had been elected and she wanted the new Council of State to meet to get to know her and each other — that was an informal meeting. We'd have a cup of tea beforehand and afterwards. Any Bill or part of any Bill the President felt uneasy about, she would consult with the Council of State. She does not have to take the advice, but she does listen. You can see people's minds changing as it goes round the room. People will say, "I came here with a certain view but, now that I have heard so and so, I have to agree with him or her."

I made a conscious decision not to play golf. It's a total time- waster. There's pressure from my wife and from buddies to take it up and I say, "Why does nobody go to a professional golfer and say, 'Why don't you take a break from this and get into business?'"

There was a time in the first few years when it was virtually a full-time job — there was really no leisure. When we were working on a Saturday, I would say to the guys that our competitors were out sailing or on the golf course and we had the edge on them. You got out of the habit of having leisure time. You got out of the habit of taking holidays. That was never right. What we've done now, for the last number of years, we go away as a family at Christmas — all the family and now the extended family. I have two grandchildren. Their mother, Fiona, is my eldest child and only daughter. She also owns and runs Donnybrook Travel. The whole world closes down at Christmas so it's a time when you can go away, when the faxes and the phones switch off. I enjoy spending time with the family. Something I have always done, from way back, is to have a one-to-one chat with each of the children during that Christmas break. We would go away to a restaurant together and talk things through, just the two of us. As they got older, that became more important. Even during the year they would say, "We'll keep that till Christmas and talk about it then." Two of them are now married and gone but, written into the diary is that one weekend per month they come home and we have Sunday lunch together in Stackallen, with their wives and the extended family. It's too easy not to do these things, to let them drift.

With this old Irish fatalism we have, I often say to myself, I don't deserve to be this lucky. You're waiting for the kick in the arse. I'm happily married, I enjoy good health, I love what I'm doing — a lot of blessings. I have a large number of acquaintances and I have a few friends. A friend since we were at school together, Ronnie McCaffrey, is now running a hospital for Harvard in Boston. He's just had a by-pass. The divil advises everybody else: he had seven different check-ups planned for himself and he cancelled them all. He was always so bloody busy. He said that he has now discovered that the crowd has to stop while you take a stone out of your shoe. They have to wait for him now.

For my fiftieth birthday, I was given a portrait by Derek Hill. He came to the house for three days; he would work only in the mornings. While he was painting we gossiped and he told me that he had painted Mountbatten, who told him that he had only three friends. I said, "That's really very few friends, isn't it?" Then I began to count my own true friends and, when you've gone past the fingers of one hand, you find it hard to think of many others. A true friend is someone you call if you've murdered your wife! You ask him to bring the van around and a shovel and he would say, "I'll be there in ten minutes!"

Very few people have real "business" friends. You'll see the same crew at every function, people in high places, the best of buddies. Suddenly, they're gone and you never see them again. It's as if they've been kidnapped or left the country. They are suddenly off all invitation lists.

I've never liked the "Celtic Tiger". There's an arrogance about it. It's raised expectations to a level where some people feel it's left them behind. There's a selfishness coming into our character which is not to be welcomed. The economic performance of the country has surprised many of us, yet there is no reason why, if we don't lose the run of ourselves, we can't keep on going. I believe we have intelligent young people now, different from my time — they are more educated, more widely travelled and have a damn sight more self-confidence. They have a comfort with technology — and with being winners, leaders. That becomes a habit. I would have far more optimism than pessimism about the country.

Because I grew up near the border, I was always interested in the happenings in Northern Ireland. I crossed the border every day through all the rough times. I have a sense of gratitude for the support I got when I started first. Following on the Good Friday Agreement I was asked to chair the cross-border body on trade and business. The automatic response that comes into your head is, I can't do it, I'm too busy. On this particular occasion, I said "Yes" immediately. The politicians have all taken risks, a lot of people have taken risks, and the business community has to play its part as well. We are in temporary buildings in Newry — we shall be moving into permanent buildings. Our Board consists of six people from the North and six from the South — a very fine board with people like Kieran McGowan and the Duke of Abercorn. They have blended well together and take the work very seriously. We meet once a month. We shall have a permanent staff, just now being recruited — 44 people. The whole intention is to increase trade and business between the two parts of the island. There has been an economic border there for the past number of years. There's been a sea-change in the business community in the North, whom I know very well, as I was on the Board of the IDB in Belfast for several years. They're now keen to do business in the Republic. I enjoy being involved — it is taking up time but it's worth it. I have a bit of a passion about it. I see things getting better — we can never go back. Year after year, you'd turn on the news in the morning to hear what the latest horror was. It got to a stage where you became immune — it had to be a really big horror before you were disturbed by it. Now, normality has crept back and I'd be very hopeful.

We're here in the middle of County Louth — there is no other industry within a ten-mile radius, so we do have a natural catchment area. And, also, because we are the largest electric heating manufacturer in the world, we have a seasonality to our business. We are creatures of darkness and cold — we enjoy listening to the weather forecast when there's a cold front coming in and deep depressions. That cheers us up. We always had a position where we could take people in for the winter and then, after Christmas, they would leave us. We haven't that luxury any more — we've got to plan things a bit better. There's now, for us, a tightness in the labour market rather than a shortage. We are trying to even out the seasonality, by doing a bit of stock-building, by better planning, by trying to sell in the southern hemisphere, Australia, New Zealand, South Africa, South America.

We have a factory in Hungary where we make products and we're doing a lot of business into Eastern Europe — there's a big pent-up demand there from people who want Western appliances. We don't regard ourselves as an Irish company — we are an international company. We have several "home markets": the UK, Germany, France, Canada, Holland. They are markets where we have manufacturing, distribution, after-sales service. There is hardly a country we don't do business with.

You tell me the story of Glen Dimplex is not widely known. That's part of our style. We are a private company — we don't have to go out and try to hype our shares. Most people in Ireland would be surprised at our size. Some years ago, nobody would have believed that we could run from the middle of the countryside a company that can meet competition from China, Eastern Europe, the Far East. We keep going by doing it right and keeping at it. I don't lie awake at night worrying about my business.

Because I am an old-fashioned manufacturing man, one of my greatest joys is being involved with the engineers on designing and developing new products — I like making things. I like being a manufacturer, but I will still be totally realistic — I don't do things for pigheadedness or to prove anything. So long as we can design them, make them, keep improving them, and making profits, we'll keep on manufacturing. If it becomes impossible, and we put our finger in the wind to see which way it's blowing, we will tack and we will change. We do import products and put our brands on them — I don't get the same joy from that. OK, we do it, we trade, we buy, we sell but we still make over 80 per cent of what we sell. The kick I get personally is in the joy of making products. There's a lovely satisfaction seeing a sketch on a piece of paper or a wooden model and then to be walking down the street in Oslo and seeing the product in a shop window, or going into somebody's house, or into a hotel, and seeing your products there. When you go into a room, the first thing you do is look around for friends — to see whose products are there.

13

Denis O'Brien

Communicorp

Photo: © Fennell Photography

"The key thing that helped us was getting the right management team. You can't run a business on one person. We would prepare and prepare and prepare. We had ferocious discipline."

Denis John O'Brien is Chairman of Communicorp.

He was born in Dublin on 19 April 1958. His father is Denis O'Brien, Chairman of Plusvital Ireland Limited. His mother is Iris Lavinia Quinn. He is third in a family of four; his three sisters are Abigail, Joanne and Kerry. He is married to Catherine Walsh, a former CEO of Ireland Radio Sales Ltd. They have a son, Jack, and a daughter, Alva.

He was educated at St Killian's German School; The High School in Rathgar; University College Dublin (BA); Boston College, Massachusetts (MBA).

His first job was as an assistant manager in Trinity Bank Limited, a small merchant bank run by Brown Shipley. He joined GPA as PA to the CEO, Tony Ryan; later, vice-president for Satellite Development for GPA; worked for his father in North America as vice-president of Plusvital. He was joint chief executive of a Shopping Channel in the UK. Chairman and chief executive of 98FM, Radio 2000. Chairman of Radio Investments NV, an overseas holding company. Chairman and chief executive of Esat Telecom plc. He is now chairman of Communicorp Group.

He is chairman of Digicel (Bermuda) Ltd., a Caribbean cellular operator; a member of the Technical Advisory Board of 360 Networks, USA; a member of the board of E Via, an Italian network infrastructural company laying fibre optic cable; and a member of the Court of the Bank of Ireland.

He is chairman of the Special Olympics 2003 World Games in Ireland. He was Entrepreneur of the Year, 1998.

The conversation was recorded on 29 January and 6 February 2001 in Denis O'Brien's office in Communicorp Group, Grand Canal Quay, Dublin 2.

Denis O'Brien

I was interested in business from age eight. My father was the sales director of a company in the pharmaceutical business. During the holidays, he'd bring me off down the country to meet customers. I got a business education in the front or back of a car for maybe 12 years after that and every Saturday he'd bring me up the mountains for long runs and he'd tell me everything that was going on in business: a fellow wasn't paying him or a guy had let him down on a contract or problems with staff, sales reps crashing cars, people fiddling expenses, products having to be recalled — all of that I got from an early age.

Around eight in the morning my father would give me a lift to school and, all the way in the car, he would tell me what was going on: the difficulties he had with his partner, financing problems, how he was going to deal with the bank when a payment did not arrive and they were over their limit. All of these small things were big things in reality because any one of them would have a serious impact if they fell the wrong way.

It's still the same because my father is still in an office across the corridor. He would be in on every major decision I make. When I was 36, he saved me with a loan from going wallop. My business has always been intertwined with him. He's been an investor in everything I've done. I also worked for him for two years in America, selling — he taught me how to sell.

There was never any question of my not setting up a business. There was never any question of my working for somebody for the rest of my life. To get the tools into the bag, I did the MBA in Boston College, Massachusetts, immediately after the BA in UCD. Instead of doing the MBA in two years, I did it in 18 months, I was so keen to get out there and do something and make some money. I picked Boston College because I got a scholarship. That meant I got free tuition, which was fantastic. I borrowed the rest of the money. It was also going to be cheaper if I was there for 18 months instead of two years

— I could save myself ten grand. That was in 1980 and they were tough times. My first job — for ten grand also — was in Trinity Bank and I thought I was made.

When I got the job, I got an American Express card the next day and went mad on it for about a month. I made some money out of Atlantic Resources and cleared the overdraft. I made two-and-a-half grand and was over the moon. Trinity Bank was not in securities so there was no question of insider trading but you could come by tips. I went up to the liquidators of Ashenhurst Williams, who had the Citroen franchise, bought a couple of cars and flicked them on. Unfortunately, I could never live on a salary — I always had to have something else on the side. Even when I came back after my MBA, of which I was proud as Punch, I could not get a job for three months. I ended up painting offices to keep the show on the road. You ask was I any good — I *was* good! We would do a room of a Georgian building in one day and you'd get a couple of hundred quid. "We" was a school friend of mine, Barry Maloney.

There was always something going on where you would make a few quid. When I was 14, I worked in the Central Hotel for Andy McGlynn, who was the General Manager there. When I was 15 I went to England to do stone cleaning using power hoses. I had a variety of jobs every year. I always found that having a few quid in your pocket felt pretty good. I spent it pretty quickly too. I'm lucky now that I can afford to spend but, all along, even in business, we'd always spend the capex, we'd reach the capex without having the funding. We did that for the first four or five years of Esat — we spent the money before we had it. Once you become a public company, you can't do that, because the Yanks, in particular, want to see a fully funded business plan. If you don't have one, they get very nervous. So we always had £100 million in the bank with Esat. It was an embryonic company that needed the cash in case the capital markets closed.

For the past six months here, the high yield bond market has closed and that is why a lot of the telecom companies in Europe have seen their share price crater. They were not fully funded. In Esat, before we sold it to BT, we could always have survived for nine months, still building out our network and not running into difficulties.

Even in UCD, I worked three days a week, painting in the afternoons and evenings. I thought it was the easiest money going and one customer would recommend you to the next one.

I played rugby for Wanderers, way down the ranks — that was good craic. I was recruited by Michael McLoughlin, a great old friend of mine for whom I did some part-time work. I had a great set of friends — which I still have. I have not recycled my friends. I've seen people who have made a lot of money and they recycle their friends. They move to what they see is the next echelon of people. That was never my game. I've had the same friends in good times and in tough times. I struck up fantastic friendships in UCD — they are still the pals I hang around with now at weekends. I have been going away with one friend, Kieran O'Reilly, for 25 years. One of the great bene-fits of going to college is friendships. If you go straight into work at 18, you may make business friends but they are absolutely different from the real friendships you make in college — there's no tie-up. Business friendships are not that durable: fellows get married and their wives don't like their business partner. Everything gets convo-luted, particularly when there's economic rivalry — he's got a bigger car or a bigger house than we have and all that kind of stuff. When you all have nothing, you make much stronger friendships. All my friends started with nothing. None of them were lucky sperms; most had not a sausage. When you go off to Greece on a holiday, and you're living on fifty quid a week, you see the cut of a person. My wife and I get invited to all sorts of stuff, like going to the Derby — forget it. I'd rather be in Hartigans having a pint.

Anyway, that's how I got going — things were means-to-an-end. The reason I took the job in banking is that my old man said I would see how the banks worked. He felt that, if I could learn how the bug-gers thought, it would be easier when I went in the front door looking for money. Trinity Bank was interesting. The man who trained me in the foreign exchange side of the bank is now a colleague of mine here, David Sykes. The bank wanted to get into the business of bonding builders and they got me to write a report. It went on for months. I was bored out of my mind but I worked for a very nice man who gave me great flexibility, John McGilligan. He has unfortunately died. He was a smashing man to work for because he knew the game. He knew I was treading water, getting a bit of experience. He would bring me with him to meet clients. Then I'd go out with Kieran Walshe on business development calls and we'd end up in a bookie's shop be-tween calls. Life was easy. It was a little bit like what banking still is, a nice lifestyle, nine to five. There was a dining room at the top of the bank and everyone would drink wine at lunchtime. I had a sunny office and, after a couple of glasses of wine, I would open the window, get on the phone to run my Wanderers 3B's rugby team and get a suntan at the same time.

One day, I told John McGilligan that I was leaving for GPA. John said he was delighted for me, that it was a great company — I should go. He was totally supportive. That was interesting, because, when somebody wants to leave a company, you should never persuade them to stay. If they do stay, it's for the wrong reasons. They stay because they've been bribed. If somebody's mindset is even 10 per cent out the door, you've got to push them out that door and let them do their own thing. In a lot of cases, people that I have worked with have come back with more experience. I went off to work for Tony Ryan.

I had written to him. My means-to-an-end there was that I wanted to start an airline. In a case study in Boston College, I had read about Herb Kelleher in Southwest. He set up an airline in Texas and did brilliantly well. Ryanair is modelled on Southwest and has out-Southwested Southwest. Ryanair is more efficient. I thought, if I went into GPA, I would learn the economics of aviation. When Tony at interview asked me what I'd like to do and I told him, he said I was bloody mad. Little did I know that he had himself wanted to do it — it was always in the back of his mind. Even though he had Aer Lingus as a shareholder in GPA, he was looking for an angle to compete with Aer Lingus. He came from Aer Lingus.

Tony saved me because, if you're not working hard, you get into bad habits and I had not worked hard for a year. It would have been dangerous if I stayed where I was for year two or three. Working with Tony was a different pace of life — it was extreme. I worked six or seven days a week for him and you always had to attend the Monday morning meetings in Shannon, no matter where in the world you had to come back from. I did not like the particular style of management — maybe it was necessary because they were under such pressure. If they were taking an aircraft onto their balance sheet they had to get it off it quickly. There was some management by fear — like the French Foreign Legion. Maurice Foley brought a different dimension to it — he is a consummate pro manager. I thought to myself that you can get people to deliver, whatever the metric is, without having to beat them up, but, by God, it was a very successful company. They did things nobody ever thought they could do. They created a whole new financing instrument — people were just not doing operating leases for aircraft. They bought their first 747 from China Airlines for only $14 million and it stood on the ground for four months. I remember Tony threatening that he was going to have a Monday morning meeting on the aircraft on the apron at Shannon Airport unless somebody moved it. Then they soared upwards and bought a pile of new aircraft — they did bigger and bigger deals. They created their own canvas. One thing about the Paddies, we're not famous for commerce. The fact was phenomenal — that this Mickey Mouse Irish company with $50,000 in capital could go on and become the biggest lessor of aircraft. There were very few exciting Irish businesses at the time. Bailey's Irish Cream — Gilbeys — were just about to get going, CRH was moving nicely in the US, but there were not that many really attractive employers around, maybe four or five. Now, there's probably 50 — people you would really want to work for.

I stayed with GPA a couple of years and then said to myself, I'm outta here. I had had the worst and the best job. Every morning I travelled for an hour into work with Tony. That was a hell of an experience; he'd ask you all sorts of questions. I was involved in his farm, in the *Sunday Tribune*, which was going abysmally, I was doing some of his stuff in GPA where he would get mountains of paper . . . there were just so many things going on. In my bag I had lists of things I had to do. Tony could do 100 things at one time. If you did not know how many gallons of milk went into the creamery the previous month, he'd be pissed off — that would be a big black mark — that kind of detail. But it was great training. He also gave you the confidence that in Ireland we can do anything. It gave me a wider picture and it also gave me a window on the capital markets, because GPA had a ferocious appetite for capital — every year they were raising more money. Subsequently, in some ways we modelled Esat's capital fundraising on GPA, with one difference: all our money was ten-year bond money. GPA's money was for the most part short-term and that's what ultimately got them into the crunch. They were funding expensive asset purchases on short-term finance.

Then Tony had an idea that you could lease the transponders off satellites (a transponder is a channel on a satellite). Satellites would be like aircraft. In other words, if GPA bought a satellite, they could lease the capacity of it. He was probably five years ahead of his time.

Another guy who brought me into the communications business was Fred O'Donovan who used to be chairman of RTE and the Gaiety Theatre. He mentored me. He was a very future-focused person. He'd sit down and say, "This is what I think is going to happen over the next five to ten years." Invariably, he was on the money. He would have made a splendid analyst. Fred also gave me great encouragement.

When I left GPA, I went to work for two years for my father, on the road, selling — excellent experience. After 18 months in GPA, I felt that I had learned as much as I was going to learn. I was in London in a hotel with my father and he heard a phone call with Tony Ryan and he said, "You're outta there." He called it right. I think Tony is a fantastic operator but, if you're working for somebody who spends most of their lifetime at 35,000 feet, when they come down to earth, they're jet-lagged, short-tempered and don't remember what they last said to you. If you happen to be 100 per cent in the right and that person thinks you're wrong — you're wrong.

My father was trying to expand his business into North America. He said, "You know all the products — will you set it up for me?" He manufactures horse-care veterinary products, so I went from GPA into the horse-care business: thoroughbreds, show jumpers, eventing horses. In America, they thrash the horses, they bring them to the track too early and they end up bleeding. One of my father's products was designed to stop them bleeding — a bleeder can't run.

We set up six regional distributors in the States. We shipped them container-loads of the product — they would have maybe 100 sales reps each. What we did not realise was that they were merchandisers — they were not sales people at all, they were just order-takers. So the product stuck on the pallets of the distributors. We had to go out and train their sales reps, give them what's known as a $5 spiff incentive per case of product. I had to drive and hit maybe 15 dealers a day, go in, set up points of sale, tell them about the products, go through the pricing, give them rudimentary product knowledge. You could not give them the full download, they'd just get blurred. I did this for two years up and down the States, East Coast, West Coast, everywhere. I drove about 1,000 miles every week. It was selling, the best experience; it's what I did until I left Esat — that was just selling as well. You're selling telecoms to investment bankers and customers. Salesmanship is a forgotten criterion going into business. Most people coming out of university now don't want to go and sell. They want to go into marketing, not into sales — which I think is bullshit. If you can sell, you can sell anything.

Selling to horse-trainers was unique. They're the toughest people you could meet. They have a canary's attention span. You've got to say, "This will make your horse run faster." "OK. I'll take three cases." It was the Ballinasloe Horse Fair every day. I'd go to Belmont Park at six in the morning, hit all the trainers, then get into the car and drive to upstate New York and hit all the dealers.

The dollar was bouncing all the time. One month, margins would be 50 per cent; next month, they were down to 30 per cent. We decided we would licence a North American company to make the products.

During that time, I raised 150 grand from six investors — Paul Power from Novum; Ray McKenna, who is sadly deceased; Larry Shields, the solicitor; Ray McLoughlin; and then the Gallagher family, Seamus Gallagher, who is unfortunately deceased as well. I did this with Fred O'Donovan — the idea was that we would have an entertainment company on satellite for the whole of Europe.

I left my father's business because we restructured how we would sell the products in the US. I had worked myself out of a job. I was still interested, since my GPA days, in the satellite business. Fred O'Donovan and myself decided to set up a general entertainment channel for the whole of Europe using satellite. We were 50/50 — we sold 50 per cent of the company, called Esat Television Limited, to the six investors. (Esat comes from Eire Satellite.) Fred and I used most of the £150,000 for a feasibility study. The feasibility study showed that it would cost between two and three hundred million quid. It was one of those ideas that you just throw in the bin; it was never going to work.

The concept was for us to create an RTE for the whole of Europe using channels on a satellite and then beaming it down to people with dishes on their roofs or with cable television. It was like a precursor to Sky Television. We were ahead of the posse but with no twine. We had to go back to all our investors to tell them the idea didn't work. They took it pretty well.

Then one night I was in Lexington, Kentucky, working for my father — I was still working for him part-time. I saw a thing called The Home Shopping Network, which was selling jewellery and household goods on TV. It was American-style hard-sell. I said to myself, "This is it: we'll set up a shopping channel for the whole of Europe" and forget about going to Hollywood and buying movies and rights and so on and having hundreds of people with ponytails making programmes. Next day, I flew down to Tampa, Florida, unannounced, into Home Shopping Network, met this guy, a vice-president or something, and he walked me around a big barn of a place. They did not even have a studio. In one corner, they had a couple of cameras and two women flogging jewellery. In the background, you had three or four hundred people taking orders. I was staggered. I went back to the six investors and said, "Lads, this is it." We just needed to put the jigsaw together. Fred O'Donovan was more of an entertainment person and he did not like it — it did not fit what he wanted to do. He sold his shares to Paul Power and Paul became the chairman of the company. Then we tried to get a mail-order partner. What we were trying to do was to use everybody else's assets — we did not have the money to create the assets. A mail-order partner would have the infrastructure, the stock and a call centre. We went to Littlewoods and spent the best part of a year getting tossed about by them. They could not make up their minds. I became friendly with the guy I was dealing with in Littlewoods and, one day on the way back to the airport, he said, "My fellows are never going to do it — you should go down the road and deal with Next." He was that honest.

So I went down the road to Grattan Next, the number three mail-order company in England. I went in the door to a guy called Whitmarsh who was the deputy chairman. I made a presentation to him and to a pile of other punters in the room. They said they were interested. A week later, Whitmarsh told me they were definitely in. Five days later, he called me to say that they were not going ahead. Of the £150,000, we had only five grand left. I just could not believe it. I was at home lying on my couch and I thought the world was ending; the six investors were going to be very unhappy. I rang Tullys in Carlow, a travel agent we've used for years, and I said, "Joe, get me on a flight to Bradford." Next morning, I took the 7.30 to Bradford and arrived at your man's office unannounced. The security people asked me if I was there to see Mr Whitmarsh. They rang up and told me, "We have no appointment with a Mr O'Brien today." His secretary came on the phone and said the same thing. I said, "Look — I've come all the way from Ireland to see him and I'm here for the day if he can meet me. I've got a good book with me." An hour later, she came down and told me Mr Whitmarsh would meet me for five minutes. I went up to your man's office and gave him the same pitch I'd give to a horse trainer. I told him that if he didn't do it, Great Universal, their biggest competitor, would do it and he'd look silly: "This is a great strategic move on your part. You'll have millions of new customers." He got up from his chair and walked out the door. I said under my breath what might be called a prayer. After about 20 minutes, he comes back in. He said, "I've had a word with the CEO and the finance guy. We're in. We'll do the deal." I said, "John, you told me that last week and I'm signing up with Sky for the channel space. I need to know if you're in but I need also a good-faith down-payment of 15 grand on your shares." He walked out the door again, came back ten minutes later with a cheque for 15 grand. I went back to the airport in his Bentley, got on the plane back to Dublin, called in to Paul Power in Novum on the way from Dublin Airport. He asked, "What the hell happened?" I just flicked the cheque across the desk. He said, "You're some bollocks — how did you get that?"

We went into business with Grattan Next and then got six hours a day from Sky. We would use all Grattan's infrastructure so that we did not have to carry stock and we would make the programmes ourselves in Sky's studio in London. Grattan sold everything from jewellery to electrical goods.

We raised £1.5 million from the Smurfit Group, half in loan, half in equity — that was a trip down to Monte Carlo with Paul Power to see Michael Smurfit. Paul was a great help — he had done business in Libya. We complemented each other. He was very committed — even though it was a tiny investment for him, he wanted to see it work. We made just one mistake, we omitted one vital ingredient: where were the viewers? Murdoch, at the time, had made outlandish estimates of the number of viewers Sky would have — he said that they were going to have 4,000,000 viewers by April and this was in December. Murdoch was going to give away dishes — which they didn't do until two years later.

Cablelink would not take us — typical, Paddies not helping Paddies. That would have been a quarter-of-a-million homes. All the small cable companies in the UK did take us, but we were still waiting for the dishes. Sky became successful only when they bought the sports market in 1990. We started with a core of 2,000 to 3,000 homes — *if* they turned on the telly. We needed something like 1,000,000 to break even! We went for 13 months and then ran out of cash. It was at the time of a recession on the High Street. Next said that they were not putting up any more money and, to step up, we would have had to buy a 24-hour channel, which would have cost us 12 million quid. The business folded. It was a great idea but four or five years ahead of its time. Nowadays, QVC is a huge success on Sky with a shopping channel. Being first is sometimes not the smartest. The entrepreneur's motto is, "Always be second." I learned that the hard way.

We had a slam — everybody ran for cover. The Grattan managers ran out the door, so I had to deal with all the staff — which was an experience. Luckily, I had done an each-way bet — moonlighting from London, I had got a radio licence here, 98FM. My six investors said, "We don't want to be in the radio business." I said, "Lads, we gotta do this", so I kind of disobeyed them and we got a broadcasting licence for Dublin, which became profitable after seven months. We had a lousy investment in the UK and a profitable one in Dublin. The problem for me was I owned only four or five per cent of the radio station. I did a management buy-out. I bought Esat Television from my six investors — they got their money back plus a twist, so it was not too bad. The management and I bought 98FM, effectively for two million quid. We borrowed money from Anglo Irish Bank, which I personally guaranteed. It was a gutsy loan for the Bank to make but they stuck with us. I got the other four managers with me to buy one or two per cent each and, at the last minute, one of my six original investors, Seamus Gallagher, backed me. Bryan Phelan asked him to put up about £375,000, a lot of money in 1990 — no questions asked. He just said, "I'll do it." Then Ray McLoughlin lent me 60 grand for a year, interest-free, otherwise the MBO wouldn't have happened. That's how I got going.

We bought the business in December 1990, and 1991 was the first full year of having a half-million borrowing on the company — so the other buy-out managers and myself were obviously pretty motivated to get the revenues in. We were totally focused on revenues because the radio business is very much a fixed-cost P&L. It was the first time we had a serious amount of debt and massive obligations. If the business was not meeting its budget, we could not pay the loan back and the bank would not take the radio station as security.

The other buy-out managers were Lucy Gaffney, Jeff O'Brien, Padraic Boland, Caroline Davies and Miriam Matthews. They had borrowed, ranging from 60 grand, which was Jeff O'Brien, Lucy had borrowed 27.5, Padraic Boland the same and the others 20 grand each. Then the company had a half-million borrowed as well.

98FM made £350,000 that year and we thought we were fantastic. It was a good achievement for a two-year-old radio station. We paid back the loan to Anglo Irish inside two-and-a-half years, way ahead of schedule. Then we had another situation where the bank, for lending, had an option over five per cent. I had to pay personally a hundred grand to them to buy that option out. They were looking for a kicker on the half million, which was very fair. We were beginning to get a bit of oxygen. If you've got a business that's making money, you feel good, your confidence lifts and you begin to see things in a different light. Instead of gazing out the window and everything looking grey, you can see a sparkle of sunshine.

In 1991, we set up a Dutch holding company called Radio Investments and got a radio licence in the Czech Republic. We had tried to buy other radio stations around the country but the IRTC would not allow us. The irony is you can own 60 per cent of the newspapers in this country but you can't own or control a second radio station even in a small local area like, say, Galway. Rather than getting into a barney with the IRTC, we decided to let the hare sit. You can't beat these guys; you're beholden to them because they're the licensing body.

We got into bed with two local Czech guys who to this day are great partners. They did not have any capital of their own but they were wealthy in a different way. They had a great entrée and we got a licence for the city of Prague, with a population of about 1.5 million. We launched the business in 1992. We raised between £350,000 and £500,000 from private investors in a company called Radio Investments NV. We used the money to set up the station in Prague. It was done on a shoestring and we used a lot of the Irish staff to train the Czech people. We brought 25 of them to Dublin by car to work with their Irish counterparts. We launched the station with a huge bang. We hired 400 students to give out car stickers and t-shirts. We covered the whole city in banners. The Czechs could not believe this aggressive marketing. The station took off and, in the first year, it made a profit of a hundred grand. Then it lost money for four years because we had to move from being a local station to becoming a national proposition. We had to buy other radio stations. The cost of doing that and integrating them caused the loss. This national coverage was driven by the media buyers. Initially they were satisfied with a station for Prague but then they asked for a one-stop solution for the whole country. We now have an audience of about 1.2 million a day and 20 stations in the network — that's 12 per cent of the population. During the four or five years that we lost money we asked ourselves if we should give up. This was in parallel with the start-up of Esat. I had one great business in 98FM, which was making a lot of money; I had a business in the Czech Republic, which was losing three or four hundred grand a year; and I had Esat in its gestation period from 1991 until it got capital in 1994. It was a tricky time between balancing loss-making businesses and raising capital for a completely new venture.

In 1994, we raised $10 million. It was supposed to go into the radio business to expand it. The scheme was devised by Paul Connolly, a close associate of mine and a very good finance guy. My co-founder and pal, Mark Roden, since 1991 was busy plotting the downfall of Telecom Eireann on the ground floor. He had a team of 15 people and no revenues but he had a beautiful logo. A 21-year-old law graduate, Jarlath Burke, who was our Head of Regulatory Affairs, was running rings around Telecom Eireann's 30-person Regulatory Affairs Department. It took us three years to get a licence for Esat. The craic was mighty. We were really raising money for the radio business and hiding Esat away from the venture capitalists. One day, Massimo Prelz, from Advent International, the venture capital company with whom we were going to do the deal, was led by the receptionist by mistake into the Esat office. He saw all this activity and the logo and everything. He came up to me afterwards and asked me what this Esat was all about. He said, "I don't want to put my money into a radio business and then have you spend all your time on a telecoms business." Eventually, Paul Connolly came up with a scheme while I was on holiday in South Africa. He rang me and said, "We'll have one holding company and we'll put the radio and the telephone business into it and we'll get the venture capital guy to put the $10 million in the top company." I told him I thought that was a brilliant idea because it would leverage my shareholding upwards to 66 per cent.

It was a nightmare at that time, because I had minority shareholders in 98FM such as James Donnelly and Downtown Radio who knew I was in a weak position. Even though they were shareholders in the Czech business, they were leveraging against me and they went to the High Court for what's known as a Section 205, which is an oppression of minority interests. Even though they took a board decision in 98FM to lend money to the Czech business, they forgot about that and put on their shareholders' hat and said, "Hey, you can't do that." We called them "the Bosnians" because it was at the height of the Balkan crisis. We had a "Bosnian crisis" in Dublin with three or four shareholders who really leveraged on us at the last minute while we were trying to close the deal with Advent.

Everything was going wrong at the same time. We had a loss-making business in the Czech Republic and in Esat which was losing maybe £600,000 a month and I had all these "Bosnians" taking me on in the High Court. Then I had six banks from whom I had personally borrowed cumulatively a million quid to keep everything going. I was like Red Adair, running from one fire to another. I don't know how we did it but ultimately we signed the deal with Advent in October 1994. It was the last day of the month and I had to pay salaries and a down-payment on a broadcasting licence that we bought in Sweden — I was shy 60 grand, but I knew on Monday morning I was going to get $10 million. I went to Woodchester Bank, who had been 98FM's bankers for some time. I saw Michael Tunney — and this is after being up all night with lawyers in William Fry's. Aidan Phelan, my accountant, came with me for cred. I told Michael we were going to get $10 million on Monday and asked him for a loan of 60 grand. I brought also Gerry Halpenny, our solicitor, and he told them we were about to close the deal. Michael Tunney just went out, got a cheque for 60 grand and gave it to me.

I got the money on Monday morning — I got a million quid out of it myself. I drove around town throwing envelopes into the banks to whom I owed money: Anglo Irish, Equity Bank, Woodies, AIB, every bank basically, because I was borrowing from one to pay the interest on capital to another. It's a vicious circle — it was a bit like the funny money game.

We then decided to expand Esat. Instead of it being a Dublin-based, long-distance company where we would deliver calls from Dublin offices to New York or worldwide, we decided we'd also do national trunk calls. We had to put switches all around the country and then lease lines to create a network. We raced ahead and spent the money. We spent £1 million and put four switches into Galway, Limerick, Cork and Waterford. At last Mark Roden and his growing sales team had something to sell. Eircom then dropped their prices, so our losses increased because we had a leased network — we did not own our own network. Eircom kept dropping prices because of us. We'd arrive in and they'd drop prices by 20 per cent, which is a lot. If you have a run-rate from customers of £1 million a month and Telecom Eireann drop their prices by 20 per cent, you're down two hundred grand at the beginning of the following month because you have to make up the two hundred grand even to stand still. A tough game — we had to match them each time, and more.

Meanwhile, Telecom Eireann would not give us an interconnect — in other words, we were paying, rather than a wholesale rate, what Mrs Murphy in Fethard would pay to make a local call. We then put two million quid into an application for a GSM licence. We had a partner in Deutsche Telekom and South-West Bell — they did not put any money in, they were working with us on an application. They would fly their guys across the Atlantic first-class, which would cost them X thousand, they'd be collected by a chauffeured limousine, brought to the Berkeley Court and they would all have suites — but they would not spend 50 grand on a piece of research, something I could never understand. In the end, we ditched them. Secondly, they wanted us in for only 10 per cent, just a touch of green in the application — they never really rated us as a significant partner. We felt a bit more confident than that — we had broken the monopoly in taking on Eircom. We should take our seat in the front row, why would we get into the second row?

It was a nervous time for the board of Esat. It was, in some ways, a mirror image of the board of 98FM — about 70 per cent of the directors from 98FM were on the Esat board. We'd all been together for a number of years and all the board had written cheques to fund their shares. We never had any rancour. The problems were big but the "Bosnians" were gone and we were beginning to have a bit of craic.

We were rolling out Esat and then we started the radio business in Sweden, which was losing a hundred grand a month. We made a miscalculation. We got our station, Klassiska Hits 106FM, to number three in the Stockholm marketplace. It sounded fantastic, with loads of listeners, but there was no revenue. The Swedes would not buy radio advertising. They were press-centric. I now had a business that was improving slightly in the Czech Republic but still losing money, I had a business losing a hundred grand a month in Stockholm and then I had Esat burning cash. By July 1995, we had run out of money;

we had spent the $10 million. I went to London with Paul Connolly to see my venture capitalist. I said, "Massimo, I've good news and bad news. Which do you want first?" He said, "I want the good news." "Well, the good news is we have a great chance of winning the GSM licence." He said, "Ah yes, sure, sure." I said, "The bad news is we've no money left." The guy just died, his face drained; we had forgotten that he had to go to his credit committee to tell them the bad news — he was going to be the messenger who would be slaughtered. I told him I needed $5 million and asked him how much he would lend it to me for. He said, "I'm not lending it — I want this to be in equity." I knew if I brought in $5 million in equity, my 66 per cent shareholding would be heavily diluted.

Maybe it was a stupid thing, but I always felt I had to have more than 51 per cent and be in control — that was ingrained in me for a long time. I could never get over that. However, when you create a large-scale business, you have to cross the bridge and accept that you will never own 51 per cent forever and realise that, if you can own a slice of a bigger pie, it's going to be better ultimately. At that stage, however, that was anathema to me. He had the usual one-sided venture capital agreement with all clauses in his favour. Really, I was not in control, he was in control. At the end of the day, he had the twine. John Callaghan, Paul and I debated for hours with Massimo and I eventually asked him, "What return per annum would you expect if you were putting in equity?" He said, "30 per cent." I said, "OK. I'll borrow the money from you at 30 per cent per annum." He said, "OK." He had calculated that I'd be bolloxed another six months down the road and he'd be converting his $5 million anyway, so he saw me as only putting off tomorrow. What he did not realise was that, if I won the licence, I'd never have any problems about finance — I'd have other options at a higher price. We took the $5 million off him and it fuelled us to go ahead with the licence application.

We had 25 people in a separate building working on the licence application — that was a huge expense. Plus, we had consultants by the busload because, in 1995, we did not know anything about the cellular business and we needed a dose of expertise. Six weeks before the application was due, we got Telenor in, the Norwegian PTT state-owned company, as a partner. They started to contribute their money but they would not give any for the work that had been done to that date — so we funded the whole bloody thing. They would do only the incremental, 50/50.

I remember going on holidays to Portugal in July 1995. I was up on the roof of the rented house, hiding from my future wife, on a mobile phone going through sheet upon sheet of the bid, every chapter of the application — there were thousands of pages. We just kept honing it and trying to load the dice to impress the assessors. Lucy Gaffney, who led the bid team, and all the Board members, including Pádraig Ó hUiginn, would sit around the table working on how we could improve the application in the eyes of the assessors.

D-Day came and we were supposed to put in the application — and they cancelled the competition at the last minute because the EU said that, if the Government were going to have an auction, they would have to charge Eircell for their licence. That was ring-a-rosie — money going out of Eircell into Government coffers and back. However, while they were reconsidering, we used the four weeks to send our application to consultants in London and we got them to score our bid and to improve it. We did a dummy assessment procedure using them. They had assessed other bids around the world but they were not involved with the competition here in Ireland. We paid them 50 grand to read our application and to tell us where it didn't hang together — numbers, inconsistencies in the text, the strategic direction. We used the month to polish it. We also used the month to get more planning permissions for towers because we wanted 150 planning permissions in the application box. We had a brand name in Esat Digifone, with which we went up front. From our point of view, it was a critical break — the fact that the Department changed their mind at the last minute on the terms of the competition.

The begrudgers will say that Ó hUiginn used his influence in Brussels to kill the auction and have a beauty process instead. We had nothing to do with that. In fact, it was some other bidder who went to Brussels to say that the competition was unfair — we were too afraid to do that, even though we agreed with them. We felt that, if we had made any intervention in Brussels, it could backfire on us.

We had an oral hearing for the licence. Preparation was going to be key. We took a room in a hotel and we had the six people who would be presenting and we had a dummy interview panel all day the day before we met the assessors. The dummy panel was chaired by Pádraig Ó hUiginn and he asked us the most difficult questions. We felt we had made a pretty good presentation, but Pádraig said, "You've missed the point, all of you. You've got to take out the competition. You've got to draw attention to your competitors' weaknesses and contrast that with your strengths." It was good advice. We spent the rest of that day nailing our competition. We knew who the other bidders were and their weaknesses. We knew the assessors would identify the weaknesses and if we, in contrast, had solutions for those weaknesses, we were always going to be in a stronger position. We did extremely well in the oral hearing — it lasted three hours to the minute. It was brutal. I led the team: a couple of Telenor guys, Peter O'Donoghue on finance, Barry Maloney, John Hennessy on human resources. We did not have Pádraig on the team because we felt the civil servants might feel a bit of pressure!

Waiting for the decision, we were running out of twine again. We sent people around Dublin to get cheques from the advertising agencies for 98FM. The camaraderie that had developed in preparing the bid was fantastic — every two weeks we would find a reason to have a huge piss-up and, even on the night that we put in the bid, we went on the lash. We didn't have a party — we decided we'd have a knees-up and get locked. We always had events which got everybody together. While we felt we had done a good job, the pressure was immense because everything was riding on this. This was putting all your money on one horse. We could not make a mistake.

I don't know if, in your lifetime, when you look back you see that you have had a purple patch where you say, God, we were brilliant for a month. One of my highs was winning a Third B's medal in Wanderers; we had a month where we were all together as a team. This was one of those months where everything was coming together. The other month where things came together for us as a team was when we were doing the BT deal, between Telenor's hostile offer and the sale of the company. We were right on our game, we were razor sharp and we'd everything prepared. We hit the purple patch at just the right time. You see it in football where a team does really well coming into the end of the season.

We were waiting around for what seemed like an eternity but it was only about six weeks. I have seen so many difficulties being overcome through being clinically prepared — you can excel in one area even if you have a desperate weakness in another. The weakness we had was finance. When we went to the institutions, they said, "Get the licence and we'll give you the money." We said, we need the money now to show the assessors. The institutions told us to get lost. I went to Dermot Desmond[1] and told him I needed somebody to underwrite 20 per cent. He said, "I'll do it." We agreed a fee and he did it.

The licence, I thought, was the first sign of the new Ireland. In the old Ireland, it would all be chicory with politicians becoming involved, nudge nudge, wink wink. The GSM licence was the first example of a transparent process, independently assessed. It didn't matter whether you were Fianna Fáil, Fine Gael or Labour. It must have been the first time in the history of the State where there was no agenda.[2]

In parallel with all this, by the first week of October 1995 we were out of dough. There was a scramble for cash. Eircom were about to cut us off. Two weeks before we won the licence, we needed 50 grand to pay the bill. I knew we had to survive those two weeks to hear the licence result before we would go back to the venture capitalist or take drastic measures.

In the middle of all this, I had made two million quid out of a building in the IFSC. I bought the Stack B site, built it, rented it to AIB and then flicked it and made the two bar. I was going to put the two bar into Esat when my father nearly physically restrained me. Owen O'Connell from William Fry, who was a close adviser, said, "You're out of your bloody tree! Don't put it in, because if this all goes south, you'll need the £2 million to get going again." I didn't put it in and we struggled on.

One day I got a call from Andrew Hanlon to say that the Department were making an announcement on the licence result that afternoon. Everybody who worked on the licence application gathered in the 98FM newsroom to wait for a call from Hanlon — all the staff of 98FM, standing in the corridors and the newsroom, waiting. Hanlon rang through and said, "We won." The place erupted. I put my hand through the suspended ceiling. We just did a dance. Half the people

---

[1] *Out on Their Own*, pp. 75–89.

[2] The relevant Government minister at the time was Mr Michael Lowry TD. On 26 September 1997, a Tribunal of Inquiry, the Moriarty Tribunal, was established by the Oireachtas (Parliament) to enquire, inter alia, "whether Mr Lowry did any act or made any decision in the course of any ministerial office held by him to confer any benefit on any person making a payment [to him]". Denis O'Brien was questioned by the Tribunal, which had not concluded its investigations when this book was completed.

were crying, half the people were shouting and roaring. That was it — we knew that we were saved. We had moved from the fourth to the third division. Winning the GSM licence would bring us to the second division and we'd a great chance of getting up to the premier league — business is all about scale.

I said that we would not have a piss-up that night, we'd just have a few pints; we had to wait for the Norwegians to come from Oslo to make sure they were here to celebrate. We decided we'd have a huge fleadh the next night but that night we went up to Scruffy Murphy's and had a rake of pints. I walked home and stopped in Burger King in Baggot Street for a Whopper and chips and stuffed myself. I got into bed and could not sleep. I got out of bed and drove into the office at about four in the morning. There was a letter on the fax from Nat-West Capital Markets: "Dear Mr O'Brien, congratulations on winning the licence. We are very happy to provide you with £70 million towards your capital costs." That was a good example of the difference between the low and the high and the inch that separates success from failure. Sometimes businesses don't get the lucky break. Half the time, people just collapse. Business is 50 per cent luck and 50 per cent preparation.

We raised 27 million quid at $100 million valuation in June 1996. Then we did a high-yield bond offering for $110 million in January 1997. We had an IPO on the NASDAQ and the EASDAQ for a $223 million valuation in November 1997. That was the first time we went public with Esat. I bought my radio station back and Esat became a pure-play telecoms company. We launched Esat Digifone's GSM network in March 1997 and then did a couple of other high-yield bond offerings. We raised about £500 million in high-yield bonds. The beauty of that financial instrument is that it suits our industry down to the ground because in the telecoms business you have to build your network, put your switches in, buy everything and then turn it on and hope the customers will come to you. It's a big up-front capital investment.

We were laying a fibre optic network all around the country on the CIE railway lines. We were fibreing all the cities — we were going through £100 million in capex a year on the fixed line, another £100 million on Esat Digifone on mobile. It was like a hopper for cash — you'd throw cash in and you'd get your capex out of the other end and then you throw more cash in. In the meantime, you were growing your revenues by 15 per cent per quarter.

The key thing that helped us was getting the right management team. You can't run a business on one person — you need at least six really capable people. I brought in Sean Corkery as our COO. He had an IT background with multinationals. He brought great discipline into the revenue chain, in other words, into the predictability of the revenue line. We had to step up our revenue on a quarterly basis but we realised we had to do a drastic overhaul of our systems. Everybody had to be geared up into delivering numbers. When you're a private company you can miss your numbers. If you're a public company, you can never miss. Sean Corkery tightened the whole thing up, which allowed me to sleep at night, but also to go out and raise money, buy companies and move the thing forward. He was a very important guy. Then there was Neil Parkinson, our chief financial officer, a key manager. He brought discipline into the numbers and how we spent the company's capex budget. We had Lesley Buckley, who was the problem-solver. He was a mentor to the management team. When you are increasing your business by 15 per cent every quarter, you have huge growing pains. Having a guy in his fifties with lots of industrial management experience was vital. We were in our thirties or early forties — none of us had that kind of experience. Lucy Gaffney launched and ran a separate consumer division and she was also instrumental in the successful launch of Esat Digifone. Brenda O'Keefe was our key treasury person responsible for all our capital markets fundraising deals with Paul Connolly. Everybody had a key role in building the company.

The board was a Jack Charlton line-out — it was not a very fancy board, it was workmanlike. Most of the people were very experienced, a contrast with a very young management team. We never had a vote in ten years. The average age of the board was 60-plus, but each individual Board member had something to offer. Take John Callaghan, former managing partner in KPMG: he brought credibility that the numbers were going to be right and had a lot of public company experience. He was chairman of the Audit Committee. Tom Keaveney advised the Board on capital market aspects and had credibility in the eyes of our US investors. Padraig Ó hUiginn brought credibility from a government and European point of view — the investors could see that he knew the whole government and licensing side. Brendan

O'Kelly was a long time advisor since 1988. Richard O'Toole had worked in the European Union as Chef de Cabinet for Peter Sutherland.[3] Mark Roden was with me from the outset and was incisive on strategic issues. My father was always with me — in the Board's eyes, he was the guy who would keep me under control. Ironically, he would never be totally for everything I was saying. The lads would know that, after the Board meeting, he would button me down. Paul Connolly was on the fund-raising side. We raised $900 million over five years. He was studying the market perspective, how we would raise money and keep the story right. He always accompanied me on the roadshows — we did them every three months. We did two or three offerings a year. Massimo Prelz, as I mentioned, was my venture capitalist and he was also on the Board all the way through. When he sold Advent's shares in a secondary offering, I asked him to stay and I gave him share options. That was unusual — you normally get rid of your VC but I thought he had something to contribute and he did.

As a management team we had always felt that Irish companies, with a few notable exceptions, had done a lousy job in the capital markets. Look at the number of Irish companies that went to London and floated and then blew up — there were a lot of them over the years, particularly in the eighties. Ryanair, Elan[4] and ourselves were the first three NASDAQ-quoted companies. If we did a good job in the capital markets, the share price would go up and we would all be very wealthy. We'd do a lot of preparation before we hit the road — I'd be preparing my handwritten notes, key messages to juice up the fund manager to catch his/her attention. We would prepare and prepare and prepare. We would have a sheet from previous meetings on each of the fund managers, what they did not like, what investments they were in, what their questions were the last time and what our answers were, what predictions we made. We had a ferocious discipline — we would see our investors three or four times a year. Most companies do it only once or twice a year. Then we'd fly in to high-yield conferences where twenty companies would present in a day. We'd go anywhere — to Denver, Colorado or Columbus, Ohio — anywhere we could get an audience. It all paid off and let me tell you why.

---

[3] See Chapter 16, pp. 313–334.

[4] See Chapter 5, pp. 85–102.

In September 1999, our stock was about $30 per share. Then it went up to $40. We went to the Board and told them that somebody out there was looking to buy us. You hear rumours — we knew all the investment bankers. It was pure instinct. We said to the Board that we needed to get ready for it at our next Board meeting in the middle of November 1999 and we had check lists of things to do if somebody made an offer. We had everything regimented. The Board asked if we were over-reacting. I said, "Something tells me that something is happening — the share price is moving up." It had moved by $20. On the last Monday in November, I said to Paul Connolly, "We're hitting the road." We'd come off a roadshow only six weeks previously. I said, "We're going out — we're going to talk to all our big holders." We went to London and did about eight calls in two days. We were driving out to Heathrow to take the evening flight to New York, starting there the next day, when I got a call. Sally-Anne McEvoy, who has worked with me for years, said, "Terje Thon (the chairman of Telenor) has been on and wants to talk to you." I rang Terje Thon in Oslo. He said, "I'd like to see you." I told him I was in the middle of a roadshow, I could not go to Oslo. We had so many conversations about us buying Telenor out of Esat Digifone and they were going nowhere. I wasn't going to break my roadshow. He said, "I do want to see you." I told him I was on my way to New York: "I'll see you in New York tomorrow." He said, "OK, I'll see you in New York tomorrow." I rang our investment bank, Chase, and said, "Lads, this guy is coming to see me in New York." They said, "Something big is up."

I arranged to meet Terje at one o'clock. I knew the only way he'd get there was using Concorde. You take a nine o'clock flight in the morning and it gets you there at ten in the morning. There was no other flight that would get you in that early for lunch, not from Oslo. We had our guy from Chase on the Concorde marking him. He rang me at five in the morning and said, "There are three guys coming on the plane. They don't see me." When they arrived in New York, I *knew* there was something up. We had a private room in the New York Palace. We had met four investors that morning and we had an hour's break for lunch to meet the Telenor guys. I should have told you that the reason we went on the road in London and New York was to tell our investors that, if anybody made a bid for the company, we would never sell it for less than $100 and we were at $60. They kinda smiled and said, "Denis, the market's great but how are you going to get $100?" When somebody makes a hostile offer you need to get your investors to start thinking and get greedy and thinking about what number they'll sell for. That's why we were racing to see all the fund managers who held our shares.

We sat down with the Telenor people in this little room with a couple of sandwiches, Cokes and coffee. I poured the coffee for Terje Thon. I left the sugar and the milk in the middle of the table. He took the milk and I could see his hand was shaking and I thought to myself, this guy is up to something. In his Norwegian accent, he said, "We would like to thank you for seeing us. We would like to make an offer for your company. We would like to buy you out. We think it's a very happy arrangement for you. We can make an offer with a seven in front of it." I said, "Look, Terje. The mistakes you made in the last two or three years were: number one, you didn't treat us properly; number two, you were rude; and, number three, you were totally uncooperative." I explained in detail to Terje how our relationship had deteriorated once we won the GSM licence. They underestimated by 50 per cent the cost of the project. They would take no responsibility for anything, they'd never admit to a mistake — they were extremely arrogant. They screwed us around for months and months — and years. They would speak Norwegian at Board meetings. Dermot Desmond was pissed off with them — they started suing him. Terje looked at me in shock.

I said to him, "Hold it right there — I'm never going to sell to you, even if you're the last offer in the world. You've insulted us; you've insulted your partner, Dermot Desmond; you have been totally miserable to deal with and totally incompetent. You have a nerve trying to buy our company. I'm going off to see my investors. Goodbye. You're welcome to stay for lunch."

Both Paul and I wanted to sleep that night, so we drank a lot of red wine. That was out of character because, when you are on a roadshow, the last thing you want is drink. I guess the pressure of it all had to be released somehow. I got a call in bed at two in the morning from Terje Thon. He said, "This is Terje Thon. I would like to tell you we are making an offer for your company at $72 and we are announcing it this morning." I said goodbye and put the phone down with a bang. It was 1 December 1999. The game was on.

Luckily we had all the preparatory work done. We had a template of what to do in the first 24 hours. Normally when somebody makes a hostile offer, there is absolute chaos — what does each person do? Then you have to get your advisors revved up — you cannot reject a bid without going to them and getting independent advice. I made a number of phone calls straight away. The first was to Minister Mary O'Rourke TD to let her know out of courtesy what was happening. Surprisingly, at 7.20 a.m., she was at her desk in the Department and her private secretary put me through immediately. The second was to Geraldine Harney of RTE who had phoned me the night before and left a message. I thought she was on to the story. I called her at 7.30 a.m.— she does the business news at 7.45 a.m. I asked her if she had heard the news and she said, "What news?" So I had kinda dropped myself in it. I said, "Telenor are making an offer." She said, "What! How much will you sell it for?" Not knowing the takeover panel rules, I said, "We'll sell it for $100." She ran the story even before Telenor had announced, which was troublesome for me later because I had to go down to the takeover panel and explain my gaffe — they thought I was messing them. On air, Geraldine said, "Telenor have made an offer but it is *believed* that management will sell only for $100." It was critical to get that $100 out again to our investors — we had to get it in the public domain.

Then it was all battle stations. I dropped out of the roadshow. We went back to Dublin and did a couple of things quickly. We divided up our investment bank teams: first, we formed a defence team with Chase, Davy's and CSFB; and, secondly, we formed a White Knight team led by Donaldson Lufkin Jenrette (DLJ). With four different investment banks involved, you don't want the defence team to know what the White Knight team is doing because they're all getting phone calls from their pals in other banks: "What are you doing? Who are you talking to?" We did what Michael Collins did — create distinct information cells. I would not allow one team to talk to the other. Lucy Gaffney and myself and then, alternatively, Neil Parkinson, but always Paul Connolly — worked with DLJ on the White Knight side. We picked DLJ because we had a high regard for them and, in particular, Tony Belinkoff whom we christened "Tony Telekom". We were out looking for a White Knight within 24 hours. The first company we went to see was Sonera in Finland. They were the PTT up there, very progressive guys. They own 40 per cent of the biggest mobile company in Turkey, Turkcell, very entrepreneurial people.

We felt that, if Telenor were smart, they would have us followed, so we rented a private plane. It's a long way to Helsinki and we were feeling a bit shagged after our long meeting with Sonera. We were waiting around this little private terminal and who walks in but Ron Sommer, the Deutsche Telekom chairman. We exchanged pleasantries. We each knew what the other was at. While I was with the CFO of Sonera trying to get them interested in making a bid for us, he was with the CEO and he was trying to buy Sonera. We met about eight or nine companies over a two-week period with plenty of follow-up information meetings. The list narrowed down to two, one of which was BT. Meanwhile, Telenor had increased their bid to $85. Our defence team shot them to pieces. We would be in the media every day — the mistake they made was not to put executives in Dublin to run their offer. They tried to do it by remote control from Oslo. Eileen Gleeson ran our PR campaign. We called her Paul McGrath because there was nobody better at defending and attacking at the same time. We slaughtered Telenor in the press. We leaked all the stories about their messing over the years. We then hired the equivalent of NCB in Oslo, a local company called Sundal Collier. We wanted a Norwegian perspective on how Telenor might think and how we might anticipate them. We also hired an Oslo PR company to spin stories.

It was the time of their merger with Telia, so they made a joint offer for Esat. Their chief executive gave a journalist a toe in the backside one day and Telenor got eaten in the press. Then their merger fell apart, so we had loads of material to slaughter them with. Our defence team, particularly Eileen Gleeson on the PR front, were shooting at them every day while we, on the White Knight side, were out there trying to get another buyer at a higher price.

After our first meeting with British Telecom, I knew there was something afoot about it — you have an instinct when you are a seller. There was Paul Connolly, Tony Belinkoff, the DLJ investment banker guy, and myself. We had the BT CFO sitting opposite me, Robert Brace, a very nice, warm Welsh guy. There was also a Northern Irish BT fellow and a guy from Rothschilds, a man called Higgins. He started beating me up on price. I had said to the lads before we went in, "If we start to get beaten up here, we're going to walk" — this was all prepared. I said across the table, "I didn't come here to get beaten up. We have a very valuable business. Obviously it's just too valuable for you to buy." I got up from my chair, the two lads, suitably stage-managed, with me. Brace made a move to calm things down and asked us to sit down again. I knew then that they were interested. If they were not interested, they would have let us walk out the door. The tightrope was stretched fully, thank God.

It was all cloak-and-dagger — we had been brought through BT's basement, up in a service lift to the gin palace. That was 23 December. We went home that night on Aer Lingus and who was sitting in front of us but the whole AIB corporate finance team working for Telenor. We had our printed defence document with us with "Reject the Telenor offer" emblazoned across it. I had been in UCD with one of the AIB guys, Mon O'Driscoll. Joking, I said, "Mon, you're only a bollocks working for those tossers." He told me good humouredly to buzz off. I took our defence document out of the bag and Paul and I signed it and I said to Mon, "See you on 11 January" — the closing day — "but you'll be disappointed". I gave the offer document to Mon and shook the back of his seat all the way home across the Irish Sea. The banter was great between us all; we were not drinking but we felt as if we were drunk. We knew we were going to get a deal with BT — we were going home happy for Christmas. We had lots of pressure because the other potential bidders were coming at us but we had identified a White Knight we could do a deal with.

We were down in Mount Juliet on Stephen's Day and I said to Paul, "We're going to work today." We got on the phone in a little room in Mount Juliet and got in touch with all the fund managers in the UK and the US. Our minder, Des Carville, a young investment banker from Davy Stockbrokers, was noting our conversation so he could report back to the takeover panel. I knew we wouldn't get many of them but I left voicemails saying that I wanted to talk to them about our White Knight strategy — "Please give me a call back, here's my mobile number." It would register with them that we were working on Stephen's Day — it was just a bit of a game to keep them in the loop. We had to keep them in the ruck to keep the share price up. If one of them started selling stock, that would bring the price down and then it would be a house of cards.

On 7 January we had another meeting with BT and this was the time we were going to do a deal. We had kept the proposed deal airtight. Our defence team of investment bank advisors did not know we were doing a deal with BT. The only people who knew were Belinkoff and a sub-committee of the board. When we went to BT, there was a roomful of them surrounding Robert Brace, the CFO. Going in, I said to Paul, "If there's a pile of clowns in the room, we'll never get a deal done because they'll be pushing their testosterone over the table." They all started talking and I said to Robert Brace, "Do you mind if we just go for a walk?" I had seen this before in 1983, when I worked with Tony Ryan. Gary Wendt, President of GE Capital, and Tony Ryan were in the middle of heated negotiations where all the advisors were trying to get their spoke in. Realising this, Tony went off for a walk with Gary through the grounds of his house at Kilboy and ended up agreeing a deal between them.

A fellow can do a deal on his own much easier than he can in front of his team. I walked down the corridor with Robert. Everything in BT is labelled. I saw a door with non-executive director on it. I went in and pulled a chair out from behind the desk to sit knee to knee in front of him and I said, "Robert, I have another offer — it's a high offer, but it's a mixture of paper and cash. I don't want to take it but you're forcing me. You will wake up tomorrow and I want to know how you will feel if you let this deal out of your grasp. You won't be happy, will you?" He said, "No. I won't be happy." I said, "Give me $105 a share and I'll do a deal with you now and I'll deliver every aspect of it." He said, "I can't do it — we're at $93 or $94." This went on for about 30 minutes, toing and froing. In the end, I stuck out my hand and said, "$100 on the nail." I could see his hand coming towards me and I just grabbed it. I said, "Have we got a deal?" He said, "We've got a deal."

Rather than me announcing the deal to the roomful of advisors, I asked Robert if he would explain what the deal was. I knew he was going to sell it and nobody was going to question him, none of the bankers or anybody else. Suddenly, everybody became great friends and hugging, nearly kissing each other.

The problem was, we could not go on the lash to celebrate because the word would get out, so we went back to the airport, had a couple of pints, and knew that we had a window of five days so that BT could print up their documents and announce but also get all the conditions precedent in place, one of which was that Dermot Desmond would sell 1 per cent in Esat Digifone. Telenor and Digifone each had 49.5 per cent and Dermot had the 1 per cent swing — they were suing Dermot every week in the High Court trying to disenfranchise his vote and Dermot had told us he was with us, that he would support us

every step of the way. I would phone him each day and tell him exactly what was going on. The Norwegians and their lawyers and their
investment bankers had forgotten that Dermot, when he bought his
shares in 1996, had one free transfer without any offer-around provisions. In other words, he could sell that 1 per cent to anybody in the
world but he could not sell it to Esat or to Telenor. Dermot signed up,
and we thought the Telenor people would suspect something, because
they were in business with BT in Germany and there had been a silent
period. Owen O'Connell of William Fry, our solicitors, together with
Paul and myself, were working all night, signing up documents. On
the way home, Paul drove past AIB Corporate Finance opposite Jurys
Hotel and the lights weren't on. He rang me at 3.00 a.m. and said,
"The lights are off — they don't know what's going on."

We had called a press conference in the Berkeley Court Hotel for
that morning. The chairman of BT, Sir Iain Vallance, came over to
announce the deal. It all had to be timed to the minute. BT did not
want to sign Dermot up for 1 per cent before we made the announcement, in case Telenor sought a High Court injunction. Halfway
through the press conference, Sir Ian's equerry came up behind him
and whispered that the deal with Dermot was signed. Next thing, a
question popped up from the floor, "What about the 1 per cent?" Iain
Vallance, cool as a cucumber, said, "That's already signed up." It almost appeared as if the questioner knew what the equerry had told
Sir Iain.

There are two epilogues to all this. One, we were delighted that we
had stuffed Telenor — we never wanted to sell to them. Two, we had
done a good job in terms of the capital markets — people could not
believe that we had got the $100. CEOs always say their share price is
under-valued and all that crap. You never normally deliver the $100
— we thought we would try and get $100 and we did. That was the
main thing.

A big concern of mine was how the staff would react. If you, as the
CEO, are seen to make a lot of money, you worry how people will perceive that. You could be seen as greedy or looking after yourself, a *mé
féiner*. What I had forgotten was that everybody in Esat got the twine.
The staff of Esat Telecom got $250 million in vested share options. I
was so focused on seeing off Telenor that I had forgotten that all the
staff were on their screens watching the share price every minute of
the day — everybody had calculated how much they were going to

make. We called a staff meeting immediately — 1,000 people came into the ballroom in the Berkeley Court — this was straight after the press announcement. To me, it felt like an anticlimax. I thought I was going to get hammered for selling the company.

The place erupted. The management team got a standing ovation. We had forgotten that they all were making serious amounts of money — people who were earning 20 grand a year were going to get 50 grand in cash. How long would it take somebody to save 50 grand? We opened a free bar in the Berkeley Court and it was like a rugby international night. We had a big fleadh.

Another epilogue was when the hostile offer was launched on 1 December. I had sat in a room in William Fry Solicitors with all our investment bankers. I said, "Paul and I can get $72 per share from Telenor. I don't need you fellows to get us that. The deal is this: you get nothing up to $72, you get a certain amount up to $99, but, if you get $100 or more, you're all on jumbo fees. I assume everybody's happy with that?" They were all happy with that. They were going to make their standard fee plus a significant bonus — 50 per cent — plus we had our PR company, Eileen Gleeson, our legal advisers, William Fry, all on the same bonus fee basis. Everybody was pulling the oars at the same time. That way, we had no dissension. When you divide investment bankers and give some people the sexy bits and the others the grunt work, people get upset. Because they all shared the common goal, they were going to work their tails off for six weeks. All the advisors would make a huge amount of money for their firms and subsequently each of the lads would get their deal-related bonus. That's what ultimately happened. That's the story.

Life did not end. Normally you are much older when you sell your company. I was 41. The fact that I had made a lot of money did not have any impact at all. It didn't make much of a change. I made $300 million but, before that, with other investments and interests, I was very comfortable. But $300 million in one fell swoop was phenomenal. A lot of complications came with it, because you've got to manage it. I had to get an infrastructure, to get organised. I had to employ people to help me in a personal capacity. I had a lot of other things going on and there were the elements of an infrastructure there. I went through a sad phase because I knew the craic had gone out of it — running a public company is very demanding, but it's also very enjoyable. It's supercharged stuff. The buzz, the buying of companies, the leading of people . . . once you sell, it's all over. In some ways, I should have walked straight out the door into the sunset, but I had said to BT that I would help them into the saddle to ensure a smooth transition. Sean Corkery had resigned two months before Telenor made the offer. He wanted to go back to Limerick to his family and stop commuting to Dublin. Neil Parkinson was our chief financial officer, we had worked great together for four years and he had a big impact on the success of the company. He worked seven days a week and was exhausted. When I gave up being CEO, BT asked me whom I would recommend as CEO for the company. It was a toss up between Lucy and Neil. I recommended Lucy Gaffney, but she did not want to take the job. For ten years she had left her home at 6.30 in the morning to get into the office early — she is a ferocious worker and she was tired. The board offered it to Lucy but she declined. It was a unanimous decision to ask Neil Parkinson. Neil accepted but first took a three-month sabbatical. Lucy held the fort while he was away. She did a good chunk of the integration work while Neil was re-charging his batteries. Neil became the Group CEO from 1 July last year (2000). There was a lot of integration work — Ocean was merged in with Esat Telecom, as was Esat Digifone — we'd all these different businesses that we had to bring together under one structure. As the culture with the new ownership changed every day, every week, peo-ple I had worked with for five years and more would come in to tell me they were resigning. Eighty per cent of the management team re-signed within six months. I knew they were right to go because they felt the BT world would be more bureaucratic than they were used to. Also they all had their F.O. money.

For me, the craic was gone. I struggled on with this for about seven months and in August I told my wife Catherine I was just drop-ping out. She agreed with me. She could see I wasn't enjoying seeing the changes. I resigned on 7 September 2000 and that was it.

Three or four weeks later, Vodafone made their offer for Eircom's mobile business, Eircell. The old Esat team used to meet occasionally for lunch or at a party. At one of these gatherings we got talking in a corner. We thought — if Vodafone were buying Eircell, maybe we should have a look at buying the fixed line business of Eircom. Soon after, Paul and I got calls from investment bankers with whom we had worked before and they said, "Denis, why don't you have a look?" I thought we might have a go, why not? I never expected to go back into the telecom business. This was a financial opportunity and I decided to have a go. That's where we're at.[5]

---

[5] Denis O'Brien did have a go with a grouping called eIsland. When this book had to be finished, August 2001, the only rival group, Valentia, headed by Sir Anthony O'Reilly, was favoured to win the contest, having secured undertakings from Comsource, a joint venture between KPN of the Netherlands and Telia of Sweden, with a shareholding of 35 per cent, and, crucially, from the Employee Share Ownership Trust, with 13,000 members and a shareholding of 14.9 per cent. The ESOT consistently opposed the eIsland bid.

14

Fran Rooney

Baltimore Technologies plc

*"Don't forget where we've come from. Nothing has changed.
The same rules apply: team work, discipline and preparation."*

Francis Rooney was, at the time of this conversation, the Chief Executive Officer of Baltimore Technologies plc.[1]

He was born in Dublin on 2 December 1956. His father is John Rooney, a plumber. His mother is Dolores Godwin, a housewife. He is the eldest in a family of six: John, Joseph, Raymond, Dermot and Imelda. He is married to Mary O'Connell, who was a buyer with the Switzer Group. They have three children: Yvonne (18), David (15) and Laura (13).

He was educated at Westland Row CBS and at the Institute of Public Administration (Degree in Administrative Science awarded by Trinity College Dublin). He is a chartered accountant.

His first job was with the Department of Posts and Telegraphs (1974–1979). He subsequently worked at the Department of Transport and Power in the Air Navigation Services Office (1979–1983); An Post (1984–1989), in the finance and IT departments; National Irish Bank (1990–1993), where he headed the credit card business and also the asset finance business. He left NIB in 1993 to start a company called Meridian, where he was the first employee and managing director. He joined Quay Financial Software which was sold in 1995. He set up Baltimore in 1996. He is a director of Norkom Technologies, a private company.

The conversation was recorded on 25 January 2001 in Fran Rooney's office in Baltimore Technologies headquarters at Parkgate Street, Dublin 8.

---

[1] He resigned as Chief Executive Officer of Baltimore Technologies on 10 July 2001. See page 290.

Fran Rooney

My family background was one of strong values of honesty and integrity, and that has greatly influenced my business life. I believe in being fair and straight, with employees, customers and partners. In our business culture, the employees feel that they are treated fairly and they respond accordingly with loyalty and commitment to the company.

I was educated by the Christian Brothers in Westland Row and got a good Leaving Certificate. In 1974, most school leavers went directly into employment rather than to university. Most of the opportunities were in banks, the civil service or insurance companies. I was offered jobs in the Central Bank, Bank of Ireland and the civil service. I eventually chose the civil service, because it seemed to offer greater opportunities for advancement.

Soon after joining, I started to study. First, I studied for promotion opportunities. Most of the promotions were decided through a written exam and an interview. I was promoted a number of times. Later on, I did a number of courses to get further qualifications — first a diploma in public administration with the Institute of Public Administration followed by a degree in administrative science. I also completed various computer courses including systems analysis and software programming.

I felt that, along with computer studies, the financial arena was important. I frequently met finance professionals who did not understand technology. Understanding the two disciplines was a much-needed and rare skill. Initially, I studied Certified Accountancy but then felt that Chartered Accountancy was a stronger qualification. I persuaded An Post management to initiate a Training in Industry scheme through which I could be articled to an accountant in industry, rather than having to go the traditional route through an accountant's office.

I was now married and my day consisted of rising early to study, going to the office, coming home, spending some time with my wife and children, then back to study. I rarely attended lectures, preferring to study directly from textbooks and course material.

I continued to play sport. I think that sport, especially team sport, is the greatest character builder of all. I played football up to two years ago. Now I kick-box every Tuesday, Thursday and Saturday. The discipline and camaraderie are important. Many of the people with whom I played football are still friends with great trust in each other. There are huge bonds forged on the playing field. This and family values are probably the biggest influences on my life.

I did not find the job in the public sector very challenging but there was great discipline. I believe in discipline. Now, in business, I see that the bigger the challenge, the harder you have to work. One of the requirements of the public service was an ability to write clear, accurate, succinct and timely reports getting the facts right. Often, a report I would write could end up on the minister's desk or in the Dáil. I was also involved in drafting Air Navigation legislation. I was not stretched in the public sector: it allowed me to focus on other things like my studies and football. I always knew I would move on — it was a question of finding the right job. The transition from the public to the private sector was easy for me.

I qualified as an accountant in 1989 and took up a position at National Irish Bank, which was the old Northern Bank that had just been taken over by National Australia Bank. It was a young dynamic bank, with Alex Spain as Chairman and Jim Lacey as Chief Executive. I was attracted by the fact that they were aiming to take some of the market share held by the two main banks. The first job was to rationalise the asset finance leasing business.

When I went to the private sector, the big surprise was that things were not any more difficult. When we had sorted out the asset finance division — and that involved some hard decisions like redundancies — I took over the credit card business, which National Irish Bank were promoting aggressively and through which we were trying to attract customers. We brought in very good systems to make it easy to deliver the business.

The thing I remember best was pushing the decision-making process right down. Young people coming into the bank were able to make decisions directly with customers using a new system we had installed. Queries that previously would have come to the manager were delegated down to junior assistants, up to certain amounts of money. What it ultimately meant was that I had almost worked myself out of the job. Christmas in the credit card business was the busiest time of the year for us. For me, Christmas 1992 was the least busy period in my career.

On 23 December 1992, I got a phone call from a headhunter asking me to meet with some South African investors. Initially I wasn't interested, but the headhunter persuaded me. They wanted to invest in a business, which ultimately became Meridian. The business was to reclaim VAT for corporations worldwide. There were a lot of corporations both inside and outside the EU that incurred VAT charges outside their own country and were not aware that they could reclaim them. For example, Irish businessmen on a convention in another country would incur VAT charges on hotel bills, airfares, etc. — all of which was reclaimable. In our first 18 months, we reclaimed almost $60 million.

Initially, we needed to learn the VAT rules in every country. We employed individuals who could speak the languages of the EU jurisdiction and also Chinese and Japanese. We targeted larger global businesses such as IBM and Hitachi. The process was quite simple. They shipped us all of their invoices, which we evaluated, decided whether they were reclaimable or not and then submitted the claim to the various jurisdictions. It was a people-intensive business: the high-tech part was the process of putting the claim together. The claims had to be submitted within six months of the year-end, so we needed to make the process extremely efficient. Within a few hours of the invoices coming in, we had a claim ready to go out. We charged customers 50 per cent of their first claim and after that 20 per cent. There was also a treasury element — we were sitting each night on quite a substantial amount of cash in various currencies. The treasury was profitable in itself. The initial investment in the company was $10 million and then $20 million. I started work on 17 February but did not formally leave the bank until April. By the time I left, I had employed a complete management team for Meridian. I interviewed at night. I started work at 6.30 a.m. each morning and finished at midnight or after.

I had no premises. I found an old IDA advance factory in Tallaght, 40,000 square feet. By 3 May 1993, we had employed 97 people and had trained each of them in the process. We spent the entire Easter weekend training the first batch of 16. We asked them to spend another weekend training the next 16. When I say the 97 were all trained, there was still a lot of doubt about the depth of their training. We had to spend considerable time hand-holding people. The ability to reclaim VAT for the previous year expired on 30 June 1993, by which time we had cleared $12 million. By Christmas of that year, we had 200 people working for us. It was an especially aggressive start-up and is still going strong.

I was not a shareholder — I just had a salary and bonus. I was the managing director reporting to an international board and the only Irish person on the board. It was interesting to work with people who, whatever country they came from, had the same ethnic [*Jewish*] background. They were quite aggressive in their approach to life. There was a lot of strong discussion at board meetings. Even going for lunch or dinner with them was aggressive — they'd argue across the table. I was used to a softer approach. I went to a board meeting in New York and found that, for all their aggression, they were ill pre-pared. The more prepared I was, the more I was able to show them the facts and the trends and the more things calmed down. This preparation gives great confidence in an international environment. Some of this came from my sporting background — the more pre-pared you are, the easier things become. The shareholders were gen-erous enough to me, but it was not a surprising generosity, it was ne-gotiated.

After two years, Meridian was running smoothly and Dermot Desmond[2] asked to meet me. In 1994, he had a software company, Quay Financial Software, in Ferry House in Mount Street. Dermot wanted me to join him. Eventually, I agreed to look after Quay Finan-cial Software, which required some restructuring at that time. In 1995, we sold the company for over $20 million to CSK Micrognosis, a Japanese company. After that, I worked with Dermot setting up IIU (International Investment and Underwriting) in the Financial Serv-ices Centre.

---

[2] *Out on Their Own*, pp. 75–89.

I quickly started to research the question of security for electronic commerce, which I believed was the single biggest opportunity at that time. The research was a passion, not a chore. I wanted to drive the project. I was also confident that Dermot would invest in it. When I looked at the businessman at the airport using his laptop and mobile telephone, I saw that security was the thing that was most required. I spent all of 1996 studying this area, also in the States speaking to people in large corporations like Oracle and Novell in order to understand their requirements. I built solid relationships with them. I spent some time looking at Irish software companies, but at that stage, there had been no software successes. CBT and IONA had not yet made their names and it was not an encouraging software investment climate.

I already had a business plan: what I needed was a vehicle for it. I wanted to buy an existing company and evaluated 25 different companies. Eventually, I found Baltimore, a six-person company with revenues in 1996 of £50,000. They were losing money but there was some cash in the balance sheet from previous deals they had done. Dermot, some other investors and I bought it for a net £240,000. Baltimore was not a product company at that time, but rather provided contracted outsourced programming. As part of the deal, we got 40 per cent of a house in Fitzwilliam Square, which we sold back to the majority owner. That gave us £200,000 cash into the balance sheet. We started to build the products that we had identified in the business plan. The EU had advertised a project for the security of electronic commerce. One of the reasons for buying an established company rather than having a start-up was that it gave us a nameplate. We put a presentation together for the EU and won the bid. That gave us €750,000, which allowed us to build the products.

One of the things I had learned at Quay Financial Software was that building huge systems products took a long time and they were very difficult to deliver. If you build products that are going to take two years to deliver, they may well be outdated. I fundamentally believed that the correct way to build software was in smaller modules that you could sell individually. If you needed to build something big, you built a lot of smaller modules that could plug together. It was like building a house — you use building blocks to get there. As a result, at Baltimore we undertook to deliver the first version of our products within 12 weeks. It was to show the customer the functionality product — not the final version, but it was not a prototype. It was a fully functioning product. We could then tell the customer that the next version would have additional features. We showed him the roadmap for the product and allowed him to influence it. We spoke to the customers a lot and we learned their requirements. Our philosophy was that we would not even start to build a product unless it was: The First, The Only or The Best — in the World. Our people knew that if a product did not meet these criteria, they were not even to start to build it because somebody else had already done it.

We immediately announced that we were a global company and all the staff had to adopt that view. I remember passing a desk and hearing somebody say, "We're a Dublin company." I said, "No, no, we are an international company headquartered in Dublin, Ireland." We might have only been ten people but that was the way we were to describe ourselves. If anybody wanted to know about our US office, we were to tell them that we were opening it as soon as possible. We almost identified our own roadmap by telling people what we were going to do. If we were asked whether we were going to open on the east or the west coast, our answer was, "Probably both." I think we were the first Irish company to open offices on both coasts.

In January 1997, we went to the RSA Conference, the most important event in our industry. Most of the large international corporations were exhibiting. It cost $40,000 for a booth for the week. We could not afford that sort of money. However, two of us attended and we had a lot of Havana cigars with us. There was a welcoming reception the night before the conference and we gave out the Baltimore cigars. It made a big impact. Everybody knew the Baltimore guys were there. There were less than 15 people in the company at the time. The one thing we had was a very impressive website and we encouraged people to visit it. We got thousands of hits during the week. We captured information about the people who were visiting the site. Then, during 1997, we started to deliver the products to market.

At this stage, I was looking after everything. The first senior person we hired was Paddy Holahan who was highly experienced in US software marketing. We hired him before we hired a sales manager. Paddy came on board in December 1996, at which stage I was the only person selling product. Then we hired Aidan Gallagher as sales manager. He asked me, "What's the target for the year?" I gave him a target and, typical sales guy that he was, he asked, "Is that orders? Is it pipeline? Or is it invoices?" I told him he had to fulfil the order, book the revenue and get the money in — cash is king. We were running the ship so tightly that everything was cash-based. This meant we had no such thing as "revenue recognition issues" which had gotten some companies into trouble.

In 1998, we went to the RSA show again and this time took a booth. We still had only about 30 people working with the company. We had 15 of them in San Francisco with us. With 15 people on the booth, we looked like a very big company. We had our own uniform, a red golf shirt with a logo on it — everybody could see the Baltimore people. We also gave them out so there were lots of people walking around in our red shirts. We took a big suite in a hotel and had a really good party for all our potential customers and the CEOs of our competitors. We had people looking after the CEOs — they were kept at one side of the room. The customers were seeing the competitor CEOs at the party while we were mingling with the customers, telling them who we were. This was the night before the convention started. During the week everybody was talking about the great party the Baltimore team gave. Making us look big meant that we had to get as big as we were acting. During 1998 we had to adopt what I call the GBF factor — Get Big Fast.

At this stage, we had received offers to buy the company — $30 million, $40 million, and $50 million. A number of large corporations looked at us, including IBM and Axcent. My own philosophy was to grow the business ourselves rather than sell it. The key question was how we would get to the scale we wanted. It was too early in our life cycle to go public, as we did not have the consistency or strength of revenues. An option was to get some technology companies to invest in us. Another option was a merger and that's the approach we decided on. We merged with a company called Zergo, a UK public company. I was trying to get to a valuation of $50 million. Zergo at the time was valued at $90 million. They had been valued at $90 million for a long time and there was no movement in their share price. Zergo were much bigger than we were in revenue and people. They delivered hardware products to customers like the Ministry of Defence and the banks — very high end, mission critical systems. This was not exciting technology but the products were of a high quality. Because they were security products, their customers were obviously potential customers for us, but the real reason for our interest was to give us access to capital. I could have arranged capital of $5 million, $10 million or $20 million, but I wanted to get $100 million and I wanted to bring the company ultimately to the US market.

The Zergo people were not prepared to give away more than one-third of the company for $45 million in an equity deal and $5 million in a convertible loan. This loan ultimately became worth a lot more than the original deal, valued at over $100 million. We agreed to take 33 per cent of the equity of the merged, enlarged company. Once we announced the deal, their share price went up. Technically, they acquired us but, in reality, it was a reverse take-over, because we became the management team.

We shook hands on the deal on 3 September 1998. The day after, Bill Clinton was in town to do a digital signing with Bertie Ahern. I shook hands on the deal very late at night and had to be in Dublin Castle at six o'clock the following morning. The signing was on every TV station, including CNN, CNBC, Sky and Fox TV and gave us a lot of media exposure — a great marketing ploy.

We announced the Zergo merger externally on 16 December 1998. Between the announcement and the closing, we negotiated, first, who was going to manage the company. We agreed that Henry Beker, the Zergo CEO, would become chairman of the company and I would become chief executive. Initially, for a couple of months, I was president and chief operating officer. Interestingly, we gave the Zergo senior management people significant roles and, in some ways, diminished the roles of the Baltimore people. However, they were all still reporting to me. Aidan Gallagher, who had been in charge of global sales, was now responsible for European sales. John O'Sullivan, our executive vice-president of engineering worldwide, reported to a Zergo manager. Within three months, the Baltimore management emerged as the obvious leaders. Under Aidan, Europe became the shining star of the global organisation. He was obviously the guy to manage global sales. John was running all the product groups. These men were humble in their own way. They were not personally ambitious but ambitious for the company: they were simply the most talented people around and they all assumed the key global roles.

Zergo management had a very optimistic outlook on the market and on their revenue expectations. However, we were more cautious and I went out and told the market, "Here's the reality as we see it", and reduced expectations. The share price dropped within 20 minutes and, within a couple of hours, started to come back. People's first reaction was "Oh, the expectations are down." Their second reaction was, "These guys are giving us a straight steer. These are good guys." So, after a few hours, they started to respond very positively to the conservative news we were giving them.

One of the issues in the merger was branding. The Zergo people wanted to call the merged entity Zergo — there were 300 of them and 70 of us. They were a publicly listed company on the London Stock Exchange with $15 million in the bank. We felt we had built up quite a bit of collateral with the name Baltimore, particularly in the States. We sat down to have a genuine open debate with the Zergo management. Then something happened. We met at Heathrow Airport to discuss the branding issue. I felt that the management of both companies had come to the view that Baltimore was best. But, when we met with the board of Zergo, they had brought along a branding company to advise them. This was a surprise for us. The conclusion of the branding company was that the real brand was in the name of the public company, Zergo. We listened to everything they had to say and then I was asked for my views. I said I'd like to digest what had been said and consider it over the weekend. This was not really my style but I didn't want to get into a debate with a lot of people. I didn't want to put my cards on the table at that stage — this was one that had to be handled delicately, as it was taking place before the merger.

I was going to Vienna — Baltimore had won the European IT prize to be presented by the Austrian Prime Minister. In the hotel in Vienna, I got a call from the Zergo chairman saying that he had decided that Zergo was the name they were going to roll out. I told him I'd think about it. In the next 48 hours, each of the Baltimore managers wrote to me expressing concern that, if we dropped the Baltimore name, it could have a serious impact on our revenues, particularly in the States. I gave this information to two of the board members at Zergo and said I was very concerned about the decision process. I believed it was something for the board. I told them that we felt we could not go ahead with the merger — and this was the week we were going to close the deal. It would be very difficult for me and the management team to proceed with such a style. At that stage, we were inclined to walk away.

Zergo held an emergency board meeting. I asked for an assurance that any such decisions would be properly debated at board level, as I had been asked to become a member of the board. At 11.30 on that Saturday morning, I got a phone call to say they agreed that the name would be Baltimore. I said, "Hold on. That's not what I asked."

I like a strong board — strong as a group, as a team. Things should be fully debated and agreed together. Most of the decisions made by the Zergo board were myopic, with no US influence. Baltimore has a very American style in management and marketing. When we were performing due diligence on Zergo, I was looking at the expenses. Curiously, there were lots of travel but very few accommodation expenses. The reason was that most of their travel was one-day trips — they would travel to Europe and come home the same day.

Baltimore people tended to go to the States. Our management team has been away for the past two weeks in the States and I'm off to Australia and Hong Kong at the weekend. In time, we brought on some American non-executive directors — people who have a totally different point of view. It's a good board now — we have some heavy hitters, like George Powlick. George was head of Intel Capital in Europe. He's now managing director at Doughty Hanson, major fund managers — they own companies that are household names. We have John Cunningham, the CFO of Citrix. Our chairman is Peter Morgan, formerly IBM. Before that, he was director general of the Institute of Directors in the UK. I believe in bringing really talented people onto the board — it raises the ante and gives me a capacity to grow the business because these people are so clear in their thinking. With the original board, I had to explain ambitious thinking at a very low level.

In 1999, Baltimore was a public company listed on the London Stock Exchange. In November 1999, we decided to list on the NASDAQ and raised $150 million in the process. We're now one of the leading European software companies. We went into the FTSE 100 twice last year. That was never a stated ambition, it just happens once your share price goes to a certain point.

We decided that the best way forward was by acquisition. During 2000, we completed five. The first was Cyber Trust, a division of GTE Corporation and a key competitor of ours in the US. They used a service-based model as well as providing products. We bought the company for $150 million because we felt that we should enter into the services area. They were based in Boston and also had operations in Japan. They had 240 people. We identified 60 people we did not want, so we just kept 180. Out of the 180, we probably lost about 20. We pruned a bit at the senior level. As a result, a lot of talented people came through: we found that there was a layer of management holding talent back. Once you took that layer out, the talent started to bloom.

We acquired NSJ in Japan, followed by Cyber Trust Japan. We bought Content Technologies and a company called Nevex in Toronto. In total, we now have over 1,300 people worldwide. This was our Get Big Fast plan. This industry is moving so quickly that, if you fall behind the pace, you are out of the game.

We had learned a lot from the Zergo merger. The reason it went well for us was that we prepared meticulously. We brought our entire management team together and went through every single detail in our 100-day plan in terms of roles, responsibilities and actions. We had a plan for actions from the time we announced a deal up to the time the transaction closed, as well as a separate marketing plan and a post-closure plan. It was a comprehensive integration plan that covered all functions. We brought the Zergo management team over to the Country Club in Portmarnock and spent four days there. We did not leave the hotel until everything was agreed. We broke the conference up into small groups. Our team was thoroughly prepared, but the Zergo management were not and our plan survived. Each of the working groups had to come back to me with a plan and I would question them. At the end of the week, everything was agreed. We then presented our plan to the Zergo board. They were given an avalanche of meticulous planning which they could not question. Well, it could be questioned, but we had every answer.

We learned the value of planning everything. We have used the Portmarnock Formula for each acquisition since then. The first thing is usually to measure the value of the technology we are acquiring and how it interoperates with our products. Once you get the technology match right, other areas flow naturally from that. The second thing is how the management of the acquired company fits in. We don't retain any brands from organisations that we acquire. We still have the Cyber Trust name if we want to use it for a product but we would not use it for the group.

We also buy market share via our acquisitions. With the acquisition of Cyber Trust, we gained about 10 per cent of the US market. Content Technologies has 40 per cent of the content management market. Baltimore has a system that issues digital certificates to authenticate people. Content had a different product that sits at the periphery of an organisation and monitors all the traffic coming in and going out. For example, the company policy might be that the sales forecasts should not be distributed outside the company, so the system stops them being distributed. Equally, if there is malicious traffic coming in, such as a virus, you can stop it at the perimeter.

We would now have 20 per cent of our market worldwide, with 50 per cent of the European market and 45 per cent of the Asia Pacific market. However, you're looking at a market that's less than $1 billion now — it will eventually go up to $10 billion. You have to be well positioned for the opportunities and to capture the market growth.

Today, we have over 1,300 people globally. They are divided into engineering, who account for around a quarter of staff; direct sales, who account for another quarter; the remainder are dedicated to professional services and marketing, with a small number involved in general administration. There are about 200 people here in Dublin, 500 people in the rest of Europe, over 100 in Japan and 100 in the rest of Asia Pacific, with 250 in the US. In total, we operate out of 46 offices worldwide.

I'm a great believer in surprising people with generosity. In the business here, most people have been surprised at how well-looked-after they are. When I was setting up Baltimore and was hiring people, I asked each individual, "If this company is very successful in five years' time, and I was to give you then a lump of money to share in the success, how much would you like that to be?" Most people had the objective of paying off their mortgage. Every single one of them has received at least ten times more than they expected. We have probably made 20 or 30 millionaires. That was great, because we were not hiring people who just wanted to make money but who wanted to make the company successful.

Some of our employees were last year given options that are currently under water. I told them that I was concerned that they would be properly incentivised, but they wouldn't even enter into discussion with me. They know I'll fix the problem for them. They don't even want to debate it. None of them ever asked me for options, even though most people joined the company on salaries less than they were earning outside, on the basis that we told them they would be rewarded in the future.

The one thing I know I have is the trust of all the employees in the organisation. They trust the management team. They trust me as an individual. It's important to me that people trust me — in that way I can lead and they don't have to worry about things like remuneration, bonuses, being looked after . . . all of those things are taken as read. A strong value is that money is not the motivator — success is, the joy of seeing the company on the world stage, seeing the company's name in international newspapers. My picture was on the front cover of the business section of the *New York Times*. For the employees to see a picture of their CEO on the front page of the *New York Times* — Wow! You might see my photograph in *The Irish Times* or the *Financial Times*, but not many get onto the *New York Times*. The employees get a lot of pride in seeing the company being successful.

Round about April 2000, we saw a downturn in the markets. Technology companies were targeted as failures. Dot.coms were going belly-up. I said, "We've got to distinguish ourselves from this morass." I was doing an interview on Sky TV. A lot of people were watching it. The interviewer got around to discussing the failure of technology companies. I have to say I took a very focused approach and said, "I want to build a company that's capable of generating $1 billion of revenue in a single year." And I told him only ten software companies in the world had ever done that — people like Microsoft or Oracle. Baltimore wanted to be on that scale. The impact that had on the organisation was unbelievable, so I said, "I've said it. Now let's fulfil it." What people are saying now is, if we have to get to $1 billion, that means we have to do $350 million in the US — to do that we need so many people, so many partners, so many offices and so on. If we're going to do a third in the US, a third in the UK and a third in Asia Pacific, now everybody's focused on what they have to do in their own region to get to that $1 billion. Now everybody talks about the $1 billion company. It's a great focus for us. We said right from the outset that we wanted to be global — so we set big goals. We have no fear of being up there with the big companies.

We have also been very clear and honest with the investment community — we do not want to mislead them.

Teamwork and treating people fairly are important to me. I just gave a keynote speech to our entire sales force in New Orleans. The theme was teamwork and preparation. I thought for a few days about what I was going to say but, on the morning, all I had in front of me was a few points. I spoke in New Orleans for 40 minutes and the message was "Look guys, don't forget where we've come from. Here's how we got there — now here's the future. Nothing has changed. The same rules apply: team work, discipline, and preparation. It's just a bigger picture."[3]

---

[3] On 10 July 2001, Fran Rooney resigned as Chief Executive Officer of Baltimore Technologies, following a fall in the share price from stg£4.27 on the day the conversation was recorded to stg£0.19 on the day he resigned. Baltimore has been radically restructured. Fran Rooney is now chairman and chief executive of Nirvana Technologies Ltd.

15

James Sheehan

The Blackrock Clinic

"It's not what's ahead — today is the golden time."

James Michael Sheehan, an orthopaedic surgeon, is a founding director of the Blackrock Clinic, Dublin.

He was born in Tralee, County Kerry on 14 July 1939. His father was James Joseph Sheehan, who worked in the Dublin Port & Docks Board. His mother was Frances Mangan. He was second in a family of three girls and two boys. He is married to Rosemary Sheehan (same maiden name), a banker. They have four children: Kathy (30), Irenie (27), Michael (24) and Mark (22).

He was educated at St Mary's College, Rathmines, Dublin. In 1963 he took his primary medical degree at University College, Dublin together with a BSc in anatomy and anthropology. In 1966 he was awarded his final Fellowship in Surgery by the Royal College of Surgeons in Ireland. In 1970, he obtained an MSc in bio-engineering, University of Surrey, Guilford; and in 1982, he received a PhD in mechanical engineering, University of Surrey.

His first appointment was Resident in St Vincent's Hospital, Dublin (1963–64); Resident in Orthopaedics, St Mary's Orthopaedic Hospital, Cappagh (1964–65); Resident, St Vincent's Hospital (1965–66); Resident, Glasgow Royal Infirmary, Accident & Emergency Unit and Travelling Scholarship from the French Orthopaedic Association (1966–67); Resident, Royal National Orthopaedic Hospital, Stanmore, England (1967–68); Resident, Centre for Hip Surgery, Wrightington Hospital, Lancashire (1968–69); Consultant Orthopaedic Surgeon, St Vincent's Hospital, Dublin and St Mary's Orthopaedic Hospital, Cappagh (1970–86); Consultant Orthopaedic Surgeon, Blackrock Clinic (1986 to date). He is also director of Irish Healthcare, a health screening unit in conjunction with the Irish Management Institute. He has been awarded the following medals: McArdle gold medal in Surgery, UCD; Feeney gold medal in Obstetrics, Coombe Hospital; Bellingham gold medal in Medicine, St Vincent's Hospital; O'Ferrall gold medal in Surgery, St Vincent's Hospital.

The conversation was recorded in James Sheehan's home in Blackrock, County Dublin, on 17 May 2001.

James Sheehan

Both my parents were from Kerry and I was born there. My mother's father ran a chemist's shop in Tralee. In those days, the local chemist was where a lot of people went for advice. My grandfather on my father's side came from south Kerry, near the Healy Pass, a little town called Tuosist. My parents lived in Dublin but we spent our summers in Kerry. I happened to arrive early so I was the only member of the family born in Kerry. The midwife who delivered me was a distant relation. Forty years later, she developed a bad hip and I brought her into Cappagh Hospital. At that stage, I had an entourage of doctors and medical students doing rounds. I heard her saying to one of the junior doctors, "I brought that man into this world." I could not resist the opportunity of saying to him, "I hope to God I don't put her out of it!" It was one of those long-term relationships you have in Ireland.

I spent most of my life in Dublin. We lived in a house called "Blennerville" because that was my mother's hometown, just outside Tralee. I had a very happy upbringing. My father was working for the Dublin Port & Docks Board. Braemor Park was bordering on the countryside — there were green fields and Hazelbrook Farm was about a mile away through little lanes. None of Churchtown had been developed at that stage. My father worked in the Ballast Office where the clerical staff of the Port & Docks Board were located. The clock in the Ballast Office was known for being accurate — going back for half-a-century, it was tuned in to Greenwich and got signals twice a day. I remember seeing that mechanism when I was very young.

I went to school in St Mary's in Rathmines. I was not unhappy but I could never say I enjoyed school. I was into games in a very limited way, played rugby until I was 13, not really keen on the rough and tumble. I remember playing St Columba's College. We always felt the people from St Columba's were a little different. We were winning about 40-nil when their coach shouted from the sideline with about ten minutes to go, "Buns for tea, Columba's, if you win."

My father was keen on education. When he left school himself his father suffered a stroke and, as he was the eldest, he had to go to work to support his family and pay the mortgage. He'd love to have gone on to third level. Because he was deprived of it himself, he put a great emphasis on third-level opportunities for us.

I got a mediocre Leaving Certificate. I was interested in chemistry and physics but not particularly interested in the liberal arts. The August after the Leaving Certificate results, my father said to me casually, "What would you like to do?" "I'd like to do medicine." "That's fine — I thought you might like to do engineering." That was the total discussion about career structures — as compared with all the input children have now with career guidance and psychologists. In those days, there was no emphasis on what you wanted to do — you just picked something and did it. There's a nice story about an Irish graduate, Kevin Roche. He was in school in Rockwell. His father was a creamery manager in Mitchelstown and, when Kevin left school, it was assumed he would go into the creamery business. In those days in UCD, you signed on in the Aula Maxima — there was a little booth for each subject. When Kevin went in, he could not find the booth for agriculture. The first one he found was architecture. He signed on for architecture and became one of the world's leading architects. An awful lot of people go into things by chance. How they apply themselves later is what matters. I believe people can make a success of virtually any career provided they become sufficiently immersed and put energy and enthusiasm into it. I don't think you are predestined to be an architect, an engineer or a doctor. You can tune yourself into developing the interest.

It was a financial strain for my parents to send us to college — a few of us were going at the same time. I decided I'd really put my heart into it. Because I got a very ordinary Leaving Certificate, I was concerned that I would not pass the exams. I spent pre-med working really very hard, realising that there were bright people in the class on scholarships. One of the first days in college, we had a biology lecturer, Mabel Kane. When we were seated, there were people throwing paper aeroplanes around and a lot of noise. Mabel stood on the podium and called for attention. "I'd like everyone to look right and to look left and introduce yourself to the people on each side because you won't be seeing them next year." At that time, the weeding-out process was after pre-med — in fact, pre-med, pre-dentals and first veterinary students were all together. It was not a bad system — virtually everybody got into college who wanted to get in; the elimination took place the second year. I was worried about whether or not I would make the grade. When I got the results, I found I had got first place and first-class honours and I really felt there was something wrong. There were so many bright people in the class it couldn't be that I was better than them. I then realised that it was hard work and discipline that achieved results in college whereas, in school, the brighter people were able to achieve with much less effort. A lot of the brighter people did not do all that well in college because they were not applied.

Having set that tone for myself, it really encouraged me to continue. There were great disadvantages in that because, when you get first place, you lock yourself into a position where you have to strive very hard to maintain that position. There's a quote: "The ambitious man is seldom at peace." That could be applied to my college days — I was always striving to maintain the position I had achieved in pre-med. I enjoyed college but it was a period of intense work.

Outside college, I got involved with some St Mary's old boys in providing a club for past-pupils of Artane Industrial School. We bought a house for them in Gardiner Street. Boys left Artane at 16 or 17 with nowhere to go and no supervision. Archbishop John McQuaid asked us to provide a premises for them where they could meet together — he was super to them. My brother Joe, myself and a few others did up the house in Gardiner Street. After I met Rosemary, she joined me in that work. They were happy times. I kept that up until I left the country for post-graduate studies.

I also got involved in photography. At that time, there was not a lot of photography to record medical conditions. I was a student of Professor D.K. O'Donovan. (He was from Limerick, where his father ran a small hotel. They were raided by the Black and Tans one night. His father was taken out to the front door and shot in front of him when he was seven years of age.) He was Professor of Medicine and was interested in changes that occur in the eyes and fingers in different diseases — and I became interested in close-up photography. I did a lot of photographic work with him and also with Paddy FitzGerald, who was the Professor of Surgery, undertaking a lot of vascular work.

On holiday in Kerry, I would work in the local county hospital. I studied with Colm Galvin, who was the county surgeon. He was the best surgical technician I've come across. In those days, he did everything. My ambition was to be a county surgeon and work in the local community. I had no interest in joining a teaching hospital.

At the halfway stage, I spent an additional year studying anatomy and then went back into the general medical stream. I qualified in 1963. Just before the final exams, we had a medal exam in the Coombe Hospital. I got the gold medal. My father was pleased and proud. Next day, a pleasant spring day, he was playing golf and died on the golf course in Delgany. That was a month before my final exam. It had a significant effect on me. I always associate 1963 with the deaths of three people I admired, my father, JFK and Pope John XXIII. They all died within a short time of each other. When my father died, I lost a lot of enthusiasm for medicine. I did the final exams and got first place but the kick had gone out of it. It took me a long time to get the buzz back. My mother was a gentle soul and a wonderful mother who spent her entire life looking after the family. My father's death affected her deeply.

Towards the end of my intern year, Paddy FitzGerald called me aside and asked me if I would like to specialise in surgery or medicine or what. I had not given it a great deal of thought but I had been interested in carpentry — I liked the idea of bone carpentry, I felt it was the closest to using timber. I told Paddy FitzGerald I'd like to do orthopaedics. He said, "There are two basic qualifications for orthopaedics — you need the strength of an ox and the brains of an ass." At that stage, orthopaedics were rough and ready and Paddy said, "I'm worried about your strength!" But he said that if I was really set on it, he would do his best to help me. He suggested I go to Cappagh Hospital.

It's interesting when you look back towards the end of a professional career. Half the children in Cappagh had polio — the last case of polio in Ireland was in 1964 — 25 per cent of the patients had tuberculosis and the other 25 per cent were children with congenital deformities of the hip. What I saw and trained in in 1964 is totally irrelevant for practice nowadays. Medicine is constantly evolving. If you don't adapt during your career, you're left behind. At that time, they had a full-time school in Cappagh. Some of the children there — like little Willie of the Little Willie Fund — spent six, seven, eight years and got most of their schooling there, particularly children with polio. A lot of these kids were from the country — there were no school buses, there was no way they could have got to school when they had often to walk a few miles carrying their bags; few of their parents had cars. It was a different time. The average length of stay now in hospitals is six days.

In 1964, while I was in Cappagh, I met Rosemary. She had left school, was waiting to go into the bank and took up a temporary post in Cappagh. She has had a profound influence in my life. Among her qualities are sincerity, her sense of fun, her caring for others, her unselfishness. Most of all, a quality we are inclined to forget, prudence — she is full of common sense. In 34 years we have never had cross words. We have four great children. I have had a privileged life that Rosemary has made easy for me. She has never put any pressure on me to be at home, to look after the kids, so perhaps I've led a selfish life following my own career and not making the contribution in the home that I should have. Your wife has a far more profound effect on your life than you realise.

I've come across some dominant wives! One patient I remember was a well-known businessman. When you're checked into hospital, the nurse takes you through the routine of how many pyjamas and how many socks and were you immunised. Every question this man was asked, the wife answered. The nurse finally said, "When did your bowels move last?" The wife said, "Let me think a moment." This man was running a very large business. It was he who told me the story afterwards.

Cappagh was essentially a children's hospital with the occasional adult patient who had tuberculosis. When people had tuberculosis they were put on a frame contoured to their body. They lay on the frame for up to a year or two. Streptomycin was introduced in the 1950s — that speeded up the process of healing. The death rate from tuberculosis was totally changed. Before that, when people were put on frames, half of them survived and half died. Streptomycin brought the death rate down to almost zero.

I returned to Vincent's as a junior trainee in surgery and worked in the casualty department. That was in the old St Vincent's Hospital in Stephen's Green. There was a little elderly nun in charge, Sister Ibar. She carried the keys and whenever you wanted something you had to call her. St Vincent's had a front end and a rear end; the front was females, the rear was males. They were separated by a corridor 100 yards long. It was an old tradition that you never mixed the sexes in hospital. Around the time Vincent's was moving out to Elm Park, Sister Ibar died. She subsequently appeared, walking the corridor, to a number of people, including the Reverend Mother. She passed them by, rattling her keys, never said anything. The Irish Permanent bought the building as their head office. A secretary there was a patient of mine and I spoke to her about the lovely plastered ceilings. I asked if she worked in that part of the hospital. She said, yes, not alone that, but it was complete with its ghost — "There's this little old nun who appeared to the cleaners." She's the only ghost I've ever known in my lifetime — but a genuine appearance. Masses were said for her because there was some reason why she was reappearing. In recent years, I haven't heard of her walking the corridor.

After the year in St Vincent's, I got a scholarship to Paris for three months. I attended my first international surgical meeting. I got a buzz out of it. The great names in orthopaedics were there — Maurice Müller from Switzerland, John Charnley who was doing innovative hip work, and a Frenchman, Robert Judet. I was enthralled by the concept of artificial components which were being tried at that time.

I came back, got married that November, 1966, and went to Glasgow. If you want a successful recipe for husband and wife to get a common understanding, there's nothing like going away from the larger family circle and having time together. It did a lot for us that we were thrown together and had to work everything out together.

I went as a senior house officer to the Royal Infirmary. A few months before that, I got my Fellowship in Surgery. That was by exam and I got it in the minimum time. It does not give you a licence to operate but it is the first stepping-stone in a surgical career. Having got that, I applied for a more senior post in Glasgow and got a registrar's job.

The first night I was on duty as a registrar was Hogmanay. They really celebrate the New Year in Scotland. That night, we had 16 stabbings in the accident and emergency department, one of them fatal. I had never seen a stabbing in Ireland. The father of one boy who was stabbed — not too seriously — rushed into the casualty department. "Who did it, son?" "Jungle Boy." "OK, son, I'll deal with Jungle Boy." I called the father back and said, "We have enough problems here. If you're dealing with Jungle Boy, would you ever tell them to bring him to the Western Infirmary." It was the same on the night of a match between Celtic and Rangers. There were horrific problems — they'd break whisky bottles and go for each other's heads. Football violence now is nothing like it was in those days.

You had no job security. There were no training programmes. You changed jobs every six months. You bought the *British Medical Journal* on the back of which there were advertisements. You went down the ads and picked out what you thought might suit but no job gave you more than six months' tenure.

Paddy FitzGerald had recommended that I go to the Royal National Orthopaedic Hospital in Stanmore, one of the few full-time orthopaedic hospitals. It had a very good reputation in the past. I was disappointed because I expected it to be a dynamic place but at that stage it was run down, the buildings were old and dilapidated, a lot of them were Nissen huts with leaking roofs. I was disillusioned with the standard of surgery. It was probably a reasonable standard, but there was nothing innovative going on — the sort of people I had listened to at the Paris meeting were not represented there. Paddy FitzGerald was keen that I would go there for three or four years and do most of my training. I wrote to him and told him I was unhappy with the situation and, at that time, a job appeared in the *BMJ* for Wrightington Hospital in Lancashire, where John Charnley worked. John Charnley had been doing very innovative surgery with hips — he was at the cutting edge but, because he was, he was not a part of the Establishment. When I told my boss in Stanmore that I'd like to go and work with John Charnley and that I had applied for a job, he said, "It's the worst thing you could do. It'll be the end of your career, you'll never get another job." John Charnley was considered to be way out. Despite his advice, I went up, was interviewed and given the job to start a few months later.

The last day in Stanmore, I was in the dining-room. In those days, there was a nice white tablecloth and we were served our meals. My very British boss, said, "Sheehan, what are your most memorable thoughts about this wonderful institution?" "The chutney, sir." They had very nice mango chutney. I was never forgiven for that remark — I left Stanmore somewhat under a cloud!

There was a short interval before the job came up in Wrightington. Rosemary and I had a Mini into which we would pack all our worldly goods as I moved from job to job. The only thing we couldn't fit in was Rosemary's piano. We had bought it in Glasgow for £10. With British Railways, we would get delivery of the piano just as we were ready to move on for the next six months!

The first night I arrived in Wrightington, I met one of the residents who said, "Don't unpack your bags too quickly. Things are fairly stringent here. The person you are replacing was fired. The routine is that, when you come, you assist John Charnley for a month. Then, after a month, he assists you with a case. If he's not happy, that's the end of you. Your predecessor was sent off to Egypt." Those were the days when there were no employment tribunals — people were easily hired and fired.

John Charnley got involved in hip surgery in the early fifties. He started with a plastic called Teflon — the same lining used in non-stick frying pans. He used it for the socket of the hip because there was little or no frictional resistance. He put in about 500 of these hips but the Teflon wore out very rapidly and, while the short-term results were dramatic, the long-term results were poor because of the wear in the Teflon — and the worn product gave rise to a reaction in the tissue. When I arrived, he was using a new plastic, high-density polyethyline. It was revolutionary. He was keeping a very close eye because he didn't yet know the wear characteristics. He was a keen craftsman — he had a lathe and a workshop at home. At the weekend, he would make up different components, bring them in on Monday and put them into patients. We also had a small workshop in the hospital where we made a lot of the hip joints. When you compare that with current FDA regulations, those innovations could not occur nowadays, the rules and regulations are so stringent. A lot of the joints at that time were rejected because patients got a low-grade infection from organisms. Charnley set out to eliminate that problem. He developed operating theatres where you had space suits and the air was filtered and sterilised. A year working with him was a great experience. He was the first person to make surgery a routine mechanical procedure. He divided into 155 steps the technique of inserting artificial hips — you went through each step at a time. Up to that, surgery was considered to have a mystique about it — you had to be able to play it by ear, more art than science. Charnley said you should be able to do things like an assembly line. He was meticulous about every aspect of the patient's care.

When I was there, Joe Gallagher visited — he was subsequently a colleague of mine in St Vincent's. John Charnley would not allow anyone use his hip unless they visited him and studied the technique. Joe Gallagher put in the first Charnley hip in Ireland. There was a surgeon from Cork visiting as well. He had a stud farm and was selling yearlings in Newmarket. He got more for a yearling than I would have got for two years' salary. We were living near Wigan, Bolton and Bury. There was a huge amount of old furniture. Rosemary and I got interested in restoring some pieces. You bought old furniture for virtually nothing and most of the furniture now in our home came from there.

In Wrightington, there was no knee surgery because there were no artificial knees available. Together with a Canadian resident, I thought, if we can do something for hips, why can't we do something for knees? I decided I would do research on knee surgery but would go back to college to get a basic understanding of engineering. The whole concept of artificial joints is based on mechanical principles. I needed a basic education in mechanical engineering. The University of Surrey was running a one-year course in bio-engineering for medical graduates. I decided I would have to take a year off surgery. I had no source of funding. If I could work for the summer in a job more lucrative than the one I was in, then I could probably afford it. Rosemary saw an ad for a job in Butlin's Holiday Camp in Filey — they wanted a medical officer for the summer. Every Saturday, 10,000 people landed in. If the weather was any way fine, they lay out in the sun and got sunburnt. On Monday and Tuesday, they all presented to the doctor's surgery with sunburn. By Wednesday, they were getting diarrhoea and vomiting — Wednesday, Thursday and Friday, they all needed treatment. I was paid six shillings for every patient I looked after. I spent three months doing this job and made a reasonable amount of funding towards the following year.

We moved down to Surrey and Rosemary took up a job in a chemical company. She had worked in Stanmore for a short period but these were the only two periods she worked in her married life. When she worked in Stanmore, she was in a finance company, and, after six months, she was second in command. In Guilford, as I said, she worked for a chemical company and supported us. It was a happy year for us — I got back to academic work. We had a simple life — in a one-bedroom apartment with the cooker in a cupboard, sharing a toilet and bathroom. When I look back now, I see how uncomplicated your life can be when it's not cluttered with possessions.

I worked on the design of an artificial knee. The University of Surrey was open only a few years and had a very good mechanical engineering department. They were doing development work on Concord. The QE2 had been launched and some of the turbine blades broke off on the maiden voyage. They were doing photoelastic studies to see what caused the failure. It was a stimulating environment.

I returned to Ireland and was appointed to Cappagh and St Vincent's Hospital as consultant orthopaedic surgeon. This was in 1970 — my first consultancy. The job was never advertised. I never put in an application. I did not have a curriculum vitae. There was no interview. If that happened now, there would be a tribunal. In those days, you were recommended to do certain training and, to an extent, you were pre-selected for jobs. It did not mean that you had any security of getting the job but, if you did what you were recommended to do, you had a good chance. The appointment was by the Mother General, not by the medical board. You went up to the head office of the Irish Sisters of Charity in Milltown and received your appointment.

Cappagh Hospital was evolving — there was no more polio, tuberculosis was in decline. They were in a sort of lull period — they had started doing a very small number of artificial hip joints but they had a large number of empty beds. There was a question mark over its future. I wrote a report for the Mother General of that time — I put as the title the only bit of Latin I could remember from school: *Carpe diem, quam minimum credula postero* — enjoy the present day, trust the least possible to the future. I advocated an artificial joint department. Within a few days, she said she would make the money available for a theatre, a workshop and research facilities. There was no Department of Health funding. I designed the theatre and had it up and running about six months later.

The hospital did get a subvention from the Department of Health — per occupied bed per day. A lot of the funding was from the religious orders, from fund-raising and charitable donations. Some of the patients had private insurance. Today, people can be very critical of the religious in Ireland but they played a key role in education and in health. Without them, we would not have our present hospital structure.

We ended up with a viable artificial joint unit. It was so successful that it became for many years the centre for artificial joints in the country. It still is the second largest centre in these islands. Seventeen years after I went to Cappagh, the waiting lists were enormous. We were now into the eighties when the Government cutbacks were hitting hard. One of the areas they were able to quantify was the use of artificial joints — they decided that they would pay for only a limited number each year. I was cut back from inserting six or eight joints a week to two every fortnight. I was largely redundant in elective surgery. I was still involved in the accident department in St Vincent's, a busy component of the job. I became frustrated that I could not perform in my main area of interest.

A third of the people in the country at that time had private insurance and only a limited number were allowed into Cappagh. There was nowhere for this third of the population to go if they had any sophisticated problems such as requiring artificial joints or heart surgery. The high-tech departments were only in the public service — there were no private hospitals handling high-tech problems, with the sole exception of Mount Carmel, where they had put in a sterile air theatre and had a small joint replacement unit. I thought, why can't we have facilities for one-third of the population and let the two-thirds use the state-funded service? There was also a shortage of diagnostic facilities — if people required x-rays, if they went to see a doctor in Fitzwilliam Square, they had to travel and find a local hospital. Parking in town was becoming a problem — Fitzwilliam Square was laborious for people to visit. There was a need for new consulting rooms. Those of us practising from existing consulting rooms were served notice to quit by the Corporation. Up to then, consulting rooms did not require planning permission — people just started consulting from their home or wherever they wanted. Regulations were introduced that people could not have consulting rooms unless they were living on the premises. My custom-built rooms were across the road from Vincent's in a block of apartments. I was served notice to quit.

We had then moved to this house in Blackrock and a neighbour, Pat Campbell, was an architect. One evening, sitting at the fire having supper, we were discussing the lack of consulting rooms and facilities. Pat and I decided we'd do something about it — he would design it and I would supply the medical input. That was where the concept of a free-standing Blackrock Clinic was born. Around this time, George Duffy, a close colleague, was running the nuclear medicine department in Vincent's. He was suffering from the cutbacks and was keen to have a more dynamic nuclear medicine department. Nuclear medicine uses radio-chemicals which are labelled with radioactive material to detect disease in various parts of the body. You give a small dose of one of those labelled chemicals, then you scan the patient and see where they're taken up in the tissues. George and myself were colleagues but would not have been very close friends. Since then, we have become both close colleagues and friends, a relationship that has endured to the present day.

My brother Joe is a practising orthopaedic surgeon in Chicago. He offered to help. He had trained in the Mayo Clinic. When he went to the Mayo Clinic, he had intended, and I had always hoped, that he would come back and that we would work together. It didn't work out that way. Maurice Neligan, a cardiac surgeon, was also having difficulty with facilities — he joined in the venture. That was the initial nucleus.

Without any funds, we decided we would buy a site. Around that time, I had operated on a patient, Maurice O'Kelly, one of the managing partners of Guinness and Mahon. I visited Maurice late one night in hospital. He called me aside and said, "I see the sort of lifestyle you have, the sort of hours you work. If I can ever be of any help to you as a banker, give me a shout." Six months went by and I lifted up the phone to Maurice: "How would you be fixed for a quick million? I'd like to buy a site and build a clinic." He said, "Put me down for it." With no security, no paperwork, we bought a site in Blackrock that was for auction. We sent my cousin, Jim Sheehan, a solicitor, to the auction with his son, Jerry. We paid the highest price ever for a site at that time, just under £1 million for five acres. Once we had bought the site, we were committed.

We designed the building with Pat Campbell, Brian Conroy and his colleagues and had a very rapid construction programme of 15 months for the first stage, the consulting block. We came in on time and on cost and opened in September 1984.

The next thing was to convince colleagues that this was the way to go. We wanted to get them out of Fitzwilliam Square and into purpose-built consulting rooms. What we had then in Blackrock were consulting rooms and diagnostic services such as x-ray and blood tests but, from day one, we had always said to doctors that this was going to be the first stage of a hospital complex — we would add on a hospital as soon as we could arrange the finance.

When we bought the site and were trying to sell the consulting suites we put up a large notice across the site entrance saying, "A New Concept in Medical Care". We had it up only a few nights when a smart guy came along and blotted out the CEPT! It took us two years to raise the finance to build the hospital.

For a long time, the consulting rooms were poorly supported. We had planned it that, as the place was being built, people would make phased payments. All doctors depend on accountants. Everybody went to their accountants and asked what they should do. The accountants invariably said, "The place will never get built. It will go into liquidation and you'll lose your money. Don't buy a unit until you see what happens." We had signed a building contract, we had the building under way, but it was very hard to get the commitment. Even though people said they were supportive of it, they did not come up with the funding. We had a building loan of half-a-million pounds and that increased to £3.5 million. That loan was carried jointly and severally by a few of us, even though we could not meet it in any way. Maurice O'Kelly had confidence in the project and, thanks to him, it actually happened. He was a unique banker. It was during that time that I realised that things don't just happen, you have to make them happen. You have to really put your heart into something so that it gets off the ground. Tom Roche[1] lived across the road from us here in Cross Avenue. We had many discussions because, at that time, he was building the East Link Bridge — that was considered a way-out project as well. One of the valuable bits of advice that Tom Roche gave me was, "Remember the Golden Years — these are the Golden Years." It's not what's ahead — today is the golden time.

Because we had problems with the first phase — the consulting rooms — the banks did not want to give us money for the hospital. The original intention was that Blackrock was going to be a charitable foundation, a not-for-profit hospital, but we could not raise the finance on that basis. The banks said that we would have to have an international management group involved because they had no faith in doctors running anything. We looked around at the various hospi-

---

[1] *Out on Their Own*, pp. 323–339.

tal corporations — the Hospital Corporation of America, the American Medical Corporation and others. We finally decided that the English company, BUPA, being a provident association, would fit. They were keen to invest in Ireland and learn about high-tech medicine. Up to that, in England, their hospitals were largely nursing homes — they were not into high-tech cardiac surgery or anything like that. They thought Blackrock would be an exciting learning venture for them. They joined with us as an equity partner. The head of BUPA at that time was an Irishman, Bob Graham, who had worked for the VHI.

It took a year to build the hospital. By this stage, the consulting rooms had been largely sold and we had reduced our debt, but people were still inquiring, "Where's the hospital?" The hospital was a good example of how quickly you can build. Traditionally in Ireland, hospitals take between ten and 13 years to plan and build because they go through a series of phases with the Department of Health. They plan the hospital but don't plan the equipment — that is done as a separate venture. When eventually they come to equip the hospital, they have to rebuild a lot of it. That happened in Tallaght, it happened in Beaumont, it happens in every hospital. Tallaght was the fastest — it took only five years. They started building Vincent's in 1938 and they opened in 1970. They stopped for years during the war and then started building again. The construction programme was totally out of synch.

I got a lot of advice on construction at that time and had an American group over who specialised in hospitals. They had built hospitals in England and several other places, all of them on a 12-month schedule. They had found that if you looked at a traditional building site, about 30 per cent of the workers were not working at any one time — they were waiting for components. Their principle was that, if you were going to build anything, you pre-ordered everything, you rented a warehouse and you stored on day one everything you needed.

We had Michael de Bakey, one of the world's leading cardiac surgeons, advise us on the cardiac services.

We had many long discussions with the VHI, who controlled the purse-strings. You could not open and finance a hospital unless the VHI agreed. Following a protracted period, they agreed to cover the cost of patients in a high-tech hospital. Under legislation, the VHI were not allowed to invest in hospitals. VHI were a competitor of BUPA but BUPA were not then allowed to compete in Ireland. BUPA insisted on holding 51 per cent of the equity because, for insurance purposes in England, they had to hold a majority stake, but we had a 50/50 board relationship. We had an equal vote with an independent chairman. Subsequently, we had to refinance and BUPA increased their stake to 56 per cent. The current Irish shareholders are George Duffy, myself and my brother Joe.

The hospital was ready to open in December 1986. A month before it opened, the VHI plans were withdrawn. There was a coalition government led by Garret FitzGerald, with a Labour element. They decided that financing patients in a hospital like Blackrock would be for an élite group and that would not be acceptable to ordinary subscribers. In all our negotiations with the VHI, they agreed that there was a need for high-tech care for their subscribers — none of the private hospitals could then handle the high-tech work. We were left with the hospital complete, with 80 staff on site, and no insurance cover. We were closed until the following April. During that time, we had intense political lobbying and negotiations. The VHI finally agreed that one of the four wards would be allowed open in April and that over the remainder of the year they would allow a phased opening of the remaining beds. During the four-month period, our losses mounted to £4 million. It took us eight years to pay that off. The hospital was lucky to have survived.

Since then, the VHI have controlled all hospital beds and no new hospital beds have come on stream since Blackrock and the Mater Private. A lot of private hospitals have closed because of inadequate funding — St Joseph's in Raheny, St Gabriel's, the Bon Secours in Tuam. Hopefully, with EU deregulation and with changes in the VHI, this dominant control will disappear.

The VHI is a branch of the Department of Health — the Department controls the premiums. As recently as one year ago, the Minister for Health did not allow the VHI to increase its premiums because that would have increased the Consumer Price Index and would have influenced the rate of inflation.[2] The premiums were frozen — totally

---

[2] In July 2001, the Minister for Health, Mícheál Martin, sanctioned a 9 per cent increase in VHI premiums with effect from September. This follows on a 6.5 per cent increase earlier in the year.

illogical: nursing salaries and overheads had gone up by 16 per cent. As a result, the amount of money from premiums is not adequate to finance the cost of care in modern high-tech hospitals.

Over the last 20 years, about 3,000 beds have closed in the public hospitals, apart from the closure of private hospitals. There was an effort to create private beds in the public hospitals. Now they're trying to reverse this situation and get some of the private beds out of the public hospitals. There are no private hospitals to absorb those beds.

Only now are we beginning to face the realities of the health service in Ireland because the waiting lists are causing political trouble. One of the problems with health is that you can never satisfy demand. No matter what you provide, it's never good enough — there's always something else you can do for health care. The politicians will never satisfy the public. The biggest problems at the moment are waiting lists, either for surgery or for consultation and also the accident and emergency services. There aren't enough beds for the demand. Many of these problems have been created by the Department of Health over the years. They are tending towards being a monopoly provider. They have not encouraged anyone else into the provision of services and they've made it difficult for people providing services like Black-rock, the Mater Private Hospital and various religious orders. They insist on central control — the Department of Health likes to control not alone the public hospitals but indirectly the private hospitals through the VHI. They provide the funds, they determine the spend, they provide the public hospital buildings and the equipment, they decide on staff numbers — they are doing what the Russians did for 40 years — and that was a disaster. They have suppressed the whole element of competition. Once this is corrected, the situation will improve. Up to a few years ago, the VHI, under the Act by which they were established, could not have any competition. Under EU regulations they had to allow competition, like in the airline industry.[3]

The Department of Health introduced community rating — that meant that everybody, irrespective of age or ailment, paid the same premium. While in principle that's good, it makes it difficult for anyone else to come in and compete. Insurance is to cover you for major disasters. You should have the freedom to insure as you like; if you want to increase your life policy, you should be able to do so. The

---

[3] See Chapter 16, pp. 322–323.

premiums are kept artificially low and, as a result, the common premium that people pay, which is Plan B, is not enough to finance modern health care. Having said that, a very high proportion of the population, 46 per cent, carry health insurance. But the private hospitals cannot provide any services for the great majority of those people — most of them have to revert to the public system.

The accident and emergency services are a huge problem because people who have acute illnesses can get into hospital only by presenting themselves in the accident department. They end up in casualty, lying on stretchers until there is an empty bed. People for planned surgery are being constantly rescheduled.

Our services are far too dependent on junior doctors. We need a lot more consultants but, for every consultant you appoint, you need a huge infrastructure. That involves a lot of money. It costs about £400,000 to provide one new bed. If a consultant is working anyway productively, even with very short-stay patients, you could not have a viable job without a dozen beds. So it's millions. And that does not include the annual running costs of that bed at £500 a day. It's not really possible to give you a general global cost for a consultant because it would depend on specialty, comparing, say, a dermatologist with a cardiac surgeon, but you're looking at £500 multiplied by 365 days in the year. The problem with providing better health care is not essentially the capital cost — the capital cost is small relative to running costs. Another problem is that the response time is far too long. The current service has a lead-in time of about ten years for planning and construction. In a rapidly changing scene in medicine, where new technologies evolve, you just can't afford this time-frame.

We now have a lack of nursing staff. This results in doctors being appointed, having theatre facilities, but not having staff for them. While they are on a contract to work an agreed number of hours per week, those hours are frequently unproductive because of lack of infrastructure. We have introduced a degree course for nurses — it's really training a lot of nurses out of the practical aspects of nursing. It's like training people in electronic engineering and then asking them to work as an electrician.

The medical area is so complex that we could spend the whole night talking about it.[4]

I look at professional life as being in three decades — three decades we're often lucky to survive. The first is when you have finished your training and you get appointed, you're full of enthusiasm. The next decade, you're consolidating your position. You have lost a certain amount of the enthusiasm but you are hopefully productive in your work. The third decade is using the accumulated experience of your lifetime. You should be able to use that expertise advising others. It's now 45 years since I entered medical school — I'm entering my fifth decade.

Looking back, there are a few things that have been important. You must see the funny side of life. Medicine can be very serious but there's a lot of humour dealing with people. The second thing is to avoid negativity — you can't be a surgeon and be negative. I trained with one surgeon in Scotland and he spent so long instructing patients about what could go wrong that nobody wanted to have surgery. Joe Gallagher was a colleague of mine in Vincent's — if he wanted to talk somebody out of surgery, like a little old lady that might have a bad hip and might be too big a risk, he would look her straight in the eye and say, "Would you like a big cutting operation?"

When you're dealing with bankers and you try to mix business with surgery, you are into a different scene. It makes you realise how negative bankers are. Somebody said you should always borrow from a pessimist because he never expects to be repaid. I'm amazed how they ever end up lending money. A simple example: I wish to develop a hospital and one of the first things they want to know is what the alternative use for the building will be if it fails. You don't have to look too hard at the newspapers to find that we are clamouring for medical services. You cannot approach a project in such a negative way. I never visited again the particular banker who asked me that question. It's an indication of the different mindset with which we are trained in surgery. In surgery, you think that something is going to work but, by God, you have to make it work.

---

[4] Press reports (25 July 2001) suggested that a Health Strategy Document to be considered by the Government in September 2001 would propose an increase of 5,000 hospital beds over a ten-year period (from the present complement of 12,500); together with an additional 1,000 consultants, 5,000 nurses and a reformed primary healthcare system.

I'd like in my own life to remain constructive — sometimes people get negative as they get older. I feel that my job is to act as a catalyst — to get others to invest in better services. I don't think the Lord ever intended us to sit back — we are *homo erectus*. Man is the only species that is erect — all the other animals are bent or on four legs. Our role in life is not to sit back and take life easy.

In medicine, it's great to see your decades as decades of change — you can still perform your basic work as a surgeon but you should have a totally different emphasis. I'd like to tail out of operating over the next few years and provide more medical services, spend more time on the development side. I visited a man in a stud farm who was in his eighties — he was planting oak trees. I'd like to feel you can leave a heritage and an example of hard work, but not wealth, because I think our resources should be used productively. At the funeral of a prominent Dublin businessman, one man turned to the other and said, "Didn't he leave a lot?" The other man said, "No, he left everything." I'm a believer in the Gospel story about the man burying the talents — there are no Brownie points for any of us not remaining productive.

Rosemary said that I've always been deaf and that it is a great advantage. If you listen to too many opinions, you get confused — you have to make a balanced judgement. You have to do things with a certain amount of deliberation and prayer. I met Charlie Haughey twice in my lifetime, the first time at a charity fund-raising function. The Blackrock Clinic had opened only a short time. Someone said, "This is Jimmy Sheehan from the Blackrock Clinic." Charlie Haughey said, "That's interesting, because I'm having a problem with deafness. Is there anyone there I could see?" At this stage, he was up to his neck in problems. I said, "To be honest, Mr Haughey, with the sort of things they're saying about you, you'd be better off to stay deaf." In fairness to him, he laughed.

Public accountability is something I find upsetting — the level of accountability in health care is very poor. The costs of delivering services are not known. Construction costs are poorly controlled. Budgeting is very bad. Cost over-runs are enormous. There is a great need for a much more businesslike approach to the delivery of medical services.

I would like to encourage the development of an *independent* health service — I don't like the word private. It's an independently funded medical service for all the community, which will carry our Catholic ethos into the next generation and take up with the laity some of the work the religious have left off because of their diminishing numbers.

I have seen huge change. The patient–doctor relationship has changed — the old-time GP who was always available now frequently works nine-to-five. People are generally better informed. They look up the Internet where they can get a lot of unreliable information. They come in with all sorts of notions and demands. Subspecialisation is necessary for people to keep up with the pace of change because you can no longer deal with everything. Subspecialisation means you become interested in specific parts of people. The days of the general physician are numbered. It's very hard to get a good physician who will deal with you as a total person. Subspecialisation brings skills and care that are superb, but it has a lot of negatives. Medical students now have a mind-boggling amount of information available to them.

I'd like to build a new hospital in the west of Ireland, where the medical facilities are very poor relative to the rest of the country. My only interest there is to develop a hospital similar to Blackrock, which would be a charitable institution on a not-for-profit basis and hopefully would be available to all people living in the west.

We've got away from the voluntary effort in hospitals. I was impressed recently when I visited the Mayo Clinic to find that a lot of their staff were voluntary workers. Here, the voluntary effort has dwindled — partly caused by the trade unions. You couldn't have somebody doing a job for nothing, when somebody else should be paid for it. Now that we have full employment, perhaps we can reintroduce the voluntary element — there's an amount that people can do in hospitals. A lot of people would themselves benefit from the time they would spend helping in hospital.

I have been privileged with the friends I have had outside medicine — they have brought me out of a narrow world and enabled me to appreciate other people's thinking. I have been privileged with the people who have worked directly with me — particularly my own staff, some of whom have been with me for 25 years. I'm conscious of the privileged position I have occupied in life and no day goes by that I don't give thanks to the Lord for a fulfilling and happy life.

16

Peter Sutherland

Goldman Sachs International *and* BP plc

*"The most important thing for me in the progression of
events in my life has been the vital significance of
personal relationships. In global and political terms,
I am personally convinced that the most important thing
in advancing change is the interplay between individuals."*

Peter Denis Sutherland is Chairman of BP plc and is Managing Director of Goldman Sachs International.

He was born in Dublin on 25 April 1946. His father is William George Sutherland, who was one of the principals in Mathews, Mulcahy and Sutherland, Insurance Brokers. His mother is Barbara Nealon. He is the eldest in a family of four: David, Jill and Karen. He is married to Maruja Valcarcel. They have three children: Shane (28), Ian (26) and Natalia (22).

He was educated at Gonzaga College, Dublin; University College Dublin (BCL); and The Honorable Society of King's Inns. He is a Barrister-at-Law (Middle Temple, England) and an Attorney-at-Law (New York Bar, USA).

He has been a barrister and tutor in law at UCD (1968–81); Attorney General of Ireland (1981–84); European Community Commissioner responsible for Competition Policy (1985–89); Chairman of Allied Irish Banks (1989–93); and Director General of the World Trade Organisation, formerly GATT (1993–95).

He currently serves also on the board of directors of Investor AB, Telefonaktiebolaget LM Ericsson and The Royal Bank of Scotland Group plc.

He is associated with the following organisations: Trilateral Commission (Europe), Chairman; World Economic Forum, Foundation Board Member; The European Institute (USA), Director; The Conference Board, member of the Board of Trustees; The European Policy Centre (Brussels), Chairman of the Advisory Board; The Jacques Delors Foundation, Board Member.

He is the Honorary Consul for Uruguay in Ireland. His awards include the Gold Medal of the European Parliament (1988); the First European Law Prize (Paris, 1988); The David Rockefeller Prize (1998); the Grand Cross of Civil Merit (Spain, 1989); the Grand Cross of King Leopold II (Belgium, 1989); the New Zealand Commemorative Medal (1990); Chevalier de la Légion d'Honneur

(France, 1993); Commandeur du Wissam (Morocco, 1994); the Or-
der of Rio Branco (Brazil, 1996); the Grand Cross of the Order of
Finante Dom Henrique (Portugal, 1998); the Robert Schuman
Medal, for his work for European Integration; European Person of
the Year Award (1988); the Irish People of the Year Award (1989);
the Consumer for World Trade Annual Award (1994) for distin-
guished service; and the Dean's Medal (1996) from the Wharton
School, University of Pennsylvania. He also holds 11 honorary doc-
torates from universities in Europe and America, and is an honor-
ary Fellow of the London Business School.

The conversation was recorded in Peter Sutherland's home in Eglinton Road, Donnybrook, Dublin 4, on 26 March 2001.

Peter Sutherland

I was born in Dublin. My father was an insurance broker, one of the founders of the company, Mathews, Mulcahy and Sutherland. The family had been significantly linked to Cork with three grandparents coming from there. The name Sutherland actually originated in the Highlands of Scotland, where my great-grandfather lived. He had a business which brought him to Cork. He married a Cork girl and had children, some of whom became priests or nuns, which cannot have been easy for a Scottish Presbyterian. My grandfather was appointed City Treasurer of Dublin just before his death in 1922. He died of natural causes, I should say. My mother's father had been Church of Ireland and her mother was a Hegarty from West Cork, who had been a nurse. My grandfather owned a builders' providers in Dublin called Monsell Mitchell. The family connection that perhaps developed the most strongly for me was with the Hegartys (who, through the female side, were O'Mahonys) in West Cork. That connection continues to this day. Indeed, we have a house there just outside Goleen.

I was educated at Gonzaga College, Dublin, by the Jesuits. I had a particular interest in rugby, following my father who had been captain of Lansdowne. I captained the school junior and senior teams and paid rather more attention to rugby than perhaps I ought to have done. I went on to University College Dublin where I also captained the rugby team before joining Lansdowne. I studied law, in which I had had an interest since I was about 15, largely because of my interest in debating, at which Gonzaga was particularly proficient. I also took economics as an optional subject. I got a reasonably good honours degree, fourth place, and went on to the Bar.

I met my wife while I was still a student, though we did not get married until 1971, at which stage things were quite difficult financially, so I taught for a while part-time in UCD, in the College of Commerce, Rathmines and in Cathal Brugha Street. I taught everything from marine law, about which I knew virtually nothing and learned on the job, to hotel and catering law, about which I knew less. I struggled on at the Bar for a while and then started to make some returns. I appeared in the Arms Trial for Captain Kelly and later developed a practice in civil law. I became a Senior Counsel in the late 1970s.

In 1973, I ran for election for Fine Gael in Cabra/Finglas, which was then Dublin North-West. While I was the last person eliminated, I was never really a potential winner. I did better than I expected (which I ascribe to my wife's canvassing rather than my own) but it was a long way from getting a seat. I then dropped out of politics. I went back to the Bar and ultimately became Attorney General in Garret FitzGerald's government, having assisted in drawing up the policies for the election. I was in the job for two terms (one of them very brief). It was a difficult time both in respect of IRA violence and of the abortion referendum.

The abortion referendum was particularly difficult because the incoming Government had promised to put forward an amendment to the Constitution: to protect the life of the unborn. During the election campaign, a wording for the Constitution had been proposed by Charles Haughey and accepted by Fine Gael. When Fine Gael came to power, the Bill proposing the Amendment was immediately put before the Dáil for the purpose of legislating for a referendum. I had doubts about it and I set up an *ad hoc* committee consisting largely of people I knew personally who were not politically engaged, including a gynaecologist. I contacted some Protestant clergymen also who had been writing to the newspapers expressing reasoned opposition. I spoke also to a Catholic theologian to get a view from all angles. I came to the conclusion, privately and personally, that the proposed Amendment to the Constitution was unworkable and unsound for a range of different reasons.

The Bill for the referendum was already before the House and a lot of people felt very strongly about it — either way. I rang Garret one day and told him I had written an Opinion that expressed a negative view on the referendum and, in particular, the proposed wording. He was taken aback. My recollection is that he took the Opinion home with him that evening, came in the next morning and said, which I thought was deeply admirable, that he was persuaded not to pursue the wording already agreed.

We then moved into a fraught period because the Fine Gael party split on the question with a minority effectively voting with the Opposition. The Amendment as originally drafted was put to the people, even though the Taoiseach and myself — and indeed the Government

— believed it should not go ahead as it stood. I anticipated that something like the X Case could and would happen. I felt that "protecting the life of the unborn" raised a significant issue. Since you did not define "unborn", it could be interpreted as protecting life from conception, a purely Catholic and not even an *ex cathedra* view, as I understood it. But a more liberal Supreme Court could in the future define "unborn" as "capable of being born" so that the protection could start only long into the pregnancy.

I also said that the other part, which referred to "the equal right to life of the mother", was absurd. If two rights were equal, how could a doctor intervene to help either?

There were other difficult issues too during this time, particularly relating to extradition for terrorist offences. I cannot say that I enjoyed the job — it was, from time to time, an uncomfortable period, but I was helped by a great staff in the Attorney General's office.

In 1984, the Government nominated me as a member of the European Commission. I had told the Taoiseach that I thought it would be better if he appointed Jim Dooge or Alan Dukes. Garret told me that Jim Dooge had suggested me — Jim was Minister for Foreign Affairs at the time — and that he could not risk a by-election in Alan Dukes' constituency. I went to meet Jacques Delors, the incoming President of the Commission. I met him in a restaurant in Paris, Chez Edgar, off the Champs Elysées. It has since closed but at that time it was the place where the Left and the Press ate. We met in a private room — he was speaking French and I was speaking English. To my amazement he said he wanted me to take charge of Agriculture. I told him that I knew absolutely nothing about agriculture but, as an Irishman, if he offered me the Agriculture portfolio, I could hardly say no. I rang Garret from the hotel that afternoon and he said, "I hope you said yes." I told him that I had to say yes but that I was not looking forward to it. I came home and started getting really excellent briefings from the Department of Agriculture. After two weeks of this daunting exercise, which I was finding more and more discouraging, Delors called me and said that the Agriculture position was no longer an option. Because of the fall-out from his proposal to divide the External Relations portfolio between two other people, he needed to allocate Agriculture to someone else. He said, "Your first choice was Competition. You can have it. And, apart from that, I'd like you to take Social Affairs, Education and Health until the Spaniards come in."

So far as I was concerned, Competition was a challenging and potentially crucial position. I saw it as crucial for Europe both constitutionally and in terms of economic policy. Through the State Aid rules, it was apparent that the European Union treaties already conferred advanced supranational powers in this area to the Commission. The powers specified in the Treaty of Rome did not require constant approval or authorisations from the Member States in the Council of Ministers. The power to prohibit illicit state aid really meant that the Commission could to a great extent determine an important instrument of industrial policy. The power had been used since 1957, but not aggressively, because the Commission had been afraid to use it. With the completion of the Internal Market as the dominant theme of the new Commission, the power had to be used in order for the Commission's programme to be credible.

The second part of the portfolio was what was traditionally called anti-trust — mergers, acquisitions and anti-competitive agreements, either vertical or horizontal. This also gave the Commission real power to ensure that firms did not engage in unacceptable restrictive practices or create corporate structures that would damage competition to the detriment of consumers. Enforcement could have real bite through legal prohibitions and the imposition of fines on offending corporations. In addition, in weighing the balance of advantage when taking decisions, account could be taken by the Commissioner of the broader European public interest. Competition particularly attracted me because, for years, I had been interested in European integration and the implications of the use of the law to advance it. I viewed my portfolio as a constitutional means to develop greater federalism in an integrated internal market. Ultimately, I prepared and presented to the Council the Merger Control Regulation that has governed mergers since.

Having affirmed the portfolio, the Commission met for the first time in Royaumont, an old abbey outside Paris. The difficulty then was that the President, Jacques Delors, could not decide alone on the designation of portfolios. He could propose the composition but the Commission as a whole had to agree. (This has changed with the Amsterdam and Nice Treaties.) However, at that time, Delors had to obtain consensus. He conducted individual meetings — which he called "confessionals" in the abbey, not inappropriately. He called me in early in the process. He said that, as to what we had already agreed

between us, there was no problem. As it was about seven o'clock in
the evening and, since I was in a position that was better than I had
anticipated at the outset, I decided I would beat a tactical retreat and
go to bed early. I went to my room and asked Stanley Clinton Davis,
the British Labour nominee whom I was supporting in his ambitions
for Environment and Transport, if he would keep an eye on developments. I told him, if he needed help, he could alert me and I was prepared to come down again. I heard nothing and ultimately went to
sleep. At seven o'clock next morning, I heard the bells of the local
church and went downstairs. I saw the detritus of the night before,
empty glasses and so on. They had obviously been up till all hours. I
went for a walk in the grounds and saw Delors coming towards me
through the early morning mist. "Where did you get to last night?" I
told him I went to bed early. "Very wise. Your portfolio is intact. My
problem is that we have agreed the portfolios for now as the Commission but, formally, we don't yet exist. Our decisions cannot be taken
yet. Secondly, there was one Commissioner missing last night." I said,
"If I were in your shoes, I'd call in the world's press and announce
what the portfolios are. They will be irreversible then. We all knew
what the meeting was about and you should announce the result
now." In the event, that is what he did.

I had circulated a note throughout the Irish public service and to
some major Irish corporations asking for nominations to the several
positions I needed to be filled in my cabinet. It had been repeatedly
emphasised to me that it was vital that I got the best cabinet possible.
Amongst the people recommended to me, I had been given the name
of Richard O'Toole,[1] one of the brightest people in Foreign Affairs. He
was to become my Chef de Cabinet. Liam Hourican, an old and dear
friend, now dead, became Deputy Chef de Cabinet. I asked a Flemish
anti-trust lawyer from the Commission, Jean-François Verstrynge,
who was notoriously strong, to join me. And Catherine Day, a UCD
economist (now one of the most senior women in the Commission)
agreed to look after State Aids. David O'Sullivan, now Secretary General of the Commission, agreed to transfer back from the Commission's delegation in Tokyo to look after External Relations,
Development and Institutional Issues. Eugene Regan, who had been
chief executive of the Irish Meat Exporters and before that chief

---

[1] See Chapter 13 (Denis O'Brien), p. 262.

economist for the IFA in Brussels, joined me largely to cover agriculture, as did Michel Richonnier, a very interesting Frenchman who had written books about the future, particularly from a technological perspective. In all, I had a first-class team. I was later told by Emile Noël (the Secretary General of the Commission) that my Cabinet was the best in the Berlaymont.

At the first Commission meeting, we had something of a contretemps — my first of many with Delors, notwithstanding the fact that he has remained a close friend of mine. In fact, I am on the board of his Foundation in Paris today, *Notre Europe*. He said he was going to give an *"habilitation"* to Franz Andriessen, who was the Commissioner for Agriculture — a series of *"habilitations"*, in fact, and nobody said anything. I said, "I don't know what *'habilitation'* means." He indicated that giving *"habilitations"* was quite standard and perfectly normal. The Commissioner for Agriculture was always given delegated powers — the personal right to make certain administrative decisions without the need to revert to the Commission as a whole, decisions of a recurring kind and so on. I was concerned about this because no prior notice had been given and I was conscious of the sensitivity of agricultural matters. I indicated that I was not prepared to agree to *any* *"habilitations"* until I knew precisely what they were about. Delors told me I was being ridiculous — that we could not have a blockage like this at our first meeting. I asked him to put it back for a week so that I could discover what it was all about. Delors refused. He said, "This always happens at the first Commission meeting." I told him I was opposing it. He asked me if I was looking for a vote. I said that, if necessary, I was. He said, "Do you know that there was never a vote in the last Commission, Gaston Thorn's Commission?" I said, "I'm not looking for a vote — you are." It was getting quite contentious. He said, "Right. If you want a vote, then we will have a vote." We had a vote — not everybody was there — but it was seven to five against me. In retrospect, I do not think that I would do things differently now, although, at the time, I felt bruised by the incident. In reality, I felt that it was an important moment in establishing the fact that due process was important and that the President, however strong, was not omnipotent.

My relationship with Jacques Delors requires some comment. He and I became great friends and went to football matches together — in fact, we were at the Heisel Stadium in Brussels the night of the disaster there. Ideologically, however, we were not in agreement on a number of issues, particularly on state aids. In this area, I had started early by taking a tough line against state aids given by governments in a number of countries, including France. At one stage, the *Wall Street Journal* did a front-page article on the continuing battle between us, which sometimes resulted in Commission votes. Jacques proposed that we should spend a Saturday morning arguing out our respective positions intellectually, bringing one person each, trying to reconcile our stances — which we tried to do, unsuccessfully. Even though he favoured a French tradition of statist interventionism in the market economy and I preferred a market-based application of competition policy, I had a basic majority in the Commission and our battles became less frequent. Years later, when he was going to resign over the failure to double the structural funds, he said, after a long lunch, that there was only one other Commissioner who he felt would resign with him — and he pointed at me. (In fact, I would not have resigned.) In any event, we agreed completely on the fundamental issue of integration and federalism, although my view on a federal Europe was that it should be based on constitutional law developed by democratically accountable institutions and endorsed openly by the people — with active use of the courts to interpret application and thus to create a supranational EU identity. My proudest possession is a generous dedication written on one of his books.

Our big programme in the Commission was the completion of the internal market, the free movement of people, goods, services and capital. The effective functioning of a free internal market obviously depended significantly on competition policy and, in particular, the control of state subsidies. State subsidies could distort the market because one member state by assisting its industry could illicitly overcome inefficiencies. We also needed effective rules to stop cartels and monopolies controlling the market through the denial of competition so, early on, I started taking on national airlines and governments which were resistant to competition. That created a lot of trouble. I remember over a private dinner being warned off by the then chairman of Lufthansa. He said, "You'd better stay out of this area because you have no power to go into it." I believed I had and that was subsequently established to be the case.

There were a number of very sensitive areas which were less publicly evident in Ireland but were very important elsewhere — for example, the coal and steel sector, shipbuilding and motor vehicle manufacturing. Other areas were breaking open the telecommunications monopolies, which we did by using for the first time a power under the former Article 90 of the EEC Treaty. This is virtually the only provision which authorises the Commission to issue a binding directive on its own authority to secure member state compliance with the competition rules and without the necessity of member state specific consent. A number of member states appealed our decisions to the Court of Justice but the Court upheld the right of the Commission to use this Treaty provision. The use or threat of use of this provision was thus to play a significant role in strengthening the Commission's hand to break the monopoly power of the state sector in Europe in energy, transport, including air transport, and telecommunications. The precedent in one of those ran for all of them. I should say that in most instances Ireland in the initial years regrettably was a reluctant follower rather than a leader in this liberalisation.

There were a lot of fractious issues that arose during my four-year term. For example, I stopped the British Aerospace–Rover deal from going ahead on the terms initially proposed. One morning in Brussels I was shaving and listening to Margaret Thatcher, who was at a G7 meeting in Canada, telling an interviewer she didn't want to talk about the G7 meeting, she wanted to talk about "that man" in Brussels. She launched an attack on "the Irish Commissioner" but, at the end of the day, she compromised on terms acceptable to the Commission. I also blocked the British Airways/British Caledonian merger until we obtained substantial concessions. For years, the German Länder had grown accustomed to giving out large sums of regional aid to companies which would locate in their regions. Even very rich Land governments would do this in regions with very high per capita income. It was counterproductive in terms of regional policy and made very little sensible use of German taxpayer funds. The matter became a political hot potato between the Federal Government and the Länder. Chancellor Helmut Kohl, at a special meeting of the Commission in Bonn, made direct representations to me. I insisted on a more focused regional aid map in Germany so that available funds would be focused on needy areas and so that poorer regions in other member states would not be placed at a disadvantage in attracting investment.

Another case was that of state aid for Renault: I remember going to Paris to do a deal with the relevant minister, Alain Madelin, one of the most liberal of French politicians. He went much farther than many people would have expected in our meeting held late one night in Paris. Having completed the deal, we had a drink and smoked a cigar in his wonderful office. He said, "I want you to join a club." He gave me a tie with a head on it. I asked him what it was. He told me the head was Frédéric Bastiat, the famous French free market economist from the nineteenth century.[2] He described him as the French Adam Smith. I said, "I never heard of him." "Oh, he's very famous — now you are a member of the Bastiat Club. It's a very small club with only 22 members." I took the tie and drove back to Brussels, arriving at about four in the morning. We had a Commission meeting next morning and I was deliberately wearing the Bastiat tie. I went over to the President and said, "Jacques, I'd just like you to know that I had a very interesting meeting last night with Alain Madelin." Delors replied, "Oh, Madelin — in 1968 he was on the other side of the barricades from my daughter Martine (Aubry as she now is — Mayor of Lille)." I told Delors that the agreement I had reached with Madelin was to remove from Renault the status of a *régie* (a *régie* was a status created by de Gaulle after the last war — it meant a type of company that could never be permitted by the government to go bankrupt no matter how badly it performed). I had agreed the previous night that that status would be removed. I suspected Delors would disagree — and he did. I said, "You'll notice the tie I'm wearing." He asked what tie it was. I said, "That's the famous French economist." "What famous French economist?" "Frédéric Bastiat." "Who is Frédéric Bastiat? I never heard of him." He turned to Pascal Lamy, his Chef de Cabinet, who was sitting beside him and asked him if he had ever heard of Bastiat. Lamy said, "It rings some sort of a bell — I can't remember who he is." Lamy had got first place in ENA, a very grande école — if he could not remember Bastiat, who would? Later that day, Jacques sent me round a page on Bastiat from a reference book and had underlined in red ink a sentence which said that Bastiat hated all socialists!

In many ways, my period on the Commission transformed my life. It irrevocably formed some fundamental beliefs and provoked a pas-

---

[2] For a recent note on Bastiat, see *The Economist*, 21–27 July 2001, p. 63.

sion for European federalism. It was a time of extraordinary events. We drafted the Single European Act. We did most of the completion of the Single Market. We started for real the single currency movement. In a sense, Europe was relaunched during the late eighties and it became the great cause that excites me most of all.

I should say that I enjoyed very much also my role in charge of the Commission's Relations with the European Parliament, a role I took over after one year in Social Affairs and Education. In the year that I was responsible for education, I put through the Council of Ministers the ERASMUS Programme, which has fostered cross-border university exchanges very successfully, and also the COMET Programme, which encouraged university–industry exchange. Hywel Jones, a Welsh Commission official, deserves particular credit for both. Reverting to my role of liaising with the European Parliament, I found myself initially in a political milieu that was unfamiliar to me. I found, however, that I could get on very well with the various groupings because they felt that I was less politically aligned than a more conventional politician might have been. I decided to invest a considerable amount of time in addressing the Parliament's concerns and, together with my Cabinet member, David O'Sullivan, we argued strongly for Parliament's enhanced role in the co-operation procedure developed in the Single European Act. I was deeply honoured at the end of my term to become the first Commissioner to receive the Gold Medal of the European Parliament.

From an Irish point of view, I should say that, during that period, I piloted through the Commission the authorisation under the State Aid rules for the International Financial Services Centre in Dublin. The Taoiseach's office — Charles Haughey's — had been actively encouraging this. It was quite a controversial issue and the debate was somewhat of a forerunner of the more modern debates on taxation between Ireland and certain high-tax member states. We argued that a derogation from the normal rules on tax could apply on the basis that, at that time, Irish GDP per capita was less than 75 per cent of the EU average and unemployment was the second highest after Spain. The Treaty rules allowed state aids to be given where there was an existing significant regional disadvantage and Ireland legitimately claimed that there was. Catherine Day, who handled state aids for me, argued eloquently at the Chef de Cabinet level meeting (which preceded the Commission meeting proper) that the derogation was fully justified. Ultimately the proposal was accepted by the Commission. I never considered the support that I gave to the IFSC to be guided by nationalist motives. I believed it was eminently justifiable as a means to tackle the difficult economic problems faced by the EU's then poorer regions.

The day I left the Commission we had a lunch with my Cabinet. We discussed what everyone would do next. Most would remain in the Commission. I said that, in public policy terms, there was one challenge that I thought very interesting, and that was GATT. The majority thought that I was mad: who would be interested in GATT? But, in 1989, I felt that this was the biggest challenge anywhere. The word "globalisation" had not really been coined at that time but it seemed to me that a global market was an essential aspect of global justice. Following the European example, it was an idea whose time had come. Jean Monnet had said that the European Community institutionally was a precursor to global governance. What GATT (and the WTO) could become, if successful, was the first real instrument of global governance apart from the UN and, in many ways, would be more effective than any UN institution.

However, GATT was to be in the future. When I left Brussels, I came home and became chairman of AIB. I had in fact intended to go back to the Bar.

Incidentally, when I had moved to Brussels, my wife, my daughter and my youngest son joined me, but we had to take a difficult decision about our eldest son, who had just started school in Gonzaga. At the beginning of my four-year term, I had a fair idea that I might not be appointed for a second term because of the likelihood of a change of government. We decided that, even though we weren't particularly in favour of it, we would have to send him to boarding school. Otherwise, we would be bringing him home from one educational system to another towards the end of the secondary school cycle. We sent him to Glenstal. The second boy went to Glenstal also, having spent a year or two in Brussels with us. Our daughter stayed with us throughout.

I mentioned that I had started thinking about this world trade situation. I started writing a little and making contributions at conferences about GATT. There was no WTO on the horizon at that stage. Mike Moore, who was then Prime Minister of New Zealand, but was later to become a successor of mine at the WTO, heard about what I was doing. He asked me to join a small group of people, which included Otto Graf Lamsdorf, the head of the German Liberal Party and a former Economics Minister, to write a report on the world trade system. New Zealand was understandably very anxious that the Uruguay Round would succeed. We wrote a report, which received some favourable publicity, and then, one day in the early nineties, I was at another conference in northern Spain and Arthur Dunkel, the GATT Director General, was there. Arthur was Swiss and had been head of GATT for seven or eight years. He asked me to go for a walk with him in the grounds of the hotel. He said, "I don't know how much longer I should stay — this has been going on a long time. Would you be interested in trying to complete the Uruguay Round?" I indicated that I might well be.

One day in March 1993, I received a totally unexpected phone call from Mickey Kantor, whom I had never met. He was the Cabinet member responsible for trade in the Clinton administration. Mickey said he wanted to meet me and, he understood, so did Leon Brittan. He said they wanted separate talks with me. I asked him what it was about and he said that he would prefer to tell me face-to-face. We met — for the first time — for dinner in a restaurant in Brussels. The Irish Government, incidentally, was at the time completely unaware of this. I met Leon Brittan for breakfast. The two of them told me individually that Europe and the United States had agreed that I should become the next director general of GATT, would I take it? Leon Brittan was then Commissioner for Trade and he said Jacques Delors was in favour of the appointment.

(Delors, incidentally, had invited me to become EU Ambassador to the United States when I left the Commission, but I had declined.)

Having contributed to finding myself in this position, I became very worried about whether or not I should take the GATT job. I was concerned about disrupting the family again even though my wife, Maruja, was, as always, supportive. Initially, I said that, on consideration, I would not go. Having said no, pressure continued, including telephone calls from two prime ministers in Europe. I went to Dick Spring, the Minister for Foreign Affairs, to tell him what had happened. There was a European Council meeting to be held in Denmark where a decision about the appointment would be taken. I was out of the frame in the sense that they were still asking me but I had not said yes. I was in Greece at a Bilderberg meeting, when I rang Dick Spring and told him I had reconsidered. As a result, in the early part of 1993, the European Community nominated me, the Americans were already on board, and between them they had brought a lot of other member states on board.

The Latin Americans, however, thought about putting forward a candidate and actually did put forward a name or two. I went and met a lot of people in Geneva to gather the necessary support. In particular, I obtained the approval of a very important ambassador who was chairman of the Council, B.K. Zutchi, the Indian Ambassador. I told everybody there was a fundamental condition: I would give an undertaking only to see out the Uruguay Round and, if possible, to create a World Trade Organisation — but I was not going to commit myself to a lifetime as an international civil servant. Above all, I did not want to disrupt my daughter's education again. It was agreed that, on conclusion of the Uruguay Round, I would have the position if I wanted it, but equally that I could leave. In fact it was incorporated in the final Treaty that the Director General of GATT would automatically become Director General of the WTO on its inception. (This was to happen.) Richard O'Toole agreed to come with me as Assistant Director General. He came with me at considerable cost to himself. In the event, I became the first Director General of the WTO but stayed for only six months.

We moved into high gear very quickly when I arrived in Geneva. I went on CNN television at the beginning of July — I had been appointed Director General in May. The G7 were about to meet in Tokyo. I made the seemingly audacious comment that, if the G7 could not make real progress in moving the negotiations for the Uruguay Round, which had been going on for seven years, at that meeting, they would raise questions about their relevance to the world economy and the summit would be considered a failure. I was told afterwards that Clinton saw that interview on television and expressed some annoyance at who this upstart was. However, he gave a direction that something should happen so far as the US was concerned — and something did happen. Tokyo, which took place about ten days after my television statement, made real and substantial progress. We then created a wholly artificial deadline that the negotiating had to be finished by 15 December of that year — otherwise we would call it off. Again, that was pretty outrageous but it worked. Even though there was no real agreement for such a deadline, the US Secretary of the Treasury, in a speech, endorsed it. For the next six months there was frenetic activity. I finally gavelled the text (a total of 22,000 pages) at a meeting of all the countries in Geneva on 15 December of that year. In the intervening six months, a process of negotiation perhaps unparalleled in history was concluded. The negotiations would require a book in themselves. Suffice it to say they formed the most stimulating period of my life. It was not the end of the problems, however, because we still had to get ratification through national parliaments and, particularly, through the US Congress — I had to spend a lot of time in the United States lobbying congressmen and senators. The final signing was in Marrakech in Morocco with Al Gore, who was Vice-President, attending from the United States.

At the signing I was standing all day at a table in the palace in Marrakech as each delegation came up to sign and smile for the cameras. Ultimately we got to the United States, far down the alphabetical list. It was late in the day. There were batteries of cameras. Mickey Kantor was in a corner and I beckoned to him to come out with Gore and sign. He was a bit far away and he beckoned to me. I did not know what was happening. I walked down to the corner and said, "What is it, Mickey? Come out and sign the Treaty." "I can't." "Why not?" "I've just got a phone call from the President of the United States." "What did he say?" "Well, I could not hear. The line was very indistinct. It was something about adding new provisions along the lines of the US Foreign Corrupt Practices Act." I said, "The what? Mickey, if I have to drag you out by the hair of the head, you're going to sign this bloody agreement." He looked around at Gore and said, "I told you he'd say something like that." Then he hugged me and there was a photograph on the front page of *The Irish Times* the next day, me standing with my mouth open. The whole thing was a joke, which was typical of Mickey, who has remained a good friend.

The Treaty was signed and then I had to spend a lot of time in the States, lobbying, because the Republicans were worried about it. I particularly spent some time with Newt Gingrich who proved vital in bringing the Republicans on side. They were concerned about possible implications for the national sovereignty of the United States. We ultimately got it through and part of it was the creation of the WTO and I became automatically the first director general. When I left after the six months, I received nice letters of appreciation from Bill Clinton, Boris Yeltsin, John Major and other world leaders.

I subsequently took on positions in BP and in Goldman Sachs.

My two public policy passions have been European integration — that remains fundamental to me — and, secondly, a rule-based structure for *global* trade. By this I mean that while I think that free competition fosters productivity and growth, I recognise that all countries cannot and should not move at the same pace. I have been involved also in public issues through Jacques Delors' Foundation, in which I am active in Paris, and with the Overseas Development Council in Washington. For the last three years I have been on the advisory board of the Council on Foreign Relations in New York. I am honorary chairman of the European Policy Centre in Brussels, the principal think-tank on European integration, and have recently become European chairman of the Trilateral Commission. Those public policy concerns will remain important to me and I hope to retain a particular involvement in them through a new Institute that I have helped to create at Trinity College Dublin.

Going back to my private life, I was non-executive chairman of AIB, 1989 to 1993 — I had taken over from the late Niall Crowley.[3] When I left the WTO, I was approached by Goldman Sachs. Why? Because during the period 1989 to 1993, Goldman Sachs had set up a group of advisers, somewhat like an advisory board in Europe, which I had been asked to join. In that same period, I had also been on the board of BP. Funnily enough, I had been introduced to BP when I was a Commissioner. When I left the Commission, I suspect they invited me because they wanted someone on the Board with a particular European focus. So, my involvement with both Goldman Sachs and BP had predated the GATT.

When I left the WTO I was asked if I would join Goldman Sachs as a partner. I felt a bit doubtful because I was not an investment banker. However, I found that my experience and relationships more than equipped me for the task. BP asked me to become deputy chairman to David Simon, later to become Lord Simon.

When Tony Blair's government was formed, although David Simon was non-political, immediately after the election he was offered the House of Lords and the position of Minister for Europe, which he took. He rang me over the weekend and said it looked as if I would have to take the position of chairman of BP. I told him that I did not know that I could possibly do that — for one thing, my part-

---

[3] *In Good Company*, pp. 215–236.

ners in Goldman Sachs might not agree to it. He said we would have to try and persuade them. Fortunately, my partners were very accommodating. The position was non-executive. It was not as difficult to do both as it might appear. I could spend three hours early in the morning in BP and be back in the Goldman Sachs' office at ten o'clock, only ten minutes' walk away. The BP job has been a rollercoaster. When I first joined the board the market cap was less than $10 billion — today, it's over $200 billion. During the three years following my becoming chairman, we took over Amoco, one of the biggest oil companies in the United States, and Arco, also a very big company, and, most recently, Castrol. Those acquisitions have put us into a different league in global reach. We are now the second largest company in Europe.

I claim no responsibility at all other than being a sounding board for Sir John Brown who deserves all the credit for BP. He was Chief Executive of the Year for the last couple of years. We have a very good collaborative relationship. I believe in principle that splitting the roles of chairman and chief executive is a very good thing. If you have the chairman as CEO, you have obvious conflicts of interest. First of all, the chairman has a significant role in the appointment of the board members so they are more likely to be a club of friends. It interferes with the objectivity of remuneration policy and with governance more generally. Increasingly in Britain there are non-executive chairmen of major corporations — indeed it has become the norm, following the Cadbury and Hampel Reports. In the United States, the merging of the office of chairman and CEO remains in a way which is undesirable. I think it's also a good idea to have a minority of executive directors on the board. Even though they are unlikely to argue against each other or the chief executive, the fact that there is a communication between the non-executives who control the board and other executives is another check and balance against the excessive use of power by chief executives.

I have enjoyed my position with BP. It's a tribute to the British that there was never the faintest question mark over an Irishman becoming chairman. I have also enjoyed Goldman Sachs immensely. It has, in the interim, become a public company. At age 55, I am one of the oldest people there. Historically, the average age for becoming a partner was 40 — the average age for retirement was 47 or 48. Virtually everybody is under 50.

Peter Wallenberg, an old friend of mine largely through his support in the early nineties for globalisation and the Uruguay Round, asked if I would join the board of Investor AB, which holds major investments in companies like Ericsson, Electrolux, ABB, Astra Zeneca. Ultimately, it effectively controls about 46 per cent of the Swedish stock exchange. Wallenberg nominated me for the boards of ABB and Ericsson. I left the board of ABB when I joined the board of Royal Bank of Scotland recently.

It is a truism to say that that one of the most important causes of economic change is confidence. But confidence is a very ephemeral thing. It is sometimes difficult to know why it should be there at a certain time and why it dissipates so quickly. At the end of March 2001, while we are talking, there is nothing inherently wrong with the US economy. We have had some share price bubbles in the technology area. They were unwarranted and excessive. We have also had the longest bull market period in history. Combine those things, and when it becomes apparent that the technology stocks are not delivering as rapidly as some of those who promoted them would have argued, it created a puncturing of the bubble. This resulted in a sudden change in the confidence factor combined with an unfortunate period of electoral uncertainty. The loss of confidence damaged the market but I believe that it will recover. I am more worried about Europe, where structural problems on the continent are not being addressed quickly enough.

I think the general view still is that this should not be more than some quarters of what could loosely be described as recessionary conditions. After that we should be improving. But that all depends on creating conditions of confidence. The other big imponderable is Japan. It has been a saga of missed opportunities for fundamental reform for years. I have been very close to China's application and negotiations for membership of the WTO — they are taking far too long. China is potentially a positive catalyst for global economic growth. I hope that political tensions don't interfere with the process of getting China quickly into the WTO as a functioning and effective part of the global economy.

The process of globalisation is generally very good but I don't think it has been allowed to work to everybody's advantage — that does not mean that it has worked to their disadvantage. Regrettably, sub-Saharan Africa has just been left out of the process. The persistence of appalling problems of global poverty is not caused by globalisation but rather by marginalisation and the failure to participate in globalisation. Access to markets is important (and the developed world could do much more than it has done in sectors such as agriculture and textiles) and much freer access to developing country products is needed to stimulate economic development. Democratic accountability and strengthened institutions in developing countries are needed to underpin development. Effective development assistance is not reaching those most in need and even the inadequate amounts that are advanced are often wasted.

The most important thing for me in the progression of events in my life has been the vital significance of personal relationships. In global and political terms, I am personally convinced that the most important thing in advancing change is the interplay between individuals. Mickey Kantor was a fighter but he, like Leon Brittan, knew that history was not made by failing to reach agreements. Also, we would not have had European integration, we could have faced the collapse of the European Union, if Jacques Delors had not been President of the European Commission when he was, but as important, he needed both Kohl and Mitterand to be in position and in agreement on the basic direction of European policy. Today, Romano Prodi has a much more difficult position. When he was preparing for the Commission, I spent the weekend with him, Jacques Delors and Stevie Davignon at the European Institute in Florence planning his strategy. We discussed also with him the structure of the Commission but his real difficulty is that he does not have the same pro-European consensus among the major leaders of government which Delors had enjoyed. The conjuncture of individuals in crucial positions for the moment is resulting in stagnation in the integration process.

The evidence has been the debacle of Nice[4] and more recently the failure of the Stockholm Summit. I do not think that Europe yet has the structure right for the coming period of enlargement. In fact, I don't know how we can cope with 28 or 30 members of the EU without having a leadership which embraces reform of the institutions in

---

[4] "Debacle" refers to the Nice negotiations leading up to the Nice Treaty. The Irish Government decided to hold a referendum on the Treaty. Subsequent to this interview taking place, the Treaty was rejected by a majority of those who chose to vote.

the Union. Essentially, what the member states appear to be trying to do is to take back from the Commission the exclusive power to propose legislation. Only the Commission can serve as the motor for the integration process in the common interest of all the member states. Both the Commission and the European Parliament are open to more democratic accountability and democratic debate but the member state governments permit too big a say to national bureaucratic representatives who dominate the structures of the Council of Ministers and who are remote from true democratic scrutiny. The bigger governments are trying to play an intergovernmental bureaucratic game, which is to dictate the agenda, confine debate among themselves, and then decide themselves the direction where everybody is going. It's absolutely contrary to the interests of the smaller countries. More fundamentally, it does not work.

I believe human relations, personal relations, are very important. In this regard, it is a huge advantage to be Irish. Becoming Director General of GATT and of the WTO was for me an easier proposition than it would be in relative terms for most other European nationals because Ireland is viewed differently. We are the only developed country which is seen by many developing countries as being, in effect, a former colony. Also, we have no imperial past as a nation state. Historically, it has been a huge advantage to be Irish in Europe because there are few negative historic images associated with Ireland.

That has been very important for me. And your feet are always kept on the ground by your friends in this country who are not fooled by status or position. They see it for what it is, largely a question of fortuitous circumstance, that one is in the right position at the right time. The biggest and best decision I took was the decision to become Director General of the GATT. For many people, particularly in Ireland, there was no perception of what the GATT was all about. Taking the position was bizarre almost. It could easily have been a poisoned chalice of major proportions. In fact it was touch-and-go as to whether it would be or not because the GATT round could easily have failed — it had dragged on for seven years and looked as if it was heading for disaster. But I was lucky to have the support of many world leaders of vision who were committed to getting it done. The time was ripe.

17

David Went

Irish Life & Permanent plc

*"There is nobody more deluded than a chief executive about
his own management style. I believe in establishing clear
goals. Goals have to start at the top and work down or at the
bottom and work up — which way does not really matter.
Then, within those goals, people have to have
significant discretion to get on with it."*

David Went is the Group Chief Executive of Irish Life & Permanent plc.

He was born in Dublin on 25 March 1947. His father, Arthur, was Chief Inspector of Fisheries in Ireland. His mother was Phyllis Howell, a housewife. He was second in a family of two, with one sister, Janice. He is married to Mary Milligan, who is a law graduate. They have two children, James (25) and Kate (22).

He was educated at High School, Dublin; at Trinity College Dublin where he took a BA (Mod) in Legal Science and an LLB; and at King's Inns (Barrister-at-Law).

He worked with Citibank in Dublin and in Jeddah from 1970 to 1976; in Ulster Investment Bank from 1976 to 1987; in Ulster Bank from 1987 to 1994; with the Coutts Group from 1994 to 1997; and with Irish Life (now Irish Life & Permanent plc) from 1998 to date.

He is a member of the Board of the Trinity Foundation.

The conversation was recorded on 17 January 2001 in David Went's office at Group Headquarters, Lower Abbey Street, Dublin 1.

David Went

I was a post-war baby. My sister was a pre-war baby. My mother wouldn't bring another child into the world at a time when she thought Hitler might win. What my parents gave me was a belief that education was important. They were English. Dad had left school at 15. He went on an adult education scholarship to Imperial College, London when he was in his early twenties. When he graduated in the 1930s there were no jobs. The only thing he could do to put off the evil day was to go on for a PhD. He did it in Oslo. My parents were engaged at this stage. He was offered two jobs, one as a lecturer in Swansea and the other was as an Inspector of Fisheries here in Dublin. Thank God he came to Dublin because Ireland has been very good to my family. He arrived a week late for the interview but they were so impressed that he came all the way down from the top of Norway that they gave him the job. Education gave my father the opportunity to develop his life in a way that was better than his immediate family. Therefore for my sister and myself, education was important. My sister was a high achiever. She did medicine and, you know, when your sister who is eight or nine years older than you is a high achiever, it can be a bit of a pain in the ass. You go through life with your mother telling you your sister did this and your sister did that. (I have got over this now!)

I wanted to go to Cambridge to study English but my father said he would not support me because reading books all day would be bad for me. I probably would have ended up being a teacher — nothing wrong with being a teacher, but I needed something different. I went to Trinity to do law. From that day to this I'm not sure why I picked law. There was no logic in the decision. I'm very glad now I did. I met some interesting people, including my wife. Law does teach you to think logically and it's as good a subject as any. I qualified at the Bar. At that stage I would love to have practised but it just was not economically viable. Dad was a civil servant and while we were comfortable, when I qualified in 1970 you would have needed family support for about five years unless you had political connections or married a solicitor's daughter or the daughter of someone who ran an insurance company, so practising was not an option. To some extent I regret that. I was called the same day as Dermot Gleeson and Jack Fitzgerald, who have both been very successful at the Bar. However, I realise that I would have found being a barrister frustrating because you're always advising people and you're never doing anything yourself. So, in 1970, what should I do?

I applied to all the English banks for a job because in those days banks would have taken lawyers for the trustee department. Four or five of them offered me jobs in England but then I got lucky. Citibank had been in Dublin about five or six years and I applied to them. They had a very charismatic guy, Adrian Evans, in charge — I probably did not know what charismatic meant at that time. I was interviewed by him and Michael Meagher (who ended up in Bank of Ireland). They offered me a job as a graduate trainee, with training and the opportunity to travel. I was very glad I took the job — I had a great five or six years with them.

I was lucky that Michael Meagher was working in Citibank because I virtually followed him through much of my career and he taught me a lot. He subsequently recruited me into Ulster Investment Bank. I took over his job there when he left and when he left Ulster Bank I effectively took over his job again.

Citibank was an experience — they were revolutionising banking in Ireland. The Irish banks would not acknowledge it, but the influx of foreign banks certainly encouraged the growth of AIIB and IBI: much of their development was provoked by the kind of competition Citibank was bringing into Ireland. Citibank worked you hard but they invested huge amounts in their graduate trainees. You learned a lot in a short time. When I joined I had no financial or economic training whatsoever. They brought me through a six-month credit course in Milan, which enabled me to understand the rudiments of accounting and credit analysis. And then they just continued to pump training into you. And I met some great people there: Jim Farrell, who is now with the National Treasury Management Agency, was my training officer, my mentor. You had to go through six months' training in operations before you could become a lending officer. You had to understand how the back office worked. With hindsight, I'm glad it happened but, when you're a 23-year-old graduate, you find it a bit beneath you to be in there writing tickets. It taught me never to look down on anybody who does a mundane job, because it's very important, but I got really brassed off — it was tedious, I was 23, a barrister, knowing everything and there I was sitting writing tickets!

I got offered a job by Aer Lingus as one of their lawyers. I actually resigned and Jim Farrell talked me out of it. I'm grateful to him ever since.

I spent five years in Citibank in Dublin and ended up running the lending business in Ireland at age 27/28. They gave you great freedom and opportunity at a young age. They told me that they had a policy that they did not want a local man heading up the operations in any country so that, if I was thinking of eventually getting the top job, I'd better forget it, but they said, "Boy, do we have an opportunity for you — we'd like you to run our branch in Jeddah." This was in 1975. Mary was pregnant with our first child. She followed me out there five months after I arrived. Saudi Arabia had not really developed in those days. They had all this money and did not know how to spend it logically. I was running a branch with 250/300 people, most of whom were Arab-speaking, not necessarily locals, but Pakistanis, etc. People working immediately for me were Americans, English, Greek, Pakistani, Saudi, etc., so it was a great learning experience at that age.

I have worked outside Ireland twice in my career, once then, and once more recently when I ran Coutts. I loved the jobs I was doing when I was outside Ireland but both of them were a mistake for me personally because I didn't realise how much I missed Ireland. That may sound schmaltzy, but Ireland, as I said, had been very good to my family. My sister and I had a great education here. We had a much better life here than we would have had if my parents had stayed in London. I came home for Jamie's christening and happened to meet Michael Meagher. He asked me if I'd be interested in coming to work with him in Ulster Investment Bank. I decided to come home and resigned from Citibank. They completely misunderstood. I tried to explain to them that it wasn't money, it wasn't anything like that, it was all about the fact that I wanted to come home to Ireland. My parents were getting older and my children were the only grandchildren they were going to have. So I ran the lending side of the Ulster Investment Bank business for six years to 1982 and then Michael Meagher moved on to become the deputy chief executive of Ulster Bank with a view to becoming chief executive. That didn't work out because he left for Bank of Ireland a year or so later. I ran Ulster Investment Bank from 1982 to 1987, an interesting business. When I joined UIB in 1976 there were about 40 of us, and when I left in 1987 there were probably 250. We had moved from being narrowly focused to being a fully-fledged investment bank — corporate finance, asset management, lending, treasury, etc. We had some good people — there are now lots of people around town who had been in Ulster Investment Bank.

Michael Meagher had left in, I think, 1984 to become one of three managing directors in Bank of Ireland. My then boss, Victor Chambers, was coming up to retirement. They asked me in 1987 if I would go to Belfast as deputy chief executive of Ulster Bank to become chief executive in 12 months' time. Mary and I thought about that — though Mary would say that I thought about it and then told her what was happening! She was from Belfast originally and her mother was there; that was a positive. On the other hand, she had lived more than half her life in Dublin. The kids were being educated in Dublin. We took the kids to Belfast when they were 11 and nine which, with hindsight, is quite a good time. Jamie went straight into grammar school and Kate went into prep school and then into the grammar school.

I ran Ulster Bank for seven or eight years. The team we built there took it from making £35 million a year to around £100 million the year I left, not at all because of me but because of the team. From a professional point of view, that was the best of times. We changed the view of Ulster Bank in the Republic where it would have been seen as a bit sleepy. While I was chief executive my chairmen were Frank O'Reilly[1] and then George Quigley.

People used say, "God, you were very brave to go to Belfast." The reality was that, if you were middle-class in Belfast, none of the troubles touched you, unless you were very unlucky. I had a tennis partner who was shot dead. That was dreadful, but people in Belfast were genuinely very welcoming. I'm not sure that the people in Dublin are as truly welcoming as the people in Belfast were when we went there. For us, it might not have been quite the same as for others. When I was in Trinity about one-third of my class were from Northern Ireland, so we had friends. Mary still had school friends. I

---

[1] *In Good Company*, pp. 259–278.

could not speak highly enough of the ten years in Belfast. The kids were educated there. This was now 1994 and Ulster Bank was performing well in the NatWest Group. I was happy at what I was doing.

The Ulster Bank had been acquired by the Westminster Bank, subsequently NatWest, back in 1917. For the period I was there, NatWest were a great parent company. We had considerable freedom and discretion. We had excellent people, a lot of whom are still there.

In 1994, NatWest asked me if I would like to run their private banking business, Coutts, in the UK. I was 47 — I could have said that I'd like to stay where I was, but I could not envisage doing the same job for the next 13 years. It would be bad for me, for the organisation and for the people working for me. I did not leave Belfast — I commuted to London. I told NatWest I was not prepared to live in England. Kate was in her last year in school. It would not have been logical to move. Mary would be stuck down somewhere in England with no friends and I don't like living in a city. I'd end up in a flat in London — I might as well have the bank pay for the flat. I commuted Monday to Friday for three-and-a-half years. To be honest with you, I realised again that I did miss Ireland terribly. I missed the people I worked with in Ulster Bank — that may sound soft, but it's true. I missed knowing people very well. Ireland is such a small country that you get to know well both the people you work with and your competitors, whereas in the UK, in London, at best you'd see your competitors at black tie dinners and that would be it.

Coutts was not in the shape that NatWest thought it was when they asked me to do the job. Coutts had about 4,000 people working, with offices in 16 countries. There was Coutts in the UK, the well-known private bank associated with the royal family and all that stuff. There were about twenty-odd branches in the UK. It had a bank in Switzerland with about 500 people. It was in the Bahamas, Cayman, Jersey, Guernsey and the Isle of Man, Hong Kong, New York, Miami. It had expanded in a higgledy-piggledy fashion. NatWest thought it could be a really big contributor to profits but we didn't have the foundations. A lot of the time when I was first there we were cutting costs. That's something I don't find attractive. We took the bank in Switzerland down from 500 to 300 people. And I did not like the commuting. When someone rang me and asked me if I would like to come back to Ireland to run Irish Life, I thought I'd won the Lotto. I believed that, when I left Ulster Bank to go to Coutts, I had made myself unemployable in Ireland. I recognise my limitations; I've made my career in the financial services business and that's what I enjoy doing. I'm very much a generalist, not a specialist. Having run one of the clearing banks in Ireland, I felt there would hardly be any other opportunities in banking in Ireland. I had not thought about the insurance business at all. I did not even know that David Kingston was due to retire.

Irish Life had been privatised in 1991/92. I met Conor McCarthy, whom I knew for a long time. Conor had been the chairman since privatisation. I met the Board and came back here in 1998. Sometimes you get lucky in life!

Irish Life had gone through a difficult period. It had been a dominant player in the eighties. It was privatised on a wave of success. Then there were difficult years — the GPA issues, the Mespil flats problem, problems with investment performance. The people in the company had lost confidence. What I had to do first of all was to get everybody facing in the same direction. I was lucky because, for the first three months, I had no job — David Kingston was still there. I went around talking to the top 40 people in the organisation for hours on end. I remember one of them asked me what my ambition for Irish Life was. When I told him that I'd like to get everybody facing in the same direction, I could see that he was thinking, "Is this all we get from this aggressive, ambitious man?" But, if you can get everybody facing in the same direction, and taking the first step together, then it does not take long until they walk together and then perhaps run together. They're not head-butting each other and spending energy on internal politics.

When I joined, the strategic vision of Irish Life was to have been a financial services business. I guess the analogy would have been a three-legged stool: Ireland, Europe and the US. There was a business in the US and there had been some forays into Europe which hadn't been all that successful. These had contributed somewhat to the loss of confidence. I sat down with the people who now run the company and the first thing we said was that we were living in Ireland, in the fastest-growing economy in the Western world. Where do we have natural advantages in distribution? If you look at the financial services value chain, about 85 per cent of the profit goes to the person who distributes the product. About 15 per cent goes to the people who do all the hard bits, developing the products — that's the unfortunate reality. We had this great market here and yet we were spending our energies going off to Europe and the US. We decided to redefine ourselves and to be focused on Ireland. We might grow organically in the US but we were not going to invest further there. To reinforce the point we said we were going to have this Ireland First strategy. That may not describe exactly what we wanted to do but most people in the organisation had to have something clear and simple that they could understand. That applies also to the analysts and the market: they found it difficult to understand what Irish Life was. Irish Life had been in France and Norway and had just bought 25 per cent of a bank in Hungary (which we subsequently sold to Krediet Bank of Belgium). And you didn't have to be a rocket scientist to know that Irish Life as an insurance company was at a huge disadvantage relative to the banks. If you look back, in 1988 none of the banks sold insurance in Ireland. Ten years later, in 1998, about 30 per cent of the entire life and pensions market was supplied by the banks. Irish Life had lost out because it did not own and control its own branch network. We needed to get into the branch distribution business because that was where the growth was — bancassurance. At first, we tried to sell our products through other people's branches like First Active, which was a tied agent, but, in those relationships, you end up teaching the banks all they think they need to know about selling insurance and they just squeeze you for more and more commission. Ultimately they screw you. It became clear that we needed to own and control our own branch network.

In August 1998, I had a conversation with Roy Douglas about the possibility of a merger between Irish Life and Irish Permanent. They were then a demutualised building society which had a five-year protection from being taken over. That was running out in about 18 months' time. They were looking for their strategic future. With Irish demographics, a merger looked like a marriage made in heaven: they were the largest mortgage lender in the country and we were the largest life and pensions business. We would have been about twice their size in terms of market capitalisation. Roy and I had that conversation in London and then we brought the proposal back to our boards. We agreed to merge in December 1998. It had leaked out in October 1998. The merger closed in April 1999. It's worked better than we could possibly have expected. We committed ourselves to savings which we've exceeded. The bancassurance model through the branches has been successful. We have an integrated management team from both organisations — we brought together two cultures. And now we've just agreed to buy the TSB.

For several years before its privatisation, Irish Life had operated in the real world. There was not a "semi-state" culture. They were as aggressive in the marketplace as any private sector company. In any event, the people who are running the business now, you would not recognise them as public sector people. Equally, in Irish Permanent, demutualisation has inculcated in its people a strong commercial ethos.

What did we learn from the merger? We learned, first of all, to sort out the important issues up front. The key jobs were agreed. We had joint chairmen for a period. The positions of chief executive and finance director were decided and Roy Douglas was director in charge of integration for the 12-month period — that was another lesson we learned. In a merger or integration, there is an enormous amount to do: you have to have somebody who's running a business on a day-to-day basis — that was me — and you also have to have someone responsible for the integration/merger process. Having somebody senior who is spending 100 per cent of his time on the merger was a very big plus for us. We had twenty-odd work-streams dealing with marketing, our broker business, finance, HR, etc. Each one of those was sponsored by an executive. Roy effectively acted as chairman of that process. He was able to spend days at a time in very detailed meetings about, for example, how we were going to construct the finance function in the reorganisation. I was able to get on with the work of the business. You can't do both. That's the model we're using now while we are integrating the TSB — Billy Kane is acting as the director of integration. Harry Lorton will be running the bank. Integration is about designing an entirely new business. For us, it was not just Irish Life and Irish Permanent squashed together. You have to be thinking about all the interdependencies. You have to have somebody of sufficient seniority and credibility sitting there with people who are coming from two different cultures. We formed a team of about 40 people taken from the brightest and best of both Irish Life and Irish Permanent almost equally. You have these natural axe-to-grind problems and somebody has to put manners on that. If there were absolutely critical integration decisions, I was involved in them, but only insofar as I had to. We worked through a high level committee: Brian McConnell, the chief operating officer, Peter Fitzpatrick, our finance director, Roy and myself.

When we bought TSB, essentially what we bought was the opportunity to exploit — if that's the word — a customer base. We bought the opportunity to bring our skills to play with 300,000 customers and 80 branches. Market share is important to me, but even more important is the customer base. When we finish the acquisition of the TSB we shall have a base of over 1,000,000 personal customers. One of our strengths is that we are good at exploring the opportunities to sell to a customer base. We're good at managing the distribution of products to a customer base. TSB comes with other things: a name as a savings franchise, access to the clearing system, but ultimately what we're buying is the relationship of the bank with its customers. Anything we buy in Ireland will be about a customer base and the opportunities to explore what we can do with those customers.

I don't really think very much about the next step. What we want to be is the number one provider of personal financial services in Ireland. Maybe, in time, our elbows will be hitting off the boundaries of Ireland, but there is still an awful lot we can do to improve our business here. I can see what we've done over the last three years almost week-by-week. There is an opportunity to compete with Allied and Bank of Ireland in a business tightly focused on the personal customer. A lot of Irish people are brassed off with the AIBs and Banks of Ireland. We have an opportunity to create something different here — a different customer experience. And then there's a very benign economic climate — the demographics support our business: we're going to be building 50,000 houses a year for the foreseeable future; the employed workforce has increased by nearly 60 per cent. Those people will want pensions and mortgages and life insurance and savings. It's as if there were a spotlight on our business: mortgages, car finance, life and pensions. When you know this is a good place to do business, why in God's name would you go elsewhere where you have no natural advantages? Remember, we will now have the best distribution network of anybody in the country: an excellent branch network, the largest direct sales force, the largest force of brokers . . . we literally cover all of the ways in which a customer can buy a product from us. Some of our competition have some of them; none of the competition has all of them like we have. We've tried to build up distribution in the UK and found it very difficult. It's very difficult to build it up from scratch. So we have this natural advantage here, we're a big player, we're good at it.

My immediate objective is to make a go of the TSB. Over the long term I think the financial services business will become pan-European. The so-called Single Market has failed to lift all the barriers in the financial services business. There are lots of hidden barriers, like tax, regulation, etc. Over time, ourselves, Bank of Ireland, Allied will probably become part of some pan-European organisation. Whether that is as the consolidator or the consolidated, I don't know. Size-wise, we might be the consolidated but that's not necessarily a bad thing. Nowhere implicit or explicit in the way my team and I run this company is the assumption that we will be independent forever. What we want to do is what's right for our customers, our staff and our shareholders. If, at the end of the day, our shareholders decide they want us to become part of Deutsche Bank Europe, well, that's fine by us. The reality is there is not much I can do about it if I am going to be the consolidated. If I were to lie awake at night worrying about it, all I would get is bags under my eyes. You simply run the business as best you can.

Why do businesses get taken over? They get taken over because there's some kind of management arbitrage, i.e. other people think they can run it better than you, sweat the assets better than you can. Put it this way: I would be surprised if the three major financial institutions in Ireland, Bank of Ireland, AIB and ourselves, were to remain the way they are now, i.e. Irish publicly quoted companies. We're well managed, we're pretty sophisticated, we have great market positions, so we could be a very attractive proposition — if it happens, it happens.

All of our management have a significant stake in the business, either through shares that they own or have under option. Thirty per cent of our shares are held by retail investors in Ireland — a hangover from the privatisation and demutualisation. Thirty per cent are held by Irish institutions. The rest are held by European and US investors. Obviously, what's happening is the Irish investors are selling and the European and US investors are buying. We have a very active investor relations programme — I commit 30 days a year to it. Peter Fitzpatrick, our finance director, would have a similar commitment.

In fact, he's off this week in Europe talking to investors. We have a dedicated IR guy who's done a very good job — there's no doubt the IR business in Ireland has become much more sophisticated over the last five years, because we've had to be. The model for all of us is CRH: when you talk to people in Toronto and ask them who do you know in Ireland, they always say Cement Roadstone.

There is nobody more deluded than a chief executive about his own management style. I believe in establishing clear goals — I think all the people who work here understand what's expected of them. That has to cascade all the way down the organisation. We're a big jigsaw puzzle — every piece has to fit, otherwise it doesn't work. Goals have to start at the top and work down or at the bottom and work up — which way does not really matter. Then, within those goals, people have to have significant discretion to get on with it. I'm fortunate in the way our corporate governance is structured. I have significant discretion to run the business myself. In turn, I delegate substantial discretion to my colleagues. I can get involved to a very low level of detail if I feel it's significant. I suppose people find that a curious mixture: I can be very hands-off but, if I feel I need to be hands-on, I'll be in there to the lowest decimal place! I'm an exceptionally frank person — what you see is what you get. Some people find my frankness difficult but the way I see it is I don't have time to be flim-flamming around, trying to dress something up in a nice way. I genuinely believe that you're much better off to explain things in words of one syllable, where there's no misunderstanding, rather than have subsequent recriminations. That's something my father had as well.

I have very strong values and views on the world. Honesty and integrity for me are not hygiene factors — they are *the* critical values. I remember my father saying to me, "Son, if you ever feel uncomfortable about doing something, will you be able to look yourself in the mirror in the morning while you're shaving?" People probably think I have very Calvinist views on things. For example, I had no problem in our making a voluntary disclosure of directors' remuneration. We were the first to do that and some people thought we should be drummed out of the club! It was genuinely surprising to me that this was an issue that aroused enormous passions. The argument is that this is an invasion of privacy: why should anybody know what you earn? When you're in a public company, you're not the owner, you are an employee and the owners have every right to know what they pay you. Now that it is mandatory, I think those people who are sticking to the bitter end to non-disclosure are a bit laughable. The man-in-the-street thinks that everybody in big business is on the take. The sooner we can get over that and have a much more transparent situation, the better.

But integrity and fairness are critical. I think I have high standards. I expect to be judged by high standards and I expect high standards of the people who work with me — not so much performance standards, but telling the truth. I can't think of anybody who worked with me who would have worked for very long if they had not told me the truth.

I have always said to people, "None of us get sacked for making a mistake." What you get sacked for is covering things up, not sharing with your boss at the first possible opportunity. However, if you keep making the same mistake, you're probably not in the right job. But, if there's an issue, tell me — the last thing I want is a surprise. I think people who know me know I don't shoot the messenger, but I get very, very cross if people know something and don't tell me and then it festers and ultimately explodes. You can't run the risk in today's world of something exploding because people have kept it down in the bowels of the organisation and hoped it would go away. If you have a problem, share it with your boss. Then it's two people's problems, not just one.

I'm just enormously optimistic about this country. When I left Dublin for Belfast in 1987, it was grim here — it was almost like, "The last guy going out of Ireland, turn off the lights." When we rented a floor in the south block of the IFSC from Dermot Desmond, we felt there was nobody else going to be there. When I came back here and saw what had happened to the IFSC or, when you walked through Temple Bar, or you drive up Aungier Street, it's just a different city.

The most exciting part of it is the fantastic kids we are producing now — they're so self-confident. It's very frustrating for us when we have, say, a smart actuary in his or her middle twenties and they come in and tell you they're off to Australia for a year, where they're going to surf and find themselves. When you ask them if they would like leave-of-absence, they say they'll give you a ring when they come back. That's very frustrating for us as employers but, God, it's wonderful for the country.

I'd like to see the economy slowing down from ten per cent to five per cent growth because that's more manageable long-term. The infrastructural deficit, the traffic and all that, are really the price of success. We've got full employment, we've got all the money we need, now what we need is project management skills, which we don't have. I sometimes wonder whether, in the twenty-first century, we've got the balance right between the rights of the individual and the common good. When Liam Cosgrave was Taoiseach, I'm told he said there would be a ring road linking the airport with Dun Laoghaire in five years. Twenty-five years later, we're still waiting for it. Because of our Constitution, our legal system, it seems to take forever to get things like that done. When you see what the Lee Tunnel has done for Cork, don't you wonder why the Dublin Tunnel has not even started? There's something wrong.

The first thing I say to young people is: "Get educated." After that, the world is your oyster. When my sister qualified as a doctor in the mid-sixties, most of her class graduated for the mail boat and they were never coming home. Now the kids can go away, but they can also look forward to coming home. The opportunity to go away now — and come back — must be fantastic.

Index